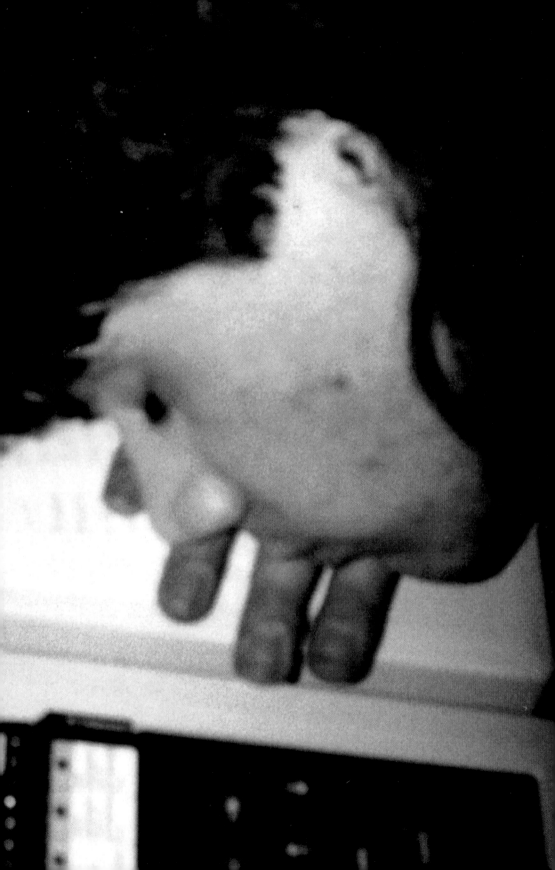

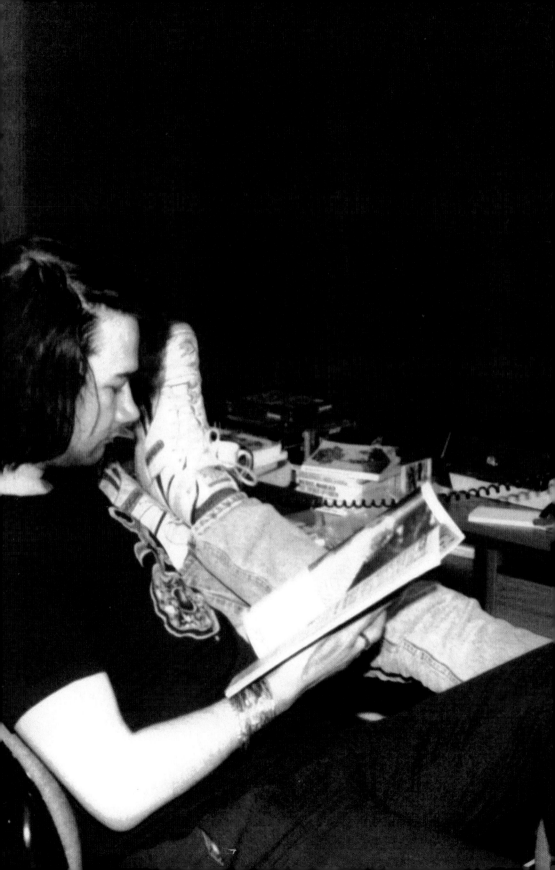

The Britain of the late 1970s
and early '80s is often
remembered through its youth
cultures, for punks spitting
at the establishment and the
rise of electro. A generation
of kids was taking hold of
technology, from early
synthesisers to cheap electric
guitars, and doing things
for themselves.

Less famously, but no less significantly, a quieter revolution was happening in living rooms and bedrooms all over the country. The microprocessor had entered the home, and nothing would be the same again. Anyone with a spark of imagination could express themselves through a new language of code, coloured light and bleeps, making their TVs their very own playgrounds. While punks wanted to break the system, these revolutionaries wanted to hack around with it and see what they could create.

In a troubled world of industrial
strikes and economic downturns,
of IRA bombing campaigns and
a war in the Falklands, computers
were helping a generation to take
control, and in so doing, to
expand the boundaries of a
brand new cultural medium and
forge the beginnings of a
vast industry. It crackled with
incredible invention and
opportunity, introducing
new wealth into regions that had
become all too used to decline.
The products of this peculiarly
male-dominated field reflected
a generation bemused by the
world around it, often anxious
to submerge itself in escapist
fantasies about being the
hero, and also curious to explore
new forms of self-expression.

But it only existed for a short
window. From its explosive
beginnings, the early videogame
industry was built on a shifting
foundation of constantly
developing technology, and
existed in an increasingly
globalising world. The fortunes
of Britsoft's pioneers flourished
and declined in waves, and
their success would become the
source of their greatest threat.

These personal accounts of the rise and fall of the early British game industry are by no means complete, but they come from some of its leading figures. Filled with insights into the technical intellect, business acumen and creative genius that lies behind a raft of treasured and sometimes legendary titles, these are the voices of people who helped fashion the modern videogame.

Introduction

Britsoft
An Oral History

Edited by
Alex Wiltshire

Based on the documentary feature film
*From Bedrooms to Billions*, written and
directed by Anthony and Nicola Caulfield

# Contents

# Foreword

Between 2010 and 2015 we shot hundreds of hours of footage and spoke to nearly a hundred people, in the process of researching and making what became the documentary feature film *From Bedrooms to Billions*. The film was our humble attempt to tell the story of the British videogame industry that developed in the early 1980s. The distinctive features of the period — the small development teams and lone bedroom coders, the independent spirit, the youthfulness, the creativity, the humour, the idiosyncrasies of the British market — all coalesced in the movement that has since come to be known by some as Britsoft.

For us, the project was an incredible journey. We met some remarkable individuals, and we were privileged to hear a host of wonderful stories along the way. We also worked harder than we had ever done before. But the toughest task of all, we found, was cutting out so much fantastic footage in order to keep to the eventual two-and-a-half-hour running time of the film.

This book is a tremendous opportunity for so much more of that material to see the light of day. It is designed to be read any way you wish: you can go for the lucky dip method, dipping in at a page of your choosing to discover an interesting passage; you can read it from cover to cover, following the story of Britsoft from birth to maturity, from the early days to the advent of the NES and the Mega Drive; or you can follow the story of each interviewee, using the page references at the top of each entry to find that interviewee's previous and next appearance. There is also a full list of interviewees, with their biographies, and references to each of their entries, at the back of the book.

We are delighted to present these stories to you now; not through the lens, but on the page. We hope you enjoy reading them every bit as much as we enjoyed gathering them.

Anthony and Nicola Caulfield
August 2015

# First Contact

I can remember on the Acorn Atom
getting a pixel to move off
screen. You know, it was
as close to sexual satisfaction
as you could possibly get.
It was unbelievable, that dot
turning into something else,
just in that very, very simple
game there.

I can remember so clearly the first moment I saw a videogame. It was in a shop window on Guildford High Street, a Binatone *Pong*[x] machine, and I stood in front of that window with my mouth open, seeing this white paddle go up and down in demo mode. I was 17 at the time and had no money at all, and I just thought, 'I don't care what I have to do, I have to own that.' So I immediately went back home, stole money from my grandmother's purse, returned and got my Binatone *Pong* machine. Then I played three games, thought it was rubbish, took it apart and it never worked again.

It was the seminal moment in my life. Before that moment I was a husk of a human being and after that moment I became who I am today. I don't care what anyone says, I don't care how many rose-tinted spectacles you put on, Binatone *Pong* was a rubbish game. It was too hard, it was unplayable and it had a terrible *Pong*-type noise. It had some *Pong*[*] variations, but I just wanted more. There it was, it was the future of entertainment for me, and I just wanted more. It set my whole imagination firing off.

[x] UK electronics firm Binatone released the first in its TV Master range in 1976, making it one of the first TV game makers in the UK. TV Masters came loaded with a *Pong* clone and variants approximating the likes of squash and football.
[*] Al Alcorn's iconic arcade classic for Atari, launched in 1972. It was inspired by a game that came with the Magnavox Odyssey console.

## Archer Maclean    37→

The first time would be *Pong* on a school trip in the early '70s to Bude in Cornwall. I was less than 10. I went through an arcade to get to an ice cream van and instead of all the mechanical machines there was this yellow thing with a dot bouncing around. Back then I had never seen anything like it. I just stopped to think, 'What on Earth is that?' I put all my ice cream money into that *Pong* machine over the next 20 minutes or so, and the teachers sent out a search party trying to find out where I was.

So yeah, that was a pretty inspirational moment. It was the lure of the moving white dot. I had never seen anything like it. There were no other videogames at that point, because everything else was all electromechanical. It was the game that started the whole industry, *Computer Space*[⌐] came just before it, but

[⌐] The world's first coin-op videogame, *Computer Space*, which was based on *Spacewar!*, was first released in 1971, produced by Ted Dabney and Nolan Bushnell at Nutting Associates.

unfortunately, as iconic as it was, *Computer Space* wasn't a success at all, whereas *Pong* sold hundreds of thousands of machines all around the world.

## Julian Rignall

My earliest videogame memory is playing *Pong* in Woolworths in around 1976, '77. Woolworths had two or three *Pong* games, and of a Saturday afternoon my mum would drop me off there and I'd just sit and play *Pong* as long as possible before I got kicked off by some fat kids.

I just loved videogames. I got completely obsessed. I remember seeing *Pong* and *Breakout*  in cafes and I would play them. But my first real moment was seeing *Space Invaders*  for the first time. I was a little bit far back from the machine, so I was just looking at the screen with these invaders on it, and my first thought was, like, how the hell is he controlling all of those things with just those buttons? Then I looked in and saw the thing at the bottom of the screen was firing, and just suddenly it hit me what was going on. It really was, like, 'Holy crap, that is just so awesome!'

I sat there and watched him play a couple of times, and I had 10p, put it in and started playing. It had such a huge impact on me. As I walked away from the machine, I was thinking, 'What do I need to do next time? How does it work? Can I use those bases?' Just thinking and obsessing, and I couldn't wait to play it again.

* Atari's 1976 arcade game was inspired by *Pong*, designed by Nolan Bushnell and Steve Bristow, and its prototype was engineered by Apple founders Steve Wozniak and Steve Jobs.
* Tomohiro Nishikado's 1978 classic, produced by Taito.

## Fred Gray

The first game I played was *Space Invaders*. I've got an addictive personality, so I played it endlessly in pubs and arcades. I was playing in a band and I put the money I earned from it in the *Space Invaders* machine: 10p, 10p, 10p. So yeah, that was the first one, and then later on, when I was actually in the business of writing code and music, I borrowed an Atari console and I was totally addicted to *Missile Command*,  and *River Raid*.

It was the addiction to achieving something. With *Space Invaders*, the psychology that went into it was absolutely amazing. They just sucked you in, and *River Raid* was similar. In fact, the first job

* Atari's 1980 arcade game was released on the 2600 the following year.
* Carol Shaw's scrolling shooter was released on the 2600 in 1982.

I got was in an arcade because I did a course in electronics, and I just played *Missile Command* all day, putting the keys in and pressing the free credit button 100 times.

## Nigel Alderton 44 →

My reaction to seeing the arcades cropping up was just to put all my pocket money into them, everywhere I went, any excuse, because they were all over the place. They were in newsagents, not just arcades. Every little corner shop had some sort of arcade machine in it. When I should have been going to school, I was stopping off and making myself late, and instead of going for lunch I would go and spend my lunch money on these daft arcade machines.

## Oliver twins 42 →

Andrew Oliver I remember playing *Pac-Man* a lot, and we used to have competitions, sometimes in the arcade if we had a bit of money, but on a friend's Apple II computer there was a good version of it.

Philip Oliver Let's be honest, we got a bit addicted.

AO Slightly addicted.

PO We spent a good year of our lives playing *Pac-Man* on that Apple II, and in fact I'm surprised that we weren't banned from our mate's household, because we were often there past midnight. This was probably when we were supposed to be doing our O levels, so it probably did have an effect on our schoolwork.

* Tōru Iwatani's legendary arcade game debuted in 1980.

## Jon Hare 38 →

It's kind of hard to pinpoint when I first became interested in games, but maybe it was the early arcade machines I remember playing when I was hanging around in the bus station in Chelmsford when I was 13 or 14, waiting to get a bus home. *Centipede* and *Asteroids* and whatever. We all played the same games: the Japanese-made arcade machines, and one of my mates had an Atari VCS×× with the early racing games.

I mean, we didn't have any kind of games machine in my house until I was 17 years old, which maybe people would find rather stunning these days, but there weren't that many people with them back then. They were quite special. You went round your mate's house who had a machine and you were excited to be playing games. My friend with a VCS had all the latest contraptions in his house, one of those kinds of families. They also had a SodaStream, you know?

## Dino Dini

Thinking back, my first encounter with games wasn't with videogames but with pinball. We used to go on holiday to the little village in the mountainous region of Tuscany where my parents grew up, and it sounds a bit odd to find inspiration for videogames there, but when I was five they had a pinball machine in the bar, and I was always nagging my parents for more money to go and play on it.

But my first real taste of videogames was walking into an amusement arcade, somewhere maybe in London, when I was around the age of 11. There were some of the original classics there. On my left was *Blockade* with a green screen, and then there was *Space Invaders* over there. They just caught my imagination. I don't know what it was about it, maybe it was just the bright lights and the displays on the screens, but *Space Invaders* was fascinating, and it just stuck with me. I was already interested in electronics, so of course a natural thing

was to want to make a game.

Back then, home computers really didn't exist. The first time I remember them being on the horizon was watching *Nationwide* on the TV when I must have been 12. I still remember the shot of this guy in the studio and he was sitting there in his grey suit saying the future was computers. 'Soon you will have a computer in your own home.' He was talking about the Commodore PET, which came out in 1977. Of course, at that point it was out of reach of people like me, because I was still a kid.

I mean, there were two sides to my interest in computers. One side is the fact it was pretty cool to make a machine do stuff by itself. Being interested in electronics, I started soldering at the age of five or whatever, so I was making electronic machines. But there's a limit to the complexity you could achieve by soldering together chips and transistors and so on, and the thing about the computer was that it would allow you to do potentially anything without having to do all this soldering. So that was one motivation.

After having seen videogames, I realised that these computers could be used to make games, and I wanted to play them. I couldn't afford to go into amusement arcades all the time, so I suppose that became a motivator as well. So I guess it was a coming together of different things. There was the motivation to make technology work, and then there was also this idea of creating something special that people hadn't seen before.

I think it has something to do with empowerment. This new technology came along and I know when I was at school I wasn't the only one. I guess another part of it was the fact that you could take control of something that your parents didn't have any clue about. It was almost like being a superhero on a certain level; there have always been films, haven't there, about the young teenage kid who saves the universe, making gadgets or inventions or whatever and becoming a kind of superhero. I think we were actually able to live that. We were using the most cutting-edge technology that had ever existed on the planet, and making stuff work with it. It turns out that making games is actually very cutting-edge, and it has pushed forward the boundaries of computing. It was a very powerful thing; I don't know that there has been any other kind of medium that suddenly popped out of nowhere where kids led the way. But that's what happened.

←33 ## Archer Maclean 39→

I remember seeing a news report about the blossoming computer hobby market at the time, and they said something like 500 people in the UK that year would build their own home computer, a Nascom or a Compukit. [x] I joined a computer club called the ACC, the Amateur Computer Club, [*] and I was like member 200 or something. It was full of middle-aged weirdy-beardy types, and I was the youngest by far, but there were two people there who were very helpful. One was Hugh Malander, who had worked on mainframes and was a research scientist, and the other's name escapes me but he was a solicitor with one hand. I remember that he had a TI-99. I went around his house many times and we would sit there writing simple games on this TI-99, which had colour graphics! Everything else was black and white characters in those days.

I think the most primitive computer I ever built was something called an MK14 from Science of Cambridge, which ended up

[x] Nascoms and Compukits were British-designed single-board computer kits released in the late '70s, though the Compukit was based on an Ohio Scientific-designed machine.
[*] Founded in 1973 by Basildon-based Mike Lord, the ACC was 'open to all interested in the design, construction or programming of computers as a hobby.'

becoming Sinclair Research.[*] It was around 1978. It had a National Semiconductor CPU, which was 8-bit and had 256 bytes of RAM, a little hex keypad, a couple of toggle switches to enable individual program bytes to go into memory, and an eight-digit, seven-segment LED display. With 256 bytes you had room to do about 100 machine code operations, albeit at one megahertz, and you could make lights flash and great things like that. You know, really advanced stuff.

The home computer that amazed me the most was the Altair 8800.[*] It was like an MK14 but in a box with a lot of LEDs on the front. I wanted one of those so desperately. It was a good three or four years before anything like that came to the UK, and I wasn't old enough to have a credit card, but there were people I knew who were buying these things and shipping them in and paying 100% import duties. In the late '70s there weren't really any shops.

[*] Clive Sinclair's started company, and maker of the ZX80 and Spectrum.
[*] Designed in 1974 as a kit computer, the Altair 8800 is generally recognised as having kickstarted the charge in the home computer, and was the home of Microsoft's first product, the Altair BASIC programming language.

## Jon Hare

If you look at what was happening in the early '80s, when the game scene in the UK really caught fire, you need to look at the background before that, that late '70s to early '80s massively creative, vibrant, international music scene. We had all sorts of different types of music coming out: ska, punk, early electronic music and various fashions, New Romantic ...

We had this thing of being a very creative hub. We also had quite a keen electronic hobbyist scene, and we were in a position where we were ready for something to happen. We had the creative mentality that we could go out and make anything happen. We had the home computers, some of which were being made and created here. And we had all the ingredients of belief in the political change that was happening at the time. In '79, the Tories came into power, so you had this feeling that we were going to go out and we were going to make things happen with some kind of industry support.

And I know it's not a popular view, but I'll continue to say it, the average person playing and making computer games was a smarter person. They were the nerds at school, and the nerds were generally the ones in the top classes. So you got people who were quite smart, who could make stuff, and they were selling to people with a generally similar mentality. They were more open to new ideas. They were turned on by new stuff. They were people who were excited by something they'd never seen before. They weren't scared of their friends thinking that they weren't cool because it had never been seen before.

## Archer Maclean

←37 57→

We had unfortunately a massive economic disaster, courtesy of a certain political party, so there was the 'Winter of Discontent': power cuts, strikes here, strikes there, BBC1 and ITV were off-air all the time with journalist strikes, there were lorry driver strikes, postal strikes, there were strikes everywhere. The government had run out of money and the IMF were arguing about whether they should give us anything. Oh, and then it snowed a lot in 1980, '81, and it was just miserable. I also remember a lot of stuff to do with the IRA and there were bombs going off everywhere, but I had gone off to university, so I was sort of slightly insulated from it.

At university I was suddenly plonked in amongst a bunch of equally ambitious microprocessor fanatics, which was good because we sort of all thrived off each other. Not much educational stuff went on; it was about the parties, beer, what computer to get with your grant, and programming. It was good fun and I didn't get to see a lot of the economic depression that was going on.

## Martin Kenwright

253→

Do you know, it was the best of times, the worst of times. I grew up in Liverpool and moved out to Runcorn as a teenager. It was like *Boys from the Blackstuff,*˙ it really was. My dad was a builder, times were hard; we only ever had three channels on the telly and not much else to do.

It wasn't what computers did at the time, it was what you could imagine them doing in the future. There was no specific moment where I thought, 'Oh, computers, great! I want to make computer games!' because the business didn't exist at that time. Most of the stories of computer games were really coming from America, this vision of California and all the cool kids over there. You could never imagine them being made down the road in Liverpool, you know, by people in a bedroom. But, slowly and surely games started creeping into our lives.

˙ Alan Bleasdale's BBC drama about unemployment among Liverpool's working class.

## David Darling

I think what sparked the interest in UK gaming was really when home computers became available for the first time, so you could buy things like the ZX81 and ZX80, and the BBC Micro. There were thousands of kids all over the country who were using these new devices. Maybe they were into Isaac Asimov and science fiction, and they just loved the idea of robots and artificial intelligence and all of that kind of stuff, so they were able to use these home computers to kind of live out their fantasies. Their parents and grandparents, nobody really understood what they were doing, so it was like a real adventure. Some kids got good at it and started making games, and then the industry developed from there, really. I think it was mostly the interest in the possibility of what computers could deliver to the human race. It was a brand new kind of adventure.

## David Braben

I always loved the idea of worlds that you immerse yourself in. I was a huge fan of science fiction books and would read them avidly, and I suppose when those books started to manifest themselves in films like the first *Star Wars* it was really wonderful. You imagined that it was a consistent world that you were a part of. I suppose in parallel to that I always loved creating things, whether it was with Lego or Meccano or anything like that. So when computers came on the horizon I found them unbelievably fascinating.

## Gary Penn

The home computer gave you the feeling that anyone could do anything, though that wasn't strictly true. They used to trade on this in some of the early adverts for VIC-20s and Commodore 64s, portraying this idea that you could do your accounts on it.

Most people went from ZX81 to Spectrum, but I went the VIC-20 and Commodore 64 route. I think it was just because it felt like a richer, classier kind of experience. The ZX80 and ZX81 didn't have real keyboards, they had this weird kind of squishy pokey thing. The membrane on the ZX81 was an awful thing, and the Spectrum of course had these squishy little rubber keys. But we used to play lots of Spectrum games, though there was almost this class division which went on for years between the different computers.

I didn't understand it at the time, because if you were a games player, why would you deny yourself a means of playing them just because they're on a different platform? But the playground wars came from the fact that we are tribal, so it was kind of almost unavoidable. You get the same thing with football teams, and maybe brands of car; it seems to be a perpetuating cultural thing where people will tie their colours to a mast, and it's an excuse to compete in some way.

You had to stick to the one you could afford, and I would have probably bought everything if I could afford it. But generally one of your friends would have a different computer, and everyone would pile round their house to play. There was an interesting social quality to gaming back then, where you would take turns and try and maximise the value of the thing you had bought by setting a series of challenges. So you would be taking turns and betting your friend that they can't do it in this time, or with one hand behind your back, or without jumping.

There was a point where there were at least half a dozen manufacturers. There was the Jupiter Ace, the Oric Atmos, loads of these platforms coming out, and as a kid I was utterly fascinated by them. A friend of mine got a ColecoVision,[×] and they all had some quality that was different and interesting, and I wanted to be able to play them.

[×] If you wanted the arcade feel at home, this was the console to get, and it came with a *Donkey Kong* cartridge, but being based in the US, Coleco was severely affected by the 'videogame crash' of 1983 and withdrew from games in 1985.

## Jez San

47→

When the BBC Micro came out in '81, I worked on Saturdays for Microage Electronics,[*] the first shop that sold them, and my job was in the back, soldering up Model As to become Model Bs.[ˀ] I learned to solder the hard way, because I thought soldering was about trying to apply as much solder as possible to the soldering iron and then wiping it on to the component. But I soon learned how to solder correctly, to heat up the part and then touch the solder so it just works magically.

The BBC was extremely empowering, because previous computers were very difficult to program, almost impenetrable, but the BBC had very advanced BASIC and the ability to mix assembler and BASIC in the same program. Your code could be written in

[*] Based in Edgware, North London.
[ˀ] The difference between the two was memory: the Model A had 16K and the B had 32K.

BASIC first and then you could take bits of it and write assembler to speed it up and make it run better, and then more and more of it would be in assembler until eventually everything was. So it was a fantastic way to learn programming and to write really good code.

The thing about the BBC, and also the Sinclair computers, was that they were very cheap and easy to use, and they empowered the youth, they enabled anyone in their bedroom to write a program. I've tried programming the other computers, like the PET, and they were actually very difficult to program properly.

## Oliver twins

Our older brother decided to get a ZX81 and he put it under the family TV. Then he promptly discovered girls, which was quite convenient for us because his computer was available, so we'd come home from school and fire it up. We didn't really have any money to buy games, not that there were that many, and it wasn't ours to buy games for anyway. So, we basically just opened the manual and started typing listings in.

The computer fires up, it's got a cursor there, and you've got a nice ring binder manual and it would say, 'Type 10, print "HELLO WORLD", line 20, "GOTO 10".' So you type that and it works. 'Hey, let's change that "HELLO WORLD" to "HELLO PHILIP".' 'Oh my God it knows me!' Then you just go, 'Let's put a question in, and you put the answer in and it compares the answer and says, 'Yes, you've got that right.' Now I'm going to give it a whole bunch of questions and get Andrew to see if he can answer them. 'Hey, you only got seven out of ten! That was rubbish.' You basically just extended the list and extended it and extended it and then we challenged each other.

There was a kind of magic to it in the early days. I fear for people now because there is too much entertainment and there are too many interesting things around. We were very bored as children.

*Pac-Man* was a bit tough.

It had 1K of memory, but we could get it to do certain things. I remember a little *Pong*, getting the ball bouncing round the screen.

Yes, we made some great *Pong* games, actually. We had multiple versions.

AO Yes, two-player versions, and we were actually having fun with games we had written.

PO But the ZX81 inspired us to say, 'It's not very good, is it? 1K, black and white, all blocky graphics. We need a colour computer,' and that's when we then pestered our parents like mad to get a Dragon 32, which everybody was talking about. This was 1981, I guess. It was going to have a full keyboard and colour and 32K of memory, and it was £200, and our parents said they would cover half if we could get the other half, so we ended up doing a paper round every evening for about six months to get the money in time for when it came out. So then we had 32K of memory, colour, sound and then we started writing some really interesting games.

AO It was actually quite nice and easy to program. We did quite a few tiny games. I remember a version of *Centipede* that we did a fairly good job of.

We had a computer at school with a punch card reader where you used a pencil to fill in these boxes in the punch card. It was really laborious, but I used to stay after school because there was only one keyboard, and I'd be there until like twelve o'clock at night, until the janitor chucked me out. That was my first experience of programming. My dad had a Commodore PET, which used BASIC. He was a contact lens designer and was trying to work out the curvature of the contact lenses using equations, so he wanted us to program them on to his Commodore PET. For me it was really trying to work out how BASIC worked. Then we'd use magazine listings and try to reverse-engineer them.

Our grandparents used to get fed up with my brother and me being in the living room on our computers for hours and hours, so they would send us to the bedroom, so we just used to spend hours and hours programming away quite happily in this secret world. I was really interested in electronics. My granddad was an electronic colour TV designer in Australia and he taught us how to build crystal radio sets and gadgets to count how many people came into a room, and when we went on holiday we built a gadget to feed the fish. We used to go down to this electronics shop to buy transistors, capacitors and resistors to make all these things, so when home computers came out it was kind of logical that we'd want to work out how we could control these more advanced electronic devices.

I also had a computer studies teacher called Mr Evans. For my computer studies coursework I did a game in machine code, and he couldn't understand it, so he failed me. He said, 'Stop doing games, they're a waste of time. If you want to get into software you need to get into business software.' This carried on throughout my career, really, where people tell you that games are a waste of time.

## Jeff Minter 55 >

I ended up wandering into the wrong room at my sixth-form college, and there was some guy there who was sitting in front of a Commodore PET. It wasn't his own, it belonged to the college, and I didn't know what it was. It was this weird thing that looked like a telly with a keyboard underneath it, and I wandered over to have a look at what he was doing and he was playing some game. I said, 'You're playing a game.' I'd seen videogames, I'd seen *Space Invaders*, I'd seen *Pong* and things like that, but I'd never seen them on a computer before, so I said, 'Where did that game come from?' And he said, 'Oh, I typed it in,' and I thought, 'Bloody hell, you can type games into computers! You type stuff into computers and games come out. I've got to find out how to do that.'

So I went away, borrowed a book on BASIC from the library, and I think I'd looked at some of my brother's Texas Instruments calculator programs the night before and hand-converted them to BASIC so I could type them in when I got in the next day. I came back in early the next morning, sat down in front of the Commodore PET with my book, and I went from there really.

Until then I made no connection to how videogames were made or the possibility that somebody like me could make them. Videogames were things that were just made by some manufacturer somewhere, and they might as well have been made by God. I didn't connect them with any kind of human activity that I might get involved in.

## ‹ 35 Nigel Alderton 87 ›

I was very lucky. I went to a big school with 2,000 kids, and there was one little room, literally a broom cupboard, and a very forward-thinking teacher put some computers in it, TRS-80s. So I was walking past this room one day, not knowing even that it existed, and I saw a couple of kids wandering in and out. I just poked my nose in – it was dark inside and there were these green screens in there, and I thought, 'What on Earth is going on in there?' I managed to wheedle my way in, because there was a bit of a clique in there.

Eventually the bigger kids let you sit down, if you were lucky, and type a few lines in BASIC. But I think we even had to write the code down before we were allowed to sit. I was going home at night, writing my little five lines of code, and then waiting around for an hour after school to go in and get to sit down and type it in and see if it worked. Then, of course, it didn't work, and I'd take it home and debug it.

I was just fascinated, just enthralled, by these things that you could get to do whatever you wanted on the screen. It was as simple as that. I was just hooked. I was doing a paper round at the time, and I'd do it as early as I could, and we managed to persuade the headteacher to lend us the keys to the school. She was gobsmacked that kids were wanting to come into school and work more, but, you know, we didn't see it as work. We would come in at half-seven just to get time on the computers.

## David Perry

65→

I happened to be at my school in Belfast at the right moment. It got a huge grant to buy a lot of computers. So imagine, there was no computer department but suddenly they had to start training teachers and they had all this equipment arriving. I saw the computer room and I wanted to go in and see what it was all about, and the teacher said to me, 'Sorry, you're not old enough,' and I was like, 'Not old enough, for what? What's in there? It must be really cool in there!'

So that created the desire. When I was finally allowed to go in, everyone was working on these different machines but there was this one little Sinclair ZX81 that no one was using. I went over and sat down with it and started figuring out what it did, and I did like some really simple program, like,

'What is your name?' 'Hello David,' and that kind of thing, and I was, like, 'This is awesome!' because you realise you can do anything. That's what drew me into it, realising I can make it do whatever I want.

Over time, my programs started two lines long, and then they were five lines, and then 10, and they started to get more and more complex, and I was addicted. The only way to really learn back then was to type programs into the computer, so you'd be hungry, looking for anything with a listing on it, mostly magazines, and later I would start to buy books. You'd type it in and see if you could get it to work. We were so engrossed and invested, and so interested in how the computers worked. It wasn't just the Sinclair, we also had Research Machines

380Zs. We were able to take them apart and understand them, and the poor old teachers were trying to keep up. I remember being in a class and the teacher basically saying, 'Can you teach this class and I'll sit down and just listen?' The teachers were being told to teach computers, but they still had to go through the learning curve, and we had more time, or we were more passionate about it, I don't know, but it was an odd relationship.

## Martin Galway

My school's computer room had ZX80s, PETs, a VIC-20, a Tandy TRS-80 Model II, and it all seemed a bit alien, but there was something compelling about these little boxes. When you're 15, 16, you're looking for a way to break away from your parents, you want to become an adult and do your own thing. Computers for me were a way for me to discover and develop some knowhow on something they had no clue about. You know, all these words like bits, bytes, RAM, and all that stuff.

Home computers' raison d'être was programming from the moment you switched them on. They were approachable and friendly, like, 'Hey, come on, program me!' So I just wanted to put little BASIC statements in there and watch the program flow down from the top to the bottom. I wasn't an incredible mathematical genius, but I had a strong interest in maths and it was a great way to explore more mathematical stuff, while also being into electronics.

## Julian Rignall

My first computer was an Atari 400 that I bought from a friend. He was a student, and he blew his first-term loan on a computer and the rest on drugs, basically. About three weeks into the term, he suddenly realised he had no money, so he said he'd sell it to me dirt cheap, and I scraped the money together. I got a Spectrum a few years later, but the Atari was my first love. It had a lot of the arcade conversions, so it was like, great, I don't need to spend 10p pieces any more and I can practise endlessly at home.

In the early days, guys were doing basic games, you know, writing in BASIC, and I think through copying games, people would start thinking, 'What if I tweaked this, and made that slightly different?' You began to have original ideas coming through. Those early days of the computing industry were very much people taking other people's games and modifying them.

When you look through games of the '70s, things like *Colossal Cave Adventure*,[x] the *Star Trek* games,[•] and some of the early strategy games, nobody had any kind of commercial sense. They didn't think about selling them. A lot of the system administrators didn't even want these games on their systems, they just saw them as a pesky thing that got in the way of the proper stuff these computers should have been doing, which was crunching numbers. So a lot of those early games were deleted or lost, but these bits of code would be shared and swapped and modified and re-modified, and I think that began to build momentum into people saying, 'I don't want to necessarily modify someone else's game, I've got this great idea myself, and I want to make it.'

[x] Originally written in 1976 for the PDP-10 by Will Crowther, it was the first text adventure game, and is famous for lines like, 'You are in a maze of twisty little passages, all alike.'

[•] A very popular, for the time, set of text-based games first written by Don Daglow for the PDP-10 in 1972 in which the player takes the role of the captain of the *Enterprise*, giving orders to the crew and defeating an enemy ship.

←41

# Jez San

93→

The early forerunner of the internet was the International Packet Switched Service and we were hacking into it with our modems, you know, an acoustic coupler, and we were logging into computers all over the world for the hell of it. The prize at the time was to log into Essex University and play *MUD*,[x] and I was one of its first external players. I played it enough to attain the rank of wizard, I was Zaphod the wizard,[x] and *MUD* was very important for me in teaching me about multiplayer games and how much fun and how social they could be. I owe a lot to Richard Bartle and Roy Trubshaw, who were the innovators of that game. People asked me how I learned to type at 110 words-a-minute and it was literally because I feared for my life. I had to type 'kill troll with sword' fast enough that I wouldn't get killed myself, so it was life or death.

[x] Multi-User Dungeon, inspired by *Colossal Cave Adventure* and made at Essex University by Richard Bartle and Roy Trubshaw, became the first online multiplayer role-playing game when it was connected to ARPANET in 1980.

[x] Richard Bartle wrote of Jez San in *Micro Adventurer* magazine in February 1985: 'JEZ the wizard, or ZAPHOD as he is occasionally known, was our first external *MUD* wiz. Being one of those people who has contacts absolutely everywhere, he heard of *MUD* fairly soon after we opened it to the public and took to it like a duck to water. After several months of glorious bloodletting, and suitably impressive telephone bills, this precocious 17-year-old (as he was then) made it up to wiz.'

I really liked the idea of programming my computer, but very quickly realised I was utterly crap at it. I didn't have the mind for it. For most products, right, 99% of people consume it and 1% of people make it, more or less. Buying games was also certainly better than typing horrendous listings from a magazine, which was zero fun. I remember doing that once, and it not working, after spending hours. I checked it and it was perfect, and of course next month they printed, 'Oh, there was a bug in line 19 ...' But at that point, I'd spend five quid on a game, and it was much better than spending my entire day programming something that didn't actually work, and if it did work, it was usually a bit crap.

The early magazines were sort of nerdy specialist magazines that were written by enthusiasts for enthusiasts, but then you got this degree of professionalism that kicked in, which was inevitable because you had an industry emerging. The publishers saw the opportunity to launch new magazines, but they were usually employing journalists who weren't necessarily game players, although when you are on the outside you didn't realise it, because you were trying to find any game nugget you possibly could.

It was before *C+VG*,<sup>×</sup> so you were looking at things like *Your Computer* and *Personal Computer World*. Back then, they covered it as a novelty, almost. Maybe you would find a listing that you could enter. I remember a version of *Missile Command* for the school computer, and it was why I learned to program. You would type in the listings and they would never work, so you had to fix them. It was a fantastic process of learning, and you'd modify them, maybe changing a few sprites, and then start messing with the rules, and then you would start adding to them. It was liberating, and a great fun thing to do, messing around.

I was terribly impatient, and so once I figured out how the listings worked I could start breaking them down and know that if I did a certain bit I could get something working really quickly and I could start messing around with it before I even finished the rest of the listing off.

× Computer and Video Games magazine, the first British magazine devoted to video games, first published in November 1981.

I thought it was really amazing that you could look at a program listing and see in your mind what the result would be. So I would look at listings, not type them in or anything, just think, 'Oh yes.' It was great. Then eventually I got a computer for Christmas, an Acorn Atom, and I was hooked. My parents were very generous and then we built a lot on to it by buying an extension to its memory and all that sort of thing. It was a predecessor to the BBC Micro, but in many ways they're quite similar. And perhaps I was one of the early over-clockers because I actually sped up the speed of the Atom to be comparable to the BBC Micro. The Atom ran at one megahertz which these days seems unbelievably slow. The BBC Micro ran at two megahertz.

The beauty was that all that you needed to learn to program was in the box. So there was an excellent book with the slightly cheesy title *Atomic Theory and Practice*, written by David Johnson Davies of Acorn, that told you how to program. It took you through the steps with a fairly steep learning curve, but beautifully laid out. I think that was very, very helpful, to the extent that by halfway through the book it was teaching you how to program in assembler. It didn't hang around, but that was great. It meant that I and a lot of other people in the same generation could be self-directed, we could learn on our own. I think that is fantastic. It is really liberating because it allows you to experiment at your own pace, and really understand what you are trying to do.

My first home computer was the Acorn Atom, and then I started getting magazines, which had those listings of games which you typed in. They always had grandiose titles like 'The Ultimate Maze Game' or something, but they were always crushingly disappointing. I mean, they were the worst for mis-selling. The magazines used to say, you know, 'The best space battle game we have ever played!' You would spend six hours typing it in, six hours debugging it, and you would get to the end and there would be a little ship going around firing a little missile and that would be it.

By that time I understood enough about programming to get my hands dirty, and I can remember on the Acorn Atom getting a pixel to move off screen. You know, it was as close to sexual satisfaction as you could possibly get. It was unbelievable, that dot turning into something else, just in that very, very simple game there. It was a great time, but it was frustrating as well. The Acorn Atom had this massive heat problem so I had to have fans blowing at it to keep it cool, otherwise you would be in the middle of something and the whole thing would just shut down.

So there were listings specifically for the Acorn Atom, some for the horrible Sinclair ZX80. Anybody could have one of those, you know, it was the BBC Micro and Acorn Atom versus Sinclair wars, and you just didn't talk to those horrible Sinclair users. But I saw listings and you got the idea, 'God, I could write them!'

There were some really inspirational people around. One of them was Sir Clive Sinclair, even though, you know, his computer wasn't as good as the Acorn Atom and BBC Micro. Clive Sinclair told this incredibly bold lie, that computers were going to be *the* new form of entertainment and that every home would have one. At the time everybody thought he was a little bit crazy, but it stuck with me because I already thought I could see a kind of Moore's Law of doubling of speed and halving of price starting to come in. So my imagination was saying one day computers are going to be pretty powerful. There was a real feeling that this was the start of something big.

## Julian Gollop

My first computer was a ZX81. I bought it second-hand from a friend at school for £25. For games it was almost completely useless, because it had 1K of memory, but the 16K RAM pack made it really useful, so I got one and I could actually make games on it. So it was the computer that I first learned to program with. I would wait until the rest of my family had gone to sleep, sneak back into the living room, plug my ZX81 into the TV, and I would code until one or two o'clock in the morning, and get up very sleepy for school the next day.

The release of the Sinclair Spectrum was a major event for the British game industry. It was, I think, the first computer that was both accessible in terms of price to people like me, and it also could be a platform for relatively sophisticated games. You actually had a huge amount of memory on the 48K model. You could use 40K for your programming data, which was amazing. The other computers at the time, like the Commodore 64, were more expensive, and I think that's what distinguished the Spectrum. It was cheap, it was powerful and you could do a lot with it.

On the ZX81 there are only one or two games which really influenced me. One was *3D Monster Maze*, which was technically really advanced. It was a pseudo 3D dungeon kind of game with monsters, and I really wanted to make games at that level of sophistication in Z80 assembly language. I wasn't really that interested in all the listings in magazines. I would look at the code, and think, okay, I'm already that advanced; I need to do something more sophisticated.

## Steve Turner 61→

I was a commercial programmer and I wanted to buy a kit computer, and when I saw the ZX80, it was so cheap I had to have one. In this box were all these pieces. It was more like an Airfix kit than building a computer, and I was a bit disappointed in a way. But I put it together and it worked. I knew nothing about how to use it, so that prompted me to go down to the library and get books out on the chips, and I worked out how the machine was doing everything. I learned how it was displaying graphics characters using the Z80 and a little timing chip, and I deduced that if I put a splice across two of the lines to short out the number of the timing chip, I would get the top half of the character twice.

The ZX80 used the same circuitry to put the video up as it did for the programming, so it was very, very hard to do both. I learned that you had to use the interrupts[*] of the machine and make the game exactly in time with the video of the TV, which meant every instruction of your game had to be exactly the right length. I was trying to do *Asteroids*; I got a little asteroid floating across the screen and that was about it on that machine.

That really got me into it, and I disassembled the operating system to learn how the machine was actually working. That gave me a big advantage when the Spectrum came out. I think homemade games really started with the ZX81, but that was a machine I missed because I was so fed up when it came out, because it made all my work at getting moving graphics on the ZX80 suddenly redundant. I'd spent perhaps a year pulling the machine to pieces. Suddenly people could write moving games on a cheap computer, and they were very good very quickly, much more like the arcade games.

[*] Interrupts are a fundamental part of programming and cause the processor to pause what it's doing to work on another task, allowing the computer to play music, animate images and take controller inputs, all apparently at the same time.

I always loved art. At school I was always in the art room and maths was my other major, and English too, but they didn't really know what to do with me. I went to art school and trained to be a silversmith, so I was looking at an art-based career, but I hadn't had anything specific in mind. Then I got married and started a family so it sort of went on the back-burner.

Shortly after I became a full-time mum, I became a single parent. I married again, had a second son, and then became a single parent again. So I was looking to work from home or something, but it was difficult to find anything at the time that didn't conflict with the school holidays and so on. I was working evenings in a pub, but that was pocket money, really, and then a good friend of mine gave me a VIC-20 and told me to see what I could do with it.

It was riveting and I couldn't stop. I got to the stage where I was having to set an alarm clock to remember to go and pick the boys up from school, because once I got in that zone I couldn't get out. Days used to go by! I didn't know much else except either playing games or typing in listings from magazines, and trying to get them to work, and then working out how they were working.

It was just something I had an affinity with, and it was stretching me where I had been a housewife, really, and vegetating a bit, sitting and doing housework. I found a direction. Most of all, I wanted to work my art into it, as well as just writing bits of code. I was playing around with which character set there was when you moved the cursor around on the screen. There were two character sets, positive and negative, and the cursor flicked between the two to show you where you were on the screen. So I redefined the two sets to be a very simple two-frame animation, so I would move the cursor and I got bells ringing and a donkey kicking, and all sorts of things like that, just to amuse myself.

I would take the kids to school and I'd be thinking about what I was going to do when I got back. Maybe I would write some notes or write a little program about something, and I learned BASIC quite quickly; I couldn't put the book down. I was just, 'Yes, I can do this!' Maths came in as well, and so I started to experiment. I learned some 6502 assembler, and so I was able to handle the data, and yeah, that's where it began.

## Rob Hubbard

The first computer I got was the Commodore 64, and it was very intriguing because, you know, you would switch this thing on and you got a blue screen saying 'Ready' and a little thing blinking at you. Then you tried to do something and it didn't work and that little box was making you feel like a complete moron, so there was natural intrigue in trying to figure out what was going on with it.

Eventually, I thought I would see if I could get some music into all this, and I wrote a BASIC program. This thing started stumbling and spluttering along, you know, completely out of time because BASIC is just so slow. Everybody was talking about learning machine code to make it fast. I had bought a couple of games, so I knew the Commodore was capable of doing music. There was a company in Bridlington called Taskset,[x] which had games called *Jammin*[•] and *Super Pipeline*[▾] with some interesting music in them. So I realised I had to be able to do something better than what I could in BASIC, so learning 6502 assembly language was the way to go.

The first time I got something working in assembly I moved a sprite across the screen, a little figure, you know. You do that in BASIC and it's stuttering along, but you get it working in assembly language and you can't see anything because it's moving so fast! So it was obviously a million times more powerful than writing in BASIC. I was working on my own, struggling with this stuff every night until four or five in the morning, trying to figure what all this binary and assembly language stuff all meant.

Eventually, I figured out what the whole interrupt thing was. That was a really difficult stumbling block. There was nobody to get on the other end of the telephone, and no internet to look it up on, so I just had to keep reading about it. I had a book called *The Dr. Watson Book of Assembly Language Programming*, which I knew inside out by the time I had finished. I kept struggling on until eventually something clicked and then it all started to work, and it opened up the floodgates.

In those days, before there were as-

←46 Martin Galway 104→

I decided to learn assembly language because it was just one more step up the ladder of complexity and achievement. Really, assembly language was the bee's knees. It was where it was at, if you really wanted to program. It's the same language as what they call machine code, but machine code is just the hexadecimal values that are generated by assembly language, and so much harder and a lot more pointless to be programming in, because all you are doing is writing these numbers down all day long. Assembly language is the easy listening version of machine code.

sembler packages, you had to type poke statements, just poking numbers into memory and writing them down on paper. It was loads and loads of late nights, until five in the morning, and then you had

[x] Founded by Andy Walker in 1983, Taskset also developed the pub crawl-themed *Bozo's Night Out* before closing in 1985.

[•] A music game loosely themed on reggae, released in 1983, in which you'd move around a single-screen maze collecting musical notes.

[▾] A game in which you'd defend pipes from enemies and repair them, released in 1983, featuring a SID-powered soundtrack by Paul Hodgson.

to wait another 40 minutes to save it to tape, and then another 40 minutes to do a backup in case the original one crashed. And the next morning, the first thing you'd do was load it from tape again.

Once I started writing music routines and sound effect routines in 6502, or Z80 on some of the other machines and 68000 on the Amiga, I really loved it. You know, I had a ball. It was so much fun to have that low level control over what you were doing. I would go to bed at night and think, 'Oh, hang on, if I did that then this would happen!' I would just get these crazy ideas that would just be so intriguing that I couldn't wait to get up the next morning to try them out, and get this thing going. It would crash a few times, but it was an absolute blast.

## Geoff Crammond

I was working as a systems engineer with Marconi.[*] I had finished a physics degree at Bristol, and the first thing I had to do was programming in Fortran.[*] I was dropped in at the deep end; there was a Fortran course at university, but I didn't understand and didn't attend the rest of it. In those days, every line of code had a punched card, so a program would be a whole deck of cards with a rubber band around it. You'd take it along to the computer room, a huge room filled with a computer with 32K of memory, leave it outside in a tray, and come back half an hour later to get your printout. That's how I learned Fortran, doing mathematical modelling, and I guess my interest in simulation kind of came from there.

While I was there I had the idea, as a hobby, of getting some hardware that produces dots on a screen, a bit like the arcade games I used to see at service stations. I was also into electronics and made things like sound effects for my guitar. I had a vision of some sort of game about flying through a 3D environment. Well, I call it a game now, but I didn't think of it as one then. So I was keeping an eye open for hardware as it was beginning to come out. You could buy motherboards that you could attach to a keyboard and things like that, but what really caught my eye was the VIC-20. It had a colour display, and I realised that I didn't need to cobble something together myself. So that was what I was going to do, but I went to a show at, I think, Olympia or Earls Court, and the BBC Micro was on show for the first time. I looked at that and

[*] The Marconi Company, a long established British telecommunications firm.
[*] An early programming language created at IBM and released in 1957, used particularly in the fields of science and engineering.

everything about it just seemed to be better than the VIC-20, so I ordered it there and then and took delivery a few months later.

I took it out of the box and started looking at the manual. It had built-in BASIC, which is actually quite similar to Fortran, so it was quite easy to start creating programs. It also had built-in graphics, which meant you could very easily produce images and move them around, but after a couple of weeks of doing that I could see that it was far too slow to produce the sort of thing I had been seeing in the arcades, so I realised that I would have to work with an assembler. I knew about assembler from Marconi, though I didn't actually work with it. I bought a book on the 6502 processor in the BBC Micro, and basically started learning how to do it. I started moving things on the screen really quickly, and that in itself was quite an addictive process, because when you have success it spurs you on.

I think it was just after I got the machine that we went on holiday to Corfu, and there was a hotel with a *Space Invaders* machine. I thought it would be a good thing to try and program, because I would learn how to do a proper game, so after the first week of our two-week holiday I wanted to go home to get it going. You know, my wife didn't appreciate that sentiment, really.

←44 Jeff Minter 62→

Basically it was just me and there were a handful of other nerds who were playing about with the PET. We obviously wanted to find things to do with it, and there's only so much pleasure you can get out of programming biorhythms,˥ so we decided to start writing games, just for each other's consumption, really. At one point we actually got into trouble, because we were writing our high scores on the wall of the computer room, and we had to repaint the walls.

There was no thought at that point that it would ever be a business. It was just kind of something which we did as nerds. We thought of this as a little nerdy hobby that nobody else in the world would ever really be interested in, and it was only later on when the ZX80 came out that we started to get an idea that maybe more people would get into this, and then the ZX81 came out and it started to really take off.

The idea of having my own machine at home was so fantastic to me and I would've done anything to get hold of the ZX80. I worked cleaning bogs in offices for months to save up the money to get

˥ A now inexplicably popular form of homebrew software that purportedly calculated your emotional, physical and mental states for a given day based on your birth date and presented them as graphs.

one, and I ordered it and of course it was a Clive Sinclair mail order, which always took a long time. My ZX80 arrived on the same day as my A-level results, and it was fantastic. Having got one of those, things progressed. Later, I ended up getting the ZX81, because on the ZX81 you could actually do moving graphics, which was a big luxury.

I was entirely self-taught, basically; you learn because you're interested. I started out learning BASIC, but I found BASIC too slow for doing videogame stuff, so I heard about this thing called machine code, so I learned that. I remember writing a loop in BASIC which displayed some graphics on the screen and you could see it kind of flickering along. I wrote the same loop in assembler, my first-ever machine language program, and it did it so fast you couldn't see it. I was like wow. Such a difference.

←49
## Peter Molyneux
71→

I had a job as a computer programmer at a local company, and I was using their computers to write little games on the side. In the early days there was absolutely no thought that I could make a single cent out of what I was doing. In fact, it was insanely destructive to my life! You know, I didn't have a girlfriend, I didn't really have any friends. All my spare time I spent sitting in front of my home computer, smoking cigarettes, drinking cans of Coke and eating pizzas. You know, I think at work I got the nickname of Thunder Thighs because I had put on so much weight. I didn't think I could make any money, I mean, you don't make money out of things that are fun. That's not what making money is all about. That's what I thought back then.

## Charles Cecil
59→

I was sponsored by Ford to learn BASIC and I met a fellow engineer, Richard Turner, who'd just started a little company called Artic Software, based in Hull. He'd disassembled the ROM of the ZX80 or the ZX81, I can't remember which, and it was great because it helped people write machine code. He invited me to write some adventure games, and we didn't expect to make any money, it was just for fun.

My first game was actually called *Adventure B: Inca Curse.*\* Richard had written *Adventure A: Planet of Death*

* Released for the ZX81 in 1981, a text adventure game in which you have to collect as much treasure from a temple in a jungle as you can. *Computer and Video Games* called it 'quite a good game' but criticised its poor spelling

and so mine was called *Adventure B* and then I made *Adventure C: Ship of Doom.** The packaging was really, really basic, but the games were actually very successful. I mean, I never got paid a penny, but that wasn't the point, it was just the fun of creating things, of exploring the interactive medium. We had absolutely no idea that the industry would grow. I think we all sort of thought it was a fad, like skateboards, and so nobody really took it seriously. If only we knew.

## Mel Croucher

I couldn't afford to buy the early machines like the Commodore PET, so I had to use them through somebody who was in the educational system. But I had a bit of luck when my local radio station down in Portsmouth got one, and it allowed me to go and invent a whole new industry.

I formed a company called Automata on the 19th of November 1977, and we made our first prize computer game broadcast just before Christmas. There was no other way to get software out there then. There were no shops, there were no magazines, there was no distribution system, but there were people with radio sets and cassette recorders, so the idea was that these people would have to stay up very late at night, because this was after hours, and record the software off the air.

They had to bang it into their computer and if it loaded, up would come a little game. I guess we had to top and tail the computer code with a prize competition, to stop people from switching off, because computer code sounds like your radio is having a fit. Clues would appear on the screen, and if you solved them and phoned the radio station, you could win a crappy prize. And that was the beginning, perhaps, of the computer game industry in this country.

## Archer Maclean

In the late '70s there weren't really any shops. The earliest one I remember was the Byte Shop in around '77, '78 in Ilford in East London. We used to drive past it on the way into central London. But that was it until really about 1980, '81. You went in there to buy American desktop PCs; the company I was working for part-time bought something called a SWTPC 6800, a Southwest Technical Products computer system with a 6800 processor; so really, really ancient. But it ran an RS232 VDU with black and white characters, a BASIC interpreter and an 8-inch floppy drive. I rapidly got into programming it in BASIC.

But there were a number of computer magazines beginning to start in the UK. *PCW* was one of them, *Practical Computing* was another, and they had lots of adverts from people running homebrew systems and little things you could buy for computers at home. Not much in the way of games, though. It was all very simple programs that did not do much more

than adding up a bunch of numbers, long before VisiCalc. Comet and Dixons and all those sort of high street shops didn't start selling readymade computers like Commodores and Ataris until probably '82 or '83.

I read a lot of magazines. Going right back to 1975, '76, watching arcade machines coming out, I was reading *Byte* magazine – I have got all of them even now – and I used to follow a column called Steve Ciarcia's Circuit Cellar, reading about his funny experiments and building some of them.

* Personal Computer World was the UK's first computer magazine, having launched in February 1978.

* First published in 1975, Byte began as an offshoot from amateur radio magazine 73 and rapidly became the most influential computing magazine in the US.

## Rod Cousens

I have never been one of those people with a conformist career path. I didn't do badly academically, but I wasn't going to be a teacher, like my mother probably wanted, and I ended up setting up an insurance brokerage, because I used to arrange insurance for yachts. But I had a school friend, who told me he'd met someone who was setting up a new business and could do with some help in terms of insurance cover. So I called this guy and arranged to meet up, and drove around looking for the name of the company, which was called Quicksilva. I knocked on the door and this guy came to the door with long blonde hair down to his knees, holey jeans, which wasn't fashionable then, and an Aran sweater, and I said, 'Hi, I'm looking for Nick Lambert,' and he went, 'Hey, you've found him, man.'

The place was an absolute shithole. There were bits of carpet, stuff jammed in the floorboards to plug holes, and there were Jiffy bags everywhere. He made me a coffee from an already used coffee mug, and I couldn't drink it quickly enough to get out of there. And in the midst of it all, the phone wouldn't stop ringing.

But I could intuitively smell that something was going to happen, and we got on really well. He started asking me about business,

* Founded in 1980 by Nick Lambert in his rented Southampton house, Quicksilva was one of the UK's first game developers.

and I asked him if he knew how to deal with VAT, and he said, 'Got it sussed, man.' He pulled this box full of invoices from under the sofa and he said, 'I'm going to give the invoices to the VAT man, and the cheque book, and tell him to write out his own cheque.' I said, 'I wouldn't do that. These guys don't have a sense of humour.'

I set him up with a girl that I knew who could get his books in order. He was making 1K RAM packs for the ZX81, which was a big deal, and school kids would pile in at 3.40pm and put them in Jiffy bags and sell them off. He used to take orders through *Popular Computing Weekly,*[×] and you'd have 28 days to fulfil them. But it was already starting to turn into a business, and he had started to design games like *Defender*[+] and *Space Invaders* and put them on the RAM packs.

So one day he called me and said, 'Hey, guess what's happened? WHSmith called me and they want 10,000 units of a game.' I said, 'Wow, that's fantastic!' and he said, 'I told them to fuck off. They wanted a 50% discount, man.' 'That's just the start of negotiation!' I said. It took me about two years to get back into WHSmith, working with a guy who was also instrumental in the games industry, John Rowland. He was the man responsible for taking videogames mainstream in the United Kingdom.

So I had a great relationship with Nick, and we started to build this whole thing together. He wanted to be creative to an extent, although he wasn't really a programmer. He worked with three other people, John Hollis, who was pretty sophisticated in his programming skills, and Mark Eyles, who, with Caroline Hayon, did marketing.

It was the most exciting and liberating thing to be in, and it occupied all of my time, so I gave up all of my other business interests. I loved it. I knew videogames were here to stay. People were talking about it in the form of fads and skateboarding, and we were criticised everywhere and never taken seriously. We were viewed with disdain and people didn't really understand, but you could see there was a whole cultural shift going on, and people's lifestyles and interests were changing.

[×] The UK's first weekly computing magazine, published from 1982.
[+] Eugene Jarvis's 1981 arcade classic for Williams.

← 56                    Charles Cecil                    64 →

Richard was the big boss of Artic, and I was just supporting him while I was at university. I drove over at weekends and we'd write games together. Then, suddenly, all this money came in and so we thought, 'This is a proper business!' But what Artic did, which was so brilliant, was to lobby WHSmith, which was the main retailer of ZX81 games at that time, and get the first order. So Artic was the first company to be able to ship directly into WHSmith.

Now, we didn't want to come across as amateurs. In those days, when you made calls in telephone boxes they would go, 'Beep, beep, beep, beep,' to tell you to put another 10p in, which felt to us desperately, desperately amateurish, so I had to scour the whole of Manchester to find phone boxes which you could pre-load with money, wait until all the cars had gone by, and we'd phone up the main buyer at WHSmith, a guy called John Rowland, and we'd pretend to be very business-like. He'd already played a number of these *Adventure* games and I'd say, 'Oh, hello John, it's Charles Cecil from Artic Computing, we've got a new *Adventure* game,' and he'd say, 'Great, is it like the other ones?' 'Yeah,' 'Send us 5,000.' He'd buy 5,000 at a go, at about £3 or £4 each.

Gary Penn

Artic Software always had this fantastic homebrew feel. As a kid, they felt like a little local business, and from the point of view of accessibility it was fantastic. It felt within reach, which was a brilliant feeling because you felt like getting into the business was an achievable thing.

We would then phone up the duplicating company that produced all the cassettes and our printer, and put them all together, send them off to WHSmith and at the weekends we'd invoice everybody. Suddenly we found we were making actually huge amounts of money. We were just kids, we weren't quite sure what to do with it. And so we wrote a few more games, and we commissioned some more, and we fell into some pretty bad company, I have to say, with some really dodgy lawyers and solicitors. Everybody saw how innocent we were, how naïve we were, and we got pretty badly ripped off.

Mel Croucher

I realised that other people were involved with computing when the first computer society was formed locally. About a dozen kids turned up and I was by then in my 30s. I thought my audience was adult, because a lot of the clues we put in the radio broadcasts were very adult and after hours. I thought they were funny and other people thought they were puerile. But we went to a computer club and there were a couple of adults there and it was mostly kids, which was a revelation.

Some of the kids at the computer clubs had hand-typed listings of computer programs, and I am sure that from those early listings being passed around from club to club, just a dozen people at a time, the early magazines were spawned and grew. Those magazines were extraordinarily important; they not only made me aware there were hotbeds of computer gaming enthusiasts in this country, but also that there were other people who were trying to do it commercially.

←51

## Steve Turner

We had a local computer club, and me and Andrew Braybrook were often asked to come and talk and show what we were doing. People used to go and show their programming efforts, swap ideas and play each other's games. It very much was a social swap shop, and it was a growing counterculture. It's surprising how quickly it happened.

The first magazines weren't actually magazines, they were hand-printed listings. And what do you advertise? Certainly not games, because there weren't commercial game producers at the time, so they were advertising components, peripherals and make-your-own-machine stuff. And so the British computer games magazine industry was born, and it grew extremely quickly into monthly and weekly magazines printed on bog paper. The standard was absolutely bloody awful, and they were great.

←52

## Mo Warden

I suppose the next turning point for me was when I started a computer club in 1983. I wanted to get together with people who had the same enthusiasm and share knowledge. All the clubs in the area in Birmingham where I lived at the time were quite distant, and I couldn't take my computer, because it was running off the TV, which was too big to carry around. So I approached my local school and I told them I had a bit of a chicken and egg situation. I'd really like to start a club, but I couldn't afford to pay for a room until I had people coming and paying subs. And they said, 'Oh, don't worry about it, have a room!' I nearly ripped their arm off.

So every Tuesday we had this meeting. To start with it was just me and the local kids playing games on my Commodore 64, and then gradually more people started to come, paying for the use of the room. We were collecting more than we spent, so we were able to make plans for going to shows. We used to hire coaches and go to London or the NEC* for computer shows.

I was blown away when we went for

* The National Exhibition Centre, Birmingham's main exhibition hall.

the first time. It was a lot bigger than I expected, very glitzy, and all these names I knew were there. I guess I was a bit overwhelmed, but I got into it quite quickly, going around, playing everything and talking to lots of interesting people. For example, I got to meet Jeff Minter. I felt I'd like to tell him that I thought his games were great and I suppose I must have sounded like an awful fangirl. 'I really like your stuff!' He was very nice about it, but we just started to chat generally and he was a nice guy. We met a few times at shows, and he was very encouraging to me. He was very important at the beginning.

## Jeff Minter

The microfairs were where we saw the new stuff that was in development, so you'd go along and it was a point of contact between the people developing the software and the people consuming it. I always really liked that, because rather than just selling games to faceless people that you didn't know, you got to actually meet these people face-to-face at a computer show, play and talk about games with them, and just get on with them as friends. I mean, a lot of these people became my friends, it was really good. For us, it became a social thing as much as a sales thing to do.

## Mel Croucher

In my experience there were few or no computer shops. Locally, I can't think of any, so the epiphany for most people in the local clubs was going to their first microfair. The microfairs were first held in a church hall or a scout hut, maybe 50 or 100 people turning up, usually on a Saturday. They weren't really buying stuff, they were talking, and some were swapping programs, either written out longhand or on cassette.

So early enthusiast clubs would have had 10 or a dozen people, and when it got to the church hall and scout hut there were maybe 50 or 100, and then some bright spark formalised the whole thing and charged people to hire a trestle table for a day, and we got to a thousand people at a microfair. So capitalism had just started in this business, and we'd soon have accountants, and lawyers, advertising executives, bankers; it would be full of parasitic shysters. But in those days that hadn't started, so it was amateurs, amateurs, amateurs. When we got to a thousand people at a microfair then commercial gamers had started to sell their software on cassette and the industry had actually hatched.

If Clive Sinclair was the catalyst to the British industry in terms of machines like the ZX80, ZX81 and the wonder Spectrum, then the catalyst to bringing people together was a guy called Mike Johnson. He was a sort of Father Christmas figure, a big roly-poly guy, very loud, very tactile. You could sit on his knee and he would embrace you after taking your money for hiring a booth. We had booths, very cheap, and he worked so hard; so hard it killed him. It was a sad day, but he exploded in fine style.

During Mike Johnson's microfair[×] days, a core of enthusiasts changed into a core of movers and shakers. The UK industry was because of the people that met for the first time then. If I shut my eyes I can picture them now in one row, no more than a dozen and a half of key people. Without him it would not have happened in the fun and successful way it did. It would have been totally different, it would have turned into the corporate shit industry it turned into much, much earlier. These guys were not only enthusiasts, they were seers. They were much smarter than me, because they made a proper living out of it.

× Johnson's ZX Microfairs took place at venues like the Royal Horticultural Halls in Westminster and Alexandra Palace.

← 58

## Rod Cousens

67 →

We would go and set up a couple of trestles with a plank across them and some black cloth over it. We'd pile the tapes high and sell them for a fiver, and that gave us a lot of cash to build the business. We went up to Manchester to the Northern Computer Fair and it just absolutely exploded and we ended up with about half a million in cash. We were standing in our hotel in Piccadilly Gardens jumping up and down on the bed, throwing it up in the air, because, you know, we'd arrived! We were on the scene.

Microfairs were one of the ways the regional markets grew and expanded. There were the microfairs put together by Mike Johnson in London, where we'd have things like Mel Croucher and the Piman[*] walking around, and the Northern Computer Fair, with companies like Rabbit Software, Bug-Byte, Artic. There was great camaraderie amongst the exhibitors and we all knew each other. We all used to play practical jokes on each other, so people would change around the names on the peg boards above your booth, so Quicksilva became 'Sickquilva'.

* Piman was a character from an Automata puzzle game and comic strip.

## Jeff Minter

There was a time before it got seriously commercialised when there was a lot of creativity in the industry. There were a lot of people having a lot of fun, and games were rated on originality as much as anything else. Later on, as it became more commercialised and game companies got bigger, I think people got less adventurous, and so I kind of missed those really early days when everybody knew everybody else; you'd all meet up at the computer shows, you'd all have a few beers. You were all in competition but it was all mostly very friendly. There wasn't the idea that somebody was out to make stupid amounts of money at the expense of anybody else. It was just all very friendly and fun.

## David Darling

I actually telephoned Jeff Minter because I wanted to understand whether there was a particular technique where you could interrupt the raster on the graphics processor to get more sprites. You had a limited number of sprites and I saw what he was doing with some of his games and thought there must be a way. I also called Jon Hare. I used to have a habit of calling other people in the industry and asking them how they did things.

It was a very cottage industry, so if you went to the trade shows you would just have a trestle table with your computer on it and some of your games, and Jeff Minter might be on the next table, and there would be somebody's Lamborghini in the car park, and everybody would be talking about whose it was. It was quite exciting; you kind of learned off other people, I suppose, like the Italian artists in the 16th century. They would be developing different techniques for shading, oil painting and doing photorealistic faces. It was the same in the game industry. People would keep discovering new techniques and so you would be constantly trying to learn off them.

## Charles Cecil

We were selling primarily through mail orders and within the UK, but there was quite a vibrant industry growing up in France and Belgium, not so much Germany, because Germany was always going to be Commodore-based, but France and Belgium were Spectrum-based. So the way that we sold, apart from mail order, was at microfairs in the UK, or actually driving over to the equivalent microfairs in Belgium or France. You wouldn't believe it now, but before we had commercial duplicators we used to duplicate all the tapes ourselves. Richard's family spent all night producing vast numbers of these things, one by one by one, putting little stickers on them and then we'd drive off to wherever the microfair was.

This was before the Common Market, well, before the UK was in it. As a student I had this Renault 10, the ugliest car ever, and we'd have to drive to the docks, and because we were commercial we'd go along with all the trucks, all those huge great trucks and there's me in my little car, and we went off all over Europe. It was fantastic! People treated us like rock stars. Because the UK so dominated the scene, these people saw us as these great stars coming over from England. We were treated extremely well, and so for a time, during the golden age, it was really, really fun.

We'd literally set up tables and sell people games for probably £10. That was quite expensive by early '80s prices, but people were so enthusiastic because they loved meeting us, and we loved meeting them. They were always wonderful, wonderful celebrations of the computer games industry and what we were doing at the time. It was very pure because there were no publishers at that point.

← 45

## David Perry

70 →

The ZX Microfairs were amazing because I was able to experience the passion for the industry from lots of other people. Imagine you're this little kid walking in and there are all these game company logos and all this buzz and excitement, all these game screens and people showing off what they were working on. It was incredible to see games for the first time – there it was, running in front of you, some game you'd been dying to see!

These shows were just so important. The CEO of a company would be selling their games in little plastic bags; it was very raw and very early. I'd be walking along and just stand there in awe, like *Jetpac* from Ultimate. I remember looking at it and going, 'How are they doing this?! The Spectrum can't do that!' It wasn't just going and listening to talks, you're there being incredibly inspired and the people who made the games are standing right in front of you.

I think we've always been very approachable; it's easy to get to the people who make the games, and there's a weird sharing in the game industry, people are open with telling you what they're working on and revealing things, sometimes before they're even finished and talking about the engineering and what technologies they use. You don't see that in lots of other fields, where if they're working on some technology, they want to keep it as secret as they can. I think it's important and part of the industry's DNA: it keeps everything moving. So when you were seeing a ZX81 or Spectrum game and you saw that someone was beating you, you wanted to learn all about it and see how they did it, be- cause then you could come back with something new, and then that would cause them to have to return fire on you. I think it's very healthy, it accelerates evolution within the industry. It was very fun times.

## Steve Turner

About 1983 or '84 we went along to a microfair. You still had the smaller stallholders around the edge, but the surprising thing was that the middle was dominated by a few huge publishers that seemed to have bought out about half the space. It was very much a them and us kind of thing, the little guys with probably family businesses selling a few copies, and big publishers that didn't have a copy on sale around the place because they weren't interested in selling at the show, they were interested in signing deals. It was a completely different feel. And, of course, the odd dolly bird in a pair of hot pants giving out little leaflets. They were turning into the car shows.

## Mel Croucher

We did three seasons of broadcasts and we were sponsored by a beer company, but by '81 I had branched out into more ambitious stuff. We had 1K of memory to play with in those days and a stockpile of C20 audio tapes, and I thought, 'Why don't we put as many computer games on a cassette as possible, and flog them for £3?' So we got eight comedy audio tracks and eight comedy videogames on one cassette, and sold it for £3, and our competitors simply couldn't compete.

By then, the first computer magazines and computer clubs were starting to happen, and the first charts were starting to be compiled. We found we were at the top of the charts, which was very nice, and totally by accident. We didn't have a clue what we were doing. Some people say that I founded the British videogame industry, and if I did it was by accident. There was no plan – and I probably didn't anyway.

It was all free before then. We had to give it away and dressed it up with prizes, and if we got a gig doing a sponsored quiz in the local pub, we weren't paid. But when it came to publishing our stuff on cassette, we were charging money. It was all done direct, through mail order. There were no shops and we never paid a penny for advertising. We used to write cartoon strips to advertise our stuff and hopefully make people laugh, and the publishers seemed to be quite happy to have a free cartoon strip which ended up as a free whole page every week in exchange for the advertising.

We had one title which was a prize game at large, which involved a cartoony character and today you call it multimedia, but back then it was just me being very silly, because out of that game, *Pimania,*[×] we had two audio albums, about two years'-worth of comic strips, T-shirts, magazines and broadcasts, so it was real multimedia stuff. So our little cartoon hero became a bit of a cult, and the rock albums, T-shirts and spin-offs went on for about three years, which was quite long-lived, I suppose.

We were running adverts and comic strips really from day one.[•] I used Letraset and stencils, things that architects used to use.[ꓹ] I did all my own artwork, which was hopeless, but then I found a cartoon genius called Robert Evans, who at the time was drawing cartoons for our multimedia maps and cassettes, and one day I said, 'Sod this, take over, I can't draw. I'm rubbish,' and he started showing me Piman cartoons and cassette covers.

[×]  A surreal and obscure puzzle game released in 1982. A player solving its cryptic clues in 1985 finally revealed its ultimate objective: the physical location of a prize golden sundial.

[•]  Automata took over the back page of *Popular Computing Weekly* from March 1983.

[ꓹ]  Before working with computers, Croucher had been an architect, designing sports arena roofs, a pavilion for the Mary Rose, and was site architect for Sheikh Rashid Al Maktoum, ruler of Dubai.

None of us had any money, so we couldn't put any huge marketing campaigns behind us. We used to take out tiny classified ads in *Popular Computer Weekly* and would be selling games at £2.99, £3.99, £4.99, and occasionally we would sell a RAM pack on the back of it. Then we'd take the money, normally in things like postal orders, bank it, and then be able to go to the duplicating company where it cost us less than 30p each. We would do a wrap-around inlay – progress was doing a full colour one – put it in a Jiffy bag and send it out, and then you would start getting letters back from people saying, 'Hey, I really liked the game, I got to level five,' or whatever. We started to build a database, and we could produce a new game every few months, and then we would go out and do it again. Later, Quicksilva became the first company to do full colour ads. We took full-page ads in magazines saying that if you had a game idea we would publish it and give you 25% royalties.

## Julian Rignall

The magazines from the very early '80s were filled with hundreds and hundreds of ads, each sent in by the individuals making the games. Very quickly, businessmen realised there are all these people making all these games, and to do it well you've got to have marketing skills, art skills, and all of this stuff. So I think the market quickly transitioned from programmers having to call up a magazine, get artwork together and send in an ad, being their own company and making the game, distributing and selling, to having business people going, 'We'll rep you. We can market your product. We can do your art, we'll manufacture.

All you need to do is just give us the game and a big cheque will roll in to you at some point in the not too distant future.' So people were like, 'Sure, that sounds good.' Very quickly I think the industry began to coalesce around those very early publishers.

If you look at some of those early ads, they have, 'Have you got a game? Send it in to us.' They included that in their advertisements because they were looking for new talent, basically. You always had people who wanted to go solo, but most people really just wanted to concentrate on doing what they knew and they did well, which was programming.

## Oliver twins

From our Dragon we started sending game listings and cassettes off to publishers to try and get them published. In fact, our very first published game was in '83, a type-in listing in *Computer and Video Games*. We had set out to make a really good tidy type-in listing, coded it all, ran it, played it, lovely. We had to get it into the magazine, but we didn't have a printer. So, very carefully, we hand-wrote it all on lined paper, every single line.

With the brackets and the commas all in the right place.

And all the spaces, because you know what the syntax on these things was like, dreadful. We gave it to our mum, who was a secretary at the local college with a typewriter. This is before the days of the electronic typewriters. 'Mum? Can you type that in?' So, she doesn't know what all this code is, but she tries to replicate my tidy handwriting and brings it home. 'Mum, that space!'

AO We ringed a few things. Syntax errors, all over the place.

PO 'Can you do it again, please, Mum?' She takes it back, she types the whole lot again on the typewriter, comes home and it's like, 'Mum! There are still a bunch of errors.' She takes it back, out with the Tipp-Ex. So this took two or three weeks and a lot of work by our mum, and finally it was close enough and we sent it to *Computer and Video Games*. We got the phone call a few days later saying they'd like to publish it for £50. It was only two or three years later that I was telling this story to somebody when they said, 'Why didn't you send them the cassette you saved the program on to?' What a good idea that would have been.

← 56                    ## Dino Dini                    291 →

Of course, back then there was no internet, so the way that communication operated in the community, or the industry or whatever, was in magazines, and there would be adverts for games. There was a company called Timedata, and I got in touch with them. They made a book called *The Acorn Atom Magic Book*, and the first actual commercial transaction that I did was to create a number of games which people had to type into the Acorn Atom that were listed in this book.

I got £400 for that in today's terms. It was a bit of money for quite a lot of work, but when that works it makes you think, 'Okay, maybe I could do something.' So I continued to try to develop games. The next one was something called *Astro Tracker*, which was a kind of *Asteroids* clone. I did that deal by going to one of the exhibitions, it could have been an Acorn User Exhibition, and there was a company there called *BEEBUG*. [x] It was a magazine really, a little BBC user club-type thing, but they published that game and that got me £1,500. They were interested in what I was doing and that really boosted my confidence. But then nothing much more happened, to be honest. It started to get more difficult to get deals back then and I went to university. But that was how it kind of started, sort of dabbling in it.

[x] Founded by *Personal Computer World* writers Sheridan Williams and Lee Calcraft, the BBC Micro User Group published *BEEBUG*, amassing a subscriber base of 30,000 by 1985.

While I was at school I got the magazine of the National ZX80 and ZX81 Users' Club called *Interface*, and as I started making my own games I sent some of them into it. I was the happiest guy alive when I saw one show up. It was the coolest thing ever. For me, when you're in school, you know, it's hard. I wasn't great at sports or anything else, but it was cool to be in a magazine, and then one day I got a cheque in the mail for £450, and I didn't even have a bank account. I was like, 'What, someone wrote to me?! I don't even get letters and here's a cheque! You can get paid to do this? Are you kidding me?!' And so you can imagine, you're in school and what do you spend that money on? The answer is of course sweets, so I'm just buying all the sweets I can possibly eat.

So I started making more and more games. The publisher, Tim Hartnell, who was based in Australia reached out to me and he said, 'Look, we're going to make a book and we'd like to include some of your games. Would that be okay?' and I'm like, 'Of course!' and then he came back later and said, 'We're going to make a different book and we'd like to give a whole chapter to you.' Then later he said, 'Look, I've got this crazy idea. Let's not make a book, let's make something we can put in all the newsstands across the country, sell it as a magazine but it's a magazine-book.' It was just my games in that one. So each step for me was very exciting.

At the same time, the game industry was evolving as a real retail business, so the listings in magazines and books weren't quite as important as the cassettes that were starting to line up in all the stores. And so I was kind of a bit lucky. I got a little bit of a taste of both sides before cassettes took over.

* First published as a newsletter in 1980, Interface featured program listings and reader letters.
* Hartnell, who died in 1991, was a prolific writer of books and magazines about 8-bit computers and computer games under the publisher name Interface Publications.
* The book was 49 explosive games for the ZX Spectrum, published in 1983.

I suppose in '81, '82 the main connection with the industry was through magazines, but once you got to '83 or '84, thousands of independent retailers popped up all over the country. There would be shops above Indian restaurants or next to the newsagents on the corner, all these little shops everywhere. It was a bit like Games Workshop, where you notice loads of kids just hanging out for hours and hours. We would go to the shops, just talking to the shop keeper and asking what games were selling and what's the best game out, and have you heard about this new computer ... The shop- keepers were an invaluable source of information because they were right at the front of the industry and they were talking to all of the customers.

## Eugene Evans 83→

In the heart of Liverpool there was a small store called Microdigital, which had been started by Bruce Everiss.[x] Very few stores selling computers opened on a Saturday, but Bruce did open, and the result was it kind of created this environment which was almost like a computer club. People would visit it every Saturday, and a lot of individuals in the game industry now can trace their path back through to that store. Bruce hired me to work on Saturdays, to go for burgers, sweep up, pin bags of games to cork boards. But I loved it and it gave me access to computers that I otherwise didn't have.

Bruce did a few other interesting things with the store. He'd discovered how much of a publishing industry there was for computer books in the US, and there were times when he paid me in those books, and he would also let me buy them cheap. That was my education in computers, buying those books. He also was importing magazines from the US, like *Byte* magazine, and he also started one, the *Liverpool Software Gazette*, and I wrote articles for two or three issues. It really was what got me started.

[x] Bruce Everiss opened Microdigital in July 1978, in Brunswick Street, and went on to lead marketing at Imagine Software.

←56
## Peter Molyneux 84→

Not only did the shops sell all these computer games which you definitely, definitely wanted, but they were also an early gathering point for people who played and wrote games. There used to be one in Guildford, and I remember hanging out around there for hours. In fact, hanging out around there I eventually bumped into the person I formed Taurus with, because of our shared passion for computer games. So they were as much a culture as anything else, and they started popping up everywhere. I think there were first a couple in London, then one in Cambridge, and then – I couldn't believe it – one in Guildford. Almost every month there were these little independent stores popping up.

## Gary Penn

My local shop wasn't actually that local, it was in Hemel Hempstead, a few miles down the road, and we had a WHSmith with a small game section. It was the classic thing, the shop was a hub, this kind of nerdy culture that evolved. It felt like there was this, I wouldn't call it an underground movement, but there was certainly something in the air that was outside of convention. So you would go into the stores and lust after a computer and sample the games vicariously, just looking at them on the shelves. The shops were part temple and part wine cellar. There was almost a degree of worship when you went there to just be among these things that you couldn't necessarily afford, or they were on different platforms that you didn't have access to. You saw the title and the box, and you were almost playing it in your head as you read the back description of how it worked.

The shop in Hemel Hempstead was tiny, because that was about all the owner could afford, but you would have all the newer computers in there, one of each sort hooked up, and then wall-to-wall games of all different formats. They had some trading scheme where you could buy a game and take it back but lose a percentage of the value. It was a great way of trying stuff out, particularly if you were grouped together. You would buy one game between you and pass it around.

## Peter Stone and
## Richard Leinfellner

I left Virgin to set up a retail operation at the very beginning of VHS video. We were initially on Kensington High Street, and then we moved to 100 Oxford Street, which later became a Virgin Game Centre. I think it's a Boots now, but that was the Video Palace. Our main line was video, but we started to have this sideline of computers, starting with selling Apple IIs and all the bits and pieces that went with them.

I actually met Pete because I got a Saturday job at the Video Palace. We used to sell Atari VCS and VIC-20s.

We also used to sell ZX80s, so we used to have kids coming into the store to buy them. They took them home and made games themselves, and came in with them. On Saturday afternoons it was a bit like a youth club. They would swap games on cassette that they made, and that's where I think we started to get involved with the kids that were making the games.

RL There were no real distributors of games then. We used to sell Llamasoft games, and Jeff Minter's mum used to come in and bring a box of them for us to sell, so it was kind of bizarre.

PS So we were seeing the kids coming in and swapping the games they had made, and then we started to sell them. We would buy from people like Jeff Minter, then later, Geoff Brown set up CentreSoft [x] and we started buying from them, so we had a range of games we were selling. Most of the games themselves in those days were pretty basic, and the marketing of them was also very basic and very cottage industry. We would get on the phone and we would order games, and this box of cassettes would turn up, sometimes even without any artwork, or sleeves, just cassettes. Having come from a background of Virgin and the Palace Group, we kind of felt that we knew how to market entertainment better than the other computer game companies and that we just needed to learn how to make the games.

[x] The West Midlands-based software distributor founded in 1983 by Geoff and Anne Brown, from which U.S. Gold emerged as a publishing wing.

# Part 2

# Money Makers

It was very chaotic and there
were a lot of people who were
just selling anything they could,
because you could sell anything
back then. There was a new
market that was desperate for
software, and people were
selling any old crap, to be
honest. But I was very fortunate.

There was this game I got really early on called the *The Fabulous Wanda.*[*] I don't know anybody who has seen this game since, but I bought it for like £2 or something and found the whole game was written in BASIC. When you got to the end of the game, nothing happened because they had simply run out of space to write any more code, and I thought, 'Well, if people can release a game like that, you know, then there is obviously some scope for me writing games.'

[*] A text adventure game written by Alan G. Osborne and released in 1983, it featured multiple choice selections and minimal graphics, and cast the player as a space traveller with the task of finding the elusive Wanda.

When I started building my own 8-bit machines, I just wanted to mimic the *Space Invaders* machine in the foyer of the company I was working for, and add things and make variations. The first proper game I wrote at home was on the Z80 Nascom machine using Microsoft BASIC. It was a car racing game, and it made use of the screen-scrolling function. It had a little car at the bottom and the screen would scroll down with objects on it, getting progressively faster. When you died it printed up a tombstone with 'RIP' written on it. I called it 'Death Race'. A few people came around my house who had similar machines, and they said, 'Can I have a cassette with it on? I'll give you £5!' So it occurred to me, well, why don't I put an advert in the back of one of the early magazines, saying 'Send off for your £5 game'?

But then the news came out that only 500 people had tried building a computer and most of them had failed. You know, the market wasn't exactly very big. Plus we had a *Missile Command* machine turn up in the pub next to the office and I was hooked on that. It was in colour, and I remember thinking, 'How did they do that?!' I was well known for building gadgets and all sorts of stuff, and I wanted to impress people with the fact that I could make what they were playing in the pub. I had a bet with a guy at university, who was writing games on a VIC-20 – £1,000 I couldn't write a game, get it published and get it into the charts. He still owes me that £1,000, because he did a runner.

A lot of the early arcade stuff was inspirational, and obviously I have always been told that *Dropzone* looks like *Stargate*[*]

[*] *Defender*'s 1981 sequel, co-written by Eugene Jarvis and Larry DeMar.

and *Defender*, but I would say it's not a copy. Inspiration isn't infringement, because you are creating your own thing on a new piece of hardware, often with a lot of variations. But I followed everything Nolan Bushnell did from '74 onwards, all the very earliest Atari games.

Anything that came out, any new game, even if it was primitive and black and white, I would go and hunt it down, or me and two friends would skive off school and get on the train to go to Tottenham Court Road, Edgware Road, find the arcades, and play these games to death. *Star Castle* was another one. We would go home and think about how to write and mimic it, or something like it but better. What we didn't know, of course, was that most arcade machines had some very impressive hardware that they kept quiet about, and I used to bust a gut trying to make a 6502 do something even remotely close. Actually, I used to have great fun doing battle with T-state timing with a 1 megahertz 6502 at three o'clock in the morning.

In the late '70s I wanted to go and work for Atari in California, making a full-blown arcade game. I believed I could, and it was just a matter of convincing the powers that be to give me a chance. I actually had an interview with Atari to do just that, but that was not long before the company basically imploded, so that was a bit of a shame. But around then, about 1980, Atari UK got established and started selling the Atari 400/800 series, and they ran an advert that offered a $25,000 prize to anyone who submitted a game that Atari chose to publish for home computers. I've got the advert somewhere. Graduate salaries back in 1980 were £6,000 a year, so you were given this four-times opportunity. I thought, 'Hey, I can make money out of something I really enjoy!'

Malcolm Evans

My wife bought me a ZX81 for my 37th birthday, because she knew that I wanted to go into software, which was something I hadn't done before. The first thing I did was to buy a Z80 software manual, and I made an algorithm that created a maze, and I wondered what it looked like if you were walking through it. So I played around with the graphics, and changed that maze into a 3D one.

Soon afterwards I met John Greye,[*] who had produced a game with a monster in it,[†] but just with ordinary text characters, like 'p's and 'q's, and he said, 'Why don't you put a monster in it?' I thought, 'How on Earth do you put a monster in a 3D game?' but I worked out how. I drew the monster out on square paper, then blocked it out and put that data in, and sorted out how I was going to put it against the background of the walls. I made it as a series of images as it got closer and closer to you.

I programmed *3D Monster Maze* in our bedroom. My computer was in the way of my wife and the children if it was in the dining room, so it ended up on a table in the bedroom. One night, while my wife was reading in bed I had the monster moving around but I hadn't yet put sound or any of the messages in. I remember it suddenly came at me without me realising, and I jumped out of my skin! My wife burst out laughing, and I thought I didn't want anyone to end up with a heart attack, so that's why I added that text on the start screen about, you know, the player going in at their own risk.

Then I thought I would scroll the message up to make it more interesting, and it had a fairground sort of feel so I ended up drawing a picture of a clown, who I must admit, to me always looked like he took his head off when he bowed. Apparently, *3D Monster Maze* became the first 3D game on a home computer, or any computer, in fact, which surprised me, because all I was trying to do was produce a game.

At one microfair, John Rowland[×] apparently overheard a young lad saying how great *3D Monster Maze* was, and he came over to see it and gave his card, saying he'd like to have a word. So I went up to London and I talked to him about my games, and we did a deal on all of them for 10,000 units each.

I remember that he mentioned that you couldn't do anything in 1K of memory, and I said that I had got a full screen *Breakout* that

←67

## Rod Cousens

88→

WHSmith in particular had one of the most progressive buyers, John Rowland. He also sensed the new world order, and he made contact with software publishers, these hobbyist companies. Half of the questions we couldn't answer, when he demanded things like discounts and retail pricing and structure. We were bluffing it, doing it by the seat of our pants, but John basically opened it up singlehandedly.

---

[*] A programmer who had set up his own publishing company, J. K. Greye Software, in 1981, which would go on to publish *3D Monster Maze*.

[†] *Catacombs*, which Greye released in 1981 and is similar to *Rogue*, was released the previous year.

[×] WHSmith's buying manager, often credited as the first person to bring computer games to the UK high street.

ran in 1K, and he said that he couldn't believe it, because you could only just about get the full screen in 1K. So I said, 'Right, I'll send you a copy!' Then I went home and what I had actually written wasn't quite in 1K, but it was close, so I spent the weekend getting it down to 1K, sent it to him, and he said, 'Great, but it's only one game, we couldn't really sell it.' So John Greye and I gave him three more, so it was three of mine and one of John's, and we said we were thinking of selling it for about £2. He suddenly turned around and said, 'That's pocket money! We will have it!' and we eventually sold 22,000 of the things.

## Steve Turner

I was working commercially as a systems analyst and programming at home. I saved like mad, like £10,000, and sent my game off to two or three publishers. Two of them offered me a publishing deal, and when I got that contract signed, I thought, 'Well, it's now or never. Even if it only lasts a year it's going to be real fun.' My employer said I could have my job back, so I almost had a safety net, and I had enough saved to last me a year, so with one game under my belt I thought I would do it.

All the games that I had seen on micros were flat, either side-on games like platform games, or top-down. I had seen a couple of 3D games on the ZX81, a little game with a Tyrannosaurus Rex running through a maze was one that I remember, and I thought you could do this with a shoot 'em up, with spaceships. It was about the time Star Wars was very big, and I thought if I did a game like Star Wars, people were bound to love it. That was the concept from the start, to make it feel like a scene from Star Wars, where you were flying into a crowd of fighters. While I was making it, no one had done a 3D game, though a couple had come out by the time it was published, so that gave me a feeling that I was on to something new.

3D Space-Wars took me six weeks of work in the evenings, so I thought I could crank out a game every six weeks. My publisher said, 'Oh, we sell between 50,000 and 100,000 games and you get between 50p and 70p for each one.' I was thinking I could get rich at this! But that's the only game that ever took me six weeks. The next one took three months, and every one after that seemed to take longer.

One of the first game companies in the UK was Bug-Byte and it was based in Liverpool. It was started by Tony Milner and Tony Baden, who I think were both Oxford chemistry grads who somehow had gotten into gaming. They produced some ZX81 and VIC-20 games, and they had hired a gentleman called Dave Lawson, who wanted to do development on an Apple II for the Spectrum. He had heard about a card for the Apple II that let it run Z80 code, the same as the Spectrum, and so he came and bought one from the shop and I delivered it to him.

He asked me what I did, and I told him, 'Well, I write some code and I work for Microdigital on Saturdays.' They asked me to show them my code, so I showed my graphics code on the Apple II and they said, 'Well, why don't you write a game for us?' And that was it. I finished up my O levels when I was 16 and went to work for Bug-Byte. My parents were very supportive when I left school, but I got a lot of questions from teachers saying, 'Why aren't you staying on? You're a good student, why don't you stay on?' I said, 'Because I love what I am doing and I want to go give this a try.'

In the period shortly before Llamasoft started up, there was a Bug-Byte *Asteroids* advertised for VIC-20 and I thought, 'I quite like Bug-Byte, this should be quite good.' So I bought it. It cost seven quid. Seven quid. And I loaded it up and it was dreadful. It was like character mode *Asteroids*: you didn't have single shots that came out of the front of the ship, you had a line of full stops that came out, and they made a noise like a hoover, and the asteroids would kind of jerk around the screen, and sometimes you'd die and then the next life would appear and an asteroid would get poked straight on top of it.

It was just terrible game design, really badly made, and I always remembered it was *Asteroids* by Simon Munnery, and it was the game which pushed me over the edge and made me think, 'Well, I could do better than this, let's do our own software house.' Bug-Byte are charging us seven quid for that. Money for old rope. Let's try and do some better games that aren't just money for old rope. But to be fair to Simon Munnery, if you actually look at some of his later output on the Spectrum, he did get better, and there is a lot worse on the VIC-20. Simon Munnery may be bad but he's far from being the worst, and it's quite funny because then he went on to become this famous comedian. Well that's good, he's found his niche, he's a comedian, just not a game programmer. Each to their own. *

I had gone to the boss of the company I was working at and said that I was going to leave. He said, 'If you leave and start up on your own I will give you £1,000 seed money. Do whatever you like, and let's see what happens.' He was a great entrepreneur, and that's exactly what I did. I had this tiny office in a corner of a warehouse in Farnham, just up the road, and the original idea was to put free software on floppy disks and sell them to schools. I don't quite know how I got that idea, but of course schools were already buying floppy disks, so they didn't want to buy them from me. But they wanted software, and that started me off creating this little suite of it. Some were educational games, very simple, and some were full games. I also used to sell these games off trestle tables at the Royal Horticultural Halls in London.

The industry as it was then used to come to this hall and we'd sell our software. I remember seeing Jez San there from Argonaut selling stuff, literally, from a market stall. There wasn't any feeling of a business, really, because there was nothing at risk. All I needed was the 17p that a tin of beans cost to feed myself; I didn't have any other responsibilities or anything. You know, life was very simple back then.

The first game that I authored was a business sim called *The Entrepreneur*, but just about nobody wanted to play a business sim. I took a little advert out in the press, and I sold two copies. But I have always loved this idea that you are playing around with a world, maybe a graphically realised world, even though it wasn't in *The Entrepreneur*. I have always loved the simulation side.

What happened next was a series of unfortunate events that started off with me making this software which allowed you to compose music. It was odd for me to do at the time because I didn't know anything about music and am completely tone deaf, but a distributor came to me and said they wanted to buy 1,000 units. Now, bear in mind that the most I had ever sold of a game until then was just a few copies. So I said fine, and then thought, 'How am I going to make a thousand of these tapes?' It was a real problem! I bought Tandy tape recorders and recorded them from tape to tape. It took me days and days, and half the batch was wrong, so I had to redo them. Anyway, I gave the 1,000 copies to the distributor and he never paid me. He never paid me! He said he was running out of money, and that was the death knell of my company.

So I closed the company down, but actually, failure was a great life experience, though it didn't seem so at the time. I went off and started a new company called Taurus, shipping baked beans to the Middle East. It isn't a big market for baked beans, but it was something, and the sort of business where you'd ship out a load of baked beans and then didn't have much more to do. That allowed me to continue to play around with games. I was completely financially irresponsible and so I was just throwing money away just to get these new machines. Today success is all about your target audience and choosing the right platform, but there was none of that then. It was just, 'Oh, the Commodore 64 has just come out! I have got to have one of those!' The same with the BBC Micro.

I suppose initially my interest in programming was a lot of just self-driven interest in the machinery, in the same way you might take interest in a board game, or a science fiction book, or a film. I suppose the first time it struck me that you could do something commercially is when I had written a number of games.

I wrote quite a few games with various themes. One was actually inspired by *Missile Command*, but different. You have a view of the northern hemisphere. It is a two-player game, where you play at either end of the keyboard, one playing Russia, the other playing America, and the idea is that you are firing nuclear weapons at the eight cities of the other guy. You get a slightly out of tune anthem once you flatten all their cities, and you have got a score which is, if you like, millions of lives lost as a result. It is slightly sick! It has some interesting design problems. You use sort of WASD-type controls at each end of the keyboard and one of the disadvantages is if the players held down certain key combinations, then their left button wouldn't work, but, actually, it was a fun game.

Another game was making use of gravity, so you have meteors coming down. I liked *Asteroids*, but I thought it was very repetitious and simplistic. So the idea is you have a landscape you can fly along, but with meteors continually coming down like in *Asteroids*, so each time they bounce they break up, so it is in your interest to keep moving to keep away from all the little bits, but you could shoot them.

There was almost nothing to buy for the Atom. Acorn produced these game packs, which had the amazingly imaginative titles of Games Pack 1, Games Pack 2, and they had I think four games in each one. I was quite surprised how simple and basic they were. I had already written things that I thought in my arrogance were more advanced. So I thought maybe I could sell some of the games I had made.

With that in mind I spoke to a company called Thorn EMI, which was part of EMI, the music publisher. I showed them what I had done, with 3D spaceships, some of which actually made it into *Elite* a lot later. They said, 'That's fantastic, that's really good, very, very interesting.' They offered me a job, but they didn't want to publish the games I had made because they said, 'Oh, the Acorn Atom, that's passé now. The BBC Micro is where it's at.' But I didn't have or couldn't afford a BBC Micro. So they said, 'Come and work for us, we've got fancy kit,' and all this sort of thing. But the trouble was, it would have required me not going to university. I already had a place at Cambridge at that point, so ironically it made the decision very easy because I wasn't not going to go to university. Had they offered something that fitted in with that, it might have been different. And then, you know, I probably would never have written *Elite*.

## Geoff Crammond

As the weeks went by making my *Space Invaders* game, I had this thought that I could produce my own cassettes, put an advert in a magazine, and sell it to other owners of the BBC Micro. So I carried on, and then I had a flyer come through from Acornsoft, advertising their games. Some were based on arcade games, but they didn't have *Space Invaders*, so I thought, well, why don't I show it to Acornsoft and see what they think? I rang them up, and I showed it to them, and they liked it, and we agreed that they would publish it.  I remember when I went up there the MD saying, 'Your nephew programmed it?' I think they were used to teenagers doing this sort of thing, and I was, you know, a little different to that. I was 28 when I got my BBC Micro.

So that was me getting my foot in the door, I suppose, and as the months went by, royalties statements came in. After, I suppose, nine months or so, I accrued about equivalent to a year's salary at my Marconi job, so I thought, 'Well, that's interesting!' After I finished *Super Invaders*, the MD at Acornsoft asked what I wanted to do next. I still had the idea of doing a flight thing, so I said, 'Well, I want to do a flight simulator.' And he said, 'Oh, okay, so, erm, great! Show us when you have got something!' I can't quite remember when we signed contracts, but I think it was fairly soon on, and I got an advance as well.

← 44 ## Nigel Alderton 101 →

After I started writing machine code on the ZX81 – I would have been about 13 – this thing called the Sinclair Spectrum was announced and it had colour, and so after much pestering of my parents I ordered one and eventually it turned up after about three months. I got straight down to learning about the hardware. I didn't bother trying to program in BASIC on the Spectrum, I just wanted to get stuck straight into machine code to see what it could do. Me and a next-door neighbour wrote a game where you were a massive big bunny rabbit chasing something round a maze. It was all block character movement, but it was written in machine code. We got some cassette tape inlays printed and recorded tapes and put an advert in a magazine. We sold none, but it was still great fun.

Then I wrote a game I think called 'Blaster' as a working title, and I had it finished but I didn't have anybody to sell it to. I was working at A&F Software at the time, making cups of tea and things on a Saturday, and I offered it to them but they weren't interested. Then, a friend of mine mentioned this guy up the road who had a shop and published games. So I got the bus up there and knocked on the door of his shop. When I got in there, he was lying on the counter, so I introduced myself and said, 'I have got this game to sell, would you like to see it?' I put it on the screen and he loved it. He thought it was fantastic and he said, 'I'll buy it. I'll give you £500.' I was just gobsmacked. I think I was 14, and I just looked at him with a blank expression, and he said, 'Okay, £600.' I thought it was hilarious that he'd up his offer, just because I hadn't said anything, so I started laughing, and he thought that was me wanting more money, so then he said, '£700,' so I said, 'Okay, I will take £700. Thanks very much.' I took the cheque home and showed my dad, and that's the first time I ever heard him use the F-word at home. My parents had no idea that this tapping around on a keyboard would ever generate an income. I'm sure they thought it was just a hobby and a bit of fun, really. Anyway, the guy released it as *Rocket Raider*.*

* Released in 1983 by C-Tech.

There was one program I came across that was a defining moment. This Jiffy bag arrived with a tape in, so we loaded this thing and this 3D Escher-like world came up, and you just knew you were witnessing something that was groundbreaking. It was written by a guy who I have got such a huge affection and admiration for to this day, Sandy White. He and his then girlfriend, Angela Sutherland, were from Edinburgh and they were art students. I called and I said it was a lovely game and asked if we could get together, and his immediate reaction was one of suspicion and defensiveness. 'Why are you so interested in it? Sinclair rejected it, so why are you so interested in it?'

I knew if he carried on sending the game out it would be picked up, so I said to him that because we loved his work, I'd like to come up and see him. But he didn't want me to, so I offered to fly him down to Southampton, and again that made him suspicious, but reluctantly he and Angela agreed. I met them by the baggage carousel carrying a newspaper under my arm so that they could identify me, and that was the start of a fantastic relationship. They met the entire team, and they loved people like John Hollis, Nick Lambert and Mark Eyles, and I wouldn't let them go back to Edinburgh until they had signed the game to us. They became lifelong friends of mine.

The technology and the art that prevailed in video games was pretty simplistic, and *Ant Attack* used 3D graphics, with these Escher-like images, with large ants that came across as scary. It was a completely different approach to gaming, with a completely different view, and it created atmosphere.

The only other game that I didn't publish that I felt was as groundbreaking at the time was *Jetpac* by Ultimate Play the Game, who became Rare. The Stampers are also good friends of mine and they were also pioneers. We went out, we raised the bar, we set new standards, and we changed an entertainment form, and we spawned a whole new generation of talent.

My interest in making games definitely carried on once I started at Cambridge. With university work it was hard, but I also met quite a few other people, like Ian Bell, who I eventually did *Elite* with, and others who were making games commercially with Acorn.

I showed some of my 3D stuff to Ian Bell and we talked. Bizarrely, I think we were both quite tired of games. I mean, it sounds silly because it was right at the beginning, but games had reached a bit of a ... I found them a bit boring, I suppose. Every game seemed to get a life at 10,000 points, seemed to involve you shooting various-shaped blobs in some way, often with some slight twist like

*Galaxian*, and they move a bit and swoop. You know? I think we both hated that. Why should you get an extra life at 10,000? I might want extra bullets! I want to choose. So I think the idea of being able to spend score was how we first talked of it. 'Wait a second, why don't we just call it money and have done with it?'

So lots of ideas came together almost as an antidote to our boredom with a lot of the games out there. I think once you get quite good at a game, especially an arcade game you are playing at home, you actually realise there is not that much to it. It gets so difficult that you can only play it a little bit further. You know what I mean? It's like in *Defender*, once you get to the green landscape, and it gets so hard to keep going. But it is artificially hard, if you see what I mean. There is a point where just getting an extra bit of score doesn't seem all that rewarding. So that is where a lot of the sentiment behind *Elite* came from. That, and seeing the very exciting community that had built up in Cambridge around creating games for the BBC Micro.

We were writing for ourselves, and writing a game yourself gives you the opportunity to fix the things you don't like. I played around with spaceships, where you have a small one, you shoot it down, you shoot down another small one and then a big one comes along and it is harder to shoot. Then you think where do we go from there? An even bigger one that is even harder to shoot? That just has a certain pointlessness to it somehow, you know? There is no feeling of progression, no reward. So in a relatively short period of time, *Elite* evolved into something that was very, very different to what was out there. The idea of saving your position. The idea of trading, which at first seemed a bit of an anathema to games, and a bit dull. But no, no, it makes you care! You want to have precious things that can be destroyed, lost. You know? You want to have that feeling like the guy who sees an oasis in the desert and crawls towards it, getting ever closer. I think that is the joy of the gameplay, especially if something attacks you and you are really afraid that they are going to kill you. So I think that is why we really wanted to make *Elite* the way we did, because I think we found ourselves not caring when we were playing a lot of the games that were out there.

The original title was 'The Elite'. We are now talking late 1982, so we hadn't been at university all that long, and it seemed like a very arrogant name, but the idea was that you were a sort of supreme pilot. You know, why are you able to kill everyone and they are not able to kill you? We thought maybe there was a secret society or group. It was that sort of logic and the name sort of stuck, but due to the restrictions of file name lengths and the fact you couldn't have spaces in them – the source files and things like that were just called 'Elite' and then a letter after it – we actually ended up just calling it *Elite*. So it wasn't like we went to focus groups or any rubbish like that. We actually thought that *Elite* was a working title.

I still didn't actually have a BBC Micro, even though I had written software for it already. Essentially, I made, I suppose you might call it today, an emulator. I could run BBC software on my Acorn Atom by just changing the way the calls worked. So I was able to write code that would transfer directly to a BBC Micro, and Ian already had one, so we put together the first stages of the game and initially showed it to Thorn EMI, because I still had contacts there.

David Braben

The programmers and the developers there were extremely excited about it. The people we unkindly later referred to as the suits talked about it and said, 'Oh yes, it's a very interesting technical demo and it shows that you are very competent, but why would anyone want to play a game like that? How long is it going to take to play it?' We said, 'Oh, quite a long time.' They said, 'What? Half an hour?' We said, 'No, no, no, weeks, and you won't really finish it,' which they didn't like either. We said, 'You just get better. You will be able to do more things, you will be able to go further and explore and ultimately you will get bored with it.' They said, 'But

There were a lot of other games based around text and things like that, but I thought 3D was very interesting because at that time there was very little around. Bizarrely, once we started writing *Elite*, we saw one or two games starting to touch on it and we started to get worried. But earlier I just didn't know that it wasn't possible to do 3D. Do you know what I mean? I had to come up with some quite efficient ways of drawing things in 3D that ran really quickly on simple computers that didn't have multiply instructions, divide instructions or anything like that.

that's not very good. You can't do that. What happens if you die?' I said, 'You die.' They didn't like that either! They said, 'Why can't you have three lives?' I said, 'Well it really doesn't fit in with the logic of the game, but we are allowing you to save your place, so that's essentially the equivalent of lives.' 'Oh, so how many times can you do that?' I said, 'Well, as many times as you like.' 'But you don't get a free life when you get 10,000?' I said, 'Well, we haven't got a score.' They said, 'You need a score.' I said, 'That's what our money is. Whatever you do earns money. If you shoot a pirate, you get a bounty. If you trade goods ...' And they said, 'That's all very complicated. No one will want to do that.' And, actually, to be fair, we were a bit worried, thinking we might be in this sort of ivory tower. Are people going to want to work out how much money they need to buy 16 tonnes of food or whatever?

So we were a bit despondent and then went to Acornsoft. The reaction couldn't have been more different. I think the best way to describe it is there weren't any suits at Acorn. Even the people in senior positions were basically developers and they thoroughly understood. They played games, they wrote software, they understood people who played games, and they were the sort of people who would buy games. So they went sort of overboard! 'How can you do that? How do you do this? How have you got ...?' We showed them the screen running in colour in high resolution and they were very surprised at that. I said, 'Oh, we have just re-written the video drivers to do colour.' It actually did something called an interrupt halfway down the screen where it changed screen mode. I'm sure many people who have tried hacking *Elite* would have found that and thought it's a bit complicated, a bit of a mess!

But anyway, the response from Acorn was really, really positive and it went on from there. They paid us with an advance, which I used to buy a BBC Micro with a disk drive, and that was phenomenal because disk drives then were very, very expensive, and it enabled us to really move forward in leaps and bounds. That would be, I think, late 1983.

We were doing a lot of university work, so we mostly worked in holidays and things like that. The game was pretty well finished at that point in the sense that you could do everything, so we ended up with the rest of the time polishing it, improving it, so what we had was what eventually became the cassette version. I think we made it go a bit faster. We added the missions. One of the things that really made a difference was honing it from something that was pretty good to something much slicker, if you know what I mean. We made sure it was absolutely solid as a rock, nothing went wrong. So it got a lot of testing as well.

Anyway, *Elite* was substantially written in what you might call stolen moments. It was a sort of guilty pleasure hobby, and I think a lot of love went into it as a result. It wasn't, 'Oh God, I have a day to somehow sort this out.' No. It was, 'Fantastic, I can sort out that problem that has been niggling me for a while. I will make it go a bit faster.' Or I might have an idea in a lecture and think, 'Actually, that would work, I am sure it would work,' and try it a day or so later, when I got some time. So actually, it took very little time because the ideas were already fully formed by the time we got them on to paper, if you know what I mean.

We solved a lot of problems. Particularly in the very early days I remember trying to come up with algorithms for how to draw a line on graph paper, you know, you go up a bit, along a bit, and up a bit. I remember working out how many cycles it took to draw each pixel and trying to reduce those numbers, and came up with various algorithms. Only later I found out that some of those algorithms had names attached to people. But quite a few, bizarrely, had names that were attached long after *Elite* came out.

I suppose at the time I didn't know where to look. It was a bit like making coffee or something, you know? You try making it and add a bit more sugar, or whatever. It might have been written down somewhere, but I just thought it would be quicker to try getting it to work than try looking it up. I did get textbooks, but they were very minimal on 3D at the time. A few books came out a bit later, but I think mostly I didn't know where to look. One of the advantages of being at university is it's much easier to find out things like that. You know, James Foley and Andries van Dam, for example, published a book, but I didn't see it until after *Elite*. I was very frustrated because I thought, 'Oh, I'm sure that would have been useful!'

I think for me the limitation of the early machines was joyous in one sense, because you had your box and you knew that once it was filled that's it. That enabled you to be much more creatively blinkered. One of the problems when you don't have blinkers on is that you get very distracted and you add lots of things. I can remember sitting in a pub with Jez San, Archer Maclean and David Braben, and it was like they were talking another language. They were using the processors in a way I couldn't even imagine, squeezing extra speed out of the machine. There was me sitting in the corner, and, you know, I just felt like the dumb kid at school.

Certainly, by 1983 we were terrified someone else was going to do something that took our thunder. We thought what we were doing wasn't that hard, and there were a few games that touched on different aspects of *Elite*, but I think we were also very lucky because we were quite early.

The other thing we were slightly afraid of was that Thorn EMI might be right, and that within the narrow community of people who worked at Acorn it would do really well and then everywhere else it wouldn't. *Elite* was so different, if you think of the sort of games coming out in '84. Most of them were very much in the same mould as games that came out earlier. One of the games Thorn EMI showed us, for example, was *Skyline Attack*, which was actually written by Fouad Katan and Jeremy San. They said,

'You want it to be more like this. This is great.' It was a cityscape where a spaceship flew left and right with little things coming down. Let's just say it had remarkable inspiration from *Defender*, and it had three lives, from memory, and doubtless you got one extra one at 10,000. Thorn EMI were saying it's bright and colourful whereas in *Elite* you were just watching white dots expanding from the centre of the screen. So we were worried that people would want to play the bright lights of things like *Pac-Man*, and that *Elite* would be seen as just an interesting, esoteric sort of sideline.

← 47

## Jez San

282 →

Friends and I produced a game in '84 called *Skyline Attack* on the Commodore 64, which was kind of a *Defender* clone but it had the skylines of cities of the world, so it had beautiful graphics. That game's claim to fame was not actually the main game, though. It was the first game that had another game to play while it was loading. Loading took so long on the Commodore 64 that you played a game of *Snake* while it was doing it, which some people cruelly said was better than the main game.

← 83

## Jeff Minter

94 →

I went to a microfair and there was a guy there selling memory boards.[×] I got talking to him, and told him I was doing some little games on the ZX81, and he said, 'Well do you want to do a deal to sell these games?' I thought it sounds like it could be a possibility. He said, 'Do you want a free 16K RAM pack to develop the games on?' I was like, 'Wow, yes, in fact I do.' So I came home from that show with a free RAM pack and this idea I could maybe, *maybe*, make some money out of doing it.

I did a little suite of games, some for the 1K ZX81, some for the expanded ZX81,[*] and the guy I met at the ZX Microfair sold them for a while alongside his hardware. I helped him with a little graphics chip, which provided the ZX81 with a set of *Space Invaders* characters and different character sets you could use, and then I wrote some games that used them, and he sold those at the ZX Microfairs and started to get a bit of a buzz about that stuff.

[×] The company was computer hardware maker dK'tronics, founded by David Heelas in 1981.
[*] The ZX81 came with 1K of memory, but could be expanded up to 64K.

## Mo Warden

One of the first pieces of art that I did on my computer was the face of the MCP from *Tron* all in facets. I was so proud of it! The computer was so slow that you could actually see it drawing the lines and filling in the areas between. Then I got my first modem for the VIC-20, which was a massive thing, the same size as the computer. It did electronic messaging and things like that, all very basic compared to what there is now. Someone I got in touch with was Jeff Minter. He saw some of my early graphics and he was very encouraging, and in fact, he gave me one of my first jobs. I did a screen for *Batalyx.* It wasn't actually the intro screen, because Jeff did all his own graphics, but he was a great influence. I loved his games, I played them non-stop, and it was my first break. Somebody was taking me seriously. I was so thrilled to actually see it there. I was telling people, 'Have you seen this? It's mine, honestly!'

## Jeff Minter

I wouldn't say that I had a particularly great talent for graphics. I mean, I did what people would consider to be programmer graphics, and certainly there were times when perhaps I wished I could have worked with better graphic artists; but for me, producing a game was such a personal thing. It was like an entire whole that I kind of made myself. I never really felt inclined to farm out any part of it, apart from the music. I did, of course, work with my friend James Lisney. We grew up together, we were childhood friends, and he was a piano prodigy. He was doing grade eight piano when we were, like, in infant school, he was that good, and so it was fun to work with him, but the actual game design process and putting it all together, it was just a very personal thing, so I just ended up doing it all myself because that's how it felt right to do it.

So I'd been doing some stuff for this guy from dK'tronics, but then we had a dispute about royalties and I kind of fell out with him, and I fell in with somebody else who was the son of a local video shop operator. He was all like, 'Yeah, I'll look after the business, you just write the games, and give us 70% of the profits.' I was naïve enough to almost go for that, but my mum got wind of it and she said, 'Look, no way, it's 50/50 or not at all,' and we ended up splitting up from them.

At that point I thought, well, my mum and me were more or less together and so, rather than have to have some third-party middle-man involved, why don't we just do this Llamasoft thing ourselves? So that's what we did. Llamasoft became this family operation that was just me making the games, my mum doing a lot of the admin stuff, and my dad helping out. We all pitched in together, and we'd go up to the computer shows together.

The name goes back a long way. I was notorious for having a fascination for camels when I was at school, and llamas were like an extension of that. I'd written a character editor for my VIC-20, and I sat down with it and made this little sketch of a llama, and then I wrote underneath, just off the top of my head, 'Llamasoft' with three exclamation marks underneath it. There was no sort of design process. That's it. Everybody called their software houses something, and I thought, 'Why not Llamasoft?' The llama was a little icon which I could attach to it.

It was very chaotic and there were a lot of people who were just selling anything they could, because you could sell anything back then. There was a new market that was desperate for software, and people were selling any old crap, to be honest. But I was very fortunate. At the first show I went to this American guy was going around looking for software to sell through one of his companies in the US, which was much bigger, obviously, it was much more of an industry over there. He saw some early work I was doing which was pretty crude, but he liked it and asked me if I wanted to hook up with him and write some games for him to sell over there, which I ended up doing.

They sold significantly over there and I made a fair bit of money. VIC-20 *Gridrunner* ⁺ went to number one in the US game charts for a while. It was quite good. I don't know whether I was the very first, but possibly. ⁺ It didn't last very long, unfortunately, but it was nice while it was there. That was the first inkling I had that there was a proper industry that was going to form around this.

⁺ A single-screen action shooter, released in 1982.
⁺ Rod Cousens believes that, indeed, Minter was the first British developer to have a number one-selling game in the US.

I met a guy from a software house in Birmingham, I cannot remember the name, and he pulled together groups of enthusiasts and got them to work together, basically with the intention of setting up a studio. I don't think it ever really came to much, but I worked with a couple of other artists on a couple of games. One was *Thai Boxing* for Anco,[×] and the other was *Tora Tora* something,[*] a war game with planes bombing things. The memory is very sketchy, but I just did the planes.

I was always, first and foremost, a single mum. Everything else took a back seat, so I worked in the evenings, when the boys were in bed, until the early hours of the morning – I would have chats with Jeff Minter at one in the morning – but I didn't get disturbed, and it was nice and quiet outside, so I could just concentrate. I really put my mind into it at four in the morning. I did that quite a lot, and then up at seven to get the kids to school.

I suppose I was starting to be taken seriously at this stage and it was a good feeling, but it still really wasn't something I could make a career out of. There wasn't enough money, and it taught me one very important thing, and that was how not to get ripped off. One game company I can't remember the name of now was not very good at paying people. I learned you do not post your work to somebody unless they hand you the cash.

And also, learning about working with other artists and combining our output was very good.

There was no training. I was completely self-taught. Obviously, I read everything I could get my hands on, lots of manuals. So I used to spend lots of time in the library, because I couldn't afford to buy books. I found everything I could, and borrowed from other people as well. Maybe it was a manual for a piece of software I'd never use, but I read it anyway because I might pick something up from it.

By then I had got as far as I could go with the VIC-20. I had the expansion unit and cartridges and so on, and the modem, and the Commodore 64 had come out. It was the big brother. I can't remember how I managed to afford it, because I was still a single parent, but I managed to scrape it together.

I produced a showreel of Commodore 64 stuff, which probably didn't show a lot of the projects that I'd worked on at that point, because I can't say I was proud of most of them, and I'd take it to the shows and I started to meet more people who were making games for a living. They helped me become more confident, and I started to wonder if I might get a job. I started to go to the stands and tell them I was an artist: 'I can work on that machine; would you like to see some of my stuff?' I got a variety of receptions. Some of them quite cool, some of them were too busy at that moment and asked me to send them stuff, which I never did.

---

[×]   A 1986 beat 'em up for the Commodore 64.
[*]   Possibly a conversion of a 1980 arcade game made by Taiyo System.

# Archer Maclean

I was at university between '80 and '83, doing a degree in cybernetic electronic control systems, when I wrote the guts for *Dropzone*. I continually went back to it in my spare time and in '83 I used to go to trade shows, like the PCW Show at Earls Court and Olympia and places like that. One day, at one of the big shows, a U.S. Gold stand was there. They were then the new kid on the block, with a very formidable stand and lots of stuff coming in from America for Atari and early Commodore 64. I was a bit sneaky: I just went up to one of their machines, took the disk out, put *Dropzone* in, got it running and then stood 20ft away just to see what would happen. It built up a huge crowd and I thought, 'Blimey, well, I've got a bit of a winner here.' Then one of the senior guys from U.S. Gold came marching out and demanded to know who did it. I eventually made my presence felt, and he shook my hand, took me in for a cup of coffee, and started talking about how we could publish it.

But it was actually another whole year before anything happened. I later found out that Atari US were looking at another game written on an Apple II to become *Defender* for the Atari 400. But then they saw *Dropzone* and it scrolled an awful lot smoother than an Apple did, and they were looking at whether they could reverse-engineer it back into a *Defender* clone, which would have been another six months' work. But *Dropzone* stood on its own two feet at that point, so when it was finished we just published it on home computers instead.

# Geoff Crammond

In 1981, when I made *Super Invaders*, the perception of home computers was that it could be a fad, something that would come and go. It was all a bit unknown. My next game, *Aviator*, took me just under a year, and when it came out it generated about three years' salary. It was a lot of work, weekends, evenings and holding down a proper job, so I decided at that point I probably couldn't carry on as I was.

The next thing that happened was that Acornsoft asked me if I would like to do a racing game. Now, to be honest, I hadn't really followed racing, but they were sponsoring David Hunt, the brother of James Hunt, in Formula Three. They said that he could be a consultant and his team could provide me with data and stuff, and I agreed, and that was my decision to leave Marconi around May '84. So basically I left one week and started on *Revs* the next.

It was great. I went to Silverstone and the Formula Three team and David Hunt's engineers gave me the data I needed to make a physics model for the sim, so that side of it was really interesting, and of course David Hunt took me around Thruxton in a BMW saloon car, just to make it even more interesting.

I remember we started off with new tyres and when we finished on one side of the tread pattern it was still all there but on the other side it was right down, where the lateral force completely bent the tread over and then wore it off. It was amazing. I took a camera with me, but I was so sort of mesmerised that I forgot to take any pictures. I appreciated certain things, like centripetal force, that I wouldn't otherwise have been aware of.

He showed me how you could steer using the throttle. He could just point the car with the throttle foot and without moving the steering wheel. When you are racing you are always on a balance of grip, so using the throttle alters the rear lateral force slightly. I guess I put that into *Revs*, as well as driving around the corners on the edge of grip, and understeer and oversteer. David Hunt came round to my house a few times to test drive it. He got really into it with the BBC joystick, actually.

I wanted the game to compete graphically with the games we were used to, like *Pole Position*,* so we got solid colour, but what I was trying to achieve was a properly mapped 3D environment, so it wasn't quite as straightforward as a *Pole Position*-type game. But as I was full-time I could experiment with stuff, and I did actually manage to get a solid field environment so you could actually drive at a corner in 3D and it had a solid feel and the red-and-white curb stones and things.

I wondered how to achieve things you take for granted now, like a curved road. It took a little bit of evolution just to realise that I could have a series of straight edges and you would get the impression of a curve with perspective. It seems the easy way to do it now, but I had to experiment a bit with generating curves and things like that. It was all new, I suppose – I approached everything with an open mind; I tried to figure out the best way to do something before doing it, trying to optimise things for speed because you were always up against it with these machines. You could never do what you really wanted on the speed front, so I was compromising all the time. I was trying to simulate real life, so the design for the game for me was simply looking at the real situation and getting as much of that in as I could.

← 97
## Geoff Crammond
136 →

For my BBC Micro I had a second processor, which was another box you could buy that gave me a bit more power. By then I had a disk drive, and I used to give backups to my wife, who is a government scientist, to keep in her office so I would have something outside of the house. It reached a point where I would look at the code and I would think that it was more valuable than the house, you know, if it burned down!

That was really my approach, so everything in the game I think I expected to be there when I started, and I don't remember writing down plans. I was simply thinking about what I needed to do next to evolve the game. If that meant I had to be able to drive it, then I'd better get it working as soon as I could. If I wasn't interested in playing the game, I wasn't interested in developing it, so I was always making games that I found fun to play, and that was necessary because of the amount of hours that I had to spend testing them.

I think it was a while before I took Acornsoft anything to show. I think it was when I had a road you could drive down, and so it would have probably been six months or so into the project. I don't remember delivery pressure from them; it was fairly relaxed, certainly compared with what was to follow in years to come.

← 92
## Peter Molyneux
196 →

There wasn't really a lot of feeding off each other, because there weren't really any events where we got together and talked about things. You phoned each other up and said, 'Hey, do you fancy going for a drink?' or something, and you might chat about things, but there was no E3 or Game Developers Conference or anything like that. There were no books at all, no references, no internet. There were no experts, no courses. All of the stuff that we did we invented for the first time. It made it very frustrating. You would want to do something in a game so much but you just couldn't because the machine wasn't powerful enough or you didn't know the tricks that others knew. If you wanted to do something you had to sit down and invent it. It was incredible, you know, and there were some amazing achievements.

My first break in the industry came I think when I was 14 years old, in 1983, or something. I started off writing BASIC programs on my computer, but it didn't grab me straightaway and I had a bunch of problems trying to figure out how to use it. I bought the advanced manual, which was all machine code and a bit beyond me. I tried writing some programs and they didn't go so well, so the computer ended up on the shelf for a bit.

But it came down again. The first thing I did was to try to get the screen to scroll sideways. There were all these cool games which managed to scroll the screen sideways, like *Scramble* and a whole bunch of others. I eventually found out that the 6522 co-processor handled the screen on the BBC, and I managed to get it to scroll sideways, with a little wiggly line that scrolled off the side. The wiggly line turned into a landscape, and then there was a bicycle that went across it, and I added obstacles like rocks and it became enough of a game for me to send it to publishers to see what they could do with it, and at first it got rejected. I roped in one of my friends from school, because I didn't know at that stage how to do a high score table, and eventually found a publisher, Superior Software.

I didn't really know how much money was involved in getting a game published, but it was obviously a cool thing to do. I can't claim finances were the major driving factor, but I signed the contract and I think I made about £700, which was enough money to make me think that maybe I should look a bit further into it and do something better. I wasn't satisfied. I thought I could do a better job, and maybe make more money.

So I made two more games, and they got widely rejected. One was called 'Cosmic Debris', which was quite a lot like *Jetpac*, a sideways scrolling game over a large landscape I wrote quickly and sent off to a whole bunch of software houses, and they all turned me down. Then I wrote another sideways scrolling game – sideways scrolling was about the only trick that I knew how to do at that stage, as you can probably imagine. This one was called 'Pink', which involved a pink panther seeking out diamonds in a maze-like environment. It was a platform game, but in some respects it was a little bit of a prequel to *Repton*. That also got rejected by everybody.

A&F Software at that point was a shop mainly selling computer games and hardware, and then in the back room they had a couple of programmers writing games, which they sold with all the other games in the front.

As I was finishing off my previous game, I was already thinking of another idea. I realised that you could do pixel movement on the Spectrum, even though the received wisdom was that you couldn't, and everything had to be character movement. So I wanted to do a game which was pixel movement, which I thought was an advantage just because it was technically superior. It would be better to play and would look better, so it would make a better game. The first thing I did with *Chuckie Egg* was to get the man moving left and right through pixel movement rather than character movement. Initially it wasn't even animated, just a smooth-scrolling box, and it probably took two or three weeks to get that working.

The game design for *Chuckie Egg* was mostly nicking ideas from what I loved playing in the arcades, so it's a cross between *Space Panic*, which was a platform and ladders game, and *Donkey Kong*, and then a few ideas that I chucked in myself. When I first showed A&F I think I had the man moving around going left and right, and up and down ladders. I hadn't put any colour in at that stage so it was

all just monochrome, but most of the game ideas were done and most of the memory was mapped out. You have to have a rough plan of how much memory you're going to use for each different part of the game, otherwise you get to the end and you have run out of space.

So I showed A&F and they had a brilliant reaction. They were so pleased. To them, I was just this 14-, 15-year-old kid who made the bacon butties and tea, but when I showed them this game they grabbed people from around the office so they would come and look at it. They made a big fuss, it felt like a genuine fuss. They put me on a retainer at £50 a week, which they paid me on the understanding that when the game was finished I would give them first dibs on it.

As the game got closer and closer to being finished I started to spend a bit of time programming it at their office rather than at home, but that didn't work out because there were too many distractions, and I ended up working back at home again. The BBC version was done in parallel-ish by Doug Anderson,* slightly behind what I was doing. I would take it in to show them what I had done, and he would add it to the BBC version.

At the very end, A&F were putting pressure on me to get it finished; there were one or two things that I wanted to put in that I didn't in the end. I just said, 'Right, that's it, finished,' and they took a master and started making copies.

* Developed for Universal and released in arcades in late 1980, *Space Panic* was probably the first platform game, ahead of 1981's *Donkey Kong*, but wasn't nearly as popular.

* With Mike Fitzgerald, Anderson co-founded A&F.

They designed the cassette inlays and the names of Henhouse Harry and *Chuckie Egg* – they came up with them, I just called it 'Eggy Kong' – and they started sending it out to magazines to get reviews. I was so excited to see it in magazines, and I remember the reviews being good, you know, 80-something per cent, 90-something per cent, and really nice comments. I would have been heartbroken if they had been bad, because I had worked my socks off. I knew it was pretty much as good as I could do.

They started saying they had loads of orders, and they were so pleased. It was selling way above anything that they'd experienced in the past. They also managed to get it into the major retailers, like WHSmith, which was a big deal. You had to get in there to have the biggest sales, and it got to number one in the charts. That was beyond my wildest dreams, but even after *Chuckie Egg* I still wasn't motivated by the money; I got a real buzz when I went into WHSmith in Stockport and it was on the shelves, a big stack of them there waiting to be bought by people. I was so excited. I just looked around and thought, 'Does anybody know it's me?'

A sequel to *Chuckie* was discussed very quickly after *Chuckie Egg* was finished. I had an idea for it, which I called 'Chuckie Apple' as a sort of working title, and I was working on it, but A&F had their own idea, and I didn't like it, and I guess they didn't like mine, so I think they just went off and did their own *Chuckie Egg 2*, and it wasn't anything to do with me, really.

## David Braben

We had *Elite* agreed as finished by Acorn probably in June 1983, but it wasn't going to be coming out until September. So that was a terrifying period, when we thought it could be ripped off and that anything could change. But I think with hindsight that Acorn were right. They didn't want to release in summer because they thought it wouldn't make a splash. Also, they wanted it to have a lot of testing, and in the box a big manual, a story, a poster, and all those sorts of things, and they were all being made and approved.

Acorn wanted a lot of stuff in the box to show the game was different to what had come before. They also charged a much higher price for it. But, actually, at the last minute we changed the dashboard because the radar, the scanner that everyone knows and loves, wasn't there. It had a bizarre left view and top view which was very hard to use. We changed it at the last minute and Acorn got really annoyed. I said, 'Look, we can still go with the old version, but isn't this so much better? Look, we have only changed one small part of the code, so it won't have any knock-on effects.' So they tested it and everyone agreed it was much better, which is why in the manual all of the shots have the bottom cut off, so they have no radar showing in the screens. Actually that had a really nice knock-on effect, because when we did versions for things like the Acorn Electron, which was basically the same game, it meant the manual didn't have to be re-typeset.

So then the game was ready for release. Acorn had booked what I think was the first-ever press launch for a game at Thorpe Park, which was a theme park with the world's first underground roller coaster. It was an astonishing event. It was the first time I realised that *Elite* was a major thing because up to then it had always felt like something in our neat little Cambridge community, where we were sort of writing games for each other. There were hundreds of people and film crews and things like that. That made it really quite daunting; we got up at the front and talked like geeky teenagers, and we realised it was a really big deal. They were giving away copies of the games, piles, thousands of quids-worth of games. It sort of concentrated my mind into thinking that this is big business, not something where you put cassettes in a Jiffy bag and charge £4.99, or whatever, which is how the business had been up to then.

Then, you know, *Elite* went on to sell very, very large numbers. Acorn were really good. Even though we were teenagers they involved us in all the different decision-making processes. In the UK there were at that time two very big distributors. One was called Websters Software and one was called Terry Blood. Essentially one did WHSmith and lots of shops, and one did Boots and the other shops. But neither wanted to take *Elite* because the price was too high. We were thinking, 'Oh, that's bad, isn't it?' But we had direct orders from independent shops.

Now, Acorn had made 50,000 units, and that showed a huge amount of faith because that's a lot of money to commit. Their previous highest-selling title was a game from Geoff Crammond called *Revs*, and its total sales were 30,000! So that was very brave, and hats off to them, because all of those units were sold within the first, I think, around ten days to two weeks, which was a lot for a BBC Micro game, especially when there were only around 100,000 or so of them around at that point.

The big distributors had offered a lower price and we had said no, and with time Acorn ordered a reprint of a further 50,000 units, and Terry Blood and Websters caved on the same day we got the new stock, so we were able to supply them. It was a real eye-opener to the whole business behind the scenes: the politics of retail and trade prices. I'd entered another world.

Some of my school friends and I started to program games ourselves, basically trying to emulate *Jetpac* or something, and because of my musical upbringing I was able to add music and sound effects with no problem. But my friends would just delete their games, spending six weeks programming an arcade copy, and then deleting it and doing another, so it was very hobby-like for them.

I have got a kind of an entrepreneurial bent, though, and I was thinking we ought to be trying to sell them. I mean, you would always read in magazines that they were making millions of pounds, so one day I said to my school friend, how about you let me sell this game and I will take 10% of whatever money I can get. He said all right, because he was kind of shy and didn't really want to bother with his *Pac-Man* rip-off, which was called 'Eyes'. I would read *Personal Computer News* every week and I looked in there for someone to phone up, and on the back were Ocean Software's adverts, and since they said Manchester at the bottom, I thought it was a good place to start. So I rang them up in May of '84, told the receptionist I had got this game, and she transferred me to David Collier, who was the software development manager at the time, precursor to Gary Bracey. I was led in there and I said I'd also brought a disk in with a bunch of tunes I'd written, including a BBC version of the *Super Locomotive* tune, which I had converted into assembly language, so they knew I was a serious programmer. They liked what they saw, and they bought the game for £300, but it was never seen again. It was never published, but they gave me some work to do as a result of the *Super Locomotive* music.

They said to me, 'Well, the BBC is nice, we've got one guy doing one BBC game, and armies of guys doing Commodore 64 and Spectrum games,' and they asked if I could do it on the Commodore 64. I said, 'I will give it a try, but I don't have one,' and they said, 'Ah, no problem!' And they gave me a Commodore 64 with a cassette player, an assembler and the programming manual for it! I was astonished that they would lend me all that gear, but in retrospect it was quite cheap.

So I took it home and I got programming like crazy, trying to produce sound effects and music. It was a little while before I went back in again, maybe a couple of months later I gave David Collier a call and he said, 'Where the hell have you been?! Get your arse in here! We need you to do some work!' So I went in, and it was July of '84, and the Olympics were happening. It was roasting hot in the Ocean offices, all the doors and windows were wide open, and they were all sitting there programming *Daley Thompson's Decathlon*, which was a rip-off of *Track & Field* by Konami. They wanted some music for the cassette loader, so I sat down and did some. All I could think of was the *Super Locomotive* music so I did that, unlicensed, and they just needed me to type in the data. I did it in about an hour and a half, sitting in David Collier's chair, and they paid me £100. Not bad, even in today's money!

I had just finished my A levels, which were a disaster. I tried to do three and I only got one, and that was a D for computer science, because computers were dominating my whole mindset. So there I was in the summer holidays figuring out what I was going to do next, not really with a lot of drive, still programming, and Ocean said they had a couple of games coming up and asked me to give them a ring when I was ready to start. Around September I started at a community college and I got in touch with David Collier again. Bill Barna and Tony Pomfret were working on *Hunchback II*, and David Collier was working on *Kong Strikes Back!*, and they both needed music.

My parents saw all this with, I think, some concern, because they didn't really understand what it all was and thought it was a little bit silly. When I said I was doing music for games my dad would laugh, but later, when I first came home and dropped three £100 cheques on the table, his eyebrow went up.


## Archer Maclean

Given my experience of publishers over the years, which is not particularly brilliant, U.S. Gold were sort of terribly friendly and open-armed: 'Have a coffee, have another coffee, and have some chocolate,' you know, and very much sort of, 'Just sign here, here's another 50p.' It really was quite an interesting time, but *Dropzone* wasn't actually signed until about a year later when it was a completely finished thing on a disk.

U.S. Gold published the Atari and the Commodore 64 versions of *Dropzone*, but there was a later dispute about whether it should have gone worldwide because it wasn't in the contract. It was a fixed-fee royalty, not even a percentage with an advance. For the Commodore 64 one they gave me six weeks to convert it, or something, with a bonus payment at the end. I think I spent 5.9 of those six weeks not sleeping, trying to make this 64 do anything remotely as powerful-looking as the Atari, because the game had certain features that it just couldn't do.

I used to have arguments with all the programmers about how good the Atari was. It was always the underdog, but was the most powerful machine because it had some very fancy hardware tricks in it that Atari didn't go on about for many years, whereas the Commodore came out in '82, two and a half years later, and they instantly said it's got sprites, a SID chip, it's got this, it's got that. But the Atari had all that, and never promoted it. They just said, 'Look at our games, aren't they great?' They didn't say it's got hardware scrolling and display interrupts and a lot of other stuff which they should have. So yeah, putting *Dropzone* on the 64 was an absolute nightmare and I had to hugely simplify big chunks of the game to make it look remotely like the Atari one.

There was a later dispute with U.S. Gold about how many copies they had actually sold, but I discovered a little trick that they were doing, which was that they were overpaying me on the royalties. Naturally, that meant that you would think, 'Well, I will be quiet and wait until they ask for it back.' But then I discovered that two or three other people working as authors for U.S. Gold also had the same thing, and they all felt guilty about it. Then it occurred to me that they may be actually making an awful lot more than they were telling us, and keeping us quiet by overpaying. There was a clause in the contract about auditing, so we went and audited the sales, and it was just like blimey, really. We discovered some other interesting features too, and that's when I met the boss, who basically said, 'OK, the game's up. How much do you want?' There was a picture of a Ferrari on the wall and I said I wouldn't mind one of those. Something like that.

## Fred Gray

The newspapers then were full of articles about Eugene Evans, who lived less than half a mile away from me. I lived on one scruffy council estate, and he lived on the other scruffy council estate. This inspired me, and it was when I started thinking about money rather than just education. It was breaking news, you know, 'Kid makes lots of money programming in his bedroom,' so that's where the bedroom programmer expression was coined, and I was the same, doing things in my bedroom, except I wasn't young. I was in my 30s by then.

This new technology empowered people; when home computers came about it was amazing how kids who didn't thrive at school could thrive in the bedroom, either producing music or producing code, and make a name for themselves. The punk scene tried to make everybody a rock star, whereas the music giants were focusing on super groups and soloists, so I think the punk scene was brilliant. The time at the beginning of the computer game industry was fabulous. It was so fresh and new and exciting. I mean, it was on par with the garage band scene that came later on in the '80s, which was people doing their own music in the garage. I think there's a big analogy there. In the music industry there was the start of the punk scene and then the small record labels came along, so there were a lot of similarities between that and computer games, and there was a mutual feeling of distrust in big companies.

I started to rip off what I had seen, but, you know, ironically, I actually wrote a version of *Arkanoid* before *Arkanoid* came out,[x] but nobody was interested. So yeah, I started off writing subroutines and the games became more sophisticated, then I tried to sell them, so I got in touch with local people. I remember one guy looked at my VIC-20 games and said they were very good, but he wanted me to do some Commodore 64 work. Now, the C64 was brand new then, and I said, 'Well, what about the dough?' He said, 'Don't worry about the dough, you'll be rich when you start writing these games.' I thought that would do me, but the other person I approached was a guy called Tim Best,[*] who was a friend of a friend. He was interested in publishing it, but then he called me and said, 'Look, forget the VIC-20. I am recruiting for Imagine,[¬] and I want a musician and you're it.'

I think it was that I'd put vibrato on the music in the VIC-20 games and it sounded really eerie and spooky, very atmospheric. VIC-20 games up to that point sounded basically naff, so he saw my potential in doing music rather than writing games. That was the beginning of my love affair with the SID chip, because everybody wanted me to work on the C64. It was new on the market, and obviously it had much better hardware than the previous machines.

---

[x] Taito released *Arkanoid* in 1986 in the arcades, adding power-ups to the formula set by Atari's 1976 *Breakout*, which in turn was inspired by *Pong*.

[*] Tim Best had been a Dixons salesman before being invited to join Imagine. He went on to co-design 1987's *The Last Ninja* with Mark Cale.

[¬] Liverpool-based Imagine Software was one of the first big development companies.

# Jon Hare

My first games job was working as a consultant artist on a game that my mate Chris Yates was working on. Chris is a brilliant programmer, a genius programmer, but not that great at art. I was round his house because we were making music together, and he'd got this small contract, a gig as a programmer with a local company in Basildon, LT Software.

Neither of us had jobs in those days, and he got me to do some art, and from doing that art I managed to get a job as a consultant artist with the same company. I did graphic jobs on a number of games like *Skyfox* and an early sort of *Trivial Pursuit* game. We did *Twister* for System 3, which was great for us. It was the first original game we'd done, but of course it was through a third-party development company.

So we realised halfway through that we needed to change. At the time you had the Enterprise Allowance Scheme, which would pay us, I think it was, £40 a week for a year to set our own business up if we were young enough. You also needed £1,000 in the bank each, and you needed to have been unemployed for 13 weeks. Now, we couldn't work out how to achieve this without working whilst we were unemployed, because we couldn't get the £1,000. So what we did was to do another game after *Twister*, a conversion of an adventure game for the Commodore 64, for the same company. It didn't come out, but we signed on the dole and continued to work because we needed to get the £1,000 each. And in March 1986 we set Sensible up.

I don't think we were hobbyist at all: we were pragmatic young people in a creative industry working from the spare bedroom in Chris's dad's house, so we were bedroom programmers, but it was pragmatic to work there, and it was where we were making our music anyway. It was the same place we recorded our first couple of albums when we were younger.

# David Darling

Our dad had always been an entrepreneur, starting businesses in different countries around the world. He had contact lens companies and shops and things like that, so we had learned commercial business from him. Even in Canada, back in 1980, when we were with our friend Michael Hiebert, we formed a company called Darbert Computers, because we put 'Darling' and 'Hiebert' together, and we started making games. Michael is a book author now. When we came back to England we got separated, so we were sending our games on tapes to show him, and he was sending his games over here.

In that way we built up a collection of games and then we suddenly thought, 'Why don't we sell them and try and make some money out of it?' At the time, our mum and dad were living in Vancouver, and they used to send us £5 a week pocket and lunch money, but we didn't eat much, so we just saved it up until we had £70. I had a friend called Tim, whose dad ran an advertising and graphic design company, so we worked with him for a few days and he came up with this character called Galactic Man, who was like a kind of Superman character. Once the advert was finished I phoned *Popular Computer Weekly* and booked our first ad, saying '14 great games from North America'. We tried to put the North American angle into the marketing.

They were just simple games like tennis or shooting games, like similar to *Galaxian* and things like that. I think we charged £9.99, so they were less than £1 each, and we were trying to get across that they were value for money. I don't know how many orders we had, whether it was like 50 or 100, but cheques just started appearing through the post. Our grandparents were like, 'What's going on?'

We had to stay up all night duplicating the tapes, putting them in Jiffy bags and sending them out, and then more orders came in! There was too much to duplicate, so I did a deal with a local record company in Bridgwater who made cassette music tapes. That's how the business grew in the beginning. I would drive to Bridgwater on my moped and come back with a couple of big boxes on the back. It was a bit precarious.

It was really when our dad came back from Canada that we started to build it up. At first he was getting me to make contact lenses – we even made some green ones for one of the *Incredible Hulk* movies – but I think he saw what we were doing with the game business, and he thought he could apply himself to this new industry. So he really tried to encourage us, saying, 'Why don't you do a bigger advert and use colour?' He always has lots of bigger ideas, and crazy ones, like doing a competition where you give away a Rolls Royce. So we started doing bigger advertising campaigns and then he got his friend involved, who used to work at Comet or Currys as a sales manager. That guy went to Boots and WHSmith and said, 'These guys are selling these games by mail order – why don't you have them in your shops?' So he got us into shops.

At that stage things were going quite well, and then we got a call from a guy called Alan Sharam, who was from a new company called Mastertronic. They had been selling cheap videos, like fishing videos and all kinds of weird stuff, but they wanted to get into the game industry. They knew people like Ocean and U.S. Gold were selling games for like £10, and they were thinking, why didn't we sell our games for £1.99? So they said, 'As well as doing your own games at Galactic Software, why don't you do some games for us as well?' So we started doing games for Mastertronic, and then games for Robert Maxwell at Mirrorsoft, so that was really how the business developed.

At first, we would be programming as soon as we got back to our grandparents' house after school, about four o'clock. Then, when the business started taking off, I kind of lost track. It was our greatest passion, we just loved making games. But also, my dad is a bit of an Alan Sugar-type guy. He pushes you. He won't like me saying that. He was a bit of a slave driver, so he would get us to have 22 games finished by the end of the month, and we would be like, 'How the hell are we going to do this?!'

So we would work through the night, night after night, just trying to get these games finished, and he was saying, 'This is your only opportunity. You will never get another opportunity like this! Do games for the Mirror, for Commodore!' He had always taught us that you can achieve whatever you want, and that there is no limit to people's potential if you apply your mind. So I think he was trying to really encourage us, but then also he saw the potential in the industry. He was asking us questions: is it like skateboarding? Is it just a fad, like the yo-yo or the Rubik's Cube, that's going to be dead next year? We said, 'No it's not like that! People have been playing chess for hundreds of years.' It's like Pandora's box: you can never close it again. So we were convinced games would just grow and grow, and he got really excited about it as well.

I was 16 by that stage, so I had finished my O levels, but my brother Richard was 15, and he left school before he took them. The school kept writing my parents letters, asking why he wasn't at school. I think one of the heads came around to the house, and our dad was like, 'No, they have to finish a game.'

## David Perry

There was one game in the book-magazine I wrote that was much bigger than all the rest, so it was a nightmare to type it in. I mean, how painful is that? So I thought, 'Why don't I add a bit more and we'll sell it as a game?' I sent it to a publisher in England called

Mikro-Gen,[×] and for whatever reason they liked it and they called me up and said, 'We want to publish your game but we'd also like to offer you a job to come and work in England.'

You've got to remember, I'm this little kid in Northern Ireland who thinks he knows what he's doing, writing games in BASIC without any training. I don't know how everyone else does what they do, I just know what I've taught myself, and that's just how I think it works. So it made sense to me to move to England and make games over there, but my school teachers were like, 'Videogame what? That's not an industry, what are you talking about? It's like skateboarding or something!' It was a crazy fad as far as everyone was concerned.

So it was a very difficult decision for the teachers, and my parents were very supportive, but it was interesting, because when faced with the challenge of someone giving up their education, some of my teachers just thought it was terrible, but some of them were quite supportive. But videogames just seemed to me like a great escape trajectory that I could take. They weren't really an option before. As time has gone on I've kind of watched this whole thing evolve from what seemed like a bit of a fad, an interesting little side hobby, into a real, full industry. The only thing I regret a little is that I wish I could have started earlier and have been there from the very first, you know, the Ralph Baer[°] days, or from the Nolan Bushnell days. But, you know, I can't complain, I got a pretty early start.

My mother had bought me a ZX81 so I could program at home, and I had a little black and white TV in my bedroom, and so literally everything I made up to that point was on this little black and white TV in my bedroom, but I really wanted to get a Sinclair Spectrum. And I had a very strange thing happen to me. I was at my grandmother's house one day and she said, 'I want you to come into my bedroom. I want to talk to you,' and I'm like, 'Okay,' and she goes to me, 'You know, I'm getting pretty old now and I don't want you to think that I left you some teapots or something like that, and so I want to give you some money, just so I know that you're not going to end up with silverware.' So she gave me, like, £100 or £150, and that was just what I needed to get my Sinclair Spectrum, and by buying that computer, suddenly I was able to take off, I was able to make competitive and relevant games for that time.

× Founded by Mike Meek and Andrew Laurie in 1981, Mikro-Gen was the publisher of Pyjamarama and Everyone's a Wally. Perry's game was Drakmaze, a largely text-based adventure in which you must survive Dracula's castle, released in 1984.
° Often referred to as 'the father of videogames', Baer introduced the first home game console, producing a system known as the Brown Box in 1966 and then taking it to market in 1972 as the Magnavox Odyssey. He died in December 2014.

Demonstrating what I was able to get that Spectrum to do, I got the job offer, and it was terrible: move to England for £3,500 a year and give up your schooling ... It was a very, very difficult decision but I decided to do it. I worked in Ashford in Middlesex, and there was nothing but work. I'd get up in the morning and go to work and that was it. I don't even remember anything else. I didn't go anywhere, I didn't do anything, it was literally just work, work, work. I realised that it wasn't going well.

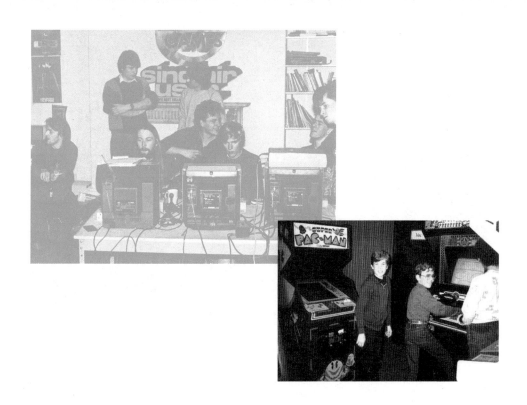

1

2

3

Britsoft

4

5

6

7

8

9

10

11

12

13

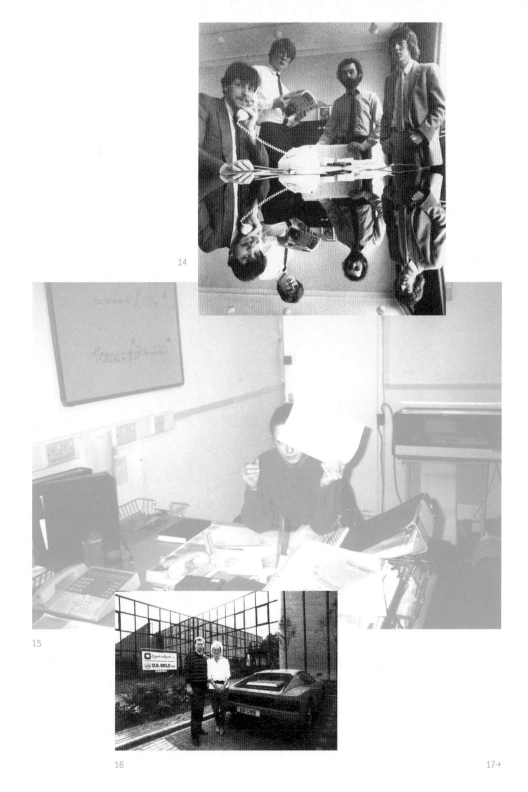

14

15

16

17→

18

19

Britsoft

20

21

22

Britsoft

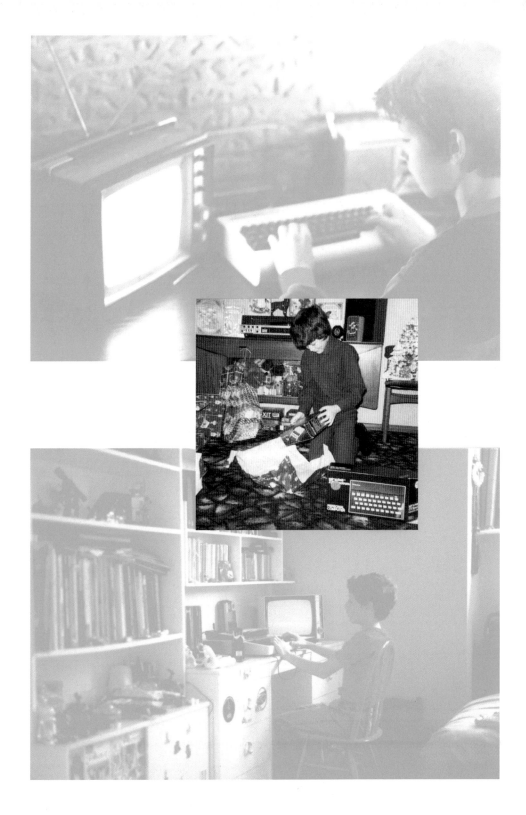

# Part 3

# Going Pro

A big change for me was that university had been my work and *Elite* was my hobby. When we released it, I think they switched, but I still hadn't finished my degree. In fact the masters for *Elite* were sent off a week before my end-of-year exams, so that was challenging.

It seems that I saw the way games were going to evolve 30 years before they did. I never questioned the fact that computer games were multimedia. They had celebrity voices and proper sound-tracks. They had real-life themes, and they were not rehashes of the same old ideas, they were funny rehashes of the same old ideas, and I always knew that these machines were for fun, and if they entertained my chums it was great.

By the time the Sinclair Spectrum arrived it was patently obvi-ous that computers were for only one thing and that was making interactive movies. The fact that I had to wait 25 years for the rest of the industry to catch up with this vision is pretty sad, by the way. That's not arrogance, it's just a statement of fact. *Deus Ex Machina* was meant to be a full-blown interactive movie. You got immersed in it, you changed the action as you went along, and it took a full hour to play, with the soundtracks totally synchronised. We had celebrity voices, we had Ian Dury. We had life and death, we had sperms, geriatrics in Zimmer frames, we had *Citizen Kane*, this was it, and we had it on a 48K Spectrum! Actually, it was a 128K Spectrum, but you could play it on a 48K.

I wanted to involve people emotionally. It wasn't even computer gaming, it was a multimedia experience. Instead of thinking up the theme myself, I stole it from this writer, William Shakespeare, who had a great idea and he called it the Seven Ages of Man. So we adapted the Seven Ages of Man and rewrote the dialogue to be spoken mostly by John Pertwee, Doctor Who. I say 'we': I wrote it. I wrote the music, the dialogue, and I played all the instruments and I got other people to do the voices, which they did very well considering we had almost a zero budget. They were just superb and they really got into it.

It was a case of total ignorance and fearlessness. I just phoned them up, like John Pertwee, and explained what it was about, and he said, 'Yeah, okay, it will cost you not a lot.' He turned up late for the recording session and I thought, 'You arrogant bastard.' But he'd just had a motorbike accident! He came in, took off his leathers, and he did it in one take. Fantastic. Subsequently, we exchanged Christmas cards and we wrote a book together, and we had a sort of friendship.

Ian Dury liked the whole non-violent idea of our games, and he liked particularly that his son Baxter was then into playing games and didn't like the violent side of them. He liked the idea that his son could say that his dad was involved in a non-violent game with a rock 'n' roll soundtrack. The themes were big: life, death, sex, all in a good way, of course, and it had disability in it, which rang a bell. He liked the music, because I did a guide track, and just did it by line-by-line.

If you're looking for a message in *Deus Ex Machina* there isn't one. Many people thought they'd found messages, but they had made them up. I wanted people to be emotionally involved with a computer game, which sounds really up my own arse, and it is up my own arse, but it's true. Using a 48K Spectrum to do it just sounds stupid, but I had a go.

When it was released it was a slow burner, and it was very difficult to pirate. After a while I was getting feedback in letters, and people really did say it changed their lives. It didn't change mine because I only played it twice. Some people would sit in a darkened room, put their headphones on, have a wine gum, and just go with it. Some would play it, some would read meanings into it which weren't there. Some really thought they were seeing, hearing and doing things which weren't programmed, which is fascinating. You can't do that with a book. So in a broad sense it sort of worked, and in a very narrow sense it did work for a few people.

So just imagine if it worked for real and you had incredible graphics, amazing audio and proper gameplay. A life on rails, if you like, from the fertilisation of an egg through to the very last moment of life into death, and then all the way around again. Totally up my own arse, but Shakespeare wrote it, not me. So *Deus Ex Machina* was very different, it wasn't an adventure, a quest or a shoot 'em up. It was a life on rails and it took exactly one hour.

I'm not proud of any of the original interactive moments in *Deus Ex Machina*, because they are all based on the same four crappy game elements, a little dice, a little chess, ping

The posters, the packaging, the second cassette for the audio, all took a very short time to think up, weeks not months. We found some vinyl cassette covers with space for two audio cassettes, so we could do it on two cassettes, but unfortunately the vinyl cassette covers were big, and WH-Smith and other high street retailers had shelves that took software in cassettes that were smaller. So nobody would touch us, we were back to day one and we had to sell it by mail order direct to the player.

pong – which was quite a lot – and bollocks, which was all the flimflam: the soundtrack, the message. So there was no great gameplay in it, but because it took you on a ride and you couldn't really get off – you couldn't pause it once you started – you became immersed, and the gameplay wasn't really the important thing.

A big change for me, and I think Ian, but certainly speaking for myself, was that university had been my work and *Elite* was my hobby. When we released it, I think they switched, but I still hadn't finished my degree. In fact the masters for *Elite* were sent off a week before my end-of-year exams, so that was challenging.

Of course the game was very, very successful, and we went on to sell it for other platforms. We saw that machines like the Commodore 64 and Sinclair Spectrum sold the big numbers, and that the BBC Micro was the sort of high-end Rolls-Royce-expensive machine that a lot of people didn't have. We wanted to make sure we could have *Elite* on all of them, but obviously, Acorn weren't going to want to publish on a rival machine. So when we agreed the contract with Acorn, we reserved all of the rights to the game, including film rights.

Now, Acorn essentially laughed, which was more or less what we thought might happen. They said, 'Why would you want film rights?' And we said, 'Well, why do *you* want film rights?' They said, 'You never know. This is a new business; where will it be in the future? But you think there is going to be a film?' I said, 'No, I think there *might* be a film. But anyway, you are not going to do anything with these rights. We are giving you the rights for the BBC Micro, and in fact all Acorn platforms.'

There was this sort of strange pause, and because they were laughing so much about it, they agreed. They

said, 'Yes, you're right, we don't think there's going to be a film.' I said, 'Well, I think there might be a film, therefore we want the rights.' They agreed, and there was no discussion at all about the other rights. So later that year, with Acorn's knowledge, we auctioned them through Jacqui Lyons' Marjacq Micro[*] agency.

One interesting thing that happened was that John Taplin, the editor of ITN News, saw that in his newsroom they were all using BBC Micros, and they were apparently all playing *Elite* in their downtime. He thought it was great and newsworthy because he found out it was from Cambridge, so they sent a news crew down. It was really bizarre. We saw the news film with us on it on *Channel Four News*, between Arthur Scargill and the miners' strike, which of course was current at the time, and something about Margaret Thatcher, I'm sure. We were the happy bit in the middle. I suppose the fact that it was national news really made us take it seriously and go, 'Wow, this is exciting. This is a career.' I think also it challenged the scepticism that friends and family had. You know, 'We saw it on the television, it must be true,' type of thing.

We went on to publish *Elite* for other platforms with British Telecom, which at that point was still a government company. It hadn't yet been privatised. We said, 'Don't you make

[*] An agency founded in 1983 specifically to serve game developers, and still operational today. The company's name is derived from its founders: George Markstein and Jacqui Lyons.

telephones?' They said, 'We're going private and we're going into software, so we might as well go into games. It's the future.' They had a new label called Firebird and they needed something to help get visibility. We got what I think was the first ever six-figure advance in the industry. We didn't get in the red tops, unlike the PR that people like to remember from that time, but it was fantastic, because with Acorn we weren't on anything like as good a deal as we were on with Firebird. Once *Elite* came out, being a professional developer was obviously a career path.

## Geoff Crammond

Towards the end of '85, certainly by the time I did *The Sentinel*, I noticed that when I was mentioned in the press it said 'Geoff (*Aviator*, *Revs*) Crammond,' saying what I had done before. I didn't have much contact with the magazines, though. I guess the publisher did all the liaising and I just got on with the games.

Working alone from home was exactly what I wanted. The telephone would go now and then and it was the publisher – in fact, in future years it would go quite a lot – but the days when I didn't get calls were good days, because I could get on with work and not be interrupted. I liked the fact that I could do the physics, the graphics, do stuff with sound: it was all things that I was interested in. Computer games just kind of brought everything together in one place.

One of the things I used to do between games was to come up with ideas. I always used to spend a couple of weeks trying to think of an idea for the next one, and invariably I would choose the best idea, start working on it, and then at some point later I would have a better idea, so I never actually thought of the game straight away. In the case of *The Sentinel*, I was sitting on the edge of the bath, running the tap, and I don't know why but that kind of freed my mind a bit and it suddenly dawned on me it might be possible on the 8-bit machines to have a 3D environment that you could move around in.

The reason I thought that was because it struck me that it was possible to have a camera in a 3D environment and rotate and pan the view, in such a way that the image just scrolls across the screen. You would have to have a slight distortion to the lens to do that but it's not really perceptible, and so I gave it a go. I started working on creating a landscape. I created a *Sentinel* terrain and I was able to pan around it.

At this point I took it to show Acornsoft. They were very interested, but this was at the time when I think Acorn got into trouble, actually. I had converted *Revs* to the Commodore for Acornsoft, but they ended up not publishing that version. Acornsoft had a desire to do it but Acorn itself didn't want to, because it was supporting another machine. So they asked Telecomsoft, which had the Firebird label, if they were interested, and that's how it ended up getting published by them. Anyway, shortly after I showed them the *Sentinel* world, in 1986, Acornsoft ceased trading because Acorn decided that games were not part of their future, and that was a signal to me that I had to go somewhere else. Telecomsoft was a natural place to go with *The Sentinel*, but I didn't go straight there; I kind of carried on developing the game. In fact, I think it was about 90% complete before I took it to them, so you could see everything that you see in the game now.

←136 ## Geoff Crammond 301→

The first headache was that although it had the same processor, in the Commodore 64 it runs at half the speed, so there was a lot of speed to be made up, somehow. In its favour, the Commodore had more memory. In the BBC, half the memory is system ROM, whereas in the Commodore 64 you can almost get all 64K for your game. So I could use techniques where I would use more space to make something work faster, so perhaps a calculation I could store in tables. I think I stored some log tables in there to speed up the maths.

Having got the landscape system up and running, I then had to think of a game I could play in it, and it took a little while to come to that design. I thought, 'Well, I have a first-person 3D game here, which is unusual ...' In most games you were talking about isometric views, overheads and side views, so I wanted a game that you can only do in first person, something you can't do with these other views. That's why line of sight became important. Then I thought about the fact I could see some tiles at certain heights and not others, so I thought about placing things on tiles and climbing upwards. Then I had the idea that you could move around in the landscape by planting your robot in a place and moving to it instantly. You couldn't do the kind of smooth moving through a 3D landscape that's in *Doom*, because my scrolling system was only updating the edges of the screen each time you moved. Updating the whole screen would have been too slow and jerky.

So this transportation idea was about climbing higher to see new tiles to plant things on, and the game kind of naturally evolved. I think when you're creating something like that, it takes on its own personality, which helps you to form all the key elements to it. The next thing was, OK, there's something very high up and you are very low down and you are going to have to get up there, and then the energy thing and boulders and trees ... it all fitted into place.

*The Sentinel* has 10,000 levels, which was a number I just chose. I'd built a landscape generator and I could control how hilly it was, how many sentries and trees there were, and all these sort of things. I thought, well, I could have 100,000 landscapes, I could have 1,000. One hundred thousand felt too many, and 1,000 didn't seem enough, so I just chose 10,000. It was literally just a number change, and 10,000 seemed, well, I hesitate to say doable, because I didn't really think anyone would do it really. Some people have, of course, but because it is a random landscape generator, and because of the complexity of the landscape and the interaction of everything, I had no way of knowing that they could all be completed. You might be starting in a low place where you can't see high enough to plant a boulder. That's why the amount of energy you had when you finished a level determined how far you jumped through the landscapes. If you came to an impossible one, you could go to a different one by going back and finishing with a different amount of energy.

Herbie Wright was the publisher at Telecomsoft and I think he was blown away when he saw it. It was so different to what they had seen before, and I think we agreed contracts on that day. The new thing for me was that they wanted to get it on as many different machines as they could. So I set about then doing conversions to Commodore 64, Atari ST and Amstrad CPC, and we outsourced the Amiga and Spectrum ones. It took about another year just doing the conversions, but actually doing them was a really nice alternative challenge to creating a game, because we had a technical challenge of how to get it to work rather than having to make something up, which, you know, in itself is quite difficult to do.

I wrote convertors to help. The main challenge with converting to the Amstrad CPC was converting to Z80 assembler code, and I wrote a program to semi-automatically convert maybe 80% or 90% of it and I did the rest by hand. Telecomsoft had a Spectrum programmer who was very keen to do the Spectrum version, so I think I gave him the Amstrad code to do that, and he could deal with the restricted palette.

David Braben

In the next three to six months we both oversaw and wrote a whole load of versions of *Elite*. I think there were eventually 16 or 17 different platforms that we covered. For some we did the coding ourselves, and for others, other people did the coding and we helped by providing source code, which was very messy.

It felt like a bit of a treadmill, in the sense that we were solving the same problems with slightly different issues, multiple times. It was also very exciting. I was very proud of some of the things we did on the Commodore 64, because even though the machine was half the speed of the BBC Micro, we managed to make it go almost as fast by using wacky things like log tables for the multi-plications, which I had never before seen written as a way of doing it. I just thought, 'Well surely it will work. If a person can do it with log tables, so can a computer.' It had a huge speed improvement, and it used a little bit of memory, but the Commodore 64 had a lot more memory. The BBC Micro only had 22K of memory because the screen came out of the memory, whereas the Commodore 64 took less memory for the screen and had 64K. It felt like a huge amount! So we also got music in, which was great, and the whole 'Blue Danube' thing. We found ways of compressing it, so we would get more in the same space.

←82

## Steve Turner

142→

Before I even got my first royalty cheque, Hewson was already asking me, 'Well, what about more versions of *3D Space-Wars*?' We used to play *Space Invaders* up our local at lunchtime, and that's how I met Andrew Braybrook. I'd heard of him from a mutual friend, but there was this long-haired guy who was absolutely bril-liant at *Space Invaders*, miles better than me.

Andrew's dad had a Dragon 32, and so when Andrew saw the kind of things that I was doing on the Spectrum he started using his dad's computer to secretly copy them. I went around there one night after a beer, and he said look at this and he showed me. He'd managed, just by seeing my game briefly, to write something, and it showed me this guy knew a thing or two. He was a com-mercial programmer, too, so it seemed a natural thing to invite him to leave his job, which he had kind of hinted about several times – 'Oh, I could easily leave my job, you wouldn't have to pay me much if you needed another programmer ...' So one night down the pub I asked if he fancied joining me. He probably came around the next morning.

Andrew worked on the Dragon version of each of the *Seiddab* trilogy, which were my first three games. He didn't just shadow each game, he looked at the Dragon and saw what it could do, because it could do some things better and some things worse than the Spectrum, and he improved the games to fit the machine. So the Dragon 32 version of *3D Space-Wars* was the definitive version, because he added some really lovely explosions, because he had the room in the machine to do it. Poor old Andrew, the Dragon games were lovely, but I think the biggest sale we ever had was something like 600 copies. It's a shame that the last couple never really got into the shops.

## Andrew Braybrook

Steve and I were in similar situations, in that we were unhappy in our IT careers, loved arcade games, and were playing in a band together. He invited me to join him in September 1983 – he was bored writing on his own, and was selling enough games to warrant expanding to a second computer format. My dad had bought a Dragon 32 and I was writing some games in BASIC on it, and took the plunge into writing in machine code. When I joined Steve to convert his Spectrum games to the Dragon 32, which was then the second most popular home computer, he was just finishing his second game. I had almost caught him up when I finished the third game.

Andrew had a friend working with him who used to act as his chief test pilot, as he used to call him. He was very much into programming and had a Commodore 64, and he was secretly programming a copy of *3D Space-Wars*. One night they invited me around to show me the progress, which was fairly good, and I think he was probably angling to join us as a third programmer but in those days there just weren't enough royalties coming in, but it did open our eye up to the Commodore 64. Andrew was very, very keen on it, and I think his dad bought him one. It was quite a step up from the Spectrum, in that it looked quite professional and it had these things called sprites, which you could move around the screen without having to plot and unplot them all the time. It really did seem the bee's knees at the time.

We used to program just about what we wanted, which was the nice thing about the early industry. We would take a copy of a game in progress to Andrew Hewson. Very often he would say, 'What on Earth is that?' I think those were his exact words for *Paradroid*. He normally wouldn't understand at all what we were trying to do, and that was the thing with publishers throughout the whole industry. They always wanted something that was similar to the last thing that sold, but we had a nice position: we didn't owe anyone any money and we never took any advances, so we did just what we jolly well liked, which basically was what we wanted to play.

I was living in a place called Virginia Water, taking the train back and forward to Mikro-Gen,[x] and I didn't know it was going to take up just about all the money I was earning. I didn't know how games were really made, and when I arrived they said to me, 'Go ahead and make a game.' So I started, with them watching, but they didn't want a game written in BASIC, they wanted it in assembly language, which I'd been teaching myself but I was no pro at.

I realised I had to learn it in a short period of time or I was out of there, having left school over this. So the pressure was pretty intense and the game wasn't turning out too good. The guy who was running the place said to me, 'I want you to take this game that someone else is writing and put that on to the Amstrad CPC.' This game was written in assembly on the Spectrum and it was such a fantastic situation for me. I got to look at somebody else's code and see how to do it.

The guy's name was Chris Hinsley and he was a very respected programmer at the time. He had just made a game called *Automania*, which was the first Wally Week game,[*] and this was the second game, called *Pyjamarama*,[ˀ] and I converted it to the Amstrad. We didn't have any proper equipment to do it. One of the guys in the office made this little thing that would pretend to wiggle a joystick to send data in through the joystick port. It was ridiculous, the work we had to go through, taking enormously long times to compile and deliver data into the device.

But my first review came in and I think it was a ten out of ten for *Pyjamarama* on the Amstrad, because it was a cool game and it had been properly converted. It was like a drug to me, it was like, 'Oh my God, I can do this! I'm not going to get fired! I actually have a career here!' I got to start making my own games, and from that point it turned into a very aggressive developing of games. The first one I did was *Herbert's Dummy Run*,[x] which was a follow-up to *Pyjamarama*, and then *Three Weeks in Paradise*,[*] and then I

[x] Mikro-Gen was based in Bracknell and Virginia Water is on the outskirts of London, a 30-minute train ride away.

[*] Released in 1984 for the Spectrum, the game features a hapless mechanic everyman who has to assemble cars from parts scattered around two levels.

[ˀ] Also released in 1984, you play as Wally's subconscious as he sleeps, attempting to find the key to his alarm clock.

[x] Released in 1985, you play Wally's baby, who is lost in a shopping centre. *Crash* awarded it an overall score of 90%, remarking, 'The production is better in some ways than the last game.'

[*] Released in 1986, the Weeks family has gone on holiday to a tropical island inhabited by questionably stereotyped native enemies. *Crash* awarded it 93%, praising its graphics.

thought I could make just about anything on Spectrum. I started to believe, like, I had the power, and that the game would sell very well.

To be clear, I didn't really know that videogames were real or going to be my future, so I was also planning my true future. I wanted to be a pilot, that was actually my whole goal, so I was trying to study. I wanted to fly Concorde some day. But making games was kind of catching my interest, I saw it growing. I felt, 'I'm supposed to be a pilot, so I should read some book on piloting and I should focus on that, but no, making games is actually more interesting.' It's very interesting to be torn and uncertain.

## Steve Turner

The royalty cheques at first were okay, but nothing to write home about. I remember between £500 and £600, enough to keep going on, but not enough to make you rich. We thought we could multiply that with several versions of each game, and the nice thing was that the royalty did go up quite dramatically. But the horrid thing was that it only lasted a few months and then dropped to virtually nothing. We didn't realise that each game would have a shelf life of six or seven weeks.

At first we used to be called ST Software, which are my initials, and we were very disappointed with Hewson's first releases. Hewson liked to pretend that our game was written by Hewson Consultants, which was an abysmal name. He used to sell little tip books on how to program the Spectrum. It was hard to find our names anywhere, and we complained about it. We said to him that programmers are part of the culture and the magazines had lots of articles about them.

About the time when *Legend of Avalon* was selling was when when royalties started really kicking off. The cheques were in the thousands rather than hundreds and I suddenly realised I was going to be taxed an awful lot at the end of the year. The money comes in all in a lump in a few weeks, and then you have a huge period where you are writing the next game and you don't have any, and I thought that was going to really be bad if I had to pay a load of tax. The answer was to put the money in a limited company, so I had a word with my accountant and he said it was ever so easy to just buy an off-the-shelf company that's set up to do computer software. He offered me a couple and one had the name of Graftgold.

* A 1984 action adventure title for the Spectrum. In the same vein as *Atic Atac* but observed from a pseudo-3D viewpoint.

He said if we didn't like the name we had **48** hours to give it a different one, and me and Andrew put our heads together but we couldn't come up with a better name. We thought Graftgold actually wasn't half bad, because there was a company called Silversoft, and one called U.S. Gold, so it sort of fitted with the industry and had a nice plush feel about it.

Right from the beginning I thought that if I was going to work with Andrew, I wanted it on an employee-employer basis, because it was my money that was effectively being invested and so I wanted to be in control. I also didn't have enough money to pay him as a full-time employee, so I hit on a royalty deal. I gave him two-thirds of a wage, and the other third would be made up with royalties. That worked very well for the first few years, and it was only when we had more employees that I needed to keep people by giving them more money each month. We had a lot of instances where our games weren't published, and so the programmer working on them, through no fault of their own, would be down on money. So we had a bonus scheme and we brought up the wages.

That kept me firmly in control of the company. I was the boss. I always used to wear a shirt and tie when I worked with Andrew, almost like a statement. Although I could get my hands dirty programming with employees, or go down the pub with them, at work I was the boss, and it was one of the things that kept us going, I think. It gave us the commercial discipline that we needed.

Having said that, Andrew was always like a partner. I never wanted him to have sort of any liability in the company because it takes away from the creativity if you're worried about money. He was always number two in the company, and an equal with me. We used to trade ideas, and something that he did in one of his games would spark off something in one of mine. It was nice with just the two of us.

We used to work in what had been my dining room. The dining table was pushed over a little bit, and there was just room for two desks side by side, with leather chairs with high backs, which made us feel sort of big and important. I used to start dead on nine o'clock every day, and I finished at five. I had a two-year-old son, and he could understand that he could see daddy at coffee time and lunch hour, and five o'clock. Andrew was on flexi-time; sometimes he would have a lie-in, and he used to like working into the evening.

It was fine, Steve had done the hard work of getting the games to market, and we got royalties based on sales, so there wasn't a lot for me to worry about in the first few years. As we took on more staff we had to move out of Steve's house and into a proper office, and Steve looked after all the payroll and things. As far as I was concerned I was saved all that extra worry, so for my part it worked very well. We always worked on our own games and ran our own teams, sometimes with shared resources. Everything stayed well focused.

## Julian Gollop

After I left school, I decided to take a year out before going to university and I decided that I was going to spend it working on computer games. I finished *Rebelstar Raiders*, and I started work on *Chaos*, working on it even after I started at the London School of Economics.

*Chaos* was my first assembly language game, which was a major effort on my part because I didn't know it. The final game, of course, had a number of interesting bugs in it, which reflect my limited experience with the assembler, but it was a very interesting project to work on. *Chaos* actually originated as a card game when I was at school in about 1980. I watched a couple of people playing a game called *Warlock*, a Games Workshop game that I never actually got to play because they didn't let me, but what interested me was that you had a hand of cards in your hand with spells on, which only you could see. I thought I could make it myself, so I made a little board game involving cards with spells on and manoeuvring a wizard around a board. Fires would spread and you would summon dragons which could breathe fire. I played this board game such a lot with friends, and I thought it would be great as a computer game.

Actually, my friend Andy Greene, who was the programmer for my first games for Red Shift, *Time Lords* and *Islandia*, had made a version for the BBC, but it was such a complicated game that you could only do it in text mode, so all the creatures were represented in blocks of four characters and it looked really ugly. When I got my Spectrum after doing *Rebelstar Raiders* I thought I really had to go back to *Chaos*. I knew it had to be in assembly language because the game was so sophisticated and I needed to be much more efficient with memory and graphics.

You could have up to eight players, but the interesting thing was that any of those players could be controlled by the AI. It had a lot of randomness because the spell selection was random, which was going back to the original card game in which you dealt the spells out to each player, and it worked out really well. People really enjoyed in particular playing together, like two or three people versus five AI wizards. Actually the name 'Chaos' is very descriptive of what the games could become.

When I was working on the game, Red Shift sort of ceased to exist. They decided to try and publish some of their remaining titles through Games Workshop, and so *Chaos* was Games Workshop's first move into computer game publishing, even if it was an original computer game, not actually based on one of their board games. Again, it came in a nice big presentation box, but I didn't really know how well the game did, and wasn't really sure of the game's impact until much later, when I got a lot of demands from people to make a sequel, which became *Lords of Chaos*.[x]

I got a bit of pressure to finish it; I had a guy called Angus who would come on his motorbike to visit me at my hall of residence and ask, 'Is it done yet? Can I have another tape?' He would keep visiting me until I got the game done. It was a little bit rushed at the end because I was supposed to be studying. I had to basically sit in my dorm for, like, a whole week just trying to finish it.

[x] Released in 1990 on various formats including the Amiga, Spectrum and Atari ST.

# Tim Tyler

When I was 15, and in the last year of high school, I mastered four-way scrolling. Probably the inspiration for *Repton* was reading a review of a game on the Commodore 64 called *Boulder Dash*,[*] which was basically the inspiration for *Repton*. I saw a maze game with a character moving around it being chased by other creatures, and there were boulders that fell down with the potential of crushing the creature, and there was earth that could be moved out of the way. So those were the basic elements in *Repton*. *Boulder Dash* seemed a bit kind of more arcadey than what *Repton* wound

[*] Originally released in 1984 and written by Peter Liepa and Chris Gray for the Atari 400 and 800, *Boulder Dash* ended up being very widely converted.

up being, with not as many puzzle elements; I thought about the games that were available on the BBC Micro, and there didn't seem to be anything much like *Boulder Dash*. I thought I could do a pretty good job of it.

Churning out another game wasn't an enormous project for me, so it took something like three months, and a fair amount of the time was designing the levels in huge notepads. I sent it to Superior Software, and they accepted it pretty much instantly. They put all their energy behind the marketing machine, made adverts, and when it was released the reviews were all positive.

*Repton* came out when I was 16 or 17. I programmed it when I was at school, and I wrote *Repton 2* over the next summer holiday, when I was at college, over a period of a month and a half. I calculated my hourly rate at one stage, and I was earning £40 an hour while I was doing that work, which was more than anybody else in my family was making at the time, so I was quite pleased.

So I was quite keen to do *Repton 2*, and Superior Software wanted the same. I had just written a successful computer game and I thought I could probably do better, and one of the ways in which I thought I could do better was by cramming in more levels. One of the problems with *Repton* was that it wasn't that hard to get to the end of it if you were a keen game player. You could play the same levels over and over again, but that would just be boring. Part of the reason for that was the cramped memory space in the BBC B. I used one byte for each little square in the game, and that wasn't very efficient. But I figured out that because I only had 32 tiles I could probably get away with using five bits for each tile in a maze, and it was part of my plan to make a bigger *Repton* by using compression techniques to cram in more level space.

For *Repton 2* I didn't have a level designer; *Repton 3* did, and I should have had one for *Repton 2*, but what I actually did was type in binary the five digits that were required for each of the 32 different tiles. I hadn't grasped the basic computer science principle that you should spend about half your time making tools for you to use to make your life easier. I didn't do that at that stage, I just confronted the machine and went straight to the bare metal.


Jeff Minter

When I first got into coding games, I learned to program and programming was really satisfying, and that sustained me for a while. But I then developed this feel for the kind of gameplay I liked, and ever since then that's what I've always pursued. I've always tried to make a game that feels right to me, that I want to play. I always feel that if I finish making a game and then I don't play it any more because I'm fed up with it, then I've done something wrong, whereas if I finish making a game and then I play it because I really wanted it to exist in the first place, then I've done it right.

On the VIC-20, I would sit down with a piece of graph paper and sketch out roughly what I thought I wanted to happen, but it was always fairly rough, just a rough guide, really. The game itself would really come together when you actually sat down and started coding it. Always, the first and most important step, still to this day, is to get the player character in there and under control, because once you've got controls, you're always going to be refining them as you make the game, then build the rest of the game around them. There are always significant moments, like when you first get shots firing, when you first get things that you can shoot at, when you first get points in, all these different things, but first start with the rough sketch and then build it up and let the game fill itself in. A lot of the game creates itself as you go along.

A lot of my games are shoot 'em ups, but they tend to be shoot 'em ups in a very abstract context. I'm not really into the depiction of realistic murder or anything like that. I think I just like my games to be a bit humorous and not take themselves too seriously. Games are games after all, and the moment you start getting too serious about them, then I think they lose some of their appeal. At least they do to me.

‹ 141          ## David Perry          207 ›

Back in the old days, to play games you had to have imagination, looking at a 'V' and thinking how it's a spaceship. You would basically look at what you've got available to you, and try to imagine what it could become. You would be limited by your own ability to develop; so if, for example, you could work out how to scroll the screen, a whole new world opened up to you and now you could do scrolling-screen games. Or if you could find a way to animate something a little larger than normal, you started designing a game around that and that's basically how it went: you would look for the hook, like, 'What is this game going to be based upon?'

The games, to be honest, started out very simple. I remember making games like *Zombies*,* where zombies approach and you just try to get them to fall in holes. When you start and you're trying to learn how to program,

* One of the games Perry wrote in 1983 for the book, *49 Explosive Games for the ZX Spectrum.*

it's actually very good to make something really simple, just to get you that first thing, so you can complete it and then you can move on to the next thing.

Another element of game design is the concept of inspiration. You would see somebody do something and you'd go, 'Wow, I didn't even know that was possible!' It's inspiring to see people break new ground. For many years, I'd play a game and I'm like, 'Oh, I like some aspect of that gameplay,' and then transfer that across into a game that I happened to be making. I think that's very important. I mean, it's a hotchpotch; you don't know where it's all coming from but there's a mix of inspiration that ends up creating whatever it is you're doing.

I started with the Sinclair ZX81, and we went from 1K to 16K in the first Spectrum. A lot of people can't grasp just how mind-bending that was, to go 16 times more in one leap. It was such an enormous leap that people really didn't know what to do with all that space. It was such an amazingly different time, and to be limited by these blocky graphics and no colours and 1K of memory, and then suddenly the Spectrum comes out, with 16K or 48K and colour. We didn't want to go back, we always wanted to go forward. So that was probably the moment when I think games started to look more beautiful. If you were very careful with the colours and the way you created the graphics, you could create beautiful loading screens and things like that.

Before that, people like me, who are really lame artists, could stay undercover; I just did simple little blobs and things, but the Spectrum was where you could plot every dot and my graphics were just terrible. I realised I needed help with art, the moment, actually, that the concept of having a team of two: an artist and a programmer came into being. Nigel Brownjohn was my first artist and he helped make *Three Weeks in Paradise*. Some of the graphics were really very good and it was thanks to having a real artist work with me.

One thing we were always thinking when I was working at Mikro-Gen was, 'So we've got 48K of memory, and everybody else gets 48K of memory. If we could find a way to get a little more we would have an advantage, and we could make better games.' So my boss at the time, Andy Laurie, was really good at electronics, and he found a way to add 16K of memory to a Sinclair Spectrum. We called it the Mikro-Plus, and it allowed us to swap out the data in the Sinclair Spectrum's memory that runs the computer, which makes BASIC appear and everything else, and put our game in there. I wrote a new version of *Three Weeks in Paradise*, which was bigger, with more levels, more detail and everything else.

While I was developing it, another guy, Dale McLoughlin, made a game called *Shadow of the Unicorn*, which shipped before me. For whatever reason, the game didn't sell well, so the boss of Mikro-Gen said, 'Kill it! Done! No more Mikro-Plus,' and I'm like, 'Wait a minute, I need it, because I've made all this!' They were like, 'Under no circumstances. We're done. You've got to finish that game without the extra memory.'

It was actually the best thing for me. It taught me something very important, to make more than you need and then pick the best parts. It means admitting that not everything is good, but if you chop out a bunch of stuff and cherry-pick, the result is usually better. In this game I did exactly that and it got 90-plus percent reviews.

## Oliver twins

PO I guess what was different about the way we tackled games was that we thought hard about what people wanted to buy. There were people at school who made games, but they did them to impress themselves or their techy friends. Then we thought, 'What is the most efficient way to deliver that?' So we didn't do the hardest code in the world because we thought, well, it wasn't necessary. If we needed five characters on the screen we wouldn't push it to seven just because we could. We'd keep it as simple as possible because it told the story and gave the entertainment we needed.

The other thing we did very early was create tools and a pipe-line to make things efficient. So we created a sprite package and modules that we knew we could take from one game to the next. When Codemasters sent us a Spectrum to convert *Ghost Hunters*, we immediately set about just redeveloping our engine so that every game we ever wrote on the Amstrad automatically ran on a Spectrum, and it really did. It was an hour's conversion. We didn't actually use the Spectrum as our development kit, we used the Amstrad and its disk drive, and had a cable from the Amstrad to the Spectrum, which basically pumped the game straight into the RAM. We'd test it, and if it crashed we could go back to the Amstrad where it was all saved on disk.

AO We were always only writing these early games on one computer, so we were taking turns. But actually it was a really good thing to have time away from the computer. I would doodle little tiny flow diagrams and little tiny pieces of code for problems that were on my mind, and I'd be thinking about them all day. You really got things straight in your mind because of that.

PO If he nipped away to the toilet, had a cup of coffee or went to bed to get some sleep, it was, 'Right, it's my turn.' Before we knew it, we were basically doing time shifts: 'Okay, I'll go to bed for four hours, you get it all working. When you're done, wake me up, I'll crack on.' We actually worried, really worried, about the computer overheating and blowing up because it was left on for 12, 14 hours at a time, and you really didn't have to do much to break one. A lot of people back in those days said, 'You turn computers on for an hour or two and then you have to give them some cooldown time,' and we weren't giving our computers much cooldown time at all.

## Steve Turner

You used to kind of jealously guard your little secrets at first, but a little later on we used to phone each other up and kind of almost trade our secret knowledge in the machine, as long as you got something back. You would never let on about your latest thing, we'd tell them about how we did something in the last game, like a new way to scroll, or how we found another 4K of memory under the I/O devices. There was much more under the surface than you thought.

The early machines were very limited but in a way that made you strive to use the limitations. I think we found out how to do things with the machines that the manufacturers never ever dreamed of. We were constantly looking at them and thinking about what we could do that no one had done yet. That was really exciting, when you were on the cusp of something; it was like riding a wave, like a drug. No matter what you did, you would think at the end of the game that you could make that graphics routine faster. You always wanted to rewrite it, but you never had time. So you'd change the graphics routine, see that it's faster, slicker, that you have less flicker, and that leads you on to your next game.

In the early days I used a rubber-keyed Spectrum, and it was always a hit and miss affair, because you tended to have to have devices on the back, like a joystick port and later I had a disk drive. So you had a queue of things on the back of your machine and if you typed a little bit too hard then you used to lose everything. Even when I upgraded my 16K machine to a 48K machine, I had 32K of RAM sitting on the back of my machine. One little wobble and it would fall off just enough to

## Julian Gollop

I remember watching Live Aid as I was debugging *Rebelstar*, with a roll of this silver printout from the ZX Printer, debugging by hand the assembly language. You think of debugging now as running debuggers and break points and stuff, but I was actually debugging by hand, literally going through the computer printout trying to figure out where the errors were. It was actually quite a reliable method, and it really made you think about your coding; in a way, I still use it today, but without the printouts.

wipe everything. That was commonplace. I can remember writing a tip to a magazine about how to keep a RAM drive on, because I found that if you bent one of those coat hangers from dry cleaners you could make a little clip.

One of the other problems we used to have was the Spectrum overheating all the time, especially when you had your gizmos on the back. I heard of people standing a glass of ice water by them; we used to use fans in the office for a while but switching the fans on and off sometimes could make your machine crash, so they weren't terribly popular. In the end I bought another keyboard for the Spectrum and lay the circuit board right inside it, which gave it a lot of room. That's how I spent most of my time programming.

We used to save the games on to cassettes, which weren't very reliable, so I used a cycle of six. Every time I saved, I saved on to the next one, so if it didn't load back you could go back up to five versions. The disk drive on the Commodore 64 was just as bad, or perhaps even worse than the cassettes. Very often it would save disk errors, and you had to get a little piece of card to align the disk heads, clean the disk, and eventually it would load. Although it looked a much more professional machine, in effect the technology really wasn't up to much.

When I saw the adverts for Microdrives, they seemed to be the answer. There were these little gizmos which were like disk drives but they had tiny little cartridges that you put in. But when I got one, I just took one look at the tape – whatever possessed them to use a tiny little strip of tape, twice as thin as a cassette tape, which everyone knows used to kind of jam up and stretch? These little things didn't stand a chance. The tape stretched and it wouldn't play back, so the one thing that it needed to do reliably it couldn't really do. I really got near to smashing one with a hammer, but they went back to Sinclair and I actually got my money back!

## Julian Gollop

Developing games on the Sinclair Spectrum in the early days was a little bit difficult, a little bit unreliable. My 48K Spectrum had dual ZX Microdrives, which were amazingly primitive devices, you know, little cassettes which had this endless tape inside them. The cartridges that you put in, either you got a reliable one, which you could use a lot, or you got an unreliable one, which you had to throw away after a while. It's actually surprising how reliable they were, considering how basic the technology was. The biggest problem I had was that the keyboard would give out, so I had to buy a separate Spectrum keyboard, fit it in, and then it would break so I would have to get another. So, surprisingly, the Microdrives proved to be the most reliable bit! I didn't have too many problems developing *Chaos*; it worked; it wasn't very fast, but it did work.

So we backed up just using cheap tape recorders which had nothing except the volume control, with that magic setting that was neither too loud nor soft, and once it was set you put a bit of tape over it so that it never changed. That was much more reliable than you would have thought.

## Rob Hubbard

What was being talked about on the TV was educational software, and I thought getting this stuff into schools could be a business, so I made some music education stuff and showed it to a few people. We had things like a musical fruit machine, where you could pull the handle and then you had to nudge the fruits to get three quavers to equal a dotted crotchet and things like that. The music teachers I showed it to thought it was great, but it was never going to fly because the schools couldn't afford books, let alone computers.

So I got involved in writing a game. People thought the graphics were okay, because I wrote all my own graphics utilities for sprites and backgrounds and that was a lot of fun, but they thought the game sucked. But they also thought the music and sound were great. I had seen some other games which had the 'Blue Danube' on them, but half the notes were wrong. I mean, can you get the notes wrong on the 'Blue Danube'? It's such a well-known tune! If you get the notes wrong there's no hope, is there? So I thought I would get the notes for 'Blue Danube' right, but the values in the manual for the SID chip were actually out of tune, and I created a table of values that were in tune. I don't know how they got them wrong.

After this, I thought there had to be a market of people who wanted to get the notes right in their games. I got all the magazines for the addresses of all the game publishers and I did a massive mailout. The first thing I did was *Action Biker* for Mastertronic and then *Thing on a Spring*. *Thing on a Spring* was an intriguing game because its weird little character thing got the imagination going, which was why I created the little weird springy sound in that tune.

I was doing a lot of work for a guy called John Maxwell at Mastertronic; I did a lot of work for the Darling brothers, too. One of the funny things that happened was I went down to London to see John Maxwell just after *Thing on a Spring*, and he said, 'Rob, you are only charging £150 for this stuff. You want to double that at least.' That has got to be the first time in history that somebody actually said to a contractor they're not charging enough.

My view was still that I had seen this *The Fabulous Wanda* game, you know. I thought these games that Mastertronic were making basically had a shelf life of six weeks, and I had no idea how many copies would sell. I thought all these surplus copies would end up in a skip and that would be the end of it and had no idea that any of this stuff would last for as long as it did. I mean, if I did, I might have worked harder.

The first games I really got much exposure to were the Ultimate games like *Jetpac* and *Atic Atac*. It seemed like they were the first professional products, where you could sit back and relax: professionals had gotten together and made a safe, reliable product. They had great graphics and great animation, and great humour. They had scary monsters and comedy monsters, and they were very concise and very efficient in terms of everything that was on screen. Every key press, every function and every feature of the game was only enough to make the game a big hit. There were no extra levels or other stuff that you didn't enjoy, you enjoyed every part of those games evenly from start to finish. So it was always great to play those. It was like immersing yourself in a sumptuous leather seat, compared to a harsh bench, which is the comparison to its rivals.

When I was taking the *Pac-Man* game to Ocean, the same friend, Paul Proctor, had also done a rip-off on the BBC of the Ultimate game, *Cookie.*[1] I put a bunch of custom music in, like 'Food, Glorious Food', and we were all about sending this to Ultimate, if only just to offer it up to the gods like a sacrificial lamb, because they were the gods of the games business. We phoned them up to find out the name of a person to send it to – the lady just said to address it to 'Mr T Stamper', so I sent a floppy disk off with a letter, and they actually liked it, but *Cookie* was one of their older games at this point and they didn't want to put out a conversion then. They were more interested in having a more modern game converted, which we were ecstatic about. We were over the moon: me and Paul were selected by Ultimate to do one of their games!

They wanted us to do *Sabre Wulf*[x] on the BBC. Converting a 48K Spectrum game to a 32K BBC game required compression skills the likes of which even Ultimate weren't using, so we had to cut some things out, but broadly speaking we did an amazing conversion, complete with my music. I did a classical piece like they had in the Spectrum version,[*] and we fit the

[1] Published in 1983 for the Spectrum, the aim of Cookie was to flour bomb marauding ingredients and knock them into a giant mixing bowl.

[x] Originally released in 1984 for the Spectrum.
[*] It was Bach's 'Prelude in C Major'.

music data for the tune into 60 bytes, finding ways of using the notes over and over, because there's a mathematical way of using data over and over to save a lot of space. We also got rid of the BBC operating system for sound and programmed the chip directly, because that takes up 256 bytes of RAM.

Anyway, we got the game done and they were very happy with it and they put it out, so basically we had ascended to the level of Ultimate conversion folks. I can't remember what we got paid, but I got a small amount of money, like £170, and Paul made more because he was the main programmer and worked on it for several months over the summer.

Paul ended up getting a full-time job there, and he told me they were looking for an audio person, so I went there for an interview. It was a nicely done up converted farmhouse with some computers in, and Tim and Chris Stamper gave me like a six-hour interview. They made me sign a non-disclosure agreement to get a tour of the place; that's how secretive they were. They told me that they had released *Underwurlde* first even though it was made after *Knight Lore*; they sat on *Knight Lore* because it was so good  and they explained to me their quality ramp, that they wanted each of their games to be better than the last. They didn't care about just releasing a game because it was done, and then doing another. That's what Ocean were doing, and everybody else. All these concepts were just blowing me away. They were the pros. They really knew what they were doing. It was an incredible day.

They third-party-hacked their way on to the new Nintendo console, and they were thinking globally. This was the first developer I ever talked to that was thinking about the global market, that the world is one market. It was just amazing. They showed me the first game that they developed for NES. It wasn't released, just a test game, and they sent it to Nintendo to say, 'Hey, look, we just did this on the NES with no manuals, all by ourselves. What do you think?' It was actually better than Nintendo's own launch titles for the platform.

Naturally I wanted to work there, I'd do anything, I was on bended knee. But one of the things I asked was whether it was okay if I talked to my friends about what I was doing or do I have to keep it a secret. They said I absolutely had to keep it a secret, and of course they would say that, but I didn't really realise, and I think that they sensed that I was going to blab about what I was doing. I think that hurt my chances of getting hired, because I think my music was fine.

## Rob Hubbard

To start writing music for a game, I used to say to the programmer, 'Well, what are you thinking? Do you want to send me a demo, and I'll come up with some ideas?' Sometimes I just got a description, and I remember talking to somebody who said, 'I don't care as long as it sounds like Hendrix, man,' and I thought 'Okay!' Sometimes you had to work completely without seeing the game. 98% of the time they thought what I came up with was perfectly in keeping with what they wanted.

I had a little Casio keyboard, an MT31 that was portable, so I could put it under my arm if I was watching TV and if I suddenly thought of something I could have a quick little play and then go into the other room and write down the ideas. Then, most of the creative work I actually did on the computer itself using a machine code monitor, where I could get lines of hexadecimal numbers on the screen and change them in real time while the music was playing. That meant that I could fine-tune to the nth degree what was going on with the music, and most importantly I could edit all the synthesiser's patch parameters on the chip in real time.

## Martin Galway

← 153
157 →

I would think about what's appropriate for the game, and if there was a flavour that was really obvious I would definitely go down that route, like a military game would have military-type music, but when other games didn't really speak to you in any particular way, it was kind of down to me to fill in that silence with some original music. I went back to my influences like Gary Numan and Sparks, who did an album with Giorgio Moroder in 1979 called *No. 1 in Heaven*, which was one of my favourite albums. It really influenced my style of music composition, with a lot of repetition of notes and lots of arpeggiators and it had kind of a disco dance feel. That was my default mode, and I could go into an ambient-style mode.

## Fred Gray

← 106
159 →

The Sinclair machines just had a single bit output for the audio, which was basically no good at all, but programmers being programmers, they came up with drivers that sounded a lot like music. People remember *Manic Miner* had a nice little tune to it but it was probably the bare minimum. Later on, somebody wrote a driver that added two voices in envelopes, although anyone who was technical would realise that this didn't always work. You had to be very careful in picking your music so you didn't get interference between the two notes.

I was greedy for knowledge. I wanted to know what the Spectrum could do and what it couldn't. I went through every instruction in the instruction set to ask what it did and think how I could use it. Later on, with the Commodore 64, lads I befriended used to come round and show me the latest demos. People started putting sprites at the bottom of the screen, where there shouldn't be any graphics, so I had a look at some of the code and realised you could use interrupts to switch the sprites back on again. I went down to Denton Designs and mentioned it to the programmer I was with at the time. He said, 'Go away, can you?' and he instantly put a control panel made out of sprites at the bottom of the game we were working on.

There was a lot of plagiarism and also sharing of knowledge. Basically, we all wanted to get on. I remember somebody saying once, 'If they are making money, that means you can make money as well.' So altruism was rife and sharing the knowledge was one way of being altruistic. It was one way of making sure that everybody got on and the game industry thrived.

It took me a while to get used to all the features on the SID chip, because it was a very sophisticated piece of hardware. It was like going from caveman to the Big Bang theory; it had pulse and ring modulation things you would expect on a commercial synthesiser, you know like a Moog or something, and it gave you so much power it was unbelievable. The Amiga had samples, but nothing else touched the SID chip. The AY chips appeared in a lot of machines, like the Spectrum and Atari ST, and basically it was like the old arcade machines, blip blip blip, without any synthesiser effects.

But then again, the programmer was never happy with that power. We always wanted more. Later on they started experimenting with multiplex and producing two tunes from one voice, or getting really good sound effects by mixing noise with pitch. Also, the big lifesaver was the fact that you could produce chords. I found this out using the SH-101, so when you held down a chord you could play a normal arpeggio, but then if you sped it up it would actually sound like a single chord rather than an arpeggio. This is the principle behind multiplex chords on the SID chip.

For the two games Ocean asked me to do, I did *Kong Strikes Back!* first, and I developed this technique for making it sound like the Commodore was playing more than three notes at once by taking one of the oscillators and going around the notes I wanted to play in a cycle very quickly, or a very fast arpeggio. I was into a lot of synthesiser acts, and one of the tricks they used was arpeggiators, just playing all these cycles of notes, and they sounded really cool to me, so I made the Commodore do it really quickly, and when you went really quickly it sounded like all the notes were being played at once, except there was a kind of wibbly wobbly phasey weirdness to the sound .

The very first tune I ever practised it with was 'Right By Your Side' by Eurythmics, which has this little marimba synthesiser part, and so I started this little technique and really quickly wrote a custom piece of code so I could program it to play any chord, working each base note around three offsets: the base note, then the note plus four, and then the note plus seven.

So I left school with *Chuckie Egg* under my belt and thought I'd better get a proper job, so I applied to work at Ocean. They looked like a proper company, professional and organised, and to join a proper company felt like I was growing up and getting a proper job. My first game there was with Joffa Smith* on *Kong Strikes Back!* Joffa was multi-talented. He could do everything: the graphics, the coding, the sound. I think I was a bit older than him and more experienced, and I sort of bullied him a bit. I feel a bit guilty about that now, but I made myself the boss and we didn't really work together very well, because I was too big headed, probably because of *Chuckie Egg*.

\* Prolific Ocean programmer Jonathan Smith, whose first game was *Pud Pud*.

I hadn't composed any original music before, I'd just done other people's, and that was a big boundary I had to cross. *Kong Strikes Back!* was set in a kind of fairground, and I came up with some Scott Joplin-style music, basically what I was playing on the piano at the time that sounded fairgroundy, and they were happy with it. It used this arpeggiation technique, which, if you listen to a lot of what they call 8-bit music, it all uses.

\* An action game in which you have to avoid rollercoaster cars as you ascend to rescue a *Donkey Kong*-style damsel, published in 1985.

One thing that people used to do was to look in the documentation and get these 8-bit registers which had bit patterns to toggle certain aspects of the sound. Sometimes you could set two bits and get something completely different, a strange new waveform coming from it which wasn't in the documentation. There were also certain things on the SID chip, where you could do hard sync and ring modulation, which is something that I knew about because I had worked with SIDs.

The SID could play three simultaneous voices, but later on I could get four, because I could get a sample channel playing as well, but mainly all the early stuff was three voices. But it was all about how you arranged the music to use the three voices to try to make it sound like there was a lot more going on. There was a game called *Ghostbusters,*  * which had a sample sound saying, 'He slimed me!' so I knew that they could get a sample sound out of it. I kept plugging away until I figured out that they were actually modulating the volume register from a fast non-maskable interrupt to do it.  † So I expanded it to try to use it musically, which was quite a challenge. Being a non-maskable interrupt, there was only a short range in which you could change the pitch you were getting.

*   David Crane's 1984 game for Activision, based on the film.
†   When software changes the volume of a voice, the SID makes a little click, so by changing the volume register tens of thousands of times a second, a fourth sound channel is created, able to handle sample data.

## Martin Galway

The SID chip, as we all know, is the heart of the Commodore 64. Who cares about the other stuff? But communication between developers and Commodore really wasn't that robust. They might send us manuals or free Commodore 64s, but they would never really tell us about hardware updates or firmware revisions. We would sometimes buy new computers and we heard a distinctly different sound coming from our games on the Commodore 64C, a cost-reduced version. They had changed the SID quite significantly. I still haven't kept up to date with the history of what Commodore did with all of those different revisions, but basically the problem with the SID from the outset was that quality control was not managed as well as it could, and each SID came off the assembly line sounding a little bit different.

We probably had 40 Commodore 64s, 128s and 128Ds at Ocean, so I was able to compare and they definitely sounded different. It impacted my music quite significantly when I started to use the filter part of the SID, because the filter part was what was different on every SID. With the Commodore 64C it sounded very, very dull, while the older SIDs had this variable flavour. I made sure to make my music on a SID chip that sounded great, and I didn't care about the ones that sounded bad. As long as it sounded great in my studio, then I was happy.

Everyone had their own techniques, so I came from the old-school so I thought I would have a bass sequence, a middle sequence and a top sequence, which for me was like classical music. But obviously other people were listening to more radical music and had completely different approaches. They were listening to actual synthesisers and that type of band. This was the nice thing about the SID chip, everybody approached it differently and you could come out with all sorts of things.

To be honest, when I was at Imagine Software I didn't know any other musicians. I thought there must be people out there, but nobody ever mentioned any names and said, 'Can you produce sounds more like so and so?' or, 'So and so is doing this, why don't you try it?' It was when I got involved with the local lads who used to bring me demos and games, and they started mentioning names like Rob Hubbard and Martin Galway. I thought, 'Ah, this is the competition!' And I listened to

their music, like *Rambo* and what Martin was doing, and thought, 'Wow, he is doing really strange stuff.'

Later on, when I met him, he said he used to play an awful lot with the pitch in real time, whereas my music was basically portamento.` I set up a system so the notes were automatic for ease of use, but for Martin it was an exact science and he would fine-tune everything in real time. He would be sat in this little room, listening to every minute detail and you could see the concentration on his face. He was definitely a perfectionist.

*Thing on a Spring* was the first thing that hit me with Rob Hubbard, and I could hear in Rob's music that he was a very talented musician. He knew music and his programming was equally as good, so most people would say that Rob was number one. I totally agree, he is basically a genius.

` A musical technique where notes move from one to another, typified in compositions for slide guitar or violin.

Around the time I was doing *The NeverEnding Story*, Colin Stokes came in with a cassette and he goes, 'Mart, you have got to hear this!' I looked on the cassette and it said *Thing on a Spring*. So I put the game in, and it was fairly late in the evening and everyone had left, and man, I listened to that tune for like three hours looping. I was like, 'That is so good. That guy really knows what he is doing, and oh my God I've got some competition.' It was a real clarion call and I really had to get my chops together to compete with this guy. I didn't know who it was, but whoever did the music in that game was leaps and bounds over everybody else.

I had been listening to games like *Park Patrol* from Firebird Software and some of the other American games and they just had really terrible music. With *Thing on a Spring* the melody was great, I mean, this was really great composing, so I was scared. I realised somebody else who was a decent composer is now working on the Commodore 64, so it's not just me with my fiddly arpeggios. I really had to pay attention and sharpen up.

Obviously, we all know now it was Rob Hubbard, but I didn't know who it was for months, where he lived, if he worked for any particular company. I thought it was the Gremlin Graphics music guy, you know, but it was a freelancer who was working for anybody, and so his music started to crop up everywhere because he was quite prolific.

*   Released in 1985, the game to this day could've earned its composer cred for its catchy music. Fred Gray arranged the track, but it's a spectrum version, added to the version of the Commodore 64's.

## Rob Hubbard

I really didn't listen to much of other people's stuff at the time. I mean I heard Martin's music for *Rambo*, and he was doing some pretty clever stuff there. He had a really nice vibrato routine I was always trying to copy. It sounded better than mine. It was a case of doing a vibrato without doing a proper division, but division in 6502* takes a long time, and so you are trying to find a way to fudge it so you don't use a lot of processing power. So there was some of that going on, but I was so busy trying to get my own stuff done, get the invoices out and then collect the cheques, which sometimes was another task in itself. Getting paid was sometimes almost as difficult as doing the job. In fact, more difficult than doing the job.

# Martin Galway

*Rambo: First Blood Part II* did not come out at the same time as the film,* so we went to see it at a review screening. It was fun to see a movie before it was really released; we all sat in the best row in the cinema and we thought it was a great movie, and then we went back to finish off the game. I got a cassette of the film score, which is a Jerry Goldsmith score, one of his most notable, and I listened to it over and over at home and work, figuring out which tunes to do.

I got quite imaginative with the synthesiser aspects of the score, because Jerry Goldsmith used synthesisers as well as orchestra, and that appealed to me a lot. I was also driving forward my skill-set with the SID, and I came up with this electronic adaptation of the score that was pushing the SID's features, and all of my compositional skills. Adapting the tunes down to three oscillators was all I ever thought about; I never thought about a fourth or fifth part, or a situation where there would be only two, so, you know, I was really exploiting the chip to the full. Being a programmer, I was also able to get the code to do things, like I put a routine into my music player so that in the credits when it gets to a certain part in the tune they would freeze and then start moving again. I think being a programmer gave me an advantage over some other composers.

With *Rambo* they had basically been ripping off *Commando* by Capcom. We'd had the arcade machine in the Ocean office for a long time, and it was one of my favourite games. I loved the music, because it had what we now know as the FM synthesis chip, which was used in *Marble Madness* and a bunch of other games. So we had been using *Commando* as the model for *Rambo*, and once we saw the film itself we were able to build in specific stuff about it.

Then it was announced in the press that Elite was doing the official *Commando* licence, so it naturally became a rival. I am not sure if I found out Rob Hubbard was doing the music, but hearing it would have made me hit the roof. My ultimate arch-rival, that mysterious guy somewhere else in the UK who I'd never met, was working on this game that I was working on a rip-off of!

* The game came out in late 1985, produced by Platinum Productions for Ocean.

They came out around the same time, and Rob's music for *Commando* was fantastic, a great version of the tune that I was very familiar with, and much better than the version of the *Commando* tune that I privately did. But it made me really happy when I opened the pages of *Commodore User* and they reviewed both games side-by-side on a double spread, and the little point scores at the bottom gave Rob's music four stars and my music five stars. I glowed all day and thought, 'Thank God the stress is over!'

## Nigel Alderton

I managed to get an offer of a contract to write *Commando* for the Spectrum, £10,000 for a ten-week contract, so it was ridiculous money compared to what I was earning at Ocean, which was £4,500 a year. I was offered the job by Steve Wilcox at Elite, so I handed in my notice at Ocean. There was a lot of pressure; Steve was completely open and up-front and said, 'Look, this has to be out for Christmas. There is no way this can't be out for Christmas.' This incredibly lucrative contract came with a very heavy penalty clause, £1,000 a day.

It was me and Keith Burkhill on the Spectrum, and another guy, Chris Butler, writing the Commodore one. Keith and I had a great understanding right from the start, because we had both done enough development by then to know that when you're up against a deadline it takes twice as long as you think, and you have got to really hammer it. So we both just agreed to hammer it from the start. We worked really, really hard, working at Elite, the three of us beavering away in a room together. I remember Rob Hubbard coming in, and it was quite a big deal because he was this mega famous creative guy, and it was lovely to have decent sound.

Rather than going home in the evening we would go out and get a bite to eat and then come back and work in the evening. We gave ourselves the weekends off, so we would leave Friday night and come back Sunday night. During the week we were staying in a little guest house down the road called the Larches. As time went on we realised that we weren't as ahead of the game as we thought, so we started giving ourselves less and less time off, and then at the end it was getting very, very tight and very, very stressed, so we were given more people to help to test the thing.

Eventually, there was one bug left, but only one person that could get this bug to manifest itself: Karen, one of the graphic designers.

Nobody else could crash it! We tried moving her to different machines, we tried different copies of the tape, we tried moving her from room to room. Somebody decided that she had static electricity, so we earthed her at one point, and then eventually we just decided she was a witch and there was no other explanation. Of course, there was another explanation, which was that there was a bug in the code and she was playing the game in a particular way as she came up to the bridge, and the bug was in my half of the code. It didn't take long to fix, but by the time we did we were two days late. By that point we had worked two days and two nights in a row, right through the night, trying to find this damn bug because of this ridiculous penalty. But Steve did not penalise us a penny, even though he was well within his rights to.

We were trying to get the versions to be as similar as possible, but on the Spectrum in particular we had to make lots of compromises. We were trying to get the gameplay at least to be as similar as possible, even though the look was never going to be the same. But the game was a massive hit, the Christmas number one, and it stayed there for months.

← 160 ## Rob Hubbard 181 →

They called me up and told me to get on a train straight away down to, I think it was Birmingham or somewhere. I remember I got like the four o'clock train, and then we spent the rest of the day in the pub. Then they went home and left me in the office at ten o'clock at night or something. There was an arcade machine there with *Commando* on, so I had a quick listen and I used a little bit of the motif from it. I had my little Casio keyboard and my score paper with me – I always used to have proper score paper to write stuff down on, basically some musical notation splattered with lots of hexadecimal numbers which related to the actual pitches and sound patches and all that stuff. About five o'clock in the morning I finished the music and started working on the sound effects, and by the time they came in at eight o'clock I had it all done, and got the train back. I still have my old invoice book. I got paid a few hundred quid.

← 161 ## Martin Galway 164 →

I met Rob for the first time at the 1986 PCW Show. There was a gaggle of kids around him, treating him like some kind of circus guy because his photo had been in magazines. Up until that point my photo had never been in any, and I actually kind of liked that. I was able to walk around without being pestered, but Rob Hubbard had a crowd of people everywhere he went. I had to meet him, so I got close enough to say, 'Hey Rob, it's Martin Galway,' and a whole bunch of people turned around. Rob was just as much of a god for me as all the other kids standing there, but they started figuring out who I was and it kind of blew my cover. It wasn't a great moment, to be honest, because I felt a lot of scrutiny after that.

## Jon Hare

*Parallax* was inspired loosely by a couple of different arcade games, but had its own original take in the way ships kind of got sucked into little holes and spat out across the map. It was basically flying a plane around the levels with some science exploration. The exploration part of *Parallax* in my mind was going to be this massively involved thing, but it ended up being a tiny little part, but it was what we could fit in the memory.

After two or three months we had a good demo and we wanted to see some publishers. Our first appointment was to see Ocean, who were the biggest publisher in the country at the time for Commodore 64 games. So we went up there and we showed someone called Colin Gordon, and he said he liked it and we were taken to see Jon Woods, who was the boss of Ocean.

Jon Woods is a fairly intimidating guy. He looked like he'd been round the block a few times with business, definitely knew what he was doing, very canny. We were totally green, okay? We had no clue about business at all, because this was the first time we did this, and we sat down with the most experienced head of a game company in the UK. He says, 'I've been told by Colin you've got a really great game there, and we'd like to sign it.' Imagine, like, we've only entered his office less than an hour ago, our first-ever business meeting. We were given a contract to sign and they said they would pay us £5,000 and give us a cheque for £1,000 that day.

So we're like, 'Yeah!' and we signed the contract and got the cheque, and we went back on the train. In those days you could

## Martin Galway

In early '86, Gary Bracey, who was new at the time, popped his head in the door and said, 'We've got a disk here and no one's available to try it. Can you just see what it is?' It was the *Parallax* demo that Sensible Software were sending around. I could have just tossed it in the bin and said it was the biggest load of rubbish I'd ever played, and that would have been the end of that, but no, I actually played it and I thought it was a cool game. It had no sound to speak of, but it was fun to play and I thought it had potential, so I told Gary and Ocean published the game.

smoke on trains and we bought some cigars and sat in the meal carriage and we had steaks or something and a cigar. It was fantastic. Okay, it was an awful contract. We got totally burnt on royalties and all that, and nowadays I wouldn't sign it. I would have read it and taken a month or two to go through it, but the immediacy of doing business is the single thing I miss most about the industry then.

Martin Galway worked at Ocean, and Martin was a brilliant Commodore 64 musician. He was really one of the pioneers, and first time I heard his *Parallax* music, it blew me away. It was unbelievable, and I think we started to realise that we were moving into something new and exciting. When *Wizball* happened, Martin did the music for all the Ocean games, so he just came with it, which we were very lucky for. Martin was a massive Tangerine Dream and Jean-Michel Jarre fan, and he was just trying to emulate that music using the SID chip in the Commodore 64. Martin was really one of the cream of the crop people. He was brilliant.

## Martin Galway

*Rendez-Vous* by Jean-Michel Jarre came out in April '86, and I played it like crazy, and it was the first CD I ever bought, but then my CD player broke. While I was getting it repaired I worked on the *Parallax* title screen music. I was like, 'I am going to make this game big. I am going to go magnum opus,' kind of thing. I was getting a little bit egotistical at the time, and so I did this enormous intro, 11 minutes long, with nine minutes of introduction and one minute of tune, and then it dies off. So I finished it and got my CD player repaired and put in *Rendez-Vous* and I was like, 'Oh my God, I have completely ripped it off.' The basis of the *Parallax* music is one of the tracks in *Rendez-Vous*, I think 'Third Rendez-Vous', and I didn't realise it. It was in my subconscious, and I wasn't really coming up with anything original at all.

They came up from Essex to Manchester on the train, probably in May, and that's when I met them for the first time, and they heard this music, and another little tune I was doing. I knew that it would be a bit of a performance, because it was 11 minutes long. I turned the lights down in my office and just let them watch the screen in the dark, because my music software had a debugging system while it's playing so it displays a lot of information on the TV about what the music memory is doing, the RAM, the SID chip registers, and that kind of stuff, animated in time with the music. At the end it has this enormous electronic sound crash thing, and I stopped it and turned on the light, and Jon was like, 'That was the best piece of music I have ever heard,' and he was frowning, with a 'just taken a heavy joint' look to his face. So that was very satisfying, and I liked them a lot.

We signed *Wizball* to Ocean again. I think they liked *Parallax*, and we built good developer-publisher relationships, so they wanted our second game. We didn't really shop *Wizball* around anywhere. As an artist you need security to make good work. If you don't have security, you're spending all the time looking at the bottom line worrying where your money's coming from. You need to know that bit is sorted, then you can focus on the creative stuff, which requires utmost concentration, not distraction with paying bills or worrying.

With *Wizball*, the inspiration was *Nemesis* and *Salamander*, the arcade machines at the time. They were the latest things with the greatest graphics, and Chris was really into them. Chris invented this control system, and one day I went round to his house and he said, 'Look at this, what do you think?' I then made this little green head, which later became Wizball, and that was the art. We just needed something which rotated.

So we had the rotating head and then we had the thing circling it, which we called the Catellite. I really liked the controls, and the two players doing different things, working together, one controlling the Wizball and the other the Catellite, or you could play it in single-player, controlling both. Then also with the bit when you collected the paint drops, which you mixed and you could colour the landscape. This is the kind of idea that I came from, which is how can we build this into a world, so we'd have come up first of all with the colouring the landscape idea, and then okay, these things we're shooting, they could drop colours and so on.

I don't really remember how it all came together, because Chris and I would just talk. It was so natural. Design documents didn't even enter our heads until 1991. When you're making a really good game, it's an iterative process. With *Wizball*, Chris made a control system, and we went down the arcade and he looked at the flight paths and weapons and we bolted that in. I'd have been looking at colourisation of backgrounds and how that can work. Then we'd put it together. 'Now, how do we mix the colour? Oh, let's have a wizard's lab. And that little spinning spaceship, what can we turn it into?' Well, Chris had a cat called Nifta, so we just turned it into a cat. 'Oh, all right then.'

*Wizball* didn't really make a lot of sense, because it was nothing like *Parallax*, so when the time came to do it I didn't really have any ideas, so I suggested to Gary Bracey that I go down and work with them for a couple of weeks. He was like, 'Yeah, knock yourself out.' By this point I basically had free rein to do anything I wanted, because my music was getting high scores in the magazines and generally people were pretty happy, so I got on the train with all my Commodore 64 stuff and I went down to Ilford, where Jon Hare was living.

I was sleeping on a couch in a sleeping bag and I was there for six weeks and I didn't take a bath the entire time. It was the longest period of my life that I didn't take a bath. They had their guitars and their amps in the living room, like cliché rockers, and I was having the time of my life hanging out with these guys, because they were really great musicians. I couldn't figure out why they didn't do their own music, but that's just the way things are.

The time came when Ocean were like, 'When are you going to come back, Martin?' But I hadn't really got the title screen tune finished. Everyone knows the bit in the middle where it kind of trails off, that's actually where it was at when I returned to Ocean. I finished it off at work but I just ran out of ideas.

Towards the end of '87 I was getting disillusioned at Ocean Software, because they would only have me doing the music for games and I was getting quite backed up. I couldn't really go as quickly as the other programmers were doing games, and it got to the point where I think I had a queue of five or six games ahead of me. I felt like I was too slow, or that I wasn't delivering the goods, but I really couldn't go any faster. It occurred to me that they could just have more sound people, but they never really wanted to hire anybody. We had a couple of helpers, but they didn't really amount to anything, and so I was getting pretty sick of it.

# Part 4

# Booming Business

I remember seeing in the *Daily Star* a colour photograph of an Imagine programmer called Eugene Evans leaning on, I think it was a Lotus Esprit, and it said this man would earn £35,000 this year. I remember thinking, 'Yeah, I want a slice of that. It's better than writing missile code for the MOD.'

There was Silversoft in Hammersmith, there was Salamander ×
down in Brighton, and Artic Computing out of Hull, and Charles
Cecil worked for them. There was Bug-Byte in Liverpool. From
Bug-Byte you had companies that were spawned out, like Imag-
ine, but Bug-Byte was one of the very early ones, and probably
Quicksilva's biggest competitor.

Tomorrow's World did a programme on us as the fastest growing company in the UK in 1982 or '83. It was fronted by Peter
McCann, and filmed in a NatWest bank's vault, and he held the
cassette up and he said, 'This is worth more than ...' and the camera panned around the vault, '... all this.' The bank manager allowed us to do that because we were absolutely flying. It was
exploding. Videogames had been embraced by kids, 12- to 16-
year-olds, mainly male.

When we did the full-colour ad asking for people who could create programs to write into us, we got lots of responses. We took
a number of the titles and published them, and there was a kid in
Scotland, probably 12 or 13, and we wanted him to demonstrate his
game at a show at Earl's Court. His mother called me and I had to
give her a promise that as a responsible 30-year-old I would take
care of her young Ben, that he'd get to bed on time and was fed. I
did! I trailed him around London and took it very seriously.

By then some of the kids were starting to make serious money
with their royalties, and they didn't know what to do with it, so we
set up a structure where we would take care of the individual and
he would get the best tax advice and so on, and we would also
make sure that he continued to pursue his career.

× Salamander developed games for less popular platforms, such as the Dragon 32 and
Oric-1.

I stayed at Bug-Byte for probably close to a year, where I met
Dave Lawson, who was a brilliant programmer, and there was
a sales guy whose job it was to go out there and sell games to
retail and had come from Microdigital, called Mark Butler. They
decided they were going to leave, so they approached me in 1982
and we met in secret. They asked me if I would like to come with
them. I think they got about £25,000 from a government starter
agency. This was a time when unemployment among the under-
25s was extremely bad in Liverpool. Within that age group, it

was probably 20%, so there was a lot of government support and money for people starting companies.

So they were going to start Imagine. Dave left first and wrote *Arcadia* for the VIC-20 and Spectrum, then Mark left once it was done, and I left shortly thereafter. That was the beginning of a very tumultuous 18 to 24 months, when we literally went from the three of us up to about 80 full-time, to nothing and bankruptcy. It was a hell of a journey for all of us.

## Fred Gray

When I went to Imagine, I was the first in-house musician in games. They put me in this cupboard-sized room with a keyboard and a Commodore 64 and said, 'Write us some music.' I came up with *Pedro* and a few other sort of tunes that were very childish and what I thought was expected. It wasn't until later on that I realised other people were writing far more sophisticated things.

The problem with Imagine was that I was just getting paid. I was quite happy to be in work, and there was a work-load, but the stuff I produced wasn't particularly clever, and I didn't put that much effort into producing it. I was still stuck in that mindset of thinking about the Atari and what the arcade games sounded like. It was only when I became a freelancer that I realised what the competition was like, and I had to fend for myself because I wasn't getting a regular wage, though Denton Designs gave me a retainer. Denton for me was a bit of a showcase, because they were doing out-of-the-box games and I felt I had to rise to their imagination.

The working day at Imagine wasn't a working day, it was a working night. We would come in late and go home late, although usually about eight o'clock we would bugger off to the pub. Don't tell Dave Lawson that. So the people who worked of a night were sort of the freaky ones. I walked in one night with a friend of mine, Mark, who had his hi-fi playing full-blast. I can't remember what it was – Mötorhead or The Doors or something – but you could hear it down in the street. That was the sort of party atmosphere we lived in, and it was encouraged, to be honest.

The whole philosophy of Imagine was the same as Silicon Valley, where they used to say it didn't matter what people looked like: if they had long hair, employ them, because they are usually the guys who produce the work. Imagine took on anyone they knew had talent, regardless of their personality, or looks or their academic background. A lot of the staff that Imagine employed were literally kids, but they went on to develop their personalities.

So it was a lot of fun, and the people who were the most fun were the ones who came in of a night, but we didn't do an awful lot of work. We used to go down the pub, and this really seedy club called the Casablanca. We didn't go back to the office. I used to just get a taxi home; it was rock 'n' roll; we were rock stars. We had lots of money, lots of acclaim; everyone loved us and we could do what we liked.

Imagine had huge ambitious ideas about how the games industry should go. I was fascinated, and the enthusiasm that Dave Lawson used to bring to team meetings was amazing, but he always wanted more. He wanted different, he wanted new, and we were just programmers, just, sort of, the mechanics. We had to solve all the problems, and make their ideas appear on the screen. It was a new frontier and we were exploring things in public, going further and further into strange territory and trying to make the most of the hardware, almost inventing things daily.

←173

## Eugene Evans

177→

I often get asked how much was true with some of the stories about Imagine, the fast cars, parties, big houses, you know. There was a lot of it that was true. But Bruce Everiss had made a lot of innovations over the years. He had helped Bug-Byte polish their marketing, making connections with packaging companies so their products went from almost photocopied tape covers with very basic artwork to full four-colour artwork, very professional. A lot of that was Bruce, saying, 'You have got to make it more presentable as the market grows.' There were still hobbyists, but it was moving to people who were looking for a little more.

So Bruce became involved with Imagine, and he came up with this idea with his cousin: 'We need to push the cult of personality and we think the answer is him.' What was I? A 17- or 18-year-old guy in Liverpool, a city with a lot of unemployment and a lot of issues, and it's a feel-good story, you know, a success story. They came up with a salary. I wasn't making that money at the time. There was the potential to make that money, but that didn't seem to bother us.

←105

## Archer Maclean

198→

I remember seeing in the *Daily Star* a colour photograph of an Imagine programmer called Eugene Evans leaning on, I think it was a Lotus Esprit, and it said this man would earn £35,000 this year. A graduate salary at that point was about £6,000 or £7,000, so, you know, he was a bloke writing games, driving a so-called dream machine, living the rock star lifestyle, although he probably worked quite hard being the full-on geek, and earning five or six times more than a graduate! Having just left university with a 2:1 degree, I remember thinking, 'Yeah, I want a slice of that. It's better than writing missile code for the MOD.'

## David Braben

There is the famous shot of Eugene Evans and the salary and all that sort of thing. One of the things that irritated me was the dismissive way they talked about it, you know, the whizz-kid winning the lottery. But I am sure he worked very hard to get a decent salary when he was only 16. That is quite an achievement, you know? They were belittling it, almost like it was just random luck. They just put this huge pile of money next to him and took pictures of him in a Lotus.

You know, we were determined and dogged about making the company a success.

Anyway, Bruce came up with this and we wrote a press release and it went out. I don't think any of us could have ever anticipated how big the story around me became. The phone the following day just started ringing off the hook. By the end of that day I think just about every national newspaper had sent over a journalist. We were getting requests from all over to cover the story. Somewhere my parents still have a press cuttings album with it all, and it's kind of scary to look back on it. But it was a story of success at a time when there was a lot of negative news around, and it was astonishing and it put Imagine on the map. That was what we had set out to do.

People often ask about the cars. Yes, there were a number of them and it was definitely about perception. They were all leased, you know? I had a Lotus Esprit. John Gibson had a Porsche. Bruce drove around in several cars at different times, including a Ferrari Boxer. Mark Butler was a little more conservative, he had a very nice BMW. Dave at one point was driving an Aston Martin Vantage. So it was quite the collection. You can imagine in the middle of Liverpool in the early '80s, this line of cars all parked outside the front of the building.

The publicity began on the back of this press release, and it was almost getting out of hand. The next thing you know I'm invited to appear on a quiz show, and to a cocktail party at Downing Street the day Margaret Thatcher announced her intention to run for a second term. At shows, not only me but other people were being asked to sign posters and cassette covers, and you start to go, 'This isn't what we thought.' It was fame and stardom that none of us was prepared for, and it hurt a lot of people.

## Fred Gray

At the beginning Imagine were constantly reinventing themselves. If they'd only foreseen what was going to come, because they had a pretty bad system with the sale and returns and they stretched their credit too far. It was almost inevitable that they were going to go bankrupt in the end. I noticed we had far too much stock. We could go upstairs and pinch the occasional game but I was sure we weren't going to sell it all, because obviously the biggest portion of the sales would be in the first couple of weeks, when the thing was brand new. That gave me an inkling that things weren't selling as quickly as they should, but I had no idea that bankruptcy was going to happen.

It happened really fast, within weeks. Once somebody gets suspicious that there's a problem, everybody starts asking for their money back and it accelerates, and eventually the liquidator comes in. I never saw a liquidator knocking on the door, but I did notice that we were getting introduced to would-be investors, and I was thinking that they were looking for money from elsewhere and that either they were thinking what we needed to do next, or they were panicking because the company wasn't selling as many games as it needed. We had a visit from a representative from one of the big publishers, and the idea was to give the games away, but obviously we would get paid for it. But nothing seemed to come of that, and the company finally went bust.

Imagine Software had this big persona in the industry, very kind of rock star-ish, and when they were collapsing, it was sort of like, what was going to happen next? There were always stories of BMWs and other flashy cars, nice clothes and all the rest of it; when you entered the Ocean Software office you didn't see the cars because they were parked around the side, and I was just a schoolkid getting the bus, but I did see some Ferraris in the Ocean parking lot.

Let me tell you about the curve that led us to Imagine's collapse. We had started to talk about how much piracy was impacting the business, and one of the solutions that came up was the idea of creating a hardware add-on for both the Spectrum and the Commodore 64 so you couldn't play pirated games, and it would also enhance the machine with more memory so we could create a killer game. I think it was principally Dave's idea, and the games that used it became known as 'Megagames.' Bruce turned on his full marketing muscle and we started to hype them like crazy.

But it was really putting a strain on everybody, because we were suddenly going from projects with one or two people to having artists and musicians and multiple coders. We didn't understand how you have to manage a product; there was no thinking about producers, development directors or technical directors. We were hiring new people, too. We were still figuring it out as we went along.

At the same time, we had been approached by Marshall Cavendish, a magazine publisher that made partworks – you know, serialised magazines. We were going to do a gaming one, with a cover-mounted tape so every magazine would have a game, and we were going to supply them. It was another way for us to grow and get regular income and capture a market, but we had to hire a lot of programmers and artists to produce these games. The challenge was finding great people, which we did, but we didn't scale the management to go with it.

The quality of the product was not great and Marshall Cavendish decided to pull out, and we were stuck with all of these people. Dave and Mark didn't want to cut them; they wanted us to publish the games ourselves and let these people keep their jobs, but the games just weren't that great. That's not a reflection on the people who did them: it was probably more about our push. Meanwhile, progress on the Megagames wasn't what it should have been, and it started to catch up with us. Before you knew it, we were facing a visit from the bailiffs, which the TV documentary *Commercial Breaks* actually captured. They probably couldn't believe what they had stepped into the middle of.

*  How did it happened? Co-capture why wasn't ... It is ... as it was filming a documentary called *Commercial Breaks*, part of a series about companies attempting to survive ...

## Fred Gray

I was actually in the office when it happened, and I was one of the guys carrying kit down the back stairwell while the bailiffs came in the front. But the tragic thing about it was the day when the programmers and artists were told they didn't have a job any more. I remember the girls were all crying; there were quite a few female artists. Dave Lawson had selected a crack team, me included, to carry on, and we were told that they were having talks with a company in Silicon Valley and that we should keep our bags packed, because we were going to go to America.

It's quite emotional thinking back now, because I told my family that we were off to America, and everyone was like, 'Wow, yeah!' and it just didn't happen. But I also felt sorry for the people who weren't in the select few. At least I got a pat on the back and told, 'You're the best of the best.' The other people were just dumped by the roadside.

We knew the bailiffs were going to come, and that we were going into liquidation, in just a matter of days. When they came, they said, 'Everyone, grab some kit, we're going down the back stairs to try and save as much as possible!' We did relays of taking stuff. Those of us who had been chosen must have thought the kit was going to go on to form this new company, but nobody ever thought of the legal aspects of it, and I'm pretty sure quite a few people took the stuff home. I had an SH-101 and a Commodore 64, and some other bits and pieces, and when we eventually met up again at Dave Lawson's house I cheerily brought them along, being Mr Honest.

We were interested in the computers and the software and stuff that was on them, because we were basically protecting our own bread and butter. If the company did carry on we would need this stuff, and we did it not so much due to our loyalty to the company but our loyalty to our jobs; we were thinking the best way to keep your job is to try and save as much kit as possible from the bailiffs.

←177
## Eugene Evans
206→

When the bailiffs came, I was in the pub. Most of us were. I don't remember why, but we had all gone down for lunch and it was a big crowd, and the word started to come down that the bailiffs had locked the doors. I managed to get back up there and get in, but it was chaos. When it became apparent to us what was going on, John Gibson and I hatched a plot. We decided that it was really important that we were able to keep working on the games, and the bailiffs were so focused on the desks and chairs and everything else that they didn't see we had moved several of the computers to some bathroom stalls, where we had locked the doors and crawled back underneath. Those things were metal boxes, about two feet by three feet by one foot. Not exactly easy to hide. Then we came and got them later. It was with the best intentions in the world and I think the statute of limitations is up now, so I'm safe. But we decided that we were going to try and finish these games, and a small group of us started going to Dave Lawson's house to try to do that.

Dave and Ian Hetherington, who was the CFO, made a trip to the US in an attempt to raise money, and they found an investor. We started in a small office in Birkenhead figuring out what we were going to do next. The two Megagames were 'Psyclapse' and 'Bandersnatch'. 'Psyclapse' was on the Commodore 64 and was the one I had been coding with Jay Glover, but progress wasn't great and it wasn't as far along as 'Bandersnatch', so we took 'Bandersnatch' and it became *Brataccas*. We originally made it for the new Sinclair QL, which was a tech marvel. It had a 68008 processor, amazing colour graphics and I think it was only £300 or £400, which was amazingly cheap. But it didn't sell very well, because the Atari ST and the Commodore Amiga had come over from the US, but we realised they had the same processors so we could quickly port it over to them. But I didn't work on those very much. It was the beginning of me moving away from being a coder. My coding skills had been surpassed by the market and I was just not keeping up.

## Fred Gray

I always found Eugene was very extra-verted, so unless he manufactured it, he was very enthusiastic about every-thing. Later on, he asked me if I would write music for him, because he had formed a small company with another Imagine programmer, and I got the line, you know, 'If you come and work with us you'll be rich!' I thought, 'I've heard that before,' and I wasn't too sure I wanted to go there. When I worked freelance it was great because I worked for a lot of people and saw every aspect of the industry. I saw people working from home, people working in-house. The industry was starting to grow up, and people were starting to realise they had to put their business heads on.

## Julian Rignall

Any industry has a tendency for history to repeat itself, and the first major crash of the industry was perhaps Imagine. There was a lot of hype, a lot of marketing, and they'd sunk money into two games that never released. I think what they learned was that you can't necessarily control the code, that if a game's not coming together properly it can't be forced. If you promise something that you can't actually make, something bad's going to happen, and it did. They overextended, they over-published, they oversaturated the market.

They committed to 'Bandersnatch' and 'Psyclapse', these two games that were way ahead of their time, and they could never really make. They were really ambitious projects, and production costs ran on. Obviously, they'd made promises to the distribution channel that they would arrive in time for Christmas, and it never happened. Very quickly the company just ran out of money, and it all went belly up.

I remember being quite shocked when that happened, but at the same time, anybody who had been looking at what had happened in the American market had also seen the Atari VCS crash was 10 times worse. It was the same thing basically, an oversaturated market, too many people and mediocre products, and that took down the entire market. Fortunately, the UK market was small enough to weather the Imagine collapse; a lot of people knew people that were connected to it, and so the story got out quickly and people learned from the mistakes and realised we had to be careful. Of course, three, four years later, people forgot about those lessons, or just became too confident and did the same thing. We've seen it happen every five years or so, where somebody over-extends or pours money into a game that for some reason doesn't happen, and, you know, it takes them out.

Publishing in the early days was the Wild West, and some people got really stiffed, because they didn't know their own value. How could they? Somebody comes along and says, 'Ooh, hello, little Johnny,' who's still in school. 'I'll give you 3,000 quid for your game,' And little Johnny nearly has a heart attack, makes the game and then it goes and sells 100,000 ... Little Johnny's not getting rich, because he probably wasn't smart enough to negotiate a royalty deal.

It only takes one or two of those happening to poison an entire industry, because then publishers get this air of being the bad guys. I've talked to many, many publishers over the years, particularly in the early days, and yes, some of them were dodgy, dodgy dealers, you know, but they're

## Rob Hubbard

The industry in 1986 was still very much a cowboy industry, very much like the Wild West. There were some real rough characters, who would probably break your kneecaps. I won't mention any names. There was also a guy who was extremely famous, I won't mention who, who used to run a company and rip the programmers off, then set up a new company and had a Ferrari outside his new building. So there were some of those characters, as well. I had absolutely no idea of what was going on. I was just focused on doing the jobs. I had no idea that these people were selling these games to Europe or worldwide, I thought it was just England. I thought that they were maybe selling a couple of thousand of these things.

businessmen. They're looking for a great margin, and later on, when you're crying, saying 'You just made half a million quid out of me!' they'll say, 'Well, you signed the deal. You were happy at the time.'

Programmers realised their worth fairly quickly. But even so, even throughout the mid-to-late '80s, I'd hear stories of people being commissioned to make an arcade game for what seemed like good money, maybe a year's salary, but that game would make £200,000 for somebody else. Whose fault is that? The programmer for making it and thinking, 'Okay, I've just earned a year's worth of salary in six weeks, killing myself to get it to work, but I don't have to work for the next year.' But someone else is making money out of it. Ultimately, it's the same thing that happens in almost every industry that has talent, some people are successful and know their worth, but for every one of them there are a thousand people that are going to get stiffed. The bottom line is yes, there were definitely some crooks in the early days. Only a few of them, but it only takes a couple of rotten apples to ruin the barrel, right?

When you look at the real success stories in the industry, they're people who are capable of performing multiple functions. They are coders who are also smart enough to understand marketing and business, the subtleties of market demand and how to play companies off against one another. I think those people quickly transitioned from working in their bedroom to having a position at a large company, or even leading one.

But most people tend to be good at one thing, and those guys were great programmers but didn't necessarily have business sense. Look at David Braben, he's definitely gone from a bedroom coder to running a major company, producing really interesting games. But there aren't many people like him.

By 1984, certainly '85, the parasites had moved in: the managers, agents, accountants, bankers, lawyers, the publicity agents. They could see that the body was ripe for blood sucking. I had always been independent, never been involved with anybody else in terms of components, publicity, programming, just one little tiny team; it was time for me to move on and I left the videogame industry.

Rod Cousens

The computer game industry was now starting to attract a lot of media attention, and the story was always to try and identify the teenage millionaire, you know, people driving around in Ferraris and fast cars. We all drank the Kool-Aid, and there were people making a lot of money for a short period of time. Very few of them sustained it, but substantial businesses were built which formed the backbone of some of the companies that are out there today.

Young people at a very tender age were earning a lot of money in a very short period of time, and it was a bit like rock stars who were ripped off by their record labels. I was always on the side of the artist and the talent, and so we at Quicksilva were responsible in trying to guide them, but there were instances where there were people who went off the rails. There were people at Rabbit Software,[*] which was pretty tragic, and various things that went on in Liverpool. Obviously, the greatest example of that is Imagine, which blew up spectacularly, and it only went to fuel the fire that all this is here today, gone tomorrow. Of course, it was not: the game industry was experiencing what the music industry had gone through in the '60s, where it was sex, drugs and rock 'n' roll.

[*] Rabbit Software became defunct in 1985, when Virgin acquired the company name and used it to publish mid-price games.

←146

## Jeff Minter

231→

It felt weird to be famous, actually, but it was nice that people liked the games enough to want to come up and shake your hand for having made them. It made you feel chuffed. It still does to this day when I get people come up here and say, 'I really like playing the games,' and thank me or offer to buy me a pint. It's really, really nice.

I think making a game back then, especially for me, was a very personal thing. When people liked it, it was almost like they probably had the same sense of humour. People who like the same kind of music often like the same kind of bands, so I think it's the same kind of thing. Somebody likes a Llamasoft game, they'll probably like Red Dwarf and Monty Python, Pink Floyd, the same kind of stuff that I like. They probably enjoy going out for a pint or going to see a light show, or whatever.

So there was a point of contact, where you could meet these people and they could meet you, and you could actually get on socially. It wasn't just like you selling something to somebody, some kind of faceless transaction. You could actually hang out with these people and be friends with them. It was really good.

## Steve Turner

When our games got successful we started getting asked to go to award ceremonies. I mean, Andrew in particular got awards for *Paradroid* and then *Uridium*. I think the highest I got was highly commended for *Avalon*, so he outdid me. I had a suit, which was a lot more flamboyant than my normal suits, with a silver weave in it, so it was almost like a pop star's suit, and Andrew used to wear a pair of white denims and a white jacket, which used to be his publicity suit. He had his hair cut and styled, with blonde highlights, and we used to say that was his game star image, but he did actually get stopped and asked for autographs, which was a nice change from him being the unknown person who just assisted Steve in the back room.

## David Darling

I think our business really developed as soon as we got into the retailers, because every Christmas they were selling, like, hundreds of thousands of home computers. Then as soon as people got them they wanted games, so once we got our games to retailers we started generating some significant revenue, and also because we were working with Commodore and Mirrorsoft, they would pay us so many thousand pounds per game plus royalties.

Mastertronic was really working well, too, because they were getting racks of 50 or 100 games into garages, newsagents and thousands of smaller shops. *BMX Racers*, one of my brother's games, did over 300,000 units. We really enjoyed working with Martin Alper, Frank Herman and Alan Sharam at Mastertronic, but eventually they had a bit of a pile it high and sell it cheap kind of attitude, which was fine commercially but as programmers we wanted to make the highest-quality games that we could. We wanted to work on games for months or years and they always wanted us to finish them and get them in the shops.

So eventually we thought we should set up our own publishing company, so we could control our own destiny. So we set up Code Masters. We had a deal with Frank Herman so that we owned half a company called Artificial Intelligence Products, which was sourcing all of Mastertronic's games. So when we wanted to go on our own, we sold our shares back to him and used that money, around £100,000, to set up Code Masters. We moved near Banbury and then we developed about 10 games over a few months and launched the company with *BMX Simulator* and *Grand Prix Simulator* and then *Pro Ski Simulator*. Lots of simulators! The Oliver twins also did *Super Robin Hood* and the first *Dizzy* game. So we started building up a range of games, some of which we had written and some of which our friends and people that we had met had written.

We had learned a lot about the publishing business when we worked with Mastertronic, because Frank and Martin were really good business people, very good at negotiating, very good at deal-making, and they really understood how to deal with the re-tailers. We agreed with their philosophy of selling games for good value, at £1.99 or £2.99. The only difference of opinion really was that we wanted to make our own games, and have our own company and a bit more control over what we were making. My brother really likes BMX, so we wanted to make a BMX game, and I was into Grand Prix, so I wanted to make a Grand Prix game. We didn't fall out with them, it was more that it was just the next stage in our development.

In the beginning it was just me and Richard; there were a lot of brothers in the industry helping each other. Then we got our friend James Fairburn at Wadham School doing artwork for us, because he was a really good artist. Then we were working with people like Rob Hubbard to do music, so we would pay £100 or £200 or whatever, so we got into the habit of contracting out to specialists.

When we set Code Masters up we knew we couldn't write enough games on our own, so we found people like Gavin Raeburn, Andrew Graham, who did *Micro Machines*, the Olivers, and Peter Williamson at Supersonic Software. Most of them had their own companies, so we convinced them to

Oliver twins

If you look at the British games industry in particular, a lot of software companies were set up by brothers. We were all in that bedroom scenario where you want to better your brother and say, 'I'm cleverer than you.'

But it was half collaborative as well, because when you couldn't do it your brother helped you and said 'Ah! This is the way I'm better than you,' but then you've learned.

work with us as a publisher. Really, it was a bit like the way Simon Cowell sources talent: we had to spot really talented people and try and work with them.

In the first year we got to around 30% of games by unit sales, and I think we achieved that because in the previous four or five years we had been developing knowledge about the industry. We learned about business from our dad, Frank Herman and Martin Alper, and we learned about developing games from Jeff Minter, Archer Maclean, Rob Hubbard and the Oliver twins. So when we launched Code Masters we were working with lots of talented people, and we launched a lot of games in the first year. We were also working with Bruce Everiss for publicity, and a guy who worked with all of the independent retailers. In those days it wasn't just a few big retailers, it was mostly thousands of small shops, so we had a really good distribution network. In that year we really hit the ground running and made the best use of everything we had been learning.

### Oliver twins

Where we turned really commercial was when we went to a trade show in September of '85 and we met the Darlings, who were already at this point kind of famous. You'd read about them in *Computer and Video Games* as having these great bestsellers like *BMX Racers* through Mastertronic, but they were going to set their own game company up. We were already getting games published every month for £300 or £400, and we had a bunch of cassettes we took to them and said, 'These are the games we've already written and we've got some ideas for some other games. Here's one, *Super Robin Hood*. What would you pay if we were to write that for you?' David's answer was £10,000.

We'd only heard these rumours of people getting £10,000!

Our jaws just dropped to the floor. It was like, 'Okay, so can we have a contract for that?' And they said, 'Well, yes, but you've got to write it first and then we'll sign the contract.' We looked at each other and we put our heads down. We pretty much didn't sleep for the next month, to get that game done and get that £10,000. And in fact what happened was, we took it back to them. It was a really good game. It did play very well, and they did sign it. Sadly, the small print was that, 'You'll get to about £10,000 through royalties because we don't give any money upfront.' Which was a bit of a downer. But they were gentlemen, and they said they were going to duplicate a lot of copies and get it into every shop, and within two or three months it did, and in six or seven months it had exceeded it. Quite frankly, from the point of meeting the Darlings and writing *Super Robin Hood* we didn't have a social life. We just absolutely focused on making games.

AO We came out at the end of school and our friends went off to universities, and we'd found a good way of making money. We were with Code Masters for seven years.

## David Darling

← 184 189 →

We exhibited in London before we launched Code Masters, looking for people to work with, so on the stand it said something like, 'Programmers wanted'. The Oliver twins stopped and started talking to us, and they said they had this game they were working on called *Super Robin Hood*. So we asked them to come and visit to see if we can do a deal. I don't think we put it in the launch catalogue, but it was one of the next releases.

They visited the office a few months later with this idea for a game about an egg. I was always interested in things like BMXs, car racing, skiing and stuff like that, so I was quite sceptical about this egg. But I thought, well, they are really talented guys and really enthu-

siastic, so I didn't want to stifle their creativity. We said yeah, if that's what you want to do then let's do it, so then they did the first *Dizzy* game.× Almost as soon as we put it out we started getting re-orders. The kids just loved it because it was a really good puzzle-adventure game in which you could really get your head around solving all the puzzles. Lots of other games were like *Pac-Man*, where it's about skill and there wasn't much puzzle-solving, so I think people really appreciated that it was another genre.

× Released in 1987 as *Dizzy - The Ultimate Cartoon Adventure. Crash* gave it 78%, Ben Stone stating, 'Dizzy may be a little too cute and cuddly for my liking, but there's a great game hidden within those small and furry folds!'

## Oliver twins

← 186 189 →

PO The way we arrived at *Dizzy* was having had the huge success with *Robin Hood*, we'd moved straight on into *Ghost Hunters.*°

° Liked by *Crash*, especially its two-player mode. Reviewer Ben Stone said, 'I have a lot of respect for Code Masters, they have avoided releasing the sort of rubbish that emanates from other budget houses.'

We loved *Scooby-Doo* and that kind of stuff and the big movie at the time was *Ghostbusters*, so we came up with the idea that you were in a haunted house and you had a ray gun to shoot the ghosts. But while coding this game, we were also avid fans of cartoons like *Danger Mouse* and *Count Duckula*, so we thought it would be nice to do this style of game, with some really cute characters and some really nice personality, and a real adventure in a fantastical mystery world, where you didn't know what was going to be round the next corner. So we loved cartoons, and we wanted to make the ultimate interactive cartoon. Now, the first thing needed for a cartoon is to have a main character, but our coding and also the capability of the machines was such that you could actually only put a very small sprite on the screen, and it was very difficult to add any personality. We'd just drawn this man running around this haunted castle and his head was like three pixels by three pixels in three colours. So the first challenge was how do you put a personality into the main character.

It was a case of trying to draw a big face, so we were trying to draw the smallest face where you could see some kind of expression, but we ended up with something quite big, like the whole thing was a face. We decided arms and legs didn't matter, but what you do need is feet and hands. We said, 'Okay, it's a big smiley face with feet and hands.' Then, because of restrictions on colour, it ended up being a very white face, very red boots and gloves and we were like, 'Okay we'll go with this, though it's kind of looking like an egg.' It struck a chord with people, though a lot of them said it was an egg, and we ran with it. The other slightly funny thing is every single review of the very first Dizzy kept on using egg jokes, so, 'It's egg-citing!' And 'egg-cellent, egg-xhilerating'. We realised that every single twist you try and do seems to be a positive name.

So while people were trying to make their puns, they were actually bigging the game up, accidentally. But actually it was a great game as well, obviously, and it was hugely successful. We obviously had to pitch to Code Masters what the idea was and get them to buy into it, but it was relatively low risk for them. *Super Robin Hood* had been a huge success.

It didn't really matter. We were writing it. We weren't asking them for money. We were just having conversations about the next game we're going to write.

So they hadn't really said no or yes, but they were sceptical. But it was okay, because six weeks later or something we turned up with a master and our relationship was such with them that they pretty much duplicated it without really looking. There wasn't really a QA department. There was one person who did the packaging and it was like, 'Yes, just go and sit with her for a couple of hours to make a box and put the words on the back of it.' That's real cottage industry time. Code Masters literally was four, five, six people. That's it. You sat down with Richard and David and you played the game. If they liked it, they basically said, 'Cool.' If they were worried that it was a bit buggy or there might be bugs or it needs a bit of testing, that was Richard's job. For a good two or three years he played through games and said whether or not he thought they should be duplicated.

It was good because we could just make games and publish and there was no risk. We didn't go and look for any other work or go to publishers. We weren't employees of Code Masters, we just wrote a game and gave it to Code Masters every time.

```
Oliver twins
```

The actual success of games was measured in the price and the volume you were selling it at. Code Masters games were going quite cheap, which was £1.99 or £2.99, so to be successful you really wanted to be selling in the tens of thousands, but for a huge hit, something like a *Super Robin Hood* or *Grand Prix Simulator*, we were getting up to 150,000, 200,000. Pretty much if you cleared 100,000 at that price, that was a hit. If you were selling at the Ultimate Play the Game kind of price, which was £10 or £12, then they had a hit at 10,000 to 20,000, although those games were absolute classics and so some of them went up to 100,000.

```
David Darling
```

We did a sequel for *Dizzy*, the same as we did for *BMX Simulator*: any game that worked we always wanted to do another one. So we did *Treasure Island Dizzy* and then *Fantasy World Dizzy*. We used a Disney theme or something like *Treasure Island*, and thought how we could be inspired by it.

Pretty much right from the beginning we were working on multiple computers. Me and Richard were Commodore fanboys so we had a Commodore VIC-20 and Commodore 64 and things like that, but our friends at school would have a BBC, Dragon 32 or Spectrum, so we knew that we couldn't just make games for the VIC-20 because we couldn't show our friends. So as soon as it turned into a business we realised that we had to try and sell as many as we could, so it was really just working out the most popular computers and whether there were enough of them out there to really support them.

Often you would end up doing conversions after release, so there was a game called *Finders Keepers* by David Jones, and Mastertronic got my brother Richard to convert it to Commodore 64 when it had already been popular on the Spectrum. It's a much easier job doing a conversion, so often you wouldn't have to pay royalties, just a contract, whether £3,000 or £5,000 or whatever. But as the industry developed, we would invest more into marketing and to have multiple formats at launch, so the industry kind of changed in that respect.

## Julian Rignall

Marketing and the business side became important. Doing a nice bit of art for the cassette, making your ad work really well. When you look at Ultimate Play the Game, I remember the impact that those guys had because of the level of sophistication in their marketing. The iconography that they used, and the custom fonts, and these beautiful pieces of art that they created for their ads were a cut above the, 'Oh, my mate can draw us a barbarian with a sword, it's a bit manky but it looks okay.' At that time there were no real standards, it was anything goes. Fun.

Ultimate Play the Game cottoned on to the aesthetic with very effective branding, very alluring marketing. They knew how to write copy on their ads that would really get the attention of gamers. When you look back at some of those early, early ads, you'd have a crude drawing and then like three paragraphs of text to explain the game. Then Ultimate came along with a very colourful airbrushed piece of art with something very minimal underneath it, and you'd look at it and go, 'Wow, that must be really cool.'

That period of experimentation, that's when there was a jump up from the early, very nascent game publishers to the first really major publishing companies in like '84 and '85. Like U.S. Gold, you know. Geoff Brown* was very smart, he got on a plane, went off to CES in America, shook a lot of hands and began to sign distribution deals for the UK from American software companies and built a very big company off the back of that. I don't think in the early days U.S. Gold actually made any of their own games, it was just a distribution company.⁣ᵀ

## Rod Cousens

← 182 Rod Cousens 201 →

We wanted something special for *Ant Attack*, for that ant to come out and attack you from the shelf, so it could stand out and be different, and David Rowe did it. I'm a great believer in giving artistic licence to the creators, so we let Sandy White have artistic control. We had some very talented independent artists within Quicksilva, coming out of art schools like Winchester, like Rich Shenfield, and we put them together with the guys that created the programs and let them make something that they would take great pride in. I give a lot of credit to Mark Eyles for that.

It was very new. It was an industry that was sort of making it up as it went along, in many respects. There were no distribution channels; I remember WHSmith taking videogames for the first time, and it was a big thing because it was a big risk for them. They had no idea whether they were going to sell or not, but they obviously saw that there was demand through all of the ads and magazines, and these little mom and pop computer stores popping up selling games. But the infrastructure was very poor, the pricing structure was all over the place. Some games would be five quid, some 10, so there was a lot of experimentation, and people learn very, very quickly. You know, that period lasted maybe two years, tops, and it went from literally a cassette in a plastic bag with a bit of photocopied paper to a professional cassette with a printed inlay.

* Geoff Brown co-founded U.S. Gold with his wife, Anne.
ᵀ U.S. Gold's parent company was indeed the distributor CentreSoft, also founded by Geoff and Anne Brown.

## Charles Cecil

← 64 Charles Cecil 200 →

We saw the coin-ops that were coming along and we weren't quite sure whether you were allowed to use the names, so like *Galaxians*, or 'QS Zoids' for *Asteroids*, or whatever, and we thought, 'Well, what's the worst that can happen?', so we called our games things like *Artic Invaders* for *Space Invaders* and then we thought we'd go all the way with *Galaxians*,ˣ and we put little Galaxian

ˣ Both released in 1982 for the Spectrum.

things in. Of course it was totally illegal but nobody came after us. So for two or three years we just used these brands, producing them on ZX81 and Spectrum and then Commodore 64, and nobody said anything!

But from the mid '80s you had companies like U.S. Gold – which I went on to work for – and Ocean coming in, and they actually licensed and enforced those licences so we weren't able to use them illegally. It was a profound change because these companies really focused on marketing rather than actual production. Development was way down the scale; it didn't really matter what it was like, provided the licence was strong and you could market it well.

I'm not enormously proud to say that I did have a connection with all this with a game called *World Cup Carnival*, released for the Mexico World Cup in '86. Geoff Brown drove over in his Ferrari and we were desperately impressed. We were penniless, in Hull, by this stage. All the money had been wasted, squandered, and Artic had gone from being this fantastically successful pair of us to a much bigger company, just scraping out a living. And Geoff Brown turned up in his Ferrari and he asked us if we'd write this Mexico '86 game based on our *Artic Soccer* from 1983, and I said, 'Geoff, I'm sure we'd love to but why aren't you using *Match Day*? *Match Day*'s much better and that's Ocean and don't you partly own Ocean?' He said, 'Legal difficulties. We can't do that.'

Peter Stone and
Richard Leinfellner

I actually think companies like U.S. Gold had a lot to do with the growth of the industry, because they shipped American games over here and made a good business out of it. US games at that point were actually quite slick compared to UK games, quite well polished and tended to be made with better production values than the UK games, so I think that really pushed the market up quite a bit. Epyx and *Impossible Mission*, things like that.

So the deal was that they would pay us, by our standards, a huge amount of money for the rights to this game, as long as we didn't tell anybody, because there would be an uproar if it happened. So we wrote the game and we did the best we could. We added a few features but it was never going to be as good as *Match Day*, and the packaging for *World Cup Carnival* was absolutely brilliant; you had flags, posters and the game appeared to be fantastic, but once people discovered what it was there was absolute uproar. People thought they were going to get a totally new soccer game and then they realised that actually it was the re-purposed Artic one. Do you know, for years afterwards people just associated me, I think somewhat unfairly, with *World Cup Carnival* and the great scam that it was – but I'm going to put all the blame on U.S. Gold for that one!

It was a great shame because we were at one point really, really affluent as a company, but a lot of the money went into dreadful advertising. There was a bit of television advertising, the worst television advertising I've ever seen in my life, it was just awful! We were taken for a ride left, right and centre by advertising agencies, there were some sales people that came along and promised the world and took vast amounts of money. We were very, very naïve, and it left Artic in a very weak position. Then, when the new wave of marketing-based companies, the U.S. Golds, the Oceans, the Imagines, came along, there was nothing left for Artic at all. Richard took the company in a different direction and started developing kitchen software, which I had no great interest in, so I left.

## Geoff Brown 240→

I stopped at one point and thought, 'I think I am a millionaire now.' I was getting towards 40 and I said I needed a new car. I'd had Porsches before then. We'd gone out and bought two Porsches in one day, one for Anne and one for me, in different colours. A friend said, 'I've seen a Ferrari Testarossa, it looks like a pretty good car.' I said, 'Well, how much is it?' He said, 'I don't know, £76,000.' I said, 'Let's go and get one then!'

There were only nine in the country. I used to go into Birmingham city centre, I mean, it didn't change me in any way, I'd just got more money, you know, and I'd park it and go shopping with my wife and I'd come back and there'd be people having their photographs taken by the car and sitting on it. And I was that embarrassed by it, I used to wait for it to clear before I could go.

## Martin Galway 241→

By the end of '85, the industry was definitely maturing and marketing was coming into the fore. Ocean was an industry leader for getting film and TV tie-ins, and they would also really drive home the marketing. Not only having great posters but they would also advertise everywhere, and they had marketing people. I remember the marketing person for Ocean at the time thought that it was cool that I was only 19, and kept wanting to call me teenage this and teenage that, market me as some kind of whizz-kid, but I turned 20 pretty soon after that and they still wanted to use 'teenage'.

In those days they would advertise games before they were finished, so that there was built-up demand for them the day they went on sale and everyone would head to the shop. But this went wrong when games came out late. The worst example I lived through when I was working at Ocean was the *Street Hawk* game. I think they were advertising it in 1985, and for several months they had back covers, costing a lot of money, but they didn't release the game until into 1986.

At the '86 PCW Show I definitely saw the size of the stands and the money they were spending. They were putting a lot of money into building big stands, with big logos and big statues of game characters, like Rambo. It really drove home that this was a big business. The single show I had been to before was in Manchester at the Belle Vue Centre, and it was just a real cottage industry show by comparison. It had become a fully fledged business.

In '85 Ocean were on the top floor of the Central Street building in Manchester, but later on they leased more space underground. It was warmer because there were heating pipes everywhere, so it was fine in the winter but in the summer it was deadly, and they didn't have any air vents or anything. It was kind of sealed. People would smoke in the office, so there would be ash all over programmers' keyboards and the whole area would smell of cigarettes.

Back in those days development was so quick. I would work on the music for a game in a day, and half a day in some cases. Other times it might be three weeks, but games in the middle of my Ocean career might take six weeks to two months to be programmed. At the beginning of my Ocean career, games might have taken six weeks tops to get made. I know that David Collier was on a rush job to get *Roland's Rat Race*＊ done, so he went home for two weeks and came back with it mostly done, graphics and the programming. It was amazing that things took so little time. By inference there was no design phase, or greenlight phase. If there was it was one meeting where Jon Woods would go, 'Yeah, looks all right.'

I remember when I did the *Hyper Sports* music, I did the *Chariots of Fire* tune because I had just seen the film and the music was in the charts. The first two thirds of the tune was all done and sounded pretty good, and David Collier had to get Jon Woods in to listen to it. He was looking at David, probably thinking, 'What the hell are you doing having him do this tune that we haven't got the rights for?' He walked out and an hour later we had the rights to have that tune. That was one of the times that we actually got the rights to use a piece of music. So a lot of the decisions got made really, really quickly.

＊ Released in 1985.

There were too many retailers to supply, so these middleman companies set up, like Terry Blood Distribution and CentreSoft. They would try and get exclusive deals with shops, so I think CentreSoft had the exclusive distribution for Boots and Terry Blood had WHSmith and Woolworths for a time, so you would be forced to go through them. Often you would try and get around them because you could get a better price by selling directly to the retailer, so there was a lot of negotiating going on: 'We will go through you, but you have to buy 10,000 games.' I know my dad was quite tough on Geoff Brown's wife, because she wanted to buy our games to supply Boots, but he'd refuse because he didn't want us to be over the CentreSoft barrel. He always had the philosophy that it's better to have lots of customers than just a few, because you have less chance of bad debt and of things going wrong with a single big customer.

A lot of small companies failed. It was like when the car industry started, like, 100 years ago, where there were hundreds of companies and over the years the number dwindled every year until we ended up with just a handful. The same thing happened in the game industry. These small companies started dropping away; it was like, I don't know, a nuclear bomb had gone off, and you were trying to outrun the blast to survive. If you could survive then you would grow, so it was about trying to stay on top of the pile. It was quite exciting! You needed to have a release schedule with one game coming out a week, or every couple of weeks, so that you could feed the distributors and retailers and pay for advertising campaigns. So to run a proper publishing company you need releases; the same as the music industry, you didn't just have one artist, you have a catalogue of artists, so these publishing companies started evolving.

I established my first company in about 1987. I was still at university, in my second year, and I realised that I was completely wasting my time, and that I really had to get back to making games. So I decided to move back to my home town in Harlow and set up Target Games, and started being a publisher of computer games, not just a developer. I had this maybe naïve ambition at the time that I could set up a company, design and program the games, sell them and market them, get them manufactured and distributed ... So I left college, and the first game we worked on was *Laser Squad*.

After publishing *Rebelstar* with Telecomsoft, I thought their royalty rate of 10p for a £2 game was pretty abysmal, and it seemed like the royalty rates other publishers were offering weren't very good, so I thought that setting up Target Games as a publisher would allow us to have a little bit more revenue coming in. I had no idea whether we would succeed, or compete with other publishers, but it just felt like I had to try.

I was lucky, because my parents were very supportive. I set up Target Games with a friend and my father. My father actually financed the company at the beginning. Not with a huge amount of money, I think it was about £16,000. Obviously, we were living on very low wages and we had a very small office which would only fit about three or four people. The idea was that we would produce relatively quickly. I think at least my father thought that I would be able to do them much quicker than we actually did, but of course by that stage, game development was getting a little bit more ambitious, and a little bit more difficult. But with his initial investment I was able to buy a more sophisticated development system, so we had PCs, which made debugging much, much easier and quicker.

*Laser Squad* was basically an evolution of *Rebelstar* and *Rebelstar Raiders*, but I wanted to add some more role-playing elements and a

## Peter Molyneux

I've never quite had the negative relationship with publishers that maybe other people have. I think if you know publishers for what they are, that they are there to make money, not to publish games for the art form, then I think you understand them far better. The real positive side of publishers was that they started bringing money up-front, before a game was finished, and funding development. What that meant was that tiny, single bedroom coders started to expand to two or three people. They gave those people a little bit more time, a little bit more breathing space, to work on quality.

The quality of games going up was a massive positive. But the incredible negative of publishers came when they started to believe – maybe in some cases they were right to believe – that they knew more about how to make a game than the person who was making it. So they would interfere, or they would say that you should add this and that. Sometimes that worked, but very often it didn't. This problem still exists today, I think.

multiple-scenario system. The idea was that you would equip a force of soldiers, and you play a scenario in the tactical game, then load up the next scenario, which progresses the story a bit. So you could have, like, three scenarios with the game you bought in the shop, and you have a little coupon in the back of the manual and send off a cheque or postal order for expansion packs, turning the game into an expandable system.

I also wanted to add some more sophisticated features, like a concept of line of sight, so your soldiers' vision was blocked by the terrain. It made the game a lot more tense, a lot more cat and mouse. It was an element of realism in the simulation, if you like, and it really worked. It became, of course, the foundation of the later X-COM games, but at the time I was still thinking in terms of this sequence of scenarios that we would continue to work on and distribute through mail order.

The biggest challenge of devising an AI on the ZX Spectrum was the fact that you had very limited memory and a very slow processor, so I think that AI coding typically in *Laser Squad* was something like 3K or 4K of the total memory. It had to be efficient, but also plausible and playable. I think I largely succeeded, and still to this day I'm not quite sure how. I had absolutely no reference to go on; I wasn't reading any academic journals about AI, so it was completely invented by me. But it was very important for the gameplay. I think what helped a little bit was the line of sight system, so you didn't see everything the computer player was doing and you weren't quite sure exactly where they were. The computer player cheated a little bit, in the sense that it knew where your guys were.

We started publishing directly and trying to sell our goods directly to the distributors, but we abandoned it after a while, because we were running out of money, and we approached a publisher. At the time, distributors seemed to be reasonably open to new companies, but they didn't give us much feedback. We got orders in each week saying one or two hundred of this or that, and we didn't really understand how they worked or what was going on. We had very little finance for advertising and promoting the games. This was seriously handicapping us, and was one reason why we signed a distribution deal with a publisher, Blade Software, because we felt that they would be able to put some money into marketing and promoting the game.

* On its release for the Spectrum and Commodore 64 in 1988, Crash awarded Laser Squad 89%, commenting, 'Rebelstar was elegant and addictive, and Laser Squad takes it much further without losing any of its playability.'

*Dropzone* was winning awards and doing very well generally in '85, '86, and just sold and sold, and I got contacted by System 3: 'Wow great, you're wonderful. Can you come and sort out our project, do a bit of the graphics and make it shine?' I thought this was a bit weird and originally I said no, but eventually I got talked into going down to have a look. Two distinct things happened. I saw a Spectrum game that was about 3% complete, this karate game, and it was just appalling. I said, 'I can't convert that, I'm going to do something else,' because I was already thinking about a sequel to *Dropzone*.

The second thing was later that afternoon I got dragged into a bar where there was a Data East *Karate Champ* machine. The guy said to me, 'Can you copy that?' and I thought, well, yeah I could, but I could also do an awful lot better. *International Karate* was basically my interpretation, sticking loosely to what it was about, while retaining a karate feel as well. I was also a big fan of *The Way of the Exploding Fist*, * which I had played to death with my mate Barry. We would sit up until four in the morning playing it. While it was brilliant and sold an unbelievable number of units, I remember thinking I could make it better and smoother, and put a living background on it to bring it to life. As usual, they said, 'Yeah, yeah, yeah,' until I went and did it.

I reversed it into my *Dropzone* game shell to get it done as quick as possible and prettied it up. Most of the 8-bit stuff I developed was on an Atari 800, but there were no tools in those days, so if you wanted to do graphics you had to edit your own by writing a program in BASIC in which you used a joystick to slowly move around the screen, turn pixels on and off and choose a colour. It was laborious. I often started with a bit of graph paper, filled it in with a coloured pencil, turned it into hex and then typed it into a program listing. Atari did provide a macro assembler, but even that was primitive, and you had to devise all sorts of ways of getting lumps of object code into the computer and getting them talking to each other without overlapping each other, and a whole load of other nightmare stuff.

It went to number one all over Europe, and what I didn't know until someone sent me a fax from America was that it was number one in America, too. Sometime later I discovered that Data East

* Gregg Barnett's fighting game for Melbourne House, originally written for the Commodore 64 in 1985.

mysteriously took Epyx[*] to court, saying it looked like a copy of *Karate Champ*. I just kept well away from it.[†]

After *International Karate* I had the inspiration for a third fighter and thought it was a damn good idea. I tried to keep a lid on it as best as I could; I didn't tell anyone I was doing it for about six months, trying to make the third character work. On a 64 I had already run out of sprites, and it certainly wasn't going to work on an 800. I then got a call from Activision. They said, 'Why don't you come in for a little meeting, because we would like to propose 'IK2'?' I went down there, listened to what they had to say, and said, 'Well, watch this,' put a disk in the 64, and there it was. They all went, 'Sign here!'

So I signed with Activision. Trying to get the third man running on a 64 was tricky because I had run out of sprites. I pulled in a load of code from the Atari 800 version of *IK*, which was actually character-based, so I had sprites on the screen, characters behind forming a third man and then the animated backdrop behind that was just bitmap graphics. I had some fun and games with the coding making the character block man go in front and behind the other two, so I was forever switching the colours of the sprites to try and make the first, second and third order work. When it came to the 68000 versions,[×] those machines had way more power than they needed for having six men on the screen. There is a cheat mode in *IK+* 16-bit where you can have six guys dancing on the screen to disco music.

For the animation I had a program on the Atari ST called NEO-chrome. I found myself jumping around at home in front of mirrors doing my own karate moves, because I did some at university, videotaping it and then slow mo-ing it. The trick was how you then got that into the computer. It seemed fairly simple to me to put cellophane over the screen and resize the TV picture so that the figure was the same size as I wanted to edit with NEOchrome. Then I just freeze-framed and drew an outline around it on the cellophane, then advanced the tape three more frames, and drew it again. So I had all these animation cells on cellophane. Then I would spend another couple of days drawing the outlines and filling in the details, like the face, belts and other bits of clothing and stuff.

[*] Epyx was the publisher that licensed the game for the US market.
[†] The court dismissed Data East's allegations of trademark infringement, however Epyx was found guilty for infringing on the *Karate Champ* copyright, and was required to recall all copies. In 1988, the order was successfully appealed, the court holding that no discerning 17-year-old would see the two games as substantially similar.
[×] For the Amiga and Atari ST, which had 68000-based processors.

The most complex one was the backflip, because if you look at it in the game it is quite fluid. That actually came from the end of *Grease*, so if anyone wants to go and see the original *Grease* film, with Olivia Newton-John and John Travolta doing their thing at the end, there is a man in the background of the fairground scene doing a sideways-on somersault, and that's the bloke that stars in *IK+*! The other one I remember coming out of a film was the kick where the guy leaps up with both legs, and that's Jackie Chan out of *The Cannonball Run*.

*IK+* would have done an awful lot better. It was momentarily number one but then got remaindered. It went out in America as *Chop N' Drop* . I had to go there in the week of the 1987 stock market crash and sit in front of the big boss of Activision and talk about how to do an American version. I lived there for a month or two in '87 redrawing all of the animation for 16-bit *IK+*, basically shortening trousers, ripping off shirt sleeves and so on, rebuilding the game.

## Charles Cecil

After Artic, I founded a company called Paragon Programming in 1986, and we started doing conversions. U.S. Gold became very successful by importing and licensing American Commodore 64 titles, publishing them and then converting them to Amstrad and Spectrum. So I set up a development company to do this and we were reasonably successful, and then after a year I was approached by Tim Chaney, who invited me to actually become the development manager at U.S. Gold. I was so excited by this! I thought, 'This'll be fantastic! What a great company! I'm very young, I'm in my mid-20s and I'm going to be the director of this massive great department within this fantastic publisher!'

I arrived and there was myself and a tester and that was it, which is quite extraordinary, if you think about it, because we had a lot of games coming through. But they didn't have a development manager before, it was done by marketing people. So I was responsible for probably 20 games a year and there was one tester, whose job it was to test those 20 games across all the formats. It was absolutely insane. I really enjoyed working there, they were a wonderful group of people, but there was no doubt that the hierarchy was marketing first, then sales, then admin and then development, and development were a nuisance.

A lot of publishers, you know, up until very recently, really considered development to be a damn nuisance. You obviously needed development because you needed the games, but developers didn't produce stuff on time, they had sometimes variable quality, generally they were a right old pain, and to an extent I think the hierarchy of U.S. Gold went along that road.

I'd known Rod Cousens, who'd founded a company called Quicksilva and had been very, very successful. He really understood the industry, and he kept asking me to join Activision, and eventually I started chatting to him. He said, 'Look, as far as we're concerned, development means everything because without the product you can't market it, you can't sell it.' He asked me to come in as head of development, and I accepted eventually. He was absolutely true to his word. From Activision's perspective, development was everything and I came in with quite a big team, some really good guys, and we very much produced the product and fed marketing with the information.

It was a totally different set-up in terms of the way that the various departments worked with each other and it's one of the reasons probably why Activision went on to be incredibly successful and U.S. Gold ultimately collapsed. I think that over time, people came to realise that actually the product was what mattered. That was something that we didn't even realise in the Artic days and we should have. We spent money on advertising, rather than acquiring new products and that was our big, big, big mistake and that's why ultimately Artic failed.

## Rod Cousens

While I was at Quicksilva, I went to America to secure rights from Epyx for their European distribution, but the day before I left a headhunter called me about a job in the UK for an American software company. It was Activision, and I met Greg Fischbach[*] and told him I was setting up my own software company to build content in the UK.

This was at a time of diversity in formats: Commodore 64 was out, disk-based software was happening and we were still running tapes in the UK, and he had challenges taking software that Activision had created for the US market and making it relevant to the European market. So Greg figured he needed British development talent creating content for the local market. The next day he called me and offered to fund it, and said he'd meet me in London the next week to look at my business plan.

I kept thinking about what I was going to do, and when I met him I said the company was called Electric Dreams, because at the time there was the track out called 'Together in Electric Dreams.'[†] We went through the business plan and he said my costs were too

* President of Activision International at the time. He went on to found Acclaim.
† A synth song by Philip Oakey and Giorgio Moroder, released in 1984.

low, particularly on manufacturing. I said, 'No, I know those costs are right,' and he said, 'No, I don't think so,' and he called someone in. This woman walked through the door and she was pretty defiant and said to him, 'Well, Greg, all I know is that we have got the cheapest costs in the industry.' That woman became my wife, and it cost me a lot!

I made it a task to get close to all the developers of the day and see what was going on, and I knew that we had to design games in a different way. Sandy White and Angela Sutherland followed me from Quicksilva to Electric Dreams, and I published their next product which was *I, of the Mask*. I came across a guy called Paul Shirley, and he came through with a concept coming off of *Marble Madness* called *Spindizzy*, which when you picked it up you couldn't put down.

There was another game that put me on a long path into history, which we published, called *Dandy*. I tried to do a deal for the licence to *Gauntlet*, which in the end Geoff Brown picked up. He's a great friend of mine now, but was a nemesis at the time. But as I looked into it I found that actually *Gauntlet* had its roots in *Dandy*, which was based on *Dungeons & Dragons*, so 'D and DY', and that became *Dandy*. I tracked down the original creator, who came up with the idea in the '70s and lived in the Bay Area of San Francisco, and got the rights from him to develop *Dandy* in a reincarnated form for the platforms of the day.

I also dealt with Fox and got the rights to the movie *Aliens*. Electric Dreams being funded by Activision was instrumental in the introductions. John Dean, who ran Software Studios, had put this concept together. Electric Dreams was geared to the UK, and was based on the strengths of the development talent in the UK. The business wasn't as analysed, or structured as it is today; we had to trail blaze and be experimental. Not every game we published worked, but we were never 'more of the same', we were always different, we always pushed the envelope. I believe there is always a new audience out there with an appetite. The fact that *Deus Ex Machina* was pirated demonstrated that commercially people were scared of it.

* Shirley claimed in the 1992 book *Halcyon Days* that *Spindizzy* was the victim of various 'dubious commercial decisions, like selling the rights for compilation releases almost at once. [Activision] made suicidal mistakes, like refusing to pay royalties in time, prompting me to cancel the contract.'
* Electric Dreams' development wing, founded by Charles Cecil.
* Which Electric Dreams published for the Commodore 64

We had great difficulty selling the bloody game because *Deus Ex Machina*'s packaging was too big, so we didn't sell that many. Games in those days were pirated 10 to one and in many cases 20 to one, and in *Deus*'s case, 50 to one. But it was a bloody difficult game to pirate, because it needed the audio and software cassettes, and the poster with all the instructions. It was probably the first full-blown commercial game to be pirated on a large scale, because it had a premium price.

We discovered years later it was number one in Portugal, Germany and India, but we never sold any copies outside of the UK! The postage basically wasn't worth it. I have played a few of the pirate versions, and in some the soundtrack is dreadful, in some you only get half a game because they only did one side of the cassette, or you got a poster with just the front side but all the instructions were on the back.

The press embraced it, though. They said it was the greatest game ever made, game of the year, acres of coverage! But because you couldn't buy it in the shops we didn't sell very many. I was pissed off.

We'd started off very UK-based, but we recognised these machines were going to be a global phenomenon. I decided to get on my bike, so to speak, and look to take this all over the place. The British government was organising trade delegations to far-off places and one of those was Singapore, where I spent the first 10 years of my life. By this time, Quicksilva had been sold to the Argus Press Group, and on the Argus board was an MP, Michael Spence, so I had a double responsibility I was acutely aware of. We arrived in Singapore; Mark Eyles, Caroline Hayon and I were manning the stand and I was confronted by this kid who asked if I knew that all of my software was being pirated. That raised my hackles, and so I told him I didn't believe it. He said he'd show me, so I got in a car with him and he took me off through the back streets of Singapore to this place I walked into to be confronted by not only our software but other British software clearly pirated and being offered for sale.

I directly approached the store owner and I said to him, 'That's not your software!' His response was that yes, it was: 'I made it here, it's mine.' I said he had to take all that software out of all those stores, and he told me to leave, and I refused. I got into a heated argument and it got very aggressive, and we had to make our escape, being chased by very irate Singapore shop owners. I thought

I wasn't going to leave it there, so I got hold of the local newspaper, *The Straits Times*, and I told them what had gone on and they went with me back to the shop to take photographs of it all. It then transpired that the suppliers were the official distributors of Sinclair machines in Singapore, so I called Sinclair and complained, and went through their PR department, who promptly came back to the British delegation, who then met me at my hotel later that night and told me to back off and not make a public incident in Singapore. We were there to promote goodwill. I was conscious of these political powerful people on our board, so I went back and kept silent for the rest of the time, but it was an interesting time.

The medium of the day was cassette, and you could buy double-deck cassette recorders, so you could record from tape to tape very easily and whatever encryption you could build into them was pretty easily broken. So piracy was very widespread. It wasn't confined to the Far East; it was rampant in Spain and Italy and countries like that, and I would say that piracy had a negative effect on growing the business internationally, and a lot of young, talented developers did not get their just rewards and ultimately pursued careers elsewhere. It was absolute theft and it can't be interpreted in any other way.

## Tim Tyler

I formed a friendship with a guy whose father owned the local computer store, and he spent a lot of time hanging out in there, helping out. So I also went in there and chatted with him, mainly about pirating other people's games, as I remember. He ripped off a lot of the games from the shop and then distributed them to his schoolmates in order to be popular, so he was a bit like a dealer of illicit computer games. I don't know if his father knew about his activities, but anyway it made him more popular at school and I was his friend and hung out in his computer shop, which was quite an important scene for me.

Everybody was affected by piracy and everybody was concerned about it. I remember that Acorn built into their computers a digital rights management scheme and they didn't expose it to the public straightaway, so it looked as though you could just copy all the games, and that seemed to be great from the user's point of view. But then, after it had become sufficiently popular, they started distributing games which had digital rights management in them, and when you tried to load the programs into the computer you got an error message saying that the game was locked. It was the first I had seen, and I spent time trying to crack it.

It was the ultimate problem, because writing games was just dealing with a computer, whereas with cracking digital rights management you weren't just dealing with a computer, you were also fighting by remote control with another human being, who was trying to stop you from doing what you were doing. Cracking copyrighted computer programs so that you could distribute pirated copies to your friends involved a battle between yourself and a real human adversary, and they were quite crafty. That was part of the attraction. It was a bigger puzzle than computer programming, in many ways.

It was a controversial issue at the time, and I made a lot of money out of people not pirating my games and buying them in shops. But at the same time I was a pirate, and my view has always been that the copyright laws are crazy, and that information should be free. Copying things in your bedroom shouldn't be a crime, so I was really on the side of the pirates. I was a bit of a hypocrite in some respects.


## David Darling

Piracy definitely had a massive impact on the game industry. Some of it was good and some of it was terrible. In some respects you can't blame people for pirating if their friends have got a game and they can't afford it, and they think they can copy it and nobody's going to know about it. They can kind of convince themselves that there's nothing wrong because they wouldn't have bought it anyway. They can always come up with justifications, and technically it's quite difficult to stop it.

But in some ways piracy is good, because if five people buy it and then five people copy it, the people who have copied it might end up buying it. So some aspects of piracy create sales. It's a very complex area. We did try and stop it as much as we could, because we were trying to sell maximum numbers, so we developed a system called FADE, which we patented. The way most publishers stopped piracy was to put a code on the tape or CD which was hard to copy, so if you pirated it you wouldn't copy the code as well, and then the game would detect it and it would stop playing. But that was quite easy for the pirates to find because if the game didn't work then they knew that there was something wrong and they would hack out your codes.

With FADE, we thought about how in the music industry it wasn't such a problem, because when people kept copying tapes the quality deteriorated, so we tried to replicate that for games. If it didn't find the codes then it wouldn't immediately stop working, instead it would deteriorate so maybe you couldn't run as fast or your car didn't have as much petrol in. We would build things into the game to stop it being as good and the pirate wouldn't know straightaway that the game had detected that it was a copy.

## Eugene Evans

Piracy was a problem for everybody, but people misunderstand it. We weren't complaining so much about kids who were hooking up two cassette decks and copying tape-to-tape. What we were having issues with was that it was becoming clear people were doing it on scale. Retailers could send product back if it wasn't selling, and there was actually one time we got product back and we were told it was defective. We tested it and there were no problems at all, and we realised people were buying it, copying it and returning it. It was starting to really impact the business.

## Rod Cousens

We never took ourselves too seriously as an industry, though there was fierce competition and there wasn't much love lost between Bug-Byte and Quicksilva. But a sort of healthy respect grew, and we collaborated with each other on matters like piracy and so on.

In about 1983 I felt the software industry needed an awards dinner, similar to the Oscars, but I thought that no one was going to pay for it, so I called Bug-Byte and asked them if they would host a dinner with me for the industry, and everyone could attend free of charge and that we would give out these spoof awards called the Clives, after Clive Sinclair, and the awards would be acronyms, so 'Creative Use of New Technology' would be one. We called this dinner the Quick-Byte, and it went on to become the focal point of the year.

By this time we were distributed by CBS Records and I'd watched how the music industry had grown up and done various things for good. We were making our money out of very young people and so I felt that we should start to put initiatives together to support worthwhile causes, and give money back to disadvantaged young people. Around this time the Ethiopian famine had happened and was getting a lot of press, and Bob Geldof was making very impassioned pleas to the world to help save people, and I felt that it was something that we should try and collaborate with, so in 1985 I called people like A&F Software, New Generation Software, Bug-Byte, and I asked them if they would donate a title, and I put a compilation of them together and asked the retailers to support it and not take any margin. I asked the magazines to promote it free of charge. But in order for it to have credibility I wanted it to be associated with Band Aid, so I wanted to call it Soft Aid. I called Bob Geldof's record label and gave them the idea, and one night I was in the office late at night and the phone went. It was Bob Geldof, and he said, 'You've got my blessing. Go and make a lot of money.'

We held an industry dinner at the Hilton on Park Lane, which was very vocal and wacky. For example, we picked an empty bottle of champagne off a table and said that we are going to auction it off, and we were getting bids of £1,000. We raised about £350,000, which if you measured the software industry against the record industry on a percentage basis, we raised more. Every year I tried to raise £1 million for charity. The following year we did a compilation called Off The Hook, which was to help drug offenders rehabilitate themselves.

← 147

# David Perry

229 →

One day I asked Mikro-Gen for a pay rise, and they said, 'Okay.' I thought, 'Wow, that was easy!' so a short period after, I went, 'Can I have another pay rise?' and they said, 'Absolutely.' It was kind of like, 'Huh, this is interesting.' I was protected in this little building, and I didn't know that you could make good money. I think my pay went to £8,000 and then £12,000, but I wanted to leave the company and go back to developing from my bedroom again and see if I could get bigger publishing deals.

So I started to try and make games without the help of a publisher, and it wasn't as easy as I expected at all. I was making some games for Elite Systems,* like *Ikari Warriors*, and I made *Great Gurianos*.* It was hard to be your own team like that, trying to draw my own art again. The mistake that I'd made, which I should have

* Founded in 1984, Elite was well known for licensing arcade games like *Paperboy*, *Commando* and *Bomb Jack* in the UK.
* A fighting game based on the Taito arcade title *Gladiator*, released in 1987 for the Spectrum.

learned by then, is my art is terrible. I realised I couldn't do this by myself. It just wasn't competitive with what the industry was doing.

So I went to a company called Probe Software, who were based in Croydon to talk to them about what they were doing. They were making a game called *Trantor: The Last Stormtrooper* and I said I could put it on to the Amstrad CPC. They were also making a Spectrum version, but I worked really hard and Nick Bruty, the artist, was awesome, so I was getting great art. Nick ended up asking, 'Hey, can I work with you?' That was all I needed, because now I had Probe Software, which had lots and lots of game licences, and an artist.

Nick was living in Brighton and so he would come up and we would work together in a bedroom in my mother's house. We nailed up some benches on the wall so we could have an office and we ended up working night and day making games. Once I had a real artist beside me, all bets were off. We could go after the best people out there and try to make the best games we could. Probe Software gave us licences, like the *Teenage Mutant Ninja Turtles*. Putting a game out on a brand like that, we were immediately number one.

Having a number one game in the British market just opens up your whole world. Games are very much a hit-driven business, and so people want to work with you once you've proved that you can make a hit. Nick and I then had choices of pretty much anything we wanted to work on, and we made a whole bunch of different games for Probe. But as time went on, the hardware started to change underneath us. We felt like masters of the Spectrum, we could make it do anything, we could bend it to our will, but people kept talking about Amigas and things like that. What's an Amiga?

"I'm not a star. I don't think so anyway. I still go round anonymous through the playground."

## GOLD CHIP WHIZZKID

TV games genius, 15, earns £500 a week

## Whizz kid Janet, 5, scares off politicians

## ACTION
### WILL YOU BE THE 1984 CHAMPION?

### Wonder boy earns a mint
**Fifteen-year-old makes more than a director**

Julian Rignall, the 1983 Champion, with Little Lisa Travis.

## SOFTWARE SUPERSTARS

Sick humour: ''The animated toilet seats were my brother's idea. He was only three at the time.''

### YOU FANCY BEING A GAMELORD?

*Crash Competition*

**HAVE YOU GOT THE RIGHT STUFF?** Think you have? Well, get it out quick, and enter the QUICKSILVA CHALLENGE!

## WHIZZ KID ANDREW GIVES THUMBS-UP TO TOP FIRM

Matthew Smith was the person who, three years ago, created cult classics such as Manic Miner **and** Jet Set Willy. **Now he's back, with** Attack of the Mutant Zombie Flesh Eating Chickens From Mars. **We tracked down the underground hero in a warren of industrial development units in Liverpool**

Archer Maclean: a star is born

'We will be selling a computer with 256K bytes of memory by 1986'

## A great British success story

# FROM A TOYOTA

**CROWTHER: Super being a superstar!**

## Now Amstrad play at the 16-bit game

## Home computers 'are here to stay'

# BOOTS TO SELL
# BBC MICRO

# Micro User Show draws 12,500 fans

## HOW TO COPY HALF A MILLION CASSETTES

. . . every month, legally – BARNABY PAGE visited Costape, one of the country's largest duplicators of Spectrum games, to watch 'em roll

**CODE MASTERS SAVES THE WORLD**

## INTERVIEW
# THE BUSINESS OF MAKING A MILLION

" . . . we had two Christmas mornings off, that's how hard it was. We worked seven days a week, eight til one in the morning . . . "

# THE ADVERTISING GAME

Between a third to a half of any computer magazine is taken up by advertising. But who produces these masterpieces of hype, and how? To find out more, Nik Wild and Oliver Frey spoke to Stephen Blower, the man behind the Ocean and Imagine adverts.

## Going it alone

So you want to start your own software house?

## Why 50,000 people are waiting for Britain's biggest-ever micro show

# BIG BEEB DOLLAR BOOKINGS

# TO A FERRARI . . .

# NOW ACORN EMPIRE IS WORTH £134.8m

## SO, HOW DO YOU WRITE COMPUTER GAMES?

*'Every home will have a computer by the end of next year'*

**It only took five years to do it**

**❦**n the first of an occasional series examining the far reaching effects of computers on today's society, Mel Croucher uncovers the truth about:

# COMPUTER ADDICTS

## Search for the ultimate game

*"I saw an advertisement in a mag – 'I want to be rich and famous department!' I thought, oh great, I'll send my game up."*

## BEATING THE YANKS AT THEIR OWN GAME

## Record 38,000 queue to visit Fair

*'I wrote eight cassette games in one day once'*

# Now production hits 11,000 a month

**"The Japanese market's two years behind UK. It's easy to look at UK trends and see what the trends will be in Japan."**

PRODUCTION of the BBC Micro has now reached 11,000 a month at the three British plants used by Acorn, and this figure is expected to be stepped up considerably when the company starts opening up the European market.

## Knighthood for Clive

# Sinclair profit is more than £14m

# Most schools are opting for the BBC machine

# THE BIGGEST COMMERCIAL BREAK OF THEM ALL

*A look at the crash of Imagine Software as seen through the eyes of a film crew.*

# Sir Clive hits out in pub punch-up

THE RIVALRY between Sir Clive Sinclair and former employee Chris Curry, now head of Acorn Computers, developed into open warfare over the Christmas period.

Having commissioned a survey on the reliability of micros which appeared to demonstrate the superiority of the BBC over the Spectrum, advertisements were placed in two national newspapers on behalf of Acorn, implying that Spectrums bought as Christmas presents would soon be taken back to the shops, and their owners would do better to buy BBC computers instead.

The advertisement so angered Sir Clive that he attacked Curry in the *Baron of Beef*, a Cambridge pub where both are regular cus-

tomers. Sir Clive walked up to Curry and slapped him about the head, then argued with him about the advertisement. There was some shoving and jostling, and the two men later began fighting again in *Shades*, an upmarket Cambridge wine bar.

Such strong passions amazed the national press, which appear to have believed that the world of technology is populated by cold fish with few emotions. Sir Clive even fell victim to the notorious columnist Jean

Rook, who said in the *Daily Express* that she thought the fight gave him sex appeal.

The two leaders of British home computing are now said to have made up their differences, and Chris Curry was a welcome guest at Sir Clive's New Year's Eve party.

Sir Clive's brother Iain Sinclair comments, "It's nice to know our captains of industry are just as capable of letting their hair down and making complete idiots of themselves as the rest of us."

# Clive loses control

**The mad Sir Clive?**

**Cambridge ain't big enough for both of us**

# ACORN SURVIVES
## Olivetti money to the rescue

## Sinclair saved by creditors

# Amstrad axes QL in Sinclair sell out

# Rivals in hot pursuit

## QL prices plummet

### Support dies for QL

# SIR CLIVE SINCLAIR RESIGNS FROM THE HOME COMPUTER MARKET

John Minson rushed off to the press conference at which the £5million sale of Sinclair Computers was announced . . .

# Decline and fall of micro empires?

# SIR CLIVE LIFE AFTER DEATH?

Is Sir Clive Sinclair a man approaching a valuable or a doomed crackpot? A business laughingstock or a consumer saviour? Or none of the above . . . Graham Taylor interviews the men who gave this magazine its name.

## The Bubble Bursts

Imagine is dead – long live imagination.

**"** When the Spectrum came out we thought 'what a piece of garbage!'. But there's something about it, to have lasted this long is amazing. **"**

# MORTGAGE

ENTER the principal of the mortgage you wish to calculate, the interest rate, and the number of years over which it must be repaid. The computer will then calculate your monthly repayments for that time, the amount of money remaining to be repaid each month, and will draw a graph of payments.

**Mortgage** was written for the 48K Spectrum by D Barton of Keighley, West Yorkshire.

```
   1 BORDER 1: PAPER 1: INK 7: C
LS
   2 POKE 23609,10
  10 PRINT AT 6,12;"MENU": PRINT

  20 PRINT AT 8,5;"1.Input varia
bles"
  30 PRINT AT 10,5;"2.Mortgage C
alculation"
  40 PRINT AT 12,5;"3.Graph Of R
esults"
  50 PRINT AT 15,2;"Input Code N
umber To Continue";AT 16,5;"OP1
 must be completed        be
fore OPs2 and 3"
  60 INPUT P$
  70 IF P$<>"1" AND P$<>"2" AND
P$<>"3" THEN GO TO 60
  80 CLS
```

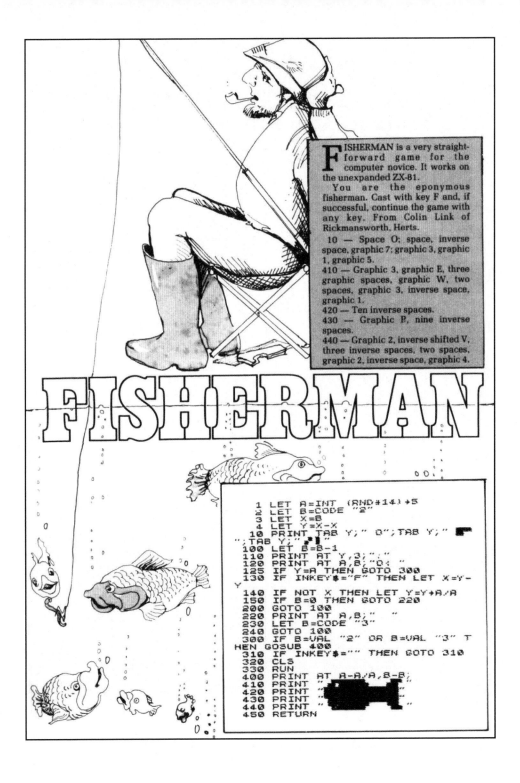

**F**ISHERMAN is a very straight-forward game for the computer novice. It works on the unexpanded ZX-81.

You are the eponymous fisherman. Cast with key F and, if successful, continue the game with any key. From Colin Link of Rickmansworth, Herts.

10 — Space O; space, inverse space, graphic 7; graphic 3, graphic 1, graphic 5.
410 — Graphic 3, graphic E, three graphic spaces, graphic W, two spaces, graphic 3, inverse space, graphic 1.
420 — Ten inverse spaces.
430 — Graphic P, nine inverse spaces.
440 — Graphic 2, inverse shifted V, three inverse spaces, two spaces, graphic 2, inverse space, graphic 4.

# FISHERMAN

```
1 LET A=INT (RND#14)+5
2 LET B=CODE "2"
3 LET X=B
4 LET Y=X-X
10 PRINT TAB Y;" O";TAB Y;" ▮
";TAB Y;"▮▮
100 LET B=B-1
110 PRINT AT Y,3;";"
120 PRINT AT A,B;"O;  "
125 IF Y=A THEN GOTO 300
130 IF INKEY$="F" THEN LET X=Y-
Y
140 IF NOT X THEN LET Y=Y+A/A
150 IF B=0 THEN GOTO 220
200 GOTO 100
220 PRINT AT A,B;"   "
230 LET B=CODE "3"
240 GOTO 100
300 IF B=VAL "2" OR B=VAL "3" T
HEN GOSUB 400
310 IF INKEY$="" THEN GOTO 310
320 CLS
330 RUN
400 PRINT AT A-A/A,B-B;
410 PRINT "
420 PRINT "
430 PRINT "▮▮▮▮▮▮
440 PRINT "▮▮▮       "
450 RETURN
```

# THE CHARTS

## TUNE IN AND RIP THE KNOB OFF

### FULL PRICE

| | | | | |
|---|---|---|---|---|
| **1** | (1) | *Teenage Mutant Hero Turtles* | | |
| | | Mirrorsoft | 90° | YS 61 |
| **2** | (NE) | *Total Recall* | | |
| | | Ocean | 84° | YS 63 |
| **3** | (2) | *Robocop 2* | | |
| | | Ocean | 93° | YS 60 |
| **4** | (6) | *Gazza 2* | | |
| | | Empire | 87° | YS 62 |
| **5** | (3) | *Hollywood Collection* | | |
| | | Ocean | 87° | YS 60 |
| **6** | (7) | *Golden Axe* | | |
| | | Virgin | 91° | YS 61 |
| **7** | (NE) | *Multi Player Soccer Manager* | | |
| | | D&H Games | 85° | YS 64 |
| **8** | (5) | *NARC* | | |
| | | Ocean | 72° | YS 62 |
| **9** | (9) | *Lotus Esprit Turbo Challenge* | | |
| | | Gremlin | 90° | YS 61 |
| **10** | (12) | *Shadow Warriors* | | |
| | | Ocean | 90° | YS 57 |
| **11** | (NE) | *Big Box* | | |
| | | Beau Jolly | | Not reviewed |
| **12** | (17) | *Pang* | | |
| | | Ocean | 94° | YS 62 |
| **13** | (11) | *Gremlins 2* | | |
| | | Elite | 72° | YS 63 |
| **14** | (13) | *Midnight Resistance* | | |
| | | Ocean | 92° | YS 65 |
| **15** | (NE) | *Rick Dangerous* | | |
| | | Rainbird | 78° | YS 43 |
| **16** | (NE) | *World Championship Soccer* | | |
| | | Elite | 80° | YS 63 |
| **17** | (NE) | *F16 Combat Pilot* | | |
| | | Digital Integration | 92° | YS 62 |
| **18** | (4) | *SCI Chase HQ 2* | | |
| | | Ocean | 71° | YS 63 |
| **19** | (6) | *Kick Off 2* | | |
| | | Anco | 60° | YS 61 |
| **20** | (10) | *Super Off-Road Racer* | | |
| | | Virgin | 91° | YS 59 |

### BUDGETS

| | | | | |
|---|---|---|---|---|
| **1** | (2) | *Double Dragon* | | |
| | | Mastertronic | 70° | YS 62 |
| **2** | (NE) | *Kenny Dalglish SM* | | |
| | | Zeppelin | 64° | YS 55 |
| **3** | (NE) | *Afterburner* | | |
| | | Hit Squad | 78° | YS 65 |
| **4** | (10) | *Paperboy* | | |
| | | Encore | 68° | YS 48 |
| **5** | (1) | *Kwik Snax* | | |
| | | Code Masters | 92° | YS 62 |
| **6** | (NE) | *Real Ghostbusters* | | |
| | | Hit Squad | 80° | YS 65 |
| **7** | (4) | *Target Renegade* | | |
| | | Hit Squad | 92° | YS 61 |
| **8** | (5) | *Dizzy Collection* | | |
| | | Code Masters | 90° | YS 63 |
| **9** | (NE) | *Defenders Of The Earth* | | |
| | | Hi-Tec | 64° | YS 65 |
| **10** | (3) | *R-Type* | | |
| | | Hit Squad | 98° | YS 61 |
| **11** | (16) | *Quattro Adventure* | | |
| | | Code Masters | 95° | YS 58 |
| **12** | (6) | *Operation Wolf* | | |
| | | Hit Squad | 87° | YS 63 |
| **13** | (21) | *Match Day 2* | | |
| | | Hit Squad | 90° | YS 57 |
| **14** | (NE) | *Rambo 3* | | |
| | | Hit Squad | 65° | YS 64 |
| **15** | (7) | *OutRun* | | |
| | | Kixx | 80° | YS 27 |
| **16** | (NE) | *Vigilante* | | |
| | | Kixx | 45° | YS 64 |
| **17** | (12) | *Track Suit Manager* | | |
| | | Hi-Tec | 79° | YS 62 |
| **18** | (8) | *Treasure Island Dizzy* | | |
| | | Code Masters | 90° | YS 63 |
| **19** | (22) | *Daley Thompson's Olympic Challenge* | | |
| | | Hit Squad | 84° | YS 59 |
| **20** | (18) | *Rastan* | | |
| | | Hit Squad | 87° | YS 59 |

Those pesky Turtles certainly are hogging the limelight, aren't they? They've been at the top for 3 months now! (And did you know that the Speccy version was the best-selling game across *all* formats last year? There's life in our old rubber-keyed chum yet!)

What else? Well, *Total Recall* seems to have fared well off the back of its movie licence, zooming in at No2, and of all things *Multi Player Soccer Manager* bows in at No7. Is there any justice in the world when a game like *Pang* lags 5 places behind it at No12? No, we thought not either.

In its third month in the charts *Double Dragon* finally jostles its way into the top spot, kicking *Kwik Snax* down to No5. In the new entry league every single game is a rerelease. *Kenny Dalglish* leads the pack with *Afterburner* hot on its heels, followed by *Real Ghostbusters* and *Defenders Of The Earth* (which has to be one of the fastest 'berg' conversions we've seen in a long while). Where are all those marvellous original games like *Popeye 2* and *Hawk Storm*, eh? (Perhaps next month will tell.)

**THE MAGIC KEY**
So how does it all work then? Well, it's all jolly simple. The number in brackets is where the game stood in last month's charts (with NE for New Entry), and the percentage at the end of the line is the score that we originally gave it, followed by the issue that the review appeared in. And finally, the YS Charts are brought to you in conjunction with Gallup (so ta very much to them).

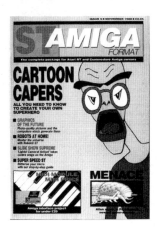

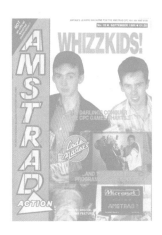

# Part 5

# Game
# Press

I was a nightmare, and so was Gary, with us throwing chairs around the office and punching walls and swearing. We barely knew we were in a professional environment. But we did know how to play games, and we had opinions and big egos, and we would write these reviews.

What was fascinating about early game journalism was that all the journalists loved games. They were as fanatical as us creators. They didn't have much background in journalism, I don't think, but when I met them there was a craziness about them, an excitement, and a lot of them were funny. A lot of the early journalists have gone on to be famous comedians and script writers in Hollywood, so they were smart and intelligent, and I think very, very influential in the success of computer games. They brought them to a bigger audience, mainly because they were a bit maverick. They were incredibly opinionated, and one of the things they were opinionated about is how you should never do a sequel. It's amazing to think that in the world we are in now, but some of the early magazines would say, 'Oh, that's just a sequel, forget that.' Us tiny little developers used to read it, and I used to say, 'Well, I can never make a sequel,' so they really influenced what my company did. They were part of the industry, very smart kids, very rebellious. They interviewed people on toilets, at the top of skyscrapers ... They were a fascinating mix of people, for sure.

The early journalists also wrote in-depth features on the developers, because they didn't really have much to write about the games. So we had those early stars of the industry, who seemed to be rock stars in my view. People like Rob Hubbard and Jeff Minter, all the early names you kind of revered. The journalists, as well. I certainly remember meeting a lot of them in the early days and thinking, 'My God, this is a superstar.'

When I first joined Mikro-Gen, I wasn't anybody. Nobody knew me; I was almost the intern. So whenever we'd go to a trade show, it wasn't like, 'Hey Dave, we want you to meet the press!', it was, 'We have this big papier mâché head and we need someone to wear it with a costume and hand out stickers, and that's you.' So I didn't get much of a break to meet any press or do anything cool at the start, but over time, when you're starting to make some money for the company, you don't need to hand out stickers any more. The press are genuinely interested in whatever you're working on next, and so I found myself going and meeting with them, like *Crash*.

I used to love *Crash*. I used to think Oliver Frey was fantastic, so I remember going to see them in Ludlow, but, you see, what's so funny is they were fans of the games, so they were excited to meet their developers, but they didn't know that we were fans of their magazine! It was like, 'Oh my God!' because the press were celebrities at the time, you know? You'd be excited to meet Julian Rignall, these people who knew so much about the industry. Magazines were our conduit. There was no internet, so we learned about the industry through what they wrote.

I did the same thing with other developers. I remember one time being at a party and looking across the room and seeing Peter Molyneux and it was like, 'Oh my God, I'm in a room with Peter Molyneux!' Do you know what I mean? What's funny about it is, and this is one of the best things about the game industry, the more people that you meet, the more you realise that everybody is cool. It's very hard to find someone who's not cool, so if you were to go up to Peter Molyneux and say hello, he'd be like, 'Oh hello, nice to meet you.' To actually get to meet these people who I respected so much, it made me start to want to attend a lot more game conferences and that kind of thing.

## Archer Maclean

I think it was early '85 when *Zzap!64* came out and carved itself a very interesting position because of the personalities that came across. There was Julian Rignall, Gary Penn, Gary Liddon and a whole load of others, enthusiastically writing pages and pages of in-depth game reviews, and *Dropzone* went out on the cover of edition number three, I think it was. It suddenly started getting incredible scores in all the other magazines, and I remember standing in WHSmith reading one of them and it gave *Dropzone* a perfect 10 or something. I was just three feet off the floor, but you can't grab someone next to you and say, 'Look at this, this is me!'

You know, after struggling for all those years, that stuff was great. You got to trust the journalists; after a number of years of reading one person's opinion you knew when something was good and the way they would talk about it became a reliable reference point. And I don't think they were as vindictive as all that. You didn't have people who had powerful personalities and just wanted to stamp over everything because they were a fanboy or something. You had people who wanted to be die-hard journalists. I mean, that was their passion. I can't remember seeing any reviews where they were deliberately trying to ruin something. They would still score it and comment on it but they wouldn't just get a thrill out of slagging it off as badly as possible. They would still give it a fair hearing.

I would look at other games that were highly rated or regarded and try and figure out whether I could have done as well, or how would I do it better, differently or add to it. So yeah, they inspired me. I definitely think they raised the standard because of the exposure of good games.

I think they were trying to find the heroes of the games creation industry. Before me there was Jeff Minter, I mean I used to look at his stuff before I had even started writing games, and he had this brilliant, sort of personal way of wearing the hippy coat and the long hair and permanently looking like he was out of it. He was producing these bizarre games with camels and lamas and sheep and all sorts of stuff, and doing very well out of it, so they obviously latched on to him.

Then, somewhere in '85, '86, there was something in *Zzap!* called the Superstar Challenge or something, where myself, Chris Butler,* Andy Braybrook, Jeff Minter and Tony Crowther* all turned up at *Zzap!* Towers and competed on each other's games. We went out that night and got absolutely slaughtered. That was a very fun weekend.

× Programmer of the Commodore 64 version of *Commando* and various other highly regarded conversions of arcade classics.
• Programmer of *Wanted: Monty Mole* and *Blagger*. Crowther was a prolific figure during the 8-bit era, creating games for Gremlin Graphics and Alligata.

← 183

## Jeff Minter

266 →

Oh, I suppose I had my famous tiff with *Zzap!64*. That was all a bit silly when you look back on it, but a lot of kids at the time, who were the main market for games, looked to *Zzap!64* and *Crash* for their opinions about games, and in the absence of YouTube, or just being able to download something and try it, how would you know about new games? Mostly it was through reviews, so they were quite important, so it would have been prudent perhaps to keep better relationships with them. They were quite powerful, especially towards the latter stages of the 8-bit era. They had a lot of clout.

I'd been writing a column, I think it was in the first issue of *Zzap!64*, and then they did a review of *Mama Llama*,* and they didn't really like *Mama Llama* very much,* and I can kind of understand why, looking back on it, because *Mama Llama* was quite heavily experimental. You were controlling these three llamas and the way you

• A shoot 'em up with puzzle elements in which you protect a mother llama and her offspring through 100 levels of enemy attacks.
× The magazine gave it a Value For Money rating of 59%, stating, 'Plenty there, but we suspect even Minter fans may not take to it.'

attacked things was by this floating droid, and you had to control the llamas and the droid together, and perhaps it might be argued it was perhaps a little bit up itself. So, looking back, I can understand why they might have liked some of my previous games but not that one. It was a bit too far out, possibly just a bit too weird for them, and to be fair it's not like they developed an enmity to me and slagged off anything I produced from then onwards. It was just that one game they didn't like very much, and I didn't take it very well. I was a bit of an arsehole about it, to be honest.

## Julian Gollop

Most of my reviews were pretty good, in the range of eights or nines. I think I was fortunate that *Crash* and *Sinclair User* appreciated what I was trying to do, and it certainly helped, I'm sure, helping the sales of my games. I never experienced the feeling or status of being a rock star, which I guess some other developers may have done. I felt that what I was doing was a little bit niche; I never really understood the true extent of the audience for what I was doing. What I did know is that the people who played my games liked them a lot, and that's what motivated me and made me happy.

I think a lot of people were sensitive about reviews because they had a fair bit of power, and so if they cut you down it could damage your sales. But I think in general they were pretty honest. I don't think there was any under-handedness or anything, especially with *Zzap!64* and *Crash*.

## Julian Rignall

It was interesting watching the evolution of journalism, certainly as a consumer in the early days, obsessively reading these very dry things in *Computer and Video Games* and getting the impression that they were written by somebody that might not necessarily know all about it. Journalists at the very beginning were basically traditional reporters who just saw these games and would talk about them. A lot of the time, they weren't particularly knowledgeable about the games and their broader contexts, and they would report on them in a very traditional, sometimes quite neutral way. You'd have this factual, 'Here's this game and it does this and this and this.' It was clearly written by someone who wasn't necessarily a real enthusiast.

Then you got *Personal Computer Games*, which was very inspiring to me because it was very obvious that the people who were writing it knew the games and were into them. Then *Crash* came along and their model was interesting, because they just got kids off the street, local school kids, 'Come in, play games and let us know what you think!' So you got these very brutally honest opinions. They weren't necessarily good writers because they were teenagers. But that worked very well for *Crash*.

← 203

## Mel Croucher

One of the reasons *Pimania* began to be featured in magazines was that I knew a lot of the journalists. We didn't have any money, so we couldn't pay for advertising, and I wrote a lot of those early reviews myself. Journalists are very lazy people – this is not a secret, it's the truth – and if you write something for them and make it readable, funny, and sometimes controversial, they will probably publish it. Then other journalists caught the bug, realising we had a little bit more going for us than some others.

← 72

## Gary Penn

236 →

Chris Anderson[*] launched a magazine called *PCG – Personal Computer Games* – and that was the first magazine that had a real sense of fun. I don't even remember seeing *C+VG* even being that much fun back then. Of course I ended up with Chris on *Zzap!64*, but he had a very different take to Newsfield.[*] *Crash* evolved from a sales thing, and for me the reason *Zzap!* stood above *Crash* was that cultish personality. We were absolutely enthusiastic, which was part of Chris's genius. The guy was a visionary, and he wanted players of games because he thought they would connect better with a readership than professional journalists.

A lot of *Zzap!* was driven by Chris and his ideas for putting the journalist front and centre, which was a very unusual and bold thing to do at the time. Without that, combined with Ollie Frey and his genius with art, those magazines would never have been as successful. I think you got this thing that was part comic book, part fanzine,

← 206

## Rod Cousens

379 →

Newsfield were unbelievably irreverent in their day, and they formed part of the character of the industry. We referred to it as the Wild West, and we knew we were trailblazing, a pioneering industry of a new form of entertainment, a new medium, and we didn't give a damn, and there were no rules.

[*] Chris Anderson went on to launch *Zzap!64*, found Future Publishing, and run the conference, TED.

[*] Newsfield Publications was the publisher of *Zzap!64* and *Crash*, as well as Amstrad magazine *Amtix!* and *The Games Machine*. It specialised in niche youth culture magazines, but games were its mainstay until the company folded in 1991.

I mean *Zzap!* more than *Crash* ended up resonating quite profoundly with readers and publishers, and we ended up in a position where it was very difficult. Everything you did had an effect: every review we ever wrote, every cover, every piece of coverage. From the way the publishers would react, and the way that the readers would react, you had something going on there.

## Chris Anderson

I got a job as editor of a magazine called *Personal Computer Games* right at the end of 1983. At that time there were only two or three videogame magazines of any note being published, and they were all being published by bigger publishers. Typically, they were hiring regular journalists who had some sort of interest in games, but they weren't really gamers. But during my year on *Personal Computer Games* we went from thinking of it as content that should be written by journalists to increasingly seeing it as content that had to be written by gamers themselves.

At the end of that year, I ran a competition in the magazine to try and find the best videogame players in Britain. The secret purpose of it was to find amazing people to bring in as writers, who were really the best of the best and who knew what they were talking about. I left the magazine when it was running into commercial difficulties, and launched *Zzap!64*, which took a completely different approach. I didn't hire any journalists, I hired people who were first and foremost gamers. We did some writing training and so on, but I wanted that authentic passion to come through.

That's why *Zzap!64*, and also *Crash* from Newsfield, had a much higher level of engagement. They were also only covering one platform instead of all of them, so there was also huge platform loyalty. Every page was devoted to your computer, and people could get obsessive, you know, almost an unhealthy level of interest, and then you had writers who were just part of the community, who didn't differentiate work from play. They were up all night playing games, figuring out tips on how to get high scores, writing reviews and so on.

So the two winners of the national videogame playing competition were Julian Rignall and Gary Penn, who I think were both 18 or 19 at the time, and so when I started *Zzap!* they were the two key reviewers, and I also hired Bob Wade, who came over from *Personal Computer Games*.

*Zzap!64* was ever so slightly different to *Crash*. We were still young but we were slightly older, and I think what Chris did was different to what Roger[×] did. Chris looked for gamers that were already out there. In my case I'd won championships, and in Gary Penn's case he'd contributed freelance hints and tips and stuff to *Personal Computer Games*, and we'd both entered a contest at *Personal Computer Games*, so it was obvious that we could play games very well and we had a certain sense of humour. So Chris took a leap of faith with trying these slightly older guys that were hard, hard, hardcore gamers, and quite a handful in the early days.

I mean, I was a nightmare, and so was Gary, with us throwing chairs around the office and punching walls and swearing. Stupid stuff because I was fresh off the farm, you know? Gary had just moved from school at Hemel Hempstead, and we barely knew we were in a professional environment. But we did know how to play games, and we had opinions and big egos, and we would write these reviews. You got that sort of honest gamer kind of journalism that I think definitely defines a period.

Throughout, certainly with my stuff and certain others, there was a great deal of humour and one-upmanship: 'I'm going to try and mock this game in as amusing a way as possible, and I'm going to say more outrageous things than him.' We'd get a bad game and we'd just kick it to death, absolutely kick it to death, and it was horrible for the person who made it but, you know, great for the readers. We over-exaggerated things, maybe, but there was always a point on the bottom line, at least I like to think so. We weren't just vicious for the sake of it.

## Rob Hubbard
← 181    251 →

I think the magazines had a lot to do with the industry going to a wider market. It was vitally important that it got a good review; I think that helped with the sales. If it didn't get a good review, it was trashed; I mean, some of these magazines were fairly ruthless – *Zzap!64* could be fairly ruthless – and if they were, the game wouldn't sell at all. But I didn't really read them. I was aware of some of the things that they were saying, which was really nice, but I had like four things lined up to do, and later on I was doing conversions on to Amstrad and Spectrum 128, Atari 800, Amigas ... So there was so much work to do.

I think as the '80s went on and more money came in, there was a period where I think the industry wanted to grow up, and it looked at the crazy journalists as being a little bit too immature and

× Roger Kean, the launch editor of *Crash*

unbecoming of a professional industry. You still had very funny, very scathing journalists writing pieces that were probably more clever than our puerile humour, but you definitely got a move towards this sort of, 'No, we've got to be professional and treat games with respect.'

## Gary Penn

*Zzap!* didn't beat around the bush with reviews. Other magazines at the time wouldn't use the full range of ratings, but this was something Chris believed in, and we shared that vision, that if you're going to rate something you use the spectrum and 50% really ought to be a strict average, and also that there aren't that many great games in the world, and that most stuff is average.

I remember we reviewed the first three games by a company, one was *Gertie Goose*, and they were dreadful. We were quite nasty about them be-cause we were cocky bastards, but we also knew that the readers would like this stuff. So the guy phoned me up and he was so angry, saying we had ruined his company. He said that no one would touch his debut games because of our review, and that it had killed his company. At the time it was hilarious and we were pissing ourselves laughing, but looking back I feel awful.

## Peter Molyneux

As time went on, the review score became hugely important, but it didn't seem quite so important as it does these days. A 10 out of 10 was very, very rare, and lots of games got 7 out of 10, and you didn't feel it was a terrible game. Journalists could really influence the sales, but I think fans influenced them as well. There were also lots of different magazines and a far bigger diversity in reviews than you get today. You also have to remember there was a lot of innovation in the early to mid '80s, and a lot of journalists had to get their head around it. Some of them didn't, and would mark games low, just because they didn't understand the game.

Reviews of games were always quoted by readers as their reason as to whether they brought a game, and so in terms of determining the game's success, publishers always felt that a review was more important than any advertising they bought. So it did lead to lots of incoming anger, when someone paid a lot of money to advertise a game and the editorial team trashed it. I got lots of phone calls. I don't know what happened at other magazines, but my background was as a journalist, and we were always crystal clear that we were editorially led and we just could not compromise on that, one iota. So we lost some advertising from time to time because they were unhappy with editorial treatment, but for the most part most people rolled with it and realised that they were playing for the long term, and that they wanted to be in magazines that had credibility.

I always think that you can have that professionalism and still be enthusiastic and still make it fun. But I also think it lost a little bit of its soul, because the business side definitely did kick in. The business side always underpinned everything that we did. People would pull ads because you said something horrible about their game, they'd call you up and ask why you gave it a certain mark, or what you were going to give it. I can't tell you how many arguments I've had where I've said, 'No, I'm not going to tell you.' 'Well, it's going to be a crap review, right?' 'No, it's not that bad.' And when they see it, it's like, 'That's a crap review.' 'No, it's not crap. 77%? That's a good review.' 'No, I wanted more. We're going to pull ads!' That's just par for the course.

The bottom line is that if you've got a magazine that sells really well, that person will hate you for that game.

And then their next game comes along, and if it's great and you write a great review, and they sell a bunch of games off the back of your review, they love you again. It's the way it works.

For me, the driving force was helping people find a game that they would enjoy. I remember the disappointment of spending three months' pocket money on *Bruce Lee* on the Atari and finishing it in a night. I remember thinking, 'Shit, great, three months until I can buy my next game.' That very visceral disappointment drove me to wanting to make sure that that didn't happen with other people, because there are always good games out there, and there's always bad ones, and we were trying to help people. 'You might not like it, just because we say it's good, but hopefully as you read the review you'll be able to pick and choose.' Or, 'Julian hates RPGs but he's actually saying this one's quite enjoyable, so since I like RPGs I'll probably love it.' Helping that good experience, that's what gets people into gaming, right?

Even in the early days, we kind of realised that we were promoting the industry. If I can recommend a game every month that you enjoy, that's going to be great for me because you're going to buy my magazine next month, and you're also going to buy games, so people will want to advertise in my magazine because you're buying a game based on my recommendation. We got that very early on. There's nothing cynical or sinister about it, it just makes sense, right? I love games, and ultimately I want the game industry to succeed; I don't want to see crap games and I don't want people to be disappointed, I'd love every games experience to be great, so perhaps we can help that. That's what it was all about to me.

## Oliver Frey

The decision to have the *Zzap!* reviews portrayed as either good or hating the game I think must have come from Chris Anderson. Of course, once you draw their faces they become recognisable, and soon their photos appeared in the magazine as well. It must have affected the reviewers, because the readers suddenly knew who they were talking to when they wrote letters, so they would attack Julian, or Gary Penn, or Gary Liddon. All the attention must have gone to their heads, I suppose, to a degree.

## Chris Anderson

With *Zzap!64* we came up with this idea of actually showing in the expression of the reviewers' faces their level of excitement about the game, so for a five-star game you would have the reviewer going, 'Woooo!' and for a one-star game they would be sort of scrunched up in agony. People seemed to like that.

## Fred Gray

The magazines, *Zzap!64* and *Crash* and the like, were very much, what's the word, the fanzine thing. It was all about catering to fans and fanatics. The only trouble is that I felt they were a little bit too critical of people. A lot of my stuff was getting 60s and 70s in the ratings, which was probably fair, but it also introduced me to the fact that Rob Hubbard and other people were getting much better reviews. I think it was all down to a few people and their opinions, and their narrow-mindedness, if you like. Obviously it's something that comes with any cultural phenomenon: you are going to get magazines and critics.

My only regret was I didn't get better reviews. They weren't so much reviewing the music as they were reviewing the actual sound of the whole package, and I quite agree, Martin was getting much better sounds, but I think musically ... Especially with Denton Designs, we weren't out to appeal like everybody else, and the fact that my music sounded different to their music didn't mean it didn't suit the game, or that the game wasn't as good. I mean, there were so many shoot 'em ups, you know, *Commando* and *Rambo* and all of this, and I think the people at *Zzap!64*, that's where their mindset was, in that type of game and that type of music.

## Steve Turner

Suddenly we had *Crash* and *Zzap!64*, and they seemed to be written by young people for young people. They were full of lovely artwork and lots of opinions, which could be really devastating. They set about reviewing virtually every game that came out, even the ones published before the magazines started. You thought that they were the voice of game players, and they were living and breathing games, and you could tell by the way they talked about their joysticks hurting their hands. It made us really want to please them, because we thought if we didn't, we weren't pleasing typical game players. They also almost treated games like the pop industry. They started having articles about the programmers and their cars and things like that. It gave a completely different feel to it.

They had a terrific effect on sales, too. If you had a bad review your game was probably not going to do well, so you opened the magazine really nervously and read the review. You wanted everything to be up in the 90s, and if it wasn't, you know, you thought, 'Oh God.' The problem we sometimes had was that if we tried something a little bit different it may not fit into the categories the magazines would want to fit you into. I remember in *Paradroid* it was a conscious decision that Andrew didn't put music in the game, as we actually hated music in games and always turned it off. He used the bandwidth to put really super sound effects in instead, yet if you look at the sound in the reviews it's marked down because it didn't have any music.

*Gribbly's* was a moderate success, but more importantly, Andrew got recognised in the magazines, in particular *Zzap!64*. They very much liked the game and gave it a good review, and they asked us whether he'd like to do a new feature called Diary of a Game, where he would write a daily account of everything he did on his next game. It was a bit of a chance because we didn't know what the next game was going to be and we had no idea whether it was going to be any good. But we thought, 'Oh, free publicity, so let's do this!'

## Geoff Brown

The magazines had an enormous power because they were reviewing the games and, you know, I think I've been pretty fair in my life but I was the biggest advertiser and I wanted good reviews. I'm not saying I bought reviews, but I wanted to know why I hadn't got a good review, you know? Our products were first class, but there were one or two that weren't, and I think Newsfield would be the first to admit that we were pretty single-minded to deal with, let's put it like that. I remember getting the front page of a magazine at one point, on a product which they'd never seen, and when I finally got the product I wasn't happy with it. I wasn't happy, they weren't happy but you can't get front page and then get a bad review.

At the time, we'd grown to have a bit of a steam-roller effect. It wasn't just like I'd taken the market and owned it; I had to really fight to get myself established and I suppose I've got that streak that I will not be beaten. If you punch me into a corner, I'll come out fighting, I won't just slump on the floor. So I'd got this streak, I'd got my wife by my side, who was extremely tough business-wise, and so the two of us were pretty formidable. I was hungry, you know, I was young enough as well, I really wanted to make that successful and I would fight anybody in the room for it, and I did.

## David Darling

With famous reviewers like Julian Rignall and people like that, people would listen to them as experts in the industry, and it became really, really important because a lot of games were quite expensive and they wouldn't want to waste their money on a bad game.

To begin with, we had quite a bad relationship with some of those magazines, because we were selling budget games, and they didn't really admit it but I think they were biased towards companies that were spending advertising money. Because we didn't spend loads of money on advertising we could mostly take that money off the price of the game, so the game was good value. But they would give us terrible reviews, even though we thought our games were really good.

But I don't think the reviews were so important for budget games. I think it was true that if you got bad reviews with full-priced games they bombed, but with budget games, often players would be buying a game a week from the local newsagent, thinking they looked good from the screenshot.

← 149 Oliver twins 271 →

PO We were quite fortunate that we were living near Bath, which was where Future Publishing was. So when we decided to switch over to the Amstrad, we actually had the official Amstrad magazine* a twenty minute drive away. We very quickly hooked up with them.

AO We were just friends with them and we always played games with them.

PO Yes, we took our next games to show them, and we got a pretty good relationship with them quite quickly. Richard and David were very friendly with the *Zzap!* and *Crash* people. We absolutely loved seeing the reviews, and we'd learn who the reviewers were, get to talk to them, write them nice little letters and stuff, and try and butter them up a little bit. We were trying to be friendly and nice, but we also wanted to try and give them material so that they'd write bigger and better articles.

* Future Publishing published *Amstrad Action*, which wasn't actually officially affiliated with Amstrad, but was one of the most respected titles available for the format. It was also Future Publishing's first magazine.

← 193 Martin Galway 275 →

The magazines, like *Zzap!64* and *Commodore User*, they were basically your only feedback. There were no forums or internet, no thousands of users giving you feedback. You really had no idea, unless you happened to stand around in WHSmith and ask people. But the magazines were specialised for games and almost like the MTV of the generation, and they just revolutionised the game industry. There was so much colour, so much pizzazz, with little headshots of the reviewers, and personalised reviews and things like that.

Now, previously I had been reading games reviews in magazines like *Your Computer*, and some of the other ones, which are a lot more for hardware enthusiasts, where you would have a wire dangling out the back of your computer to control some fish tank motor or something, and they were kind of square by comparison to these really hip magazines like *Zzap!* I remember seeing my name on *Zzap!*'s front cover because I did an interview for them, and I bought three copies and had a smile from ear to ear all day long, and showed it to my parents.

The magazines were definitely responsible for turning people into rock stars. It started in the Imagine days with Eugene Evans, but then it continued with Tony Crowther around the time he put *Loco* out. Any time there was a fantastic programmer or a fantastic game, they would try to interview the people who developed it and turn them into rock stars, even if they were kind of nerdy programmers. You would never know that from seeing a picture of a guy, and they basically got hyped up so you start to think that they are like cool rock stars. I would frequently meet them, you know, 18 months after seeing them as gods from a magazine, and they would just be normal people, just like me.

* A Super Locomotive clone released for the Commodore 64 in 1984.

## David Darling

We were definitely aware of the idea of promoting programmers as celebrities, or guys behind the creative works. Like, if you really enjoy *Manic Miner*, or you really enjoy this particular game then these are the people who are actually making it. Our dad was completely aware that it's no good just having a really good product; you have to market it. Richard Branson knows PR is a really, really good tool compared with advertising, if you can get a story to run in the newspapers or on the BBC News or whatever for nothing.

So we pushed as many stories as we could. When we signed the Oliver twins and they moved up to Leamington Spa, we did a photograph of them in a tree like they were looking for a house to move into. When we did *BMX Simulator* it was the first four-player game on the Commodore 64, so we did a picture of me, my dad, and my two brothers on a motorbike, four people. So we supplied the press with interesting pictures. We also did a game called *Rock Star Ate My Hamster,* so we were doing some controversial games too.

Even when we were at Mastertronic, Martin Alper was really good at publicity, so when we did the *Chiller* game, he got some controversial PR because we did a launch campaign on a boat in London with girls dressed in nappies, of all things. We also got on TV a few times, so Mastertronic promoted us as kind of whizz-kid programmers on *No. 73*, a kid's TV programme. They interviewed me and Richard about the games we were working on at the time.

Marketing was really hard work because you were spending all hours making games and working with lots of other people, trying to get games out for Christmas or Easter, so it was

* A management game about the music industry released in 1988.
* Inspired by Michael Jackson's *Thriller,* released in 1984.

a bit like being on a conveyer belt. But we were working with a PR company called Lynne Franks, who is basically the woman who *Absolutely Fabulous* was based on, you know, this, like, crazy PR lady. She was presenting us as these whizz-kids because it was a really good story for the papers to get round the idea that you could turn this cottage industry into a mass consumer industry.

So we had fun with the PR, but there was truth behind it because we were making games that were going to the top of the charts. The Olivers at one stage had number one, two and three in the charts with *Dizzy* games, but it never really slowed down because you were always doing the next game, and you were only as good as your last game, too. If you had a failure, you could disappear overnight. So it wasn't really like you could sit back and relax and put your feet up and go to a Caribbean island or something like that. It was very, very hectic.

←236
## Peter Molyneux
265→

Oh, I don't think PR for me happened until the '90s. For my first real, proper game, which was called *Populous*, the journalist came in to interview me after release but we never saw a journalist before then.

## Mike Montgomery
265→

There is an interesting thing about this industry, and it's that the gaming magazines came along with the industry from the start. You know, it was very much backroom stuff at the very beginning, with probably one guy doing his own magazine, until the big publishers thought, 'Wow, there's something in this.' Magazine publishers ended up having eight or nine computer magazines, probably even more. It helped the industry, and it helped The Bitmap Brothers, because that was how we got over to the public, the people who spent money on games and on the magazines to see what to buy, you know? Opinions.

We were very lucky. We had our first 10 out of 10 on *Xenon 2*, and we also had a few very poor reviews, but quite honestly, it is like bad news is still publicity, we just turned it around the way we wanted to. The publishers had PR people, and we worked with them very closely, like Cathy Campos and Alison Beasley. That was in the contract, that they had to have a dedicated PR person for us. The press was extremely important to us, and we did our marketing through the magazines, really. And if they got an exclusive, or saw stuff, it was good for them, too. Their coverage got punters picking up the magazines that our advertising paid for, if you like. We became extremely friendly with most of the big journalists in the UK and Europe, and America, to an extent. We used to go on press tours, anytime we went to the States to do a show, and we'd get a bunch of journalists and take them out to Six Flags and go roller-coasting for a day. That was our thank you to them for good coverage and reviews.

Now, of course, journalists who didn't give us good reviews? I'd get my baseball bat out and put it over the top of their heads. That worked quite well, actually. But we were pretty good to the press, and we didn't treat them like muppets, like some developers did.

The image that we wanted to give to the public was very similar to the record industry. You don't go into a shop and buy an Apple record. You go into the shop and buy The Beatles, not the label. The game industry is actually all about the labels, about the publishers, but we wanted to try and crack that, and we did it, through insisting we did some of our own PR and some of our marketing, and that the publisher paid for it. They gave us a budget to do it all and believed in us, and we went out and did all of these photographs. We wined and dined the press, retailers. We did an awful lot, you know, at one point we were doing more marketing and PR than we were doing programming and work. I think we believed that we became the first pop stars of the industry.

The only problem is that not many people followed us. That's a shame, because even though there are some very big names, it's the publishers that get all the glory. It's their brand, it's their name, you know, and they turn around and say, 'Well, we're paying for it.' You know what? That's not true, because in the music industry the financial models are almost the same, where everything is advances and front money.

One PR event worked out really well, the shot with Maxwell's helicopter. What a day that was. We got permission to do this on top of the Mirror Group building in Fleet Street. The only problem was that Maxwell was out that day – I think he was actually at the races or something – and we only had 15 minutes once it had landed to take the pictures and get off the roof. But it also meant we had to wait there all day for him to turn up. So we were there from 9 a.m., but we got the best pictures ever, because he turned up just before sunset. We couldn't have planned it, but it was fantastic. We sent that around to every magazine, and I think every single one printed it, because, you know, magazines are looking for things to print. They are looking to fill space. When you give them something as good as that, they are going to print it.

The Bitmap Brothers also introduced pop stars into the games industry. We did Bomb the Bass,[x] John Foxx from Ultravox,[•] Betty Boo.[¶] We linked up with a record company called Rhythm King; we said to them, 'We want these stars to write music for our games.' Apart from Betty Boo, all the music was actually written for the games that we had, which was just a great combination. It gave us a few extra stars on our reviews, as well.

[x] Otherwise known as Tim Simenon, who created the title track for *Xenon 2: Megablast*.
[•] Composer of the title song for *Gods*, 'Into the Wonderful'.
[¶] Betty Boo contributed her song 'Doin' The Do' to *Magic Pockets*.

←239                                                                247→

## Steve Turner

I gave Andrew a very open brief for *Paradroid*. I said I'd like for his next game to be a more technical game, featuring robots. I had seen a lot of films like *The Black Hole* and *Star Wars*, where you had these little cute robots with character, and no one had really done a game with robots, so it would be a good subject.

He didn't really like the idea. I eventually did the game in my head with *Quazatron*,[x] but he came back the next morning with a bit of paper, kind of almost like the Ten Commandments, a list of rules which basically outlined *Paradroid*. It said things like, 'Cute and tech don't go, so it's going to be a techy game. It's going to be a series of spaceships with robots that have run amok and you've got to take control of them.'

He immediately started building the spaceships, so he hadn't really worked on how the gameplay was actually going to work,

[x] Released in 1986 for the Spectrum, it took *Paradroid*'s design but opted for an isometric playing perspective.

how you're going to take over things. I remember him talking about wanting to build a ship in Lego to check that it would actually work as a three-dimensional space. He wanted it to be like a real place.

Andrew Braybrook

The design of the game actually came about in one evening walking home, all except the firing mode, which went through two over-complicated and difficult-to-use incarnations before I got something that worked, albeit something rather conventional. The whole game came together fairly smoothly, including the transfer game, everything just worked. Steve was a bit busy so didn't write any music for it, and I even had a go at doing some sound effects myself.

Our initial concept for the graphics was to get a high-tech display on the screen. In a lot of films you get these lovely futuristic graphic displays, so we thought we would try that, because it hadn't been done in a game. But we found it was something the Commodore 64 couldn't really do because you needed high resolution graphics, and early attempts looked blurred on TVs, with this herringbone effect.

Whenever Andrew had a problem he'd do something else, so he worked on the game's title. He'd come up with the word 'Paradroid' and he wanted it stamped in metal. I can remember him experimenting with the graphics of getting this word stamped in metal, and that's where the final concept came from, with walls which looked metal and rounded, which came from using three of the Commodore's colours, a light, a dark and a medium, which all kind of blended together and you got these rounded effects. He actually got me to plan the colours, because he's a little bit colour blind and was very worried about his choices, so he got me to be his painter decorator, where I chose a set of colours that went together.

Andrew used to design games as he went along, and the first thing he used to do was a character set, just to give him time to think about it. He was very much into control modes, because you couldn't do much with a joystick, and we hated games where you had to break off and do things on the keyboard. So he would spend a lot of time playing about getting extra functions in the game just using a fire button and the directions. If your fire button is used for firing, how do you use it for something else, too? He came up with some brilliant solutions, so for *Paradroid* he put little panels on the floor where if you pressed the fire button on one it did something else. That gave him the extra functionality he needed.

At first when you wanted to take over a robot there wasn't any sub-game, you just collided with it and if you were successful you took it over, or you were dead. If you were stronger than the other robot you had a much better chance, and if you were lesser it'd be less likely, so the game was like going up a series of stairs. But when we tried it we found it was a little bit hit and miss. Sometimes, you were in a firefight with one of the bigger guys and you grappled with him instead and were instantly blown up. So to solve that problem he hit on the idea of holding down the fire button for half a second or so to get into transfer mode, which got another function out of the joystick.

## Steve Turner

Andrew did all the sound on *Paradroid*. Normally I did his sound, but I was really tied up trying to get my latest game finished. I had written a sound routine, and we had a little program that you dialled hex numbers into, but he used to say, 'Oh, I'm so hopeless, it would be better just putting random numbers in and seeing what happens.' So he fired the SID chip's own random number generator back at our routine to put random numbers in, and when he came up with something that was nice he wrote down the numbers. He got some fantastic effects like that, but the routine sounded like robots talking to each other, and we liked it so much that it became the title sequence. I think it was rather special, because you had never heard a sound like it before.

To see whether these ideas worked we let other people try them. The lasers were very much case in point, in that he always envisaged having a gunsight, and right up until about two weeks before he finished, the game had one, but none of the players liked it. The gunsight allowed you to shoot in any direction but it took you ages to move it over the thing you wanted to fire at, and by that time you were dead. In the end, Andrew reverted it, almost as a necessity after exhaustively trying more and more complicated ideas. The more complicated the routines, the less we liked them, so we went right back to simplicity.

One complication Andrew kept was the speed of the robots, because it worked rather nicely in giving you a different feel for every robot. So light ones accelerate very fast and the heavy robots have momentum, so they have to build up speed, and if they hit another robot they nudge or blow it up. That almost caused a problem at first, because he coded the robots before he did the player, and the larger robots were destroying all the little robots before he found them. So he had to put in a routine that said robots had to be nice to their friends.

The first time we showed it was to Gordon Hewson, who was Andrew Hewson's brother. He used to do the game reviewing and testing side, and his reaction was, 'What on earth is that?' His very words. It was in the early days, so it didn't have much in other than the main sprite. But he had put in the routines to hide the enemy sprites when they were out of sight. That idea came from a game he had written on an IBM monitor called 'Assassin', where you creep through rooms and try and shoot at each other. He said it used to work so well because you never knew whether someone was there, giving you a real feeling of suspense.[*] So in *Paradroid* the sprites looked as though they were just disappearing and appearing and they really couldn't understand the concept whatsoever. But when we sent the pre-production copy, Gordon quickly changed his mind and rang up and said he'd been playing all afternoon.

Andrew loved doing the diary for *Zzap!*, and he used to write it up at the end of each day on an A4 pad, so that he could remember the little things, like breaking his ruler. If you read them now, the style was slightly different in the first ones because he would type them all in a word processor once a month and they went off to Andrew Hewson, who edited them because he didn't like Andrew's style and made them a little bit more comedy. Like, the bit about the ruler breaking, with the bit flying past my head, happened, but Andrew Hewson added that it nearly hit the cat, which was totally imaginary.

← 246

## Andrew Braybrook

The diary came out of a trip I made to *Zzap!64*'s office in Ludlow with *Gribbly's Day Out*. They wanted to do the diary of a game being written, and I enjoy writing, we thought it would be fun. The games were taking four or five months to write, so that seemed like a short enough series not to get boring or be too slow. The first part got edited to 'make it funnier', which didn't please me much, but the rest of the parts went straight to the magazine and were unedited. I was quite happy to do that, it only took a few minutes every evening to take some notes.

I seem to remember the game took about three months, and we had this deadline, because Hewson wanted to publish it the week that the last diary entry was in *Zzap!64*. It was the first time we had a strict schedule, and it was getting a bit nerve-wracking at the end. I went off on a summer holiday for two weeks and left Andrew at it. He was programming through the night to get the game back on track, and it was mostly finished by the time I came back. He was still changing things, like the graphic look changed at least once for the initial screenshots, and then he came up with the Heavy Metal version after we'd sent the master to Hewson. We wanted them to change to it, but Hewson said, 'Oh no! We will call that version "Paradroid Plus" or something!' He liked that idea because he'd seen it happen with things like when you buy the 16K version of a game and immediately the 48K one comes out.

[*] Written in COBOL for a mainframe system at his former job. 'Assassin' was a multiplayer game set in a multi-level dungeon.

When it was done we had a phone call with, I think it was either Julian Rignall or Gary Penn at *Zzap!64* to tell us what they thought about the game, and they admitted that they had been very worried, because of all the publicity of the diary and what if it was a dog of a game? It would really make them look silly. But they also had a reputation for being brutally honest, so if the game hadn't met the hype they would have torn it to shreds. We kind of knew that was going to happen, but when we got the phone call it was a relief. 'We love it! Julian loves it!' Julian especially loved the transfer game and learned how to master it and could do it better than Andrew. He used to reserve all his shots, then pressed the fire button faster than anyone else I had seen, this sort of thing like a machine gun effect, winning the transfer game at the last possible moment, which was brilliant.

←192

## Peter Stone and Richard Leinfellner

256→

PS *The Evil Dead* was Palace Video's big product and we had the rights, so we thought, why not?

RL We thought that because we had the video rights, we also had the videogame rights. We went to your place in Shepherd's Bush and had to watch the video. I hate horror films, so I was basically fast-forwarding the whole film, eating copious amounts of pizza and drinking beer, and thinking how we could make a game. I think it literally had one level, it was very, very basic, but it was our first professional programming job, and I learned a stack of stuff. It was a pretty awful game. In games, generally speaking, you take inspiration from a control method, or you get inspired by a storyline, but with *The Evil Dead* we didn't actually know what game we wanted to make. We just knew we wanted to make a game, It wasn't like I was a big fan of the movie, quite frankly. Pete also had the brilliant idea of making me the star of the game – he would say a rock star – because at that point we didn't quite realise it's not the same as being in Wham! or something. So my photograph was on the back cover of *The Evil Dead*.

PS You must be embarrassed about that now!

RL I was delivering the master tape to the replicators, and on the way back I got knocked of my motorbike by a van on the Euston

Road. Pete managed to spin that into a PR story about the curse of *The Evil Dead*, you know, 'The lead programmer gets killed on the way to deliver the master tapes!'

What Richard is saying is that we managed to get a fair few column inches out of the fact that we were making this game, but the reviews were terrible, and we didn't sell many. I think at that point we knew where we had gone wrong. We needed better graphics and better gameplay, and we started looking around for an artist. We put an ad in a weekly for the advertising industry called *Campaign*, because I noticed if you wanted graphic artists that's where you advertised. One of the people who came forward was a guy called Steve Brown, who became very important to the next phase of Palace Software. He was a comic artist and he didn't really know too much about computer games at that point. We got on well with him and he started to look at games and figure out how to make a good one, and from that came *Cauldron*.

We used to have quite a few meetings down the pub.

The pub was very important to Palace Software.

In fact, they should have a plaque in that pub, because I think we funded it. Steve was a very good illustrator and he really understood how you position things for marketing. I gave him a fast-forward through the game industry and we played things like *Manic Miner*, and Steve was going, 'Well, I like these bits in *Manic Miner*, but I also like these bits in *Scramble*, and I really wish it was possible to do both genres in one game.' I said there was no technical reason why you can't. People choose not to because you have to write two game engines, one for sideways scrolling and one for platforming, but we could write both engines. That's what started *Cauldron* off, and very early on, Steve wanted the witch, the main character in the game, to be the same character that's on the box.

Yeah, the box artwork came at an early stage.

I think he had the box before we had the game design.

During the making of *Cauldron*, we were able to go out and PR the making of the game. I don't think that really happened with other companies.

RL We would have journalists coming in throughout to give us feedback and to go down the pub with us, and that was invaluable. We kind of knew the game would be successful and get good reviews, because they liked it all the way through development. It wasn't like we were buying the reviews, but it was just getting feedback from people.

PS Yeah, by then, computer game magazines like *Crash* and *Zzap!64* were becoming very important. Those for us were the key magazines. We were talking to the journalists about their front covers, and how we would get on to them.

RL We did things like development diaries, you know, they would come in for the day, we would give them artwork and sketches, and we made them very much part of the development process. I think that's a little bit like the way the music business would deal with PR. Certainly, Steve loved it, because he was a very visual communicator and we always had bits of artwork knocking around.

PS With the confidence of knowing that *Cauldron* was looking good and was likely to be a good seller, we started to become more confident and we started to go overseas to do distribution deals in France, Germany, Spain and other countries, and also we started to do localised versions.

←235

## Rob Hubbard

350→

Around the time of *Monty on the Run*,[x] magazines like *Zzap!64*, *Commodore User* and *Computer and Video Games* started to talk about the music and sound, and started mentioning people's names. I remember one strange day when I went into WHSmith to pay a gas bill, and a kid says, 'Oh you're Rob Hubbard, the guy who does the music!' That was, you know, a very strange event.

But I really didn't get very much attention, to be honest. Strange things did happen, because my phone number got out to a few people, so I used to get phone calls during the night from Japan and the States, but I really didn't get out very much because there was such a lot of work coming in. For somebody who was working as a musician and not really getting a lot of work, if work starts coming in all of a sudden, you don't say no. So I was just working every hour, basically.

[x] Peter Harrap's 1985 puzzle platformer for Gremlin Graphics, featuring a mole on the run for his involvement in the miners' strike.

I loved the shows, because you had a fantastic connection with your audience, and we were also really interested in the people who made the games, and in how they made them. We were interested in the musicians, for example, and no one else gave a shit about musicians. We were the only magazine who cared.

Then you have Ollie Frey doing his fantastic comic book artwork on the front, which resonates brilliantly with an audience of mainly young males, and inside they realise that there is this richness of culture that they will not get anywhere else, and this authoritative opinion driving it forwards from people who clearly know their stuff, who can play games. I mean, that's potent stuff.

We clearly inspired a lot of the other publishers, like Emap, who seemed to be a bit slower to get behind us. When I went to work there they felt very behind, and they were trying to understand what made things work, and then when I moved from Emap to Future it was the same sort of thing. 'How are you doing this stuff? How does this work? Why is this resonating so much?' I don't know, I think it was just caring. So if you cared about what you were interested in, finding out about new games you were interested in, I think that enthusiasm feeds through.

The idea that we were treated more like celebrities than the people who made the games occurred fairly early on, in the first year of *Zzap!* There was lots of autograph signing, which in itself was very unusual, and it wasn't happening with anyone else at the time, not *Crash* or any of the other magazines. You had these guys living, from a hardcore gamer's point of view, the dream, getting to play all this stuff and meeting the people who made it.

We got fantastic things, like people writing to us and sending pictures and poems they had written about you. I used to get lots of hate mail because I was the surly one, which I really liked, because I like attention. Then I went to the shows and people were like, 'I thought you were going to be really horrible, but you're actually all right!'

I read game magazines like *Crash* and *Sinclair User* avidly, and I think they were very influential, because they were the glue that drew everything together into a gaming culture. To some extent I think they also tried to steer that culture a little bit. I took a lot of interest in what *Crash* were writing about; they were trying to create a sense of a computer games culture, which was helped by artwork like Oliver Frey's. It was almost a counter-culture, I guess. It wasn't a mainstream thing; it was like a special kind of club that you felt part of.

## Oliver Frey

←238

I think art was terribly important to the burgeoning videogame industry, because the actual pixels and the moving sprites didn't live up to whatever the games' titles were at all. You needed art to create the make-believe. You had to get the atmosphere across, so in the player's mind the little blob over there was actually Indiana Jones or whatever. My entire work with *Crash* and with computer game covers was to create the world for the gamer to imagine.

## Martin Kenwright

←39 280→

I think one of the biggest drivers of the explosion of games was the magazines. It was the fantasy artwork, the escapism. They were sending you to another world: you could in a couple of hours be fighting off alien hordes, or doing whatever.

The early computer magazines were quite dull, unless you were just interested in the hardware. They had a general trade magazine design, so one slabby photo and a boring layout, which definitely didn't suit any notion of a game magazine at all. We knew that it was teenage boys who came to buy games in person, but otherwise we just had a general feel that the magazine should appeal to teen boys. I had been involved in various comics before that as a professional illustrator, so I had all sorts of ready-made notions of what the magazine ought to be, but beyond that it was just about gut feel. I mean, you knew it wasn't going to be little girls who were reading it, or even middle-aged men or women.

So when it came to *Crash*, it was especially the cover that would make the magazine completely different to the existing ones. We were supposed to be about entertainment and the cover had to reflect that. We had to attract the readership that we wanted, and the only way to do that was to be as dramatic, in the sense of being as realistic, as possible.

Roger Kean suggested various things for the first cover, but we wanted it to be simple and straight-hitting. I suppose it hadn't been that long since *Alien* and all sorts of other science fiction, and we had the notion of combining, somehow, computer games with that image, so you see *Space Invaders* reflected in the eyes of the alien. I always thought it was a little joke that the alien was actually playing the game as reflected in its mask.

After one magazine was finished, the next one would have to be done within four weeks, but we usually didn't know what game we might want to feature on the front cover, so people would dither until we finally decided, and therefore I usually ended up having about three or four days to actually produce the picture.

The covers were hand-painted, one way or the other. I used an airbrush for backgrounds and sometimes for little highlights, but it usually started off with me doing a lot of little pencil drawings, which no one else could really understand, and then I picked the one that seemed to have the right dynamic. Then I would work it up bigger, and in the end I would do it full-size, and start inking the outline spray, the background, and then ink in the rest with a paintbrush until it was finished, or I was told that it had better be finished in time for the deadline.

Roger was quite insistent that we should bring in some form of wit or little quirk in the picture, like there was a Sherlock Holmes one where he's looking through the lens and the text is reversed so the reader had to read it backwards. We also tried to combine the Spectrum stripes or the keyboard, because we were a Sinclair Spectrum magazine, and that was what we were advertising. Later on, it became more game-specific and it became more difficult to be really witty about them, but we tried.

## Chris Anderson

A few months after launching *Zzap!64*, Newsfield moved the editorial office to Ludlow, a couple of hundred miles from the home town where I launched it. I think they liked the magazine and the team I had recruited, but I couldn't do that move for various personal reasons. So I had to figure out what to do, and happily it was the perfect time and place to start a publishing company. Specialist magazines back then were the internet of their day and they were expanding fast in terms of the number of people getting passionate about all manner of hobbyist niches.

What was also amazing about that time was that the technology of magazine publishing was changing. For the first time you didn't have to create a magazine as part of a huge company, because you could, for example, typeset on a computer. So it was possible for a small startup company like Newsfield or

Future Publishing, which followed a few months later, to launch a magazine pretty much from a living room. That hadn't been possible before.

So I hired a graphic designer right out of college to lay out a magazine, did deals with a printer and a national distributor and within three months of leaving Newsfield the first issue of *Amstrad Action* hit the newsstands. I mean, that was a really special time back then, and kind of amazing to be able to launch quickly. I only raised £165,000 or so.

There was a constant stream of new machines coming on the market, which were begging for a magazine to be published for them. This niche computer, the Amstrad CPC, didn't really have a game magazine, and off we went. It was an amazing and stressful time, and the first issue was truly atrocious but what it had was passion.

We had no real information on how well the first issue of *Amstrad Action* had done, and I guess four days after it hit the shelves I cycled into the office and the postman came in with this sack of mail. I had never seen anything like it, and these envelopes basically contained lots of letters saying how excited they were to see the new magazine and subscription cheques. Suddenly we were sitting there with a pile of cheques amounting to £3,000 or £4,000, and already our debt seemed less terrifying. That was an amazing moment.

So for issue three of *Amstrad Action* we were wrestling with how to make the magazine better. Right at the end of my time at *Personal Computer Games*, just on the last issue, I tried as an experiment putting a cassette tape on the front with demos from 10 different publishers. It was pretty much a nightmare to put together, and we got right to publication date and the publisher said we couldn't afford to do it, and I was not happy, but my secretary had the insight of raising the cover price for the issue. If you're adding a cassette tape, there is huge value to that, so we went back to the publisher and said, 'Look, we can do this if we add 50p on the cover price.' It didn't save the magazine, but I found out three months later that the issue had sold double any other issue. It was a massive hit. In a way, it was obvious. I mean, people buy computers to run software.

So for *Amstrad Action* I was able to strike a deal with Ocean to give us some demo software that they weren't planning to publish. We put it on the cover, raised the cover price, and, yes, double the sales. I think without that, Future Publishing would probably have been dead at birth, because the early issues had not sold great. The combination of that and discovering a few things about how to actually run a magazine without it looking like complete crap turned around *Amstrad Action*, and it got us thinking so that with each Future magazine we thought about cover mounts.

## Peter Stone and
## Richard Leinfellner

RL Steve had already started thinking about *Barbarian* when we were finishing *Cauldron* and because we now had staff, Steve and I could hand stuff over to them so we could be pre-prodding the next game while people were finishing the current one.

PS The other companies, like Ocean and Imagine, were churning out games, and there was us putting out one or two a year, so it seemed natural to increase our output. *Barbarian* was very much Steve's idea, and he saw it as a complete concept from the beginning, imagining the gameplay, how it looked, the packaging, the advertising, the whole PR campaign.

RL A couple of things happened around the same time, and one of them was a film called *Red Sonja* came out, with a barbarian played by Arnold Schwarzenegger with a damsel in distress, and that inspired Steve. The other thing was a whole host of fighting games, like *Yie Ar Kung-Fu*, came out. We were down the pub and Steve would just go, 'You know these fighting games? They're okay, but the characters are too small. I really want a game with huge, huge characters, like the whole screen.'
   I like challenges and I said, 'Well, there's no reason you can't have bigger sprites. You multiplex them, and so we came up with a multiplex routine and a multiplexing sprite editor.× I mean, the sprites really were huge for those days. The other thing Steve really wanted was really fluid movement, so we started experimenting with rotoscoping, filming people doing things and essentially transferring that to the sprite editor.
   There were quite a few technical challenges, but it really came down to making those characters come alive on screen. But, I tell you one thing, with that game, we knew almost from the first pixel being drawn, that it would be successful, because it just ticked all the boxes, and we had people come and look at stuff in production and they were just drooling.

× A technique by which more sprites can appear to he be displayed on screen than the hardware technically allows.

So, Steve was an avid reader of *The Sun* and he was a big fan of Maria Whittaker. It's almost like he made the game to put her on the front cover. There was never any doubt in my mind that he had thought of that from day one. In terms of the poster, it was kind of, 'Why wouldn't we have something that every little boy would put up in their bedroom?'

PS I don't think we'd ever even considered Schwarzenegger, because he was way beyond our budget.

RL And to be honest, being really tight about it, it wasn't necessary. It really wasn't. I don't think it would have really added that much, because, don't forget, he wasn't a big star then. Actually, one of the Palace videos we did was *Pumping Iron*, and *Red Sonja* was really his first big film, before *The Terminator*.

One thing, though, we never saw marketing as a cynical thing, and I don't think we fanned the flames up. What's kind of funny is when you look at it today and it is just beyond tame. That game today would probably be a U certificate, right? The stuff we had about it having blood squirting out and stuff like that, it was just a lot of rubbish about nothing, but I think it honestly doubled or trebled our sales.

PS Boots were one of the biggest game sellers in this country, and I remember having a big argument with them about the cover, because they didn't want Maria Whittaker on the cover. In the end we had to produce a separate box just for Boots, without Maria Whittaker on it.

RL The game also got banned in Germany. We got called to this court case there, and one of the funny things was that you have to show the judge what the problem is, and nobody on the prosecution team could play the game well enough to do the head chopping action, so the case got thrown out and we got another six weeks of selling the game. We went in with an ad campaign basically saying, 'Buy it before it's banned!' because we knew we would get banned the next time, and we sold stack-loads of games. Then the prosecution got a kiddy who could play the game, so we got banned, and all we did was turn the blood green and we got unbanned. Mary Whitehouse, of course, had an opinion, even though she'd never seen the game, so she had this big article about how we were corrupting kids. You could argue we were milking it a bit.

But, actually, we had less than you would have got for spending 10p on *The Sun*. When Steve phoned Maria Whittaker's agent, who was her dad, and said we would like her to be in our game, he was really perplexed and thought it was something really dodgy, so they met up. Steve probably tells this better, but the conversation was along the lines of, 'So you want to keep her bra on? Really?' And Steve goes, 'Yeah, this is for a kids' game, so we want the bra kept on.'

Steve actually made her breast plates out of little ashtrays, which apparently kept pinging off, for some reason. It was really quite tame in many ways, you know, it wasn't really rock 'n' roll, but we had a laugh.

# Part 6

# The Coming of 16-bit

The Brits were really metal-bashing, you know, getting every last ounce of power out of the old machines, and the Americans, when 16-bit came along, just stole the show. Companies like Electronic Arts really cleaned up because we were so behind the curve.

So we had started this company called Taurus Impex, [*] shipping baked beans to the Middle East, and I had been faffing around with a few hobbies at home, you know, still keeping my finger in making computer games, but not really doing anything for anybody else. The company hadn't been going very long when the phone rang and it was Commodore. They said, 'Oh, we've heard of your company Torus, and we would love to get your product on to our machine. We will send a car down to pick you up and bring you to our office. We will go out to lunch and show you this new machine we are going to release called the Amiga.'

At the time we were working on the Commodore 64 and the Spectrum and then you heard about these 16-bit machines coming out in the next year or so. I'm like, 'I want to do that. I want to be one of the top people doing that.'

I said, 'Fantastic!' What geek wouldn't? And that's exactly what happened. We had this limo pick us up, and we went round this huge office-cum-warehouse building, and they treated us like kings, really. They said, 'Right, you can have six machines and we'll support you when your products are ready. You will have a stand at shows to show them off.'

It all seemed like a dream. We were nobody. Quite how they thought that our baked beans would be of any use to them, I don't know! But of course I bluffed it, and kept saying, 'Oh yes,' but what became obvious is that they had got the wrong Taurus. There was another Torus company, not spelt like the star sign, and they thought they were talking to that Torus, not us. So I completely blagged it and managed to get to the end of the day without talking about any product at all. Sure enough, machines arrived, six of these Amigas sitting in the office. What to do with them?

Commodore at that time really wanted business applications, so I started writing a little database called Acquisition. Commodore soon realised they had sent the stuff to the wrong place, but they quite liked Acquisition so we finished it. But as we did so, it became absolutely obvious that the Amiga wasn't going to be a business machine, it was going to be a games machine. That's when I bumped into a friend of mine, and he said, 'Oh, you know a bit about the Amiga. Could you convert this game called

[*] Taurus Impex was later renamed Bullfrog Productions, which Molyneux founded with Les Edgar.

*Druid II*[*] from the Commodore 64 to the Amiga?' That's when I was introduced to my first publisher, Firebird. They gave us the princely sum of £4000 to do the conversion, which was a hell of a lot of money for me in those days.

In the process of doing the conversion I learned about the Amiga and more about writing computer games that looked good, with proper frame rates, and then I went off to do this little shoot 'em up called *Fusion*. *Fusion*[*] was a puzzle shoot 'em up, so you had to solve puzzles and shoot things. I can't remember why we did that particular game. I don't remember it being a particular passion.

*  Released in 1987 and developed by Electralyte, *Druid II: Enlightenment* was a gauntlet-style action adventure. Its original graphics were created by Dene Carter, who would later go on to join Bullfrog.
*  Released in 1988 and written by Molyneux with Glenn Corpes creating its art.

## Jeff Minter

I heard of the Amiga and it sounded fantastic, but Commodore had this weird attitude at the time that it was very definitely not a games machine. It was a business machine, and so when they started demoing it and offering development units they left out a lot of the games people. To us it was a bit annoying, because we'd made a lot of Commodore's success with the Commodore 64, and at the same time Atari, who were coming out with the Atari ST, were extremely accommodating. They were ringing me up and were like, 'Jeff, do you want to come and see the ST? Jeff, do you want one? How can we help you get developing?'

So Atari basically threw the ST at me and Commodore didn't really want to know, so for a good year or so I was very much converted to the Atari folk, and it was only later on that Commodore realised they'd made a bit of a mistake when the ST took off big time. People were buying the ST and playing games with it, even though the Amiga was a better machine. Then they realised and came out with the Amiga 500, which was much more of a games-oriented version of the Amiga, and then finally they started to catch up.

It was a little daunting at first to develop games on 16-bit, but I remember going up to London and buying a 68000 assembler manual, reading it, and thinking it actually sounded pretty good; let's just get all the right tools. Once you'd got it going it wasn't that bad, and it was actually a bit more versatile than the 8-bit machines. You weren't limited to a fixed number of sprites, you could implement software sprites, you could have a higher resolution.

But it wasn't all gravy. You couldn't scroll quite as easily and it wasn't quite as easy to set up, but at the end of the day the ST was a much more versatile system than the 64, and also you had a lot more memory and disks you could put games on, so you didn't feel so constrained as you were with only 64K and a tape deck. I enjoyed the increasing complexity of the console hardware. I did some prototype work on the Atari Panther,[*] which I really enjoyed. I worked on the prototype Atari Jaguar.[x] I just really liked messing about with new chips. To me that appealed to the nerd, the programmer in me who just liked to play with cutting-edge new stuff, and some of the best new stuff that was happening in terms of microprocessors was being thrown at games back then, so it was interesting.

[*] A 32-bit console on which work began in 1988 but was abandoned in favour of focusing on the 64-bit Atari Jaguar.
[x] Released in 1993, the Jaguar failed commercially and marked the end for Atari in the home console market.

←96

## Mo Warden

278→

Obviously, I was working on my own kit at home, and I realised that if I had an Atari ST, which was the new thing everybody wanted, I could get some proper work and maybe start to make some money. So I approached my father-in-law. It was a lot of money, about a grand, to buy an ST with a colour monitor – of course it had to be because of the graphics – and he very generously agreed to buy me the equipment and set me up.

New kit was starting to come in at an amazing speed, and if you didn't keep up with it you very quickly got left behind. Obviously, people were buying the games for the new hardware as it was launched, so you had to be there, producing the stuff before the demand arrived. So I had my eyes on the ST, I mean, I wanted to just get hold of it and play with it but I knew it would be very useful in developing my career as well. I got straight into the ST and found it very easy. I got some software with it, like Deluxe Paint. I still have the box on the shelf.

←247

## Steve Turner

271→

After we made *Uridium*[*] there was news of new machines on the block, which looked like they were going to blow away the Commodore 64 and Spectrum. Andrew wanted to program the Amiga in particular, but I had a chat with Hewson who said it wasn't going

[*] A shooter by Andrew Braybrook for the Commodore 64, notable for its smooth scrolling.

to sell. It was a problem, because there were so many machines, and backing the wrong one would be just disastrous. But we could see that the magazines were devoting more and more space to these machines, and the reviews of the 8-bit games were starting to pooh-pooh what looked like really good games, saying the graphics weren't brilliant any more. Yet they were brilliant for the Spectrum and the Commodore 64.

So we were seeing the writing on the wall for 8-bit games, and we thought we had to move on, but how do you pick the right machine? I think there were three contenders: the Atari ST, the Commodore Amiga and the Sinclair QL. I can't remember what happened to the Sinclair. I think they had technical problems, and it never sold. But it was obvious that it was a generational leap like we hadn't seen before, and it was going to change the industry. Sales started to suffer, and the last games that we did with Hewson were selling well, but weren't selling as well as before. We could see the industry tailing off, even though we were making more money than before.

## Mike Montgomery

The Bitmaps were started between me, Eric Matthews and Steve Kelly. We all got together at a company called Laser Genius, so it was almost like friends saying, 'We have a good idea for a game – let's go and do it!' Which we did. When we started, the ST had just come out and the Amiga had either come out or was very close, and we started working with the ST because we thought the 8-bit machines weren't powerful enough.

We needed finance, because we were three guys with not much money. So we decided to raise funds through the banks. What a mistake, what a mistake. We spent weeks and weeks and weeks going to bank managers asking for unsecured loans of £25,000, but everyone said, 'We don't understand what your business is!' Eventually we managed to get a bank that said if we could get a contract for an advance of £25,000 they would lend us the money. So we managed to do a deal with Mastertronic for £25,000 as an advance. Got the contract, went to the bank manager, who says, 'Fantastic, well done, boys! We must put it before our legal team.' So the contract went through the legal team and it came back and they said, 'We're sorry, we cannot loan you the money.' We said, 'Why? We've done everything that you said!' They turned around and said, 'We don't understand the industry.' Especially in the early '90s, finance was a big problem for game companies, particularly independent game companies. It was a time that the banks actually started to cut down on loans.

Now, of course, we were competing against the Americans and the Japanese. At that time it was very hard, because they had a lot of financial backing by their governments, which we didn't get at all. So this is in the '90s when independent developers began to fall beside the road because there wasn't the finance out there to actually write creative, innovative, new IP games. All these American publishers in particular, and a few English publishers, decided they didn't want new games, they wanted something they could sell like a box of cornflakes.

Eventually we got a loan, so we were up and running; we could leave the jobs we were doing and actually start working on *Xenon*. Steve Kelly, my partner, was working on the ST version and I was working on the Amiga version.

We took it into Mastertronic for its beta milestone, and they put the Amiga version on and I went, 'Wow, all the colours aren't right.' They went, 'What do you mean?' I said, 'Well, I have only got a black and white telly. This is the first time I have seen it in colour.' They went, 'You're joking! Why haven't you got a colour telly?' and I said, 'Because I can't afford it.' They sent me one the next day. That was pretty cool of them.

Finishing *Xenon* was actually quite hard work. We got to the point that, like any game, you have got to finish it, but we wanted to make it the best, so we probably overran a little bit. But we also started working on our own PR for the game as well as the publisher doing it. It worked out quite well because it was virtually an overnight success, it went into the charts at number one and sold extremely well. The ST was a bit of a problem, though, because the pirates had got hold of it and we lost quite a lot of sales, but it was great to see it on the shelves. It was so exciting. We got £25,000 from *Xenon* and we made a profit on that. Probably half went on development, so as an independent developer, we didn't have these millions. We were on very low budgets.

## Julian Gollop

← 252     353 →

*Laser Squad* did pretty well, and we stuck with the same publisher, Blade Software, for *Lords of Chaos*, which was a very big project for us, because we had three 8-bit formats, two 16-bit formats, plus disk and tape versions for each. Actually, we also gave the 16-bit version different game levels as well as different graphics.*

*Lords of Chaos* is a kind of sequel to the original *Chaos*, but I wanted to set it much more firmly in an RPG framework. So you

* The 16-bit versions were released in 1991, a year later than the 8-bit versions.

would have multiple adventures or missions and you would carry the same character forward from one mission to the next. It was a little bit difficult on the Spectrum because you had to load and save your character separately on tape, and then you had to load up the next mission, but you could configure your wizard, choosing your spells and levelling him up through experience points. It was going back to my influences from *Dungeons & Dragons* and an attempt to create a tactical RPG-style game, but with the same theme of *Chaos*.

I was very pleased with it as a technical achievement on the Spectrum. It did have its problems, for sure. It took quite a long time to play; I remember multiplayer games with up to four people would take hours, but it was a really deep game. Each creature had an inventory and could pick things up and carry them around; you could make potions from ingredients you found on the maps, and the game had a number of interesting random elements, like deployment of the objects and items that you could find, so there was a big exploration element. For an 8-bit game it was very ambitious, and it certainly had a particular audience of people who like role-playing games.

Myself and my brother were doing the bulk of the coding. We hired a third programmer for a while, but it was clearly getting a bit much for us. The Amiga version of *Lords of Chaos* was actually converted by Krisalis Software, * so we only did the ST version as well as all the 8-bit versions. But it was getting a bit silly, so we were looking to find some other way to develop games, and that's how we ended up looking towards the PC, rather than the Amiga. The thing that really helped us was the release by MicroProse of *Railroad Tycoon*, one of Sid Meier's first games on the PC, so we realised that, at least in the US, PC was going to be a big games machine, especially for strategy games. We wanted to do big strategy games, like Sid Meier was doing.

* Based in Rotherham, Krisalis specialised in porting games.

David Darling

As programmers, we were aware of the 16-bit machines like the Commodore Amiga and the Atari ST, because you are always looking for the next machine to work on, because it's got more memory or a faster processor. So when the Commodore Amiga came out it had just the most amazing graphics you had ever seen. It was a machine that we really wanted to work on.

It was like stepping stones across a pond, so you would step from machine to machine, and get your head around them from a technology point of view, and the marketing people had to understand who we were going to market them to. We had the problem that we couldn't really release games at £1.99 any more, so we had to do them at maybe £4.99, because they were on disk instead of tape.

Development resourcing on the 16-bit machines increased, but to be honest it wasn't a quantum increase. They had much higher resolution graphics so you needed better artwork, and you needed more artists. We got a guy called John Jones-Steele to convert *BMX Simulator* from the Commodore 64 to the Amiga, but it was just the same game with better graphics and sound effects. From the Mega Drive to the PlayStation, that was the bigger change because the PlayStation was the first 3D machine.

← 241 Oliver twins 328 →

AO We spent a few years working with Codemasters on the Spectrum and working out how to get our games across the different 8-bit computers. But there was the threat that everyone would move on. When the ST and Amiga came out, some of our games got converted but we weren't making them. We're not great artists, as our graphics may show, and it was very impressive what you could do on the Atari ST and the Amiga, and it slightly worried us. But we were making quite a lot of money and were very happy that we had an audience that followed us. If we left the Spectrum we'd leave our audience behind, but obviously people were moving on, and it looked quite difficult.

← 267 Steve Turner 325 →

Game prices went up from about £4 to £9.99, and when it went above £10 I remember thinking people weren't going to buy them. You used to hear of games being pirated, and I used to think, 'Well, no wonder. That's just too much for kids to pay for.' The mark-up from what a publisher paid was alarming; there seemed to be more people on the chain all of a sudden. A publisher didn't sell into a shop, it sold to a wholesaler, who sold into the shop. Everyone down the line had to have a bit of the cut, and the downside was the programmer still got about the same as when the games were selling for half the price, and games weren't selling as many. It looked as though sales could tail off altogether. We'd seen machines disappear almost overnight with the Dragon, so we were very keen on moving on to newer machines.

Hewson saw the market going a different way, though. A big thing happened with the budget industry: because the games had gone up in price, budget games at £1.50 or £1.99 suddenly sold in huge numbers again. We asked Hewson how much we would get, and he said, 'About 10p a copy, but I will be selling hundreds of thousands of them.' But if you sold 50,000 at 10p a copy I was going to make £5,000, so I could only afford to work for a little while on a game like that. It seemed to be a formula that wasn't working, and we were starting to drift apart in our philosophies of how we saw the industry going.

Hewson was good at squeezing the last bit out of the 8-bit games, but more and more he was reselling old products, re-badging our old games. We had *Uridium* with extra shit levels, he packaged *Avalon* and *Dragontorc* in a double pack. But looking at the figures, less and less was coming back. So the end was nigh.

One day we had a phone call saying, 'Look, I don't know if you know this but the two games that you're writing at the moment, Hewson's not going to publish them. He's going to sub-license them to another publisher.' That would mean we only got a fraction of the royalty, because he would get a royalty and we would get a percentage of a percentage. We thought, 'Well, he can't do that.' This person also said he was leaving the company, that Hewson was going under, and this company he was going to is willing to speak to us.

So we went up to London and Telecomsoft said they would publish our games and sort out any trouble we might have with Hewson. We said, 'Well, we haven't got a contract for these games.' In fact, the only contract I ever had was for my first game, and then we kind of just used to give Hewson a game and he used to publish it. So the publisher said, 'It's all right, there will be no trouble, and we'll give you an advance if you sign a contract to us, and we've got a legal fund that will protect you.'

It all seemed like good news to us, so we thought we were out of the fire at last, but unfortunately Hewson did contest the games, saying he had already paid money for the start off and publishing, which was tantamount to a contract. So we had both publishers saying that they were going to publish the games we were working on, *Ranarama* and *Alleykat*. They started a court action and got an injunction which at first stopped anyone from publishing them, which was a disaster for us.

## Archer Maclean

I started thinking 16-bit in around 1985. *Dropzone* had been selling well for maybe six months and I remember getting a call from
U.S. Gold saying, 'Are you going to do anything for Atari ST?' I
got hold of one and played around with it for a month or so and
rang back, and said, 'You know, I could make your socks fall off
with this!' Geoff Brown* turned around and said, 'Well, make my
socks fall off, then.'

So I started doing demo work for a 16-bit 'Dropzone 2', which
never actually saw the light of day, and then obviously *IK+* was a
conversion from the 64, although it was pretty much a re-write to
be honest, because I started throwing an awful lot more into the
game. That would have been late '87, early '88.

The Amiga had this blitter chip, which is one of a number of custom chips that sit alongside the main microprocessor to take away
some of the overheads doing things like clearing the screen and
chunks of memory, doing DMA requirements, sound effects and
various other things. They basically enhanced the game content
and made it smoother, faster, whatever.* But I always had to bear
in mind that the Atari ST had to run this stuff as well, so despite
how fancy the Amiga was I basically made everything work on the
ST and ported it to the Amiga, occasionally adding a few extra
features. I mean, 8-bit sounds were definitely better than 4-bit.

× Head of U.S. Gold.
• The Amiga was was the first commercial computer to feature a dedicated blitter chip.

## Fred Gray

Musically, the 16-bit machines, well, the Amiga, presented huge
possibilities, but unfortunately I was working on the ST and the
programmers weren't willing to co-operate with me to try to produce something better on the Amiga. So a lot of the Amiga games
I did sounded basically like an ST, but the Amiga had the possibility
of sounding like a film score because it had sampling. So really it
was a bit frustrating for me.

The other thing was that as a programmer I found the 16-bit
machines so confusing because they had such huge instruction
sets. I was never quite sure whether I should use this or this to
do a certain routine, and once I had written the software for the
Atari I got stuck in a sort of rut. I wasn't quite happy with that time,
to be honest. If you were working in-house you probably had a

better chance of creating really good drivers and getting really good sounds and emulating other machines. The problem was that the ST and Amiga were vastly different: the Amiga had amazing graphics and amazing sound, whereas the ST was a very poor relation. It was a very frustrating time for musicians, and probably for coders as well.

It wasn't that we weren't capable, or that we couldn't have got an amazing sound out of the Amiga, it was just that constantly converting things was getting to be a bit of a chore, and you never can get the same sounds on both machines. I mean, Martin was an absolute perfectionist when he came to writing for the SID chip, and I think he would have expected the same sort of perfection on the other machines, but it would've have been so time-consuming.

## Gary Penn

When 16-bit came in, it wasn't actually that bad of a transition. The 8-bit stuff was very direct, and you could make things happen pretty quickly, and 16-bit was kind of more of the same, but slightly bigger. The worst shift was definitely 3D, which was amazingly hard. I mean, it destroyed developers, a lot of the British teams. They suddenly had to go from playing in small bands, almost, then suddenly they needed these big teams, and this American mentality starts pushing its way through, of everything having to be bigger. 3D is 10 times the work of producing something in 2D, so it was worse.

The games did take longer to build on 16-bit, without a doubt, and you did lose some of that experimental immediacy, but I think you also gained from the power, so you had something like *Populous* coming out which probably never could have existed on 8-bit. But equally, it's easy to overlook the fact that there were so many innovative experiments on 8-bit.

So I think the 16-bit change was a positive one, but some of the culture got lost. It could have been that consoles were starting to come through, and the kind of person who plays a console isn't necessarily the same kind of person who plays on a computer. They aren't the kind of person who likes to feel they can make a difference to what they're playing with.

# Peter Stone and
# Richard Leinfellner

PS Even the jump from 8-bit to 16-bit, from Commodore 64 to Amiga, was quite a big leap. You saw other companies coming along, like Cinemaware˟ in the States, who were coming up with games you thought, 'Wow, that's amazing.' Psygnosis, too, and they were doing some good things, in terms of graphics, at least.

RL But there was a really interesting dynamic which I think hobbled the British industry in that transition. The US had already moved over to C,˟ everything was being programmed in it a long time before because the PC and Apple II were large machines and you used a compiler for them rather than assembler. But in the UK everything was still in machine code and everyone was doing everything in assembly language. But with 16-bit you can't do that, and really you have to write a graphics operating system and go through layers of code.

The Americans were several years ahead of the Brits in that. The Brits were really metal-bashing, you know, getting every last ounce of power out of the old machines, and Americans, when 16-bit came along, just stole the show. Companies like Electronic Arts really cleaned up because we were so behind the curve. When it came to big games, as a country we just weren't ready for it.

It was like a perfect storm: everything was bigger, but things like graphics don't scale gracefully. You suddenly make the background look better, and then you realise that the animation is not very smooth, so you make animation better, and then you realise the physics are not working, so you fix it and now the audio is a bit crap.

˟ Maker of *Defender of the Crown*, which was released in 1986.
˟ The programming language.

# Martin Galway

In October of '87 I resigned from Ocean, even though I had a great potential for making lots of money there. It was the stupidest thing I ever did, but I did have another freelance game in the offering in the US, to do *Times of Lore*˟ for Origin Systems, but I kept in touch with Sensible Software the whole time. They were my bud-

˟ An action-RPG designed by Chris Roberts and released in 1988.

dies, I was always calling them up to see how they were doing and what they were working on next, to see if I could do the music for it.

I came back to England in April of '88 and they were doing a soccer game, which became *MicroProse Soccer*. At the time they had no publisher and they were talking to the co-owner of *Commodore Computing International*, Ben Lewis, who was trying to position himself as like an agent or a producer. He would own part of the IP and get a slice of the royalties, but he would help them get a much better deal than they were getting from Ocean, because they didn't make a lot of money from *Parallax* or *Wizball*.

Sensible said they would like to hire me and the entrepreneurial guy on my shoulder chipped in and said, 'You want a piece of the action, mate, you want to be a part of the company.' The Amiga and Atari ST were in a lot of magazines and making a little bit of traction with developers, people were making lots of money, and things were starting to fall into place with publishers and developers, and I thought there was a chance to make money. I knew that they owed money to the bank, but they were great guys, some of the funniest people I have ever met. The people at Ocean were kind of plain by comparison; Sensible Software were like pop stars among the game developers. They had a great lifestyle, rock guitars, they played in a band, they had fast cars, even though they were in debt. They did whatever they wanted, and I was still living with my parents. It just seemed like a great

Jon Hare

We made the transition from 8-bit to 16-bit quite late, but very well. At the end of the 8-bit era we were probably the top developer on the Commodore 64 in Europe, coming off the back of *Shoot-'Em-Up Construction Kit*, *Wizball* and *MicroProse Soccer*. *International 3D Tennis* was our transition product, and a weird game. We saw all the games coming out that everyone was playing, like *Defender of the Crown*, generally people are excited about new markets, and people were starting to fail on the current one. We didn't want the 8-bit to change but we moved to 16-bit, and we were lucky in that it wasn't too big a technical jump for us. It was still 2D, and we could do a lot more with the art, which was great.

graduation, leaving Ocean to work with these guys. So I was very happy to work with them, even if the money didn't materialise immediately, and it actually never materialised in big spades.

So I suggested that we form a three-person partnership and proceed from there without any employees. They thought about it for a while and I thought they didn't like it, so I drew up a partnership agreement and made them sign it. Ben Lewis kind of got kicked to the side and we went to MicroProse and they snatched the soccer game IP and placed all kinds of demands on us. There was a time when MicroProse were not paying us for *MicroProse Soccer*, and the managing director of MicroProse UK resigned his job very unexpectedly. The day after that we got a cheque for £30,000. We had been suing them for that money, because they were saying no royalties were due because the game was selling horribly, and our bank manager was sending us letter after letter about our overdraft, so when that money came down we were thankful.

We all went out and got new tyres for our cars, but we were basically back against the wall, not buying new clothes, riding to work in one car. The price of petrol was terrible and having a sports car with expensive servicing costs seems like a really nutcase idea, but when you get a lot of money you spend it all at once, and then when you don't have a lot of money you kind of eke out a living. That's how a lot of developers seemed to spend their lives. Nobody ever seemed to put money back, nobody ever seemed to save money for rainy days, and nobody ever seemed to think about intellectual property and rights and proper contracts.

‹ 229                       David Perry                       533 ›

The Amiga was a whole different world: it used a different programming language, different tools and we didn't have any of it. We realised that either we evolved or died. So we got an Amiga and we started trying to make a game for it, called *Supremacy: Your Will Be Done.*

There was a little hook to *Supremacy*, like everything else. I'd found a way to make a little starfield in three dimensions and thought to make a game based on it. It turned into a real-time strategy, and it looked like it had AI but we didn't really know what AI was at the time, so it was kind of cheating. It watched what you were doing and responded to it, but people were like, 'Wow, it's incredible, it's so smart!' No, it's cheating. We were learning about the machine and it was using a different processor, called a 68000, so we had to learn a different language, and, you know, it's like you're fluent in French and now you have to speak German.

But it's funny, I had an argument with my boss, back when I was working at Mikro-Gen, when he said it only takes a day to learn

* A space strategy game in which you control a series of colonies, released in 1990.

a new language, and told me to put one of my games on a Commodore 64. He was actually right: you can learn a language in a day. You're not going to be great at it but you can have usable code, and I carried that idea throughout my career to some extent. You shouldn't look at this enormous wall: 'The 68000! Oh my goodness, it's going to be so difficult!' Just get started and you'll see there are similarities to what you already know, and then you learn some new things. In no time we had Amiga code running. We were able to get our game running on the Atari ST very quickly, too. *Supremacy* did very, very well as a game and was very highly reviewed, and so we saw that as a team we could survive and develop on other platforms.

## Mo Warden

← 267    294 →

Eventually I got to meet Bruce Jordan and Tim Bosher at Novagen. They only had a small stand at one of the shows, tucked away at the back, but it was heaving with people. It was absolutely crowded, four, five deep. They were running *Mercenary.*[*] Of course I'd heard of the game, and I went up to the stand and introduced myself as a graphics designer. Bruce said, 'That's interesting, come around the back,' and gave me a cup of coffee. He looked at my stuff and said it was good. Here we go! He was taking me seriously! He said he'd like me to meet someone, and asked me for my contact details; I came away walking on a cloud! Not long after that I met Paul Woakes[*] for the first time. They were looking for someone to do a game called *Backlash* and I was in the right place at the right time with the right attitude, you know?

Bruce came and collected me from my home, and I didn't know what to expect. We had a nice cuppa and a chat. Paul had already seen some of my stuff, I believe, and then they started to tell me about the idea for *Backlash*, which needed graphics with more interest rather than just the line shapes that they used in the past. The brief was quite difficult, because the objects had to be rotationally symmetrical. They started off in the distance and then they passed you, and they couldn't have a front and back, the only exception being the eyeball, which, as it came towards you, opened up and stared at you. I also had to design them to be able to go off

[*] The groundbreaking *Mercenary: Escape from Targ*, originally released in 1985 for the Atari 800, was a 3D game that dropped the player into an open world populated by warring factions.

[*] Woakes was the primary programmer of Novagen's games.

to the side of the camera, above and below, so they would be tilted, depending on what part of the screen they were on. It was quite satisfying, because I actually saw people duck while they were playing, as if they were zooming over their heads!

I started with some sketches and took those back to him, but it was difficult to get across the idea in my mind until I had done it. With sketches on paper it was almost impossible. But I learned quite quickly how to understand what he was after, that he wanted objects that diminished away to a horizon line, fading to grey in the distance, and then to break that into bits. I didn't play the original *Encounter!* [1] I think they gave me a copy to play, but I don't think they wanted me to be too influenced by it, and I didn't either. They wanted to see what I could do with the concept rather than say, 'Do it like that.' It was, 'Let's see what you can do.' I was guided, of course, it wasn't a completely free licence.

Fortunately, I happened to live quite locally to Paul and Bruce. I don't know what would have happened if they were London-based. I don't think it would have taken off. I visited Paul's house on quite a number of occasions, taking my work, and he would combine it with his code. When I first started with Paul I was a bit awestruck; he is an amazingly talented programmer, and it was a dream to work with somebody that good. I knew that he could do wonderful things every time I went to see him. We would have meetings which would go on all day and into the night, and we would be bouncing ideas off each other, me working on one machine and him on another. He would actually slot my graphics into the game on the spot, which was very satisfying.

Games were becoming so complex, and I think that graphics and programming needed to be separated. A lot of programmers had been doing their own graphics, and very successfully in most cases – there were a few notable exceptions, but we won't go there! But the coding was such a big job on its own, and it was taking all the time, so they needed someone else to take the

← 265 ## Peter Molyneux 289 →

You started to get bedroom artists. Now, when you mix a bedroom coder and a bedroom artist together you get games that play well and look good. So what you're really talking about is the formation of small teams. Coding is one skill, designing is another, and founding, finding and keeping your team happy is a completely and utterly different skill, which was opposite to a lot of those early coders. Some of them were incredibly introverted and having staff was out of the question. All of this happened around about the time of the transition from 8-bit to 16-bit.

[1] *Backlash* was a follow-up to *Encounter!*, which was released in 1984.

element that could be separated, and work on it. So it worked well, and Paul and I found a good working relationship. Programmers needed to be able to think in graphics, to a certain degree, and graphic designers needed to make their output very practical, so there was a lot of crossover, and there was no dividing line between what was his job and mine. We would give each other ideas; that's the beauty of working with someone. You need that crossover.

Deadlines did not exist. Paul would work on something until it was as close to perfect as he could make it, and he would just keep having ideas and he wouldn't stop. We had to wrest it from his hands, sometimes. 'You have to stop, Paul, it's got to be released!' There are some lovely stories, one about *Mercenary* when Paul insisted that the player should leave footsteps behind him on the planet surface. Bruce heard this idea and I think he must have turned slightly pale thinking about how long it was going to take, and from then forward every time Paul had another wonderful idea that he simply had to implement, we would say 'Footsteps! It's very nice but it's not necessary because the game is already fantastic! Let's get it on the market!'

Well, I not only went out to buy the magazines with the first reviews, but I still have them! I have books full of press cuttings; I kept everything. I was just over the moon. It was an amazing feeling to see my name in print, not very often because it was usually written as a Novagen game, but I was in there and I did that. Some of the magazines did actually review the graphics separately from the code, which I thought was always a bit unfair because it's supposed to slot together. But they did seem to quite like what I had done, and I was like, 'Oh, thank you!'

## Martin Kenwright

At the end of secondary school, my life circumstances changed. My parents were pensioners and they separated, and I had to go and work four nights a week in a pub, and all weekends. I got into sixth form and I almost forgot about games completely. I went into art and design, and was just working all the time to make a living. I was starting to get quite concerned about what I was going to do in the future, because I was just living on an estate in Runcorn and working all the hours just trying to get my A levels, but something remarkable happened that changed everything.

My general studies teacher was a wonderful guy called Geoff Lawson, and he had a company. It wasn't a real company, he was moonlighting, making computer games. The only reason I discovered this was that he caught me scribbling some offensive pictures of him, which had part of the class in stitches. I actually thought I was going to get kicked out of the class, and everyone put their head down, but he just sniggered and said he was going to keep them, because they were probably the best portraits anyone has ever sent him. Then he asked, 'By the way, have you ever done any computer graphics?'

Before I knew it, he had introduced me to Rod Hyde at H&H Software* and I was working at his house doing an all-nighter, trying to learn DEGAS Elite on the ST* to do some artwork. Within an hour I was trained up doing art for a game called *Strike Force Harrier.** It was a baptism of fire, but it had to be done, because their artist who had worked on it for six months had let them down. I completed it in a night, and the reviews only talked about the artwork. So obviously it was my calling, and immediately he asked me to get involved in doing games.

It wasn't a real job, it was £100 a week, and I was making cups of tea, sending faxes, photocopying and everything else, but I didn't care. I just felt it was the most amazing thing that had happened to me. I couldn't wait to get up in the morning to go to work. I felt privileged; it was like winning the lottery 10 times over. I don't know where Geoff is now. I hope he sees this one day. I've looked high and low trying to find him, because he changed my life, and I will thank him forever for that.

Rod Hyde was a technical engineer and different to the likes of me. I was probably the little scouser who talked funny, someone who could do some good graphics. I saw art packages coming out for the first time so I had glimpses of future production values and sophistication, and I could instantly see that you needed to start thinking big. People were still lost in the 8-bit mentality, and I noticed all games were the same, so I tried to do something a little bit different, a little bit fresh, and a little bit exciting in terms of the artwork.

* Hyde established H&H Software in 1984, making flight sims, before reforming as Rowan Software in 1987.
* A popular and full-featured graphics editor for the Atari ST.
* A reasonably well-reviewed flight simulator published by Mirrorsoft and released in 1986.

I would probably be a little bit obsessive and spend twice as long as I should have, having everything zoomed in and trying to create some of the best artwork I had seen, pixel by pixel. It sounds really conceited and arrogant, but there wasn't anything out there that I could emulate and say was brilliant artwork. I didn't rate most games; I felt that they had just been put in a box and had been overpriced and oversold. I thought, 'What if you could start putting together really big-scale computer graphics in 3D?'

Later, I worked with Mirrorsoft, and before I knew it I was getting involved in doing Pascal[x] for desktop publishing at Fleet Street publishers: font packages and art packages and localisation. This is someone with no form of training, and yet I am doing conversions and Pascal, just doing what I was told. But one particular thing I remember, when I was just about to turn 19, came from Russia. No one had really heard of a little game called *Tetris*, and we had a weekend to put it on to all the 8-bit and the 16-bit formats. We really thought the Slavic style was cool. Playing the tunes, flipping the R around and emulating Saint Basil's Cathedral; knocking out this design really created the start of the *Tetris* story.[*]

It was nothing to do with my graphic design, but when I saw the *Tetris* artwork flooding all over the world, it was an inkling of how big computer games could become, and it was very strange seeing all the artwork that we'd originated being repackaged and rebranded by other artists, and becoming the basis of the overall global brand for the product.

I was particularly enamoured with the 3D games, and my favourite was the original *Star Wars*[*] coin op. I just loved the way it played, the way it felt, and the way it felt like you were in space and part of the film. So actually my goal at the time was to try and get the rights to make the home version of *Star Wars*. I actually got quite far, and I was negotiating rights with the lawyers in America. They didn't know I was this 16-year-old kid. Maybe they could tell, I'm not sure, but they took me seriously.

I wasn't able to get the rights, so I thought arrogantly, 'Well, I'm going to do my own 3D game, and it's going to be better.' And that was *Starglider*. I just pivoted, kept the same technology and some of the gameplay elements of the *Star Wars* coin-op, but went in my own direction, with an original story, and that was my first big game.

I think *Starglider* took me about two years to make, but I had good art from one of my friends and some low-level code from another friend, Anna, and the 3D shapes were from someone that Rainbird had hired and the music was from David Lowe. I started on a classic Mac, and I learned 68000 assembler to program the 3D system in readiness for when the Commodore Amiga and Atari ST computers came out. When they did, I could program directly on them so I got rid of the Mac.

Our early games were negotiated through an agent, Jacqui Lyons, who was the first computer games agent, and she was responsible for much of the UK computer games industry. She was the agent of most of the top game creators, you know, Braben and Bell for *Elite* and Archer Maclean.

Jacqui introduced me to BT Rainbird, who were looking for someone that could help them get *Elite* on to the Commodore 64. Some friends and I had already programmed on the Commodore 64 in a unique way, by remote controlling a Commodore 64 from a BBC, so we would do all the programming on the BBC computer and then send it to the Commodore 64 and effectively test it in real time. So when they asked me, my fee was my own game deal for *Starglider*, and that was my entry into computer games in a commercial way. BT Rainbird paid royalties based on the retail price, which was unusual at the time, so I did well out of the game. Rainbird sold probably about 200,000 copies of *Starglider* at £2 a copy, which was very good royalties.

I put all of it into the company and hired a team, unlike my colleagues at the time who were into computer games. The early computer game creators were one-man bands like me, but some stayed one-man bands for quite a long time. They were earning similar money to me, but they were keeping it for themselves instead of paying a team, so they got to buy their fancy cars and nice houses or whatever they were doing.

I was building a team, which at the time seemed maybe not the wisest move, but I thought that was the way things were going. I thought that one great programmer couldn't make a whole computer game for very long, and I was right. Eventually you needed teams, and eventually you needed bigger and bigger teams, so I started Argonaut at the right time and I had to wait a while before I got my nice car.

Luckily my dad was a businessman, so I learned a lot of my early business skills from him. I guess I was lucky that I was a programmer, a computer game designer, and also had a bit of a business background. I kind of fell into the business side of it; it wasn't my early goal, but I could see that you could make money if you created a company, earned a reputation, and you could do more than one game at the same time. That was one of the benefits of having a larger team, and eventually we would have lots of teams and grow the business and eventually go public.

I got to hire really smart people and gave them really challenging research to do. Argonaut was very focused on technology and later became good at the creative side, so we would push the boundaries of 3D technology, which was our forte.

## David Braben

Ian and I had started working on a sequel to *Elite*, but I think we also started to go a little bit on our separate ways. Ian got very interested in martial arts and all that sort of thing, and I was interested in a lot of the techy side of where technology was going and all of that sort of thing. So we eventually shelved the work we did on the sequel, which was a shame.

Around that time, because I knew the people at Acorn very well, I knew they were working on a new chip. It was all very secret, extremely secret: we talked at length about it and I was very excited. I got a prototype of one of the first ARM chips. They're just down the road in Cambridge, a very, very successful international company now. It was actually initially a second processor on the BBC Micro, and they said, 'Well we're sure you could do something fun with it, given what you did with *Elite*.'

So I played around with it, and I produced a number of demos before they told me they were going to release a machine on a very, very tight time scale. I think I had something like three months from when they knew roughly what the machines would be like to write a game that would be on the disks that were shipped with them!

I did a game called *Lander*, which was on the disk that came free with the machine, and then a game based on it called *Zarch*.

*Zarch* was a retail game, so I had a bit longer to write it. Interestingly, *Lander* was based on one of those games that I did way back, the meteors game, in 3D. That was how it was conceived, with shadows on a sort of patchwork quilt landscape. But all of the decisions as to how we made it go fast and that sort of thing were about trying to get it working on the prototype hardware, because what I had didn't have a lot of the operating system, and didn't use a lot of its functions. A lot of people have since asked me why *Zarch* and *Lander* don't use multiple instructions, because there is multiple instruction on the ARM chip which is really quick. My feeble excuse is the multiple instruction didn't work on the first batch of ARM chips, so I didn't dare use it. So that's my story!

Ian and I had gone our separate ways, but I wanted to work on a new *Elite*. I thought that would be very exciting, but in the meantime I did a game called *Virus*˙ because, you know, *Zarch* was on quite a niche machine and it was great to see it on the Atari ST and Amiga because at that time I hadn't experience of working on them, and they were then the de facto games machines. But bizarrely it felt ... I mean, having gone on to a 32-bit machine with four megabytes of memory, which is what the Archimedes prototype had – I still have the machine I worked on – that was an unheard of amount of memory. It was comparable to the university's mainframe! Then I had to go back down to the 16-bit 68000 chip that was in both the Amiga and ST. But it was a really good way for me to cut my teeth on game writing and assembler.

I also started playing around with tools written in C, so I was learning all the time, which was great. I got an ST and Amiga; I had an Amiga before it came out, for example. It was fantastic. I used them to both learn and to write *Virus* on the ST and Amiga, which did very well. I used a lot of the techniques that I had used on *Zarch*, but way more honed because the machines were a lot slower, but it had a longer development time. I actually took 12 months to develop *Virus* for those platforms whereas the Archimedes version was done in three months.

I was still very attached to the Archimedes, and so with some friends I wrote a complier for it in BBC BASIC that supported the 68000. It supported the Amiga and ST, and it supported the PC. We showed it to Acorn and said, 'Look, if you allow us to give this away for free with your machines, you will put one of these machines on the desk of every single developer and they won't be able to resist supporting the Archimedes.' The Archi-

* Virus was fundamentally a port of Zarch for ST and Amiga. The Amiga version was made by Argonaut.

medes then was a very niche machine; it didn't really go big like the BBC Micro did and it never really went into America. But they said, 'Why would we support our competition?' So I was very disappointed about that. I then started writing for the ST and the Amiga, moving away from the Archimedes and the dust started to settle on it. I would still use it for things like email and electronic bulletin boards, which were a big thing at the time, but not much else, which was a shame.

## Martin Kenwright

It was when 3D came along that it all started to change. Mirrorsoft were tied up with Spectrum HoloByte* and did a vector wireframe game called *Falcon*. We* saw it on an Apple Macintosh and we at Rowan were asked whether we could do a conversion to the Atari ST. That was really when the floodgates opened for me personally, because up until that time everyone was using sprites, and I really felt that you could create a level of realism that no one had done before with vector graphics.

*Falcon* became a little bit of a baby for me. I gave it a lovely set of clothes, and the conversion didn't look anything like the original. I had a great team of guys at this point. Russell Payne joined me there, and Chris Orton, Colin Bell and a lot of people who went on to great things with me in the future studios. Something clicked there and *Falcon* was huge when it launched. It had incredible reviews, you know, and when I look back on it now, you know, it was the first proper true next-gen 16-bit game.

When you make a proper big blockbuster game like that you don't want to go back and do normal games again. After *Falcon* lots of opportunities opened up for me, but it was a loyalty thing for me. I really wanted to do *Falcon* mission disks and I started designing other games, like *Flight of the Intruder*, which I started doing all the groundwork on, but my career at Rowan Software was ending.

I went to the Olympia show and ended up speaking to a guy called John Symes from Microdeal. He asked if I wanted to do some artwork, and I was really loyal and honest and went to Rowan and said, 'Look, I've been offered a load of work but I am working for you. I thought you might want to do it.' The company said, 'No, we don't want to, and if you do it, you can leave now,' which kind of shocked me. Mirrorsoft were made up with the success of *Falcon*, and, you know, there were always dubious things going on in the background, and Rod came around giving bonus cheques out to all the programmers, and went past me. He says, 'Well, you're no programmer.'

What? I did all the artwork! 'Well, we

* A US-based publisher which ended up merging with MicroProse and co-published games with Mirrorsoft

* Rod Hyde had opened a new studio, Rowan Software, in 1987, which Kenwright joined.

only had you booked in for 14 weeks and it took six months.' I talked about how the reviews said it was some of the best artwork, and it was all 3D, and the techniques hadn't been done before. I just couldn't believe it. To say I didn't deserve it, you know, someone who was on £5,000 a year, I felt degraded. People in the room saw this, and I couldn't work there after that.

## Sean Cooper 348→

I got suspended from school for various reasons, and then I got expelled in my final year. I didn't do all of my exams, and I tried to go to college, but I'd had enough by that point. I ended up in a YTS scheme, the ITEC, which basically was a room full of computers, predominantly PCs, and a bunch of boys who didn't have qualifications and wanted to learn stuff. I soon started helping everyone and taught them how to do certain things. I was quite computer literate, quite good at BASIC and assembler.

Alex Trowers' was there, and he was trying to code games, and I remember looking at him and thinking, wow, he's just making them? The ITEC was set up for business software, you see, but we sat there and just created games all day long, and encouraged the others.

Then Peter Molyneux came in one day. They were just around the corner above a hi-fi shop, less than 50 yards away. He had a conversation with the head of the programme, and the next thing I know, I'm being dragged to his office and told to go and present myself to this office. When I arrived I thought it was a joke. Who are these guys up there? It could hardly be of any interest. I rang the buzzer and for 15 minutes no one answered. So I'm sat there, this polite little boy, quite shy at this point, afraid to press the buzzer too often. The final time I did it, someone said, 'Yes?!' 'It's Sean from the ITEC, they said I might be able to get a job with you?' 'OK, come up.' Of course, I'd never been through a buzzer door before, so I didn't push it. I pressed the buzzer again and a minute later, 'Yeah?' 'How do I get in?' 'Push the door!'

So I went up the first set of stairs and thought there was no one there. Then up the second set, there was still no one there. Up the final set, I ended up in the loft, and there were three guys there. I remember Glenn there, Peter, Kevin Donkin. I saw Les a week later. This was before *Populous*, so they were just putting out *Fusion*.

I proceeded to muck around for six months, drawing porno-

---

' Trowers would go on to join Bullfrog.

graphic pictures. I didn't know that Kevin had rigged up my monitor so everyone in the office could see what I was doing, this really crude pixel art, twiddling my thumbs, and they were all laughing. I wandered over and asked what they were laughing at. 'We've been watching what you've been doing for the past two hours.' I was like, 'Oh.'

Peter then went away for two weeks and Glenn said something that clicked me into action. He said, 'Let's get this whole thing done in the next week, and I reckon you'll then be secure for a job.' So we did some artwork, we made some things work, he showed me a few things. I didn't know C or 68000 at the time, which was what they were using, but Glenn and Kevin very quickly brought me up to speed. Peter came back and this thing was finished, and he was amazed that the office had got on with it without him being there.

Then Peter slowly taught me C and a bit of 68000. He always says that he's a bad programmer; I think he wants to weigh more on his creative side, but Peter's level of programming was very high, and also his teaching ability, and his trust. We were doing this game in 1988, this thing with a centipede, and he said, 'Why don't you just take this game on, Sean?' So I did. I'd shout out in the office, 'How do I do blah?' and Kevin or Glenn would come and show me, and slowly I built my skill up and we finally released the game *Flood*, which basically I had done most of the programming on, and the design, and got the artist in to do the art. I saw all the disciplines, and how to get people to do things, and describe what I needed.

I just thought it was great, and that I could really do stuff now. I stopped working for my dad, who had a pub, on Sundays, so I could spend them coding. He was a bit shocked, and my mum was a bit worried that I was choosing a career in games. I moved into a flat, once Bullfrog started paying me more than £20 a week, which was due to the ITEC. Peter bought me my first car! As soon as I passed my test he said, 'Come on, let's go and buy a car!' It was a piece of shit, it broke down two miles from the garage.

Peter Molyneux

While Glenn Corpes and Kevin Donkin were finishing off *Fusion*, I started on this crazy game called *Populous*. You have got to re-member that we were spending no money at that time. We were in this tiny, horrible office and we were all, you know, going in the sink because there was no toilet, and we were eating disgusting, cheap food.

So there was no risk involved at all, and I don't think there was an original idea. It was more like – and I still tend to develop games like this – wouldn't it be brilliant to have a game where there was a little world and these little people moving around in it? That was the first thought, and then the game kind of came about. So I think *Populous* as a game evolved rather than was designed.

It was only when I started being confronted with the real problems of creating this little world, like how to get the little people moving around the coast and around objects that I started laying game mechanics which made up for how incompetent I was as a coder. A little person would come to some water and I couldn't work out how to get them around it, so I just had the player raise the land up. That's how the game came about: because I was a rubbish coder.

There wasn't really anything much like it and this was a problem when we were taking it around to publishers. You would show the game to someone and they would say, 'Well, I don't understand what that's all about. Just go back and finish it and maybe we will look at it again.' It took about nine months to make it, me and Glenn. Glenn was doing the graphics and I was kind of doing the gameplay. It was a joy because Glenn and I used to spend hours and hours playing the game. We had this RS-232 cable linking our two machines and we would just play it and play it. I would keep changing the game so I kept on beating Glenn, and that's how we balanced the game.

I think one of the biggest reasons for *Populous*'s success is the early games that me and Glenn used to play in the office. We'd play it almost every day and then that night I would refine the game to my advantage. I think I won every single game because I used to effectively cheat. If we found the game going on for hours and hours, we'd add features which would bring the game to a close earlier. That's a lesson I learned from; all the games I have worked on since *Populous* that I have played have been far, far better than those I haven't.

It was a game of two halves; the early part was about changing the land, and you used to do this thing called 'nippling' and that's raising it, clicking up twice and down once. There was quite a rhythm to it, and it was quite relaxing. Then, after 10 or 15 minutes, then you realised there was someone else on the other side of the map and you started battling away, and that was much more exciting. It's interesting how you can have a game which has both sides.

There were also these strategies which people kind of made up, whether the flat land strategy or spreading out close to the other person's territory. It meant there wasn't just one way to solve a level, one way to get through the game. There were multiple ways, which is kind of the cornerstone of what simulation games are. You know, games like *Sim City*, *The Sims* and all of those: how you get to the objective is up to the player, and part of the joy is inventing your own strategies or your own techniques.

Firebird said no to *Populous*, so we went around to quite a few others, and eventually Electronic Arts said yes. We were very lucky when we finished it, because EA had this huge hunger for products. They were just trying to establish themselves in Europe, so they were quite into playing with lots of different products. So when we took *Populous* along to them they were fairly sympathetic about it because it was so different.

It was a double deal. These were the days where this often happened, and it was almost the death of little independent game developers. The terms on which publishers were signing developers up were just awful. I think for *Populous* we ended up getting less than 10% royalty, and then they had these terrible terms in the contract about this ridiculous, almost fraudulent thing called returns. The contract was so awful it almost meant that they owned us from day one. That happened to a lot of developers. What was even worse is – and we fell into this trap as well – they would then have recurring lifetime rights on any game you thought of, designed or created. It effectively enslaved you for years and years, and it took us a long time to get ourselves out of that.

I think it's fair to say we really didn't have an idea what the world would think of *Populous*. After all, the games that I had been involved with before had hardly been mega successes. The most successful was probably *Druid II* or maybe *Fusion*, certainly not *The Entrepreneur*. So our expectations weren't high, and at that time, you know, we were living in squalor. Electronic Arts released an initial run of the game – we never knew how many there were – and then they started sending it out to journalists. Then suddenly some amazing things started to happen.

The first was when a journalist called Bob Wade came down to Bullfrog. Now, we had never really had guests before, and certainly not someone like Bob Wade, who was a famous journalist. So our strategy was to go down the pub with Bob and to get him completely drunk to hopefully distract him from talking about the game. We didn't talk about the game at all because we were too nervous. But after countless pints we eventually plucked up the courage and asked him what he thought of *Populous*. He said this disastrous line. He said, 'It's the best game I have ever played.' The single thought that went through my mind was that he must never play it ever again, because he must have made a horrendous mistake. His review was in *Ace* magazine, one of the most respected magazines at the time, and then all these other reviews came out with incredible scores, and this guy who was one of the heads of Electronic Arts phoned up and said it was a huge success and that I'm a millionaire. That wasn't true, by the way, but I went from urinating in the sink, and owing more money to the bank than I could ever imagine, to an incredible life. Amazing.

## Dino Dini

I was repairing ST computers at a company called Silica Shop, and through that I made a connection with Anco, because they got their STs from Silica Shop. Anco were in Dartford, not very far away from where I lived. I did a small project with them, and Anil Gupta liked what I did, so we talked about what to do next. He said, 'I have always wanted a football game.'

So I said okay and went to see if I could make a football game on the Atari ST, and it went from there. I quit my job at the Silica Shop, which was definitely a leap of faith. But I had already tested it, because I had moonlighted on this other game called *Trivia Trove*, a conversion from Amiga to ST for Anco. So I kind of knew at that point I could easily get projects like that, and it paid better for the time spent than where I was working. It was kind of a natural choice, but it was also a leap: I didn't get an advance to do *Kick Off*.

I was never really a football fan. I liked to watch international matches, but the football scene, well, I'm from an immigrant family and I wasn't very social. I didn't really fit in at school very much, and this whole football thing was a bit alien to me. I knew enough about it from watching the football I had watched, and in a way actually that probably made it easier for me to design a game for it. Some people are confused by this. They think, 'Well, you created a football game and it was successful, so you must really be

An Atari-specialist based in Sidcup, Kent, which eventually opened a branch on Tottenham Court Road in London.

Gupta founded Anco Software with Roger Gamon.

into football,' and that's not actually true, and it was bad PR for me, actually. I should have realised the wisdom of picking a team to say I supported. That may have worked better, but the truth was I wasn't really a football fan.

But when I looked at football games I was able to see what it was about them that was exciting. That's the point! Then I figured out how to implement the bits that were exciting about football on the computer with its limited resources. The first thing I did was a feasibility study on whether it would be possible to do the game on the ST. It all sounds very professional, doesn't it? I got paid for doing that by Anil, but it was to see can I move, how many strikers I could move around, and what scale I would need. Can I scroll the background on this ST that didn't even have any hardware scrolling? So I checked and it would run fast enough.

So I set the constraints. I have this idea that design is basically the management of constraints, and I can connect that to what I did at the time, even though I wasn't thinking in this way. I knew how big the sprites had to be, how big the pitch had to be. I knew that to make it work I had to have an overhead view. The other constraint I set was to make the scale as lifelike as possible. That was something that was different to other games that were out there. They would have tiny pitches with huge players and it just felt wrong.

But that created a challenge, because a football pitch is very big and football players in relative size are quite small, so it's not possible to see the whole pitch. So the zoomed-in view that you get in *Kick Off* was the only solution. 'Okay,' I said. I wasn't going to worry about the fact that people can only see a small part of the screen at a time, and that is how it grew.

When I looked at other games I saw the ball stuck to your feet, and I thought that was nonsense. In real football, if you have the ball stuck to you then you might as well carry it. So I was going to figure out some way of making a ball simulation separate from the player. Actually, now when I look at the solutions that I used, they feel quite crude, but somehow it worked. It's funny how often there is a bit of stumbling in the dark required, but I think that if you stay true to the core, you have a very much higher chance of success. So I tried to stick to the core of football, so the ball didn't stick to the foot.

I put air friction in *Kick Off*, too. Some of my competitors still don't actually use it, but it's actually important to use air friction because if you want to make the ball fast enough to be exciting then without friction it will always go out of play.

More or less, I developed the game and delivered it at the end. I wish I'd had more help from Steve Screech,[x] who was more into football than me, so he was like an advisor on it. I showed Anco what I was doing, but pretty much I was on my own. That was good, too, because it meant that I didn't have to keep pleasing them, which would have affected the development process. That's one of the problems that you see now. If a publisher puts money into a game they are going to be forever looking at it and worried. You end up with fear-based development and that is just a disaster, because fear kills creativity.

The ST version took 15 months to write. Interestingly, just towards the time when *Kick Off* was getting close to being finished, Anil started to get stressed about it. It was a bit of a tense time. Part of the reason was that Anco as a company was struggling. They had actually resorted to releasing strip poker games, and you always knew a videogame company was on its last legs when it resorted to strip poker. But fortunately, *Kick Off* came out just in time.[*] I think it basically changed Anco around completely.

The way that Anil publicised the game was by going to the distributors who were selling the product to the retailers, right, and bribing them. He would tell me what he would do. He'd be there when they were on the phone, and every time someone did a deal for *Kick Off* he would give them a fiver. I guess that's the way it was done back then, I really don't know.

← 291

## Dino Dini

342 →

There were a number of things that were different in *Kick Off 2*. I did aftertouch, and you could change the colour of the shirts, which was kind of minor detail, I guess, but maybe not so much. The first game had either red or blue shirts. But I also added some other innovations, like the scissor kick. The controller only really had one button, and the stick was only sensitive in eight directions, so the problem was how I could do things like chips, passes, shooting, headers, and scissor kicks with just that. What I came up with was reversing the stick. So if you're pushing forward, the moment you hit the ball you reverse the stick and it does a lob. But if you don't have the ball and you reverse the stick and the ball is in the air it does a scissor kick. It was actually a lot of fun trying to solve these problems. So we actually got a few innovations in the controls from the first game. The other thing it had was a replay that it saved to disk. I thought it would be really great if people could replay their goals. I don't know if I was the first one to do that, but it was pretty good.

x   After Dini's departure from Anco, Screech went on to lead the *Kick Off* series, beginning with *Super Kick Off* for the Super Nintendo, Mega Drive and Game Boy.
*   It was released in 1989 for both the Atari ST and Amiga. The Amiga version took Dini two months to port.

The first review that I read was terrible. Then it got a really good review, and another really good review. Then the magazine that gave it the terrible review reversed their decision and gave it a different review. They actually changed their mind on it! It was a very different world back then. I think the sales started coming in, and then Anco could afford to do some marketing. I think it went that way around because I don't think they had the money at the time when *Kick Off* was actually originally released. Once I saw the good reviews come in I saw that it went to number one in the chart. I don't know, that was weird, that was a bit surreal.

## Mo Warden

*Backlash* was my test to see how we got along, not just for me but also for Paul to see if he was happy to work with someone like me, and at the end of the project we immediately started to talk about the next one. There was no, 'Right, well, you can go away for a while and we will talk about whether we are going to keep you on.' I thought, 'Great!'

The next project was a continuation of *Mercenary*, called *Damocles*. I think Paul always had a vision for *Mercenary* but had to fit it into the available hardware at the time, and so as the hardware became more powerful he was able to get closer to his original idea of what he wanted it to look like, to build the whole solar system and work it into the mechanics so that you had the sun rise and set and you had moons going overhead where they should.

I was quite clearly directed in terms of what it was going to be, but they wanted to take it that step forward, and for it to have textures, more colour and more solid objects and things that you could pick up and carry around, and not just the wireframes but a real first-person environment that you could walk and fly through.

We were winging it, to be honest. We were heading towards a goal we wanted to achieve but we didn't know how much of it would actually be possible. That's the best way to phrase it. We started to pull things in between us; I would do some drawings and Bruce would do some writing, and then we would brainstorm and obviously there were other people contributing as well. Paul's friends and so on would see what he was working on and they would contribute, so there were a lot of sources. It wasn't just the three of us.

The graphics were enormously complex, I mean, I had to fit them into the amount of memory that we had, so we couldn't go mad. I had to reuse designs in small tiles, then form a bigger tile which then formed an area, which then formed a city, which then formed a planet, which was in a solar system ... We had, I think, about 14 planets and moons, and most of them had four or five cities, crammed with buildings. Oh, it was huge. Sometimes it's difficult to get your brain around just how big it was. If you walked into a building and you walked around for a while, you could walk out again and the sun would have set and the moon would be up. All the time things would change. It was enormously impressive. It was your own private solar system.

I can't really remember in too much detail how he achieved it, because Paul would just go away and do these wonderful things, and then I would meet him and be just gobsmacked a lot of the time. I was wowed by what he did in such a short space of time, but it took a couple of years. We wanted to take our time because there was no point in rushing it out. It would have been obvious if we'd rushed it, but again it was a project we had to persuade Paul to part with. 'It's finished, Paul, honestly! Please step away from the game!' There was always one more thing he could do.

Bruce did original drawings for the worlds, mostly on graph paper, outlining the shape of an island and separating it into zones: commercial, agricultural, and here are the roads, there is going to be a building there, this is a port. Then he made photocopies of them and I would have half a dozen copies to scribble on. Unfortunately, because of the nature of the paper, they have not survived well, but I do still have a few of the original drawings with Bruce's writing on them showing the layout. It was only meant as a guideline though, so I could change things if it would be nice to have some farmland over there, and perhaps a building complex over here. It was all quite flexible.

Bruce also created the wonderful, sarcastic Benson character. It was Bruce: a very tongue-in-cheek, very intelligent man, very articulate. Some of his writing was just so funny. He was very well-read, and all his little jokes crept in, even down to the naming of the buildings. Those little touches are part of what made it memorable.

My job was the on-screen graphics and things like the control interfaces, so the spaceship panel and so on, and things like the drivers on the buses. Those strange characters, yes, they were my fault. I didn't do all of them, but I did most. It was a team effort, and a lot of people came in to do some work. Most of them I never met, because they would have been in the Birmingham offices, and I was working from home. I was very strict with myself all the way through, getting up at a certain time in the morning and sitting and working for hours. Everything else really had to be ignored, so you don't have time to go out with your mates because you have made a promise, not only to your employers but also to yourself. You want to get it finished; if you don't want to finish it you shouldn't be doing it, and if you don't enjoy the work, it just becomes a drudge, and I loved every minute of it. I looked forward to working, and to showing Paul and Bruce what I had done, and taking the criticism when it came. Of course it wasn't all gushing praise, but when Paul said something was excellent, I was on cloud nine.

When it came out I was fairly sure people were going to like it. I was astonished by the result; I was playing it a lot, of course, but I couldn't show it to anyone until it was ready, which was so frustrating. I showed it to my boys, and they were the envy of their schoolmates. When the reviews started to come out, they were five out of five, you know, and that was so satisfying on a very deep level. When you work hard on something and you really put most of your life into it, your social life going out of the window, to then have it appreciated like that, I can't tell you how satisfying that feels.


## Archer Maclean

The versions of *IK+* for 16-bit machines went out in late '88, and so in '89 and '90 I did various things. I moved house to a wonderful place out in the countryside, where I enjoyed endless barbecues and wine, women and song. It was very distracting, but I was supposed to be doing a snooker game. It was originally called '147', a 3D snooker game.

Now, the reason that came about is quite interesting. In 1980 I used to be addicted to watching *Pot Black*, and I remember seeing a match with Ray Reardon and Steve Davis, and halfway through it they showed a newsflash on the Iranian Embassy siege. I was getting really into this major snooker game, and I remember sitting down with my Atari 800 and thinking how on earth I could do 3D and also plot balls rolling around on a screen. I spent ages trying to make it work on a 6502 anywhere near quick enough.

I couldn't do it, which was a bit of a shame, but I spent such an intense amount of time working on it that I had a very vivid dream. For some reason it was in colour and I was like a camera on the end of a string, swooping around and around above a snooker table. I don't know why I had that, but anyway fast forward to about 1988 when I was playing around with STs and Amigas, and I had something called a screengrabber, and the very first thing I screengrabbed when I turned on the TV was yet another snooker game, a close-up of a pocket shot, in fact. I have still got that shot somewhere, of a couple of balls in front of a pocket, and it made me think, 'Hang on a minute,' and I remembered those ideas I had from 1980. I suddenly got this flash of inspiration to sit there and write 68000 code, trying to solve core problems like how to make large three-dimensional-looking balls, even though they were 2D, roll around a screen quick enough.

I spent a month or two proving that crucial part would work with various demos, and then started hawking it around in '89 and '90. Again we went back to Activision and signed up with them, but then they went pop in late '91. Then the game suddenly didn't have a home, so we signed up with Virgin in March '91 and it was still called '147'. They made a very fancy animated 147 in 3D with dots moving around, which actually looks remarkably like the front of *IK+* 16-bit, because they used the same code.

We were showing it at a trade show in mid '91, when Jeremy Beadle˙ of all people came marching out of the crowd and saw the game demo. He said, 'That plays just like Jimmy White,' and some guy from Virgin said, 'Oh, do you know him?' and before I knew it Jeremy Beadle had given him Barry Hearn's telephone number and he basically said, 'Ring that guy, he will sort you out.' Two or three days later, a bunch of us drove to Romford in Essex and had this meeting with this character who was like J.R. Ewing. He had his legs on the desk, scratching his bits, saying, 'Yeah, yeah, I will give you some money for it.' It was very strange, but Jimmy was there and we just got on really well – always have. So we changed the name of '147' to *Jimmy White's Whirlwind Snooker*, and the only thing I had to do was to change the title screen.

At the time, there wasn't really much in the way of 3D. The odd flight sim and games like *Starglider*. I remember playing that quite a bit. *Elite* was obviously a big 3D game, but that was wireframe, and suddenly this infilled polygonal snooker table came out, with all these funny little pop sounds and balls pulling faces and various other things. It looked visually stunning, and I spent ages doing camera work where the view of the game was flying all over the place, a bit like the dream I had 12 years earlier. It proved to be a hit.

˙ The popular radio and TV presenter.

The original price was £24.95, but then Virgin put the price up to £29.95, thinking it was worthy. They printed this fantastically large game box with two very fat manuals, posters, special Jimmy White chalk and all sorts of other little freebies so it had real value. The reviews were pretty amazing, and then we started winning awards. It got technical innovation, best 3D game, best this, best that. It went in the Amiga and ST charts at number one, and then the PC version, too.

The funny thing was that whenever Jimmy went on TV and started winning stuff, the game would go up the charts again, so a year later it was back at number one. That went on and on for two or three years, and the whole fan thing really kicked off massively, which really got ridiculous. I mean, myself and Jimmy White being smuggled in the back of an Oxford Street game store under blankets so that we didn't get mobbed ... I mean, it was straight-out rock star stuff. It was funny.


## Charles Cecil

I was at Activision for about a year and a half when the US side got into trouble and ultimately collapsed, and it brought down the UK side. But I really wanted to get back into development. I really missed it. If you work for a publisher it's very frustrating because you don't have a direct control over the products and you rely absolutely on the developers and if the developer's poor and you get a bad product, there's really nothing you can do about it.

I'd worked closely at Artic with a fellow called Tony Warriner, and he'd said to me, 'I'd love to set up a company.' So, in the back of my mind, I wanted to do that, and then the most amazing thing happened: my boss at Activision came along and said, 'Look, we're really sorry, we're going to have to make you redundant, but do you mind if you work for two days a week for the next six months, just helping us wind down and do whatever you can to earn money for the other three days?' And I said, 'Well, that's going to be pretty tough but I think I can just about do it,' walked out and went, 'Perfect! Perfect!'

So that gave me three days a week to set up Revolution and I founded the company with Noirin Carmody, who was the head of Sierra, so she had a lot of experience with sales and distribution, plus Tony, who is still a very dear friend and I've worked with since about 1984, and a friend of Tony's, a programmer called Dave Sykes. We decided that it should be based in Hull, because both

Tony and Dave were based there, and we had no money whatsoever. With my redundancy money I bought a 386 – it was the most magnificent PC! – and we used it for development.

Dave and Tony worked above a fruit shop, because, again, we couldn't afford to pay any rent. It was so cold, and the fruit shop guys were very mean, because they wouldn't heat it, so these guys wore fingerless gloves and typed away. It was like something out of, you know, *A Christmas Carol*.

They wrote the first demo for a game that we eventually called *Lure of the Temptress*. We had the opportunity to present it to Mirrorsoft, and this was our big opportunity. Dave and Tony drove down from Hull and I was living in London at the time and they parked, leaving the PC on the back seat overnight by mistake. The car was broken into, and I'm not sure why, but they stole the radio and they left the PC. Now, the PC wasn't insured and we couldn't possibly have afforded to buy another one. So had those thieves taken that PC, then Revolution would never have existed, which is quite an interesting idea. So we're very grateful to those thieves.

We did the presentation to Mirrorsoft and they decided to commission it. It was absolutely fantastic, and it was great working with them. Sean Brennan was the deputy managing director, so we worked very closely with him, an absolute genius at games and what sells and he sort of helped steer us.

← 268     Mike Montgomery     334 →

After we made *Xenon* we went back to Mastertronic and said, 'Look, we want to do more. We're really, really excited, and we would like you to think about providing us with a little bit of money so we can think about what our next game is.' They went, 'Well we can't really do that, but we want a game called "Real Tennis".' We thought that sounded interesting, so we went out and did a lot of research on real tennis. It's a game that is played by Prince Charles, and there are only one or two courts around the country. So we went back to Mastertronic with a full design, and they went, 'We changed our minds.' We went, 'What?' We spent like a month doing this work. 'We have changed our minds. We're not really interested.' So the relationship went extremely sour in seconds.

So the three of us went to the pub and we were like really down about it. Then, all of a sudden, I don't know how it happened, but all of a sudden *Speedball* was invented on the back of a Silk Cut cigarette packet. That was all the paper we had at the time.

We took it to another publisher. Well, quite a few publishers, actually, but we went with Image Works. John Cook was sitting there, playing his guitar, really laid back, and we just gave him the design on the cigarette pack and he looked at it and just went, 'Well, this isn't a real design, is it?' Then we spoke about it, which was when you get passionate. Then he went, 'This is good. We've got something here, boys!' Then we signed it up about a week later.

Image Works were really, really interested in us, as well as our products. They gave us a three-game contract with advances, so that meant we didn't have to go through all this trouble every time we finished a game to get another publishing deal. Okay, it probably wasn't the best deal in the world, because we were a bit green, but it gave us continuous income for a period of time and a continuation of games as well. That was when we started to expand; we started to employ people to do graphics, programming, music and stuff like that. So that was the start. I wouldn't call them good times, financially, but yeah, we were getting there.

*Speedball* was a combination of different games and different films. I am not saying that we ripped any films off, but there were a few around at the time and we wanted this science-fiction setting, but it was also working with Dan Malone on the art to get that real crisp look. A lot of games started to come out on the Amiga and the ST at that time, and they weren't using the palettes properly and were quite dull, but *Speedball* has got that nice, glossy, shiny look. Just beautiful graphics.

Over the years people have asked where that metallic look came from in The Bitmap Brothers games but it didn't come down to one particular artist, because we had three or four of them. Dan Malone and Mark Coleman were probably the biggest influences, and Dan Malone invented in some respects those steampunk graphics, and then Mark Coleman did *Xenon 2*, the original *Speedball* and *Gods*, and they're all metallic. And partly it was

Peter Stone and
Richard Leinfellner

An artist we hired around the time of finishing *Cauldron* was a guy called Dan Malone, who had a comic background. I got a phone call one day from an art college lecturer in Ipswich, and she said she had this useless student, but she thought he might be what we were looking for. That was Dan.

He came more from a gritty *2000AD*-type comic background, just a phenomenal artist. We showed him how to use our tools, and he said he had a game idea. 'I want to do this comic game.' He wanted to put his own comic in with the game, and that's how *The Sacred Armour of Antiriad* was born, as a comic book story, and that then became the game.

because we wanted all the Bitmaps games to be in a style, and that's a style we chose. It helped that the Amiga and ST could show more colours – artists could do shading, and the resolution was bigger, too, so the pixels were smaller and you could get much better shading. It comes down to an artist being really clever with the materials of the time and using them to their full.

Developing *Speedball 2* was actually quite fun, because we employed a different programmer, even though I was involved with the programming, an artist, Dan Malone, and of course Richard Joseph, who was very good at music at the time.

The thing with *Speedball 2* was it was a two-player game, which was actually how we made it, and then we put in the single-player using the AI that we had worked out from doing a two-player game. We did a lot of testing on *Speedball 2*, breaking joysticks like you have never seen before. So I did a deal for joysticks. We mention in the manual that we use their joysticks, and they supplied us with free ones; I would phone them up every two months and another case of joysticks would be delivered because we would smash the buttons. Some of the guys who were testing were actually smashing them on their knees.

I can remember one funny thing that really made *Speedball 2*. Richard came in and said, 'Mike, I want you to listen to this and I don't want you to tell me off or anything. Listen and see what you think.' He was playing sound effects from a tape recorder over the game, because it wasn't in the game yet, and all of a sudden you get this, 'Ice cream, ice cream!' And I went, 'Wow.' I mean, that just had to go in. 'I thought so, but I just wanted to test.' That was one of the things that made that game so famous. We would walk down the street in London, when we were known back in those days, and people used to shout, 'Ice cream!' at us.

← 137   # Geoff Crammond   345 →

I had done some stuff with an RS-232 interface[x] back in the days of the BBC. A university asked me for a version of *Aviator* that outputted the speed and the height as part of some experiments using it, and it occurred to me that since the Amiga and ST both had the interface, it was possible to send data across to another machine running the same program, and it might be possible to race a real person in *Stunt Car Racer*. So I basically decided to give it a go, and it worked. One of the things I was pleased with is you could link an Amiga with an ST, so you wouldn't have to worry because your mate has a different machine, so that was good. I just thought it would be a good thing to do. I didn't know whether other games were doing it.

[x] A serial connection between computers that enables transmission of data.

Not a lot of people know this, but legally, any time you add or remove partners from a partnership, the partnership has to be dissolved. So we dissolved the original partnership of Jon and Chris when we became a three-person partnership. We were in the middle of doing *International 3D Tennis* and we had all moved into houses of our own in Cambridgeshire. It was quite a nice step up, but we were in debt, interest rates were high, and the house prices were falling. But I had bought one of Chris's cars, a Porsche, so I felt pretty happy with myself, and we had a rented a house for our office.

They came in one day and said, 'Hey Martin, we just want to go our way again and be two guys again. So, you know, we are going to dissolve the partnership.' This was a shock to me and I didn't really know what to do. I said, 'Well, let's talk about this, is there any way we can work it out? What's the issue here?' But they said no, and that they were dissolving it that weekend. I was still pretty shocked, but I immediately rang up Origin Systems and asked if they were still interested in hiring me, and they said yes.

We all co-owned the IP to *International 3D Tennis* and the other games we worked on, and several months later, actually, I gave them those IPs. I was happy to. I wasn't really looking for a legal fight. I wasn't talking to them and they weren't talking to me; they were finishing off *International 3D Tennis*, even though I still co-owned it, so they had to re-jig their publishing contract with Palace Software to get me off the contract and carry on as Sensible Software. They insisted that the value of Sensible Software was zero, when of course we all know it was bloody famous and had tons of goodwill in the press. But, you know, I wasn't willing to pay a solicitor to fight, so I just said, 'All right, there you go, you can still use the title.' They could have carried on with a different name, but most people didn't realise that the partnership was dissolved.

## Jon Hare

I don't even know if Martin knows why we decided to do it. Basically, Chris and I had been used to working as a pair, right back when we were a band when we were kids. At this time, around 1988, '89, we kind of realised it wasn't quite working out, mostly for the reason that Martin was acting as the lead programmer on an adventure game called 'Touchstone' and he was struggling with it, albeit being an absolutely brilliant genius musician.

'Touchstone' was a really ambitious game, and we had signed it to Origin, but we couldn't get it past the first milestone. This was the first deal we'd done where we had to get through a greenlight process, and we couldn't get it through the gate. We had started on Commodore 64, then transferred it to PC, but Martin couldn't really get it there. It was frustrating for me, because it was a big game and the first game that hadn't come out. We didn't really have enough music work on other games to justify Martin being there as part of the partnership, and that was the main reason.

Chris and I had never had to sack anyone before, and we didn't really know how to do it. So we did it in a really, really, cowardly way, actually. In between the two offices we worked at, we used an interim one, which was some house, and we moved there one day and didn't tell Martin or give him the key. It was terribly cowardly. We ran away. He took it in good spirits because it was a really wanky thing to do, in retrospect. It's not nice to do that to one of your mates, but we didn't know what else to do. But we all left on amicable terms and he left to work at Origin in the States. We were really happy when he got that job because it made us feel less like bastards.

‹ 302

## Martin Galway

325 ›

I went to Origin in the first place because Chris Roberts[*] was a high-school friend of mine in Manchester. His dad was a lecturer at the University of Manchester and was offered a job in Austin in Texas, so Chris and his entire family moved there in '86. I thought I was never going to see them again. Origin and me got on really, really well and they wanted to hire me. Of course, I was a UK resident and didn't have a proper visa, so we had to start on paperwork, and that's when Sensible Software offered me the job.

When I got to Origin I did nothing except put my head down and work, dawn until dusk, on tons and tons of games. One of the first was *Wing Commander 2* and then I worked on *Wing Commander 3* and *Wing Commander 4*. I worked on an aeroplane game called *Strike Commander*, and Origin's first CD-ROM game, a conversion of *Ultima 6* to the FM Towns PC for the Japanese market, and then around '93 I stopped programming altogether to just create data, WAV files and MIDI files, and relied on the game programmers to do the driving software that would play back the audio. It was a sea change in my career.

[*] Roberts was the developer of *Stryker's Run* for the BBC, and went on to make *Wing Commander* at Origin.

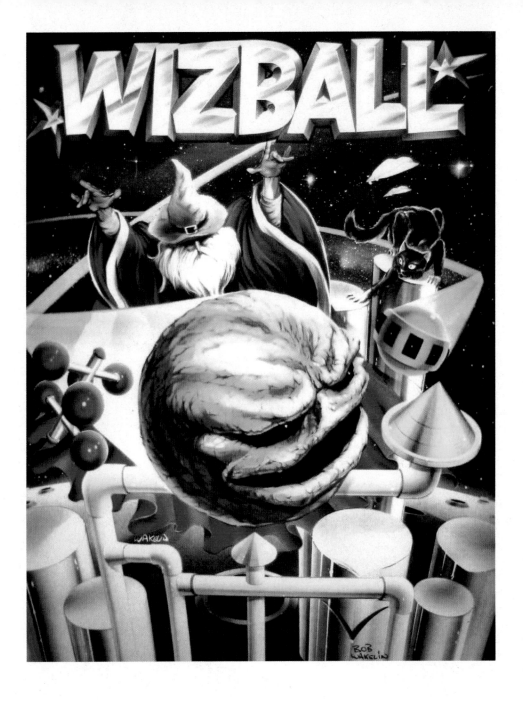

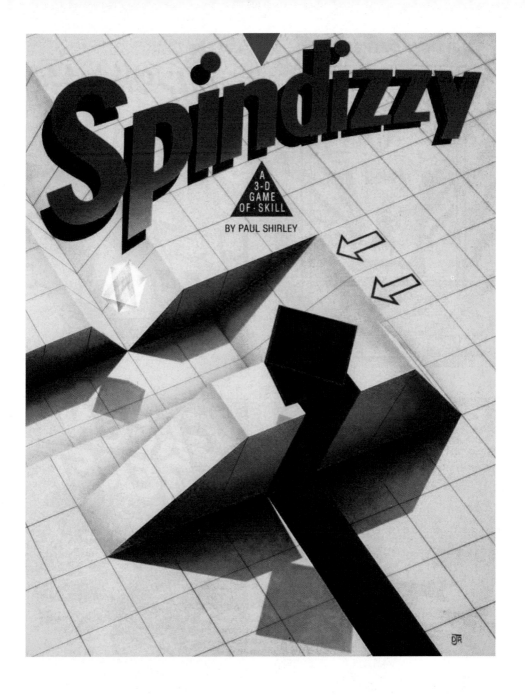

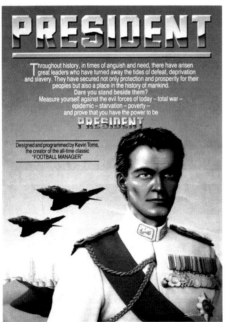

# BAZOOKA BILL

## ARCADE

**COMMODORE** £9.95

**SPECTRUM** £8.95

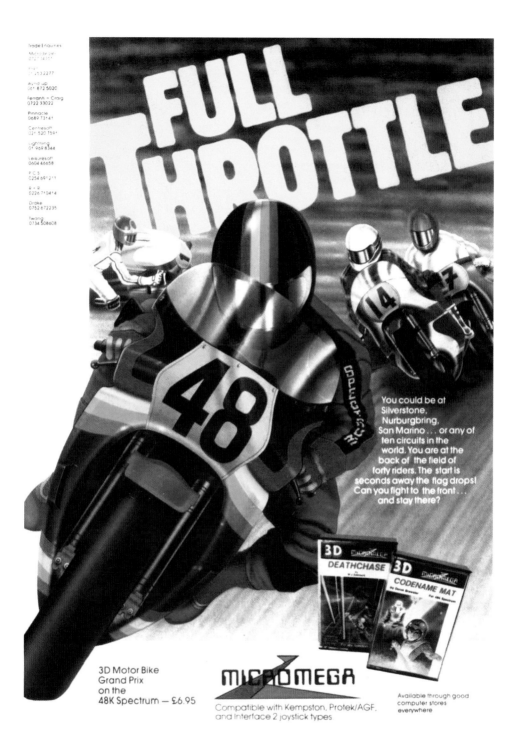

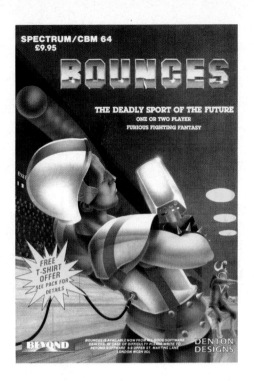

# INTERNATIONAL KARATE +

They called International Karate the
best beat-em-up so far.
And who are we to argue?
But System 3 have
come up with a stunner:
A Third Fighter. Some amazing
backgrounds. New moves. Re-mixed music.
And balls.

Commodore 64/128 Cassette (£9.99) and Disk (£14.99)
Coming soon for Spectrum and Amstrad home computers

Mail Order  Activision (UK) Ltd, Units 3 & 4 Lloyds Close,
Finedon Road Industrial Estate, Wellingborough,
Northampton NN8 4SR  Tel  (0933) 78787

Distributed by Activision (UK) Ltd

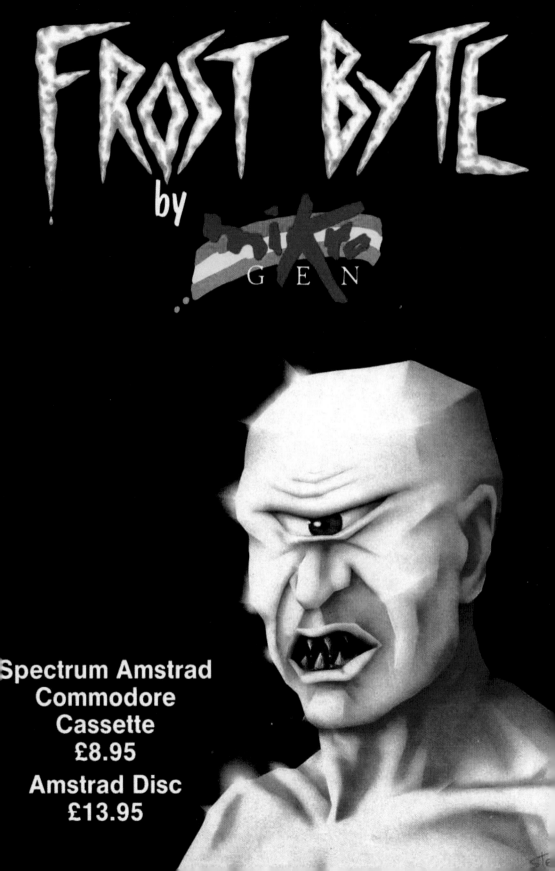

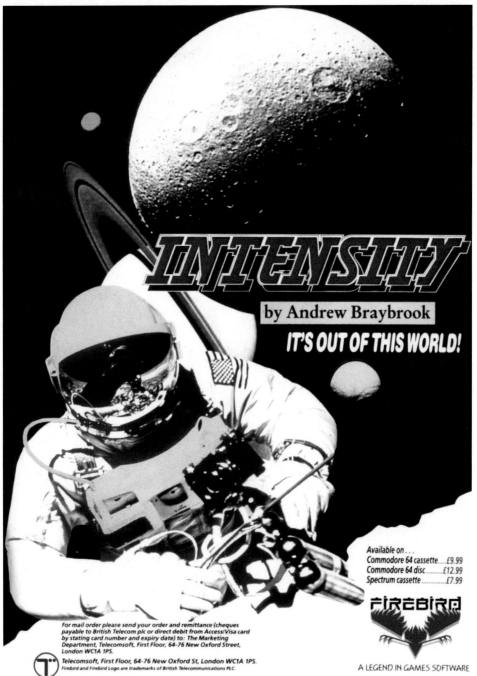

Game Artworks

# Part 7

# Maturing Industry

When the 8-bit consoles arrived
on the scene, I can remember
reading that one of my favourite
companies, Ultimate, who made
some of the best games on the
Spectrum, were giving up
and were going to concentrate
on these Japanese things.
I thought it was peculiar, but
boy were they right.

The Stampers* were some of the smartest people out there. They're obviously just brilliant creative people, and some of their products were outstanding; way, way ahead of the curve. *Knight Lore* is probably one of the most-cloned games. Also, either by luck or by judgement, they foresaw the fall of the British gaming industry, and got out of home micro programming and into consoles some four or five years ahead of the market. They saw what was happening in Japan and realised that the same thing was going to happen in America, and that if they were going to remain successful they needed to be making console games, because they were going to be the next big thing.

**Martin Galway**

They were proud and friendly enough with the other businesses to send them complimentary copies of their games, so Ocean got a box of 10 games of I think it was *Underwurlde* and we all marvelled at how cool it was. It was kind of like being shown how it really should be done. It was like, 'Wow, these guys are so confident that their game is awesome that they are sending it to their rivals on the day of release.'

I remember in the mid '80s wondering what happened to Ultimate. Had they gone out of business? They seemed to have dropped off the face of the Earth. Maybe they were just enjoying their riches! And then in the '90s when I got my first NES, I started playing imported games from America made by Rare,* and the penny dropped. These guys have been making Nintendo games at a very high premium, and selling them very well, making an absolute bank! When they became a Nintendo second-party developer in '91, '92, they were set.

The funny thing, really, was that they were possibly one of the most influential British developers, and nobody knew what they were doing in Japan and America. It was pre-internet, so nobody was looking at other markets, and no one was reporting on these games because nobody had the systems.

> ˣ Tim and Chris Stamper, the founders of Ultimate Play the Game and Rare. Ultimate was bought out by U.S. Gold in 1985, the Stampers having established a new company, Rare, which then bought back the rights to their Ultimate games in 1988.
> * Rare's first release for a console was skiing game *Slalom*, released in 1987.

When the 8-bit consoles arrived on the scene, I can remember reading that one of my favourite companies, Ultimate, who made some of the best games on the Spectrum, were giving up and were going to concentrate on these Japanese things. I thought it was peculiar, but boy were they right.

The 8-bit consoles outperformed the machines that were around. They gave a much slicker effect for a cheap price, but the problem was that the early ones used cartridges, which had to be manufactured. Some publishers told me they had to put up over a million pounds to pre-order cartridges from the console manufacturers, because you weren't allowed to order the cartridges from anyone else. You also needed a licence to sell your game, so suddenly the game industry was being closed, and the publishers were starting to get dictated to by manufacturers.

Publishers weren't interested in original games, full stop. They spent a lot of money on buying a licence for a game, and that money was going out of the industry instead of coming back into developing games or nurturing the talent that was building them. You got all this money going out to some film company, like Teenage Mutant Hero Turtles. I can remember a finance director saying, 'I know the game's crap but it's a licence to print money.' They didn't even care what the game was like. They were highly commercial and packaged, and it was completely the opposite of what we were about.

But we did send game ideas to some of the publishers that had spent excessive amounts on licences, saying we would do a proper game and match the titles they bought, but the problem was that they'd spend so much on the property that they hardly had any money left to spend on doing the game. So they'd go to a software house that didn't have a lot of overheads, which used to be the people who hadn't matured into companies like ours, so back to bedroom programmers. Sometimes they were successful, but more often than not they weren't, and they'd stop the game in progress and the poor programmer would run out of money.

You also had another sort of software house that started emerging, which was a specialist in producing those cheap games and conversions. We actually got into some of that business ourselves as a little sideline to make ends meet, underwriting the cost of our original games by producing licensed ones. But we picked and chose, so we did *Rainbow Islands,* which we liked the look of, and thought we could do a really good version of for the Amiga. You could hardly tell it from the original.

The first game console we became really aware of was the Nintendo Entertainment System. We used to go to the Consumer Electronics Show, which was in Las Vegas in January and Chicago in June. I've probably been like 25 times. One time everybody was talking about how amazing the Amiga was, and there was this tiny little company with a little grey box with a game called *Duck Hunt*, which didn't look that great, to be honest. All the retailers, like Toys "R" Us, were ignoring it because they had their fingers burned so badly from the videogame crash. They never wanted to hear about another console as long as they lived, and Nintendo was just this little Japanese company nobody was interested in.

But a couple of shows later, the NES had taken off in America, and it had gone to a mass consumer level very, very quickly. We thought we had to get into this market, because the American market is the biggest in the world. So we needed to know how to program for it. The Commodore 64 was an open architecture, so you could go into a shop and you could buy a book that Commodore published about how to program it. That's how all the home computers worked. But Nintendo kept it all a secret. So we started working with engineers and working out how to reverse-engineer the machine. Andrew Graham* worked on converting *Treasure Island Dizzy* to the NES, and another guy built one of the first development machines that we used.

Later on, we worked with Andrew to create the Game Genie. We thought it would be good if you had a game where you could adjust how many lives and things you had, and then we thought we could build an adaptor where you can actually adjust other people's games. And then we thought we could sell it to all of the game players in America who were adopting this machine. The Game

← 300  360 →

## Peter Stone and Richard Leinfellner

RL I could really see consoles coming. Nintendo had just launched the NES, and Steve and I thought it was interesting having an instant load. I thought they were really going somewhere, but Palace didn't really want to do console because it was a different ball game and we had no experience with it. Maybe the Stamper brothers had done something with them, but that was it, outside Japan. But I could really see the market would start to change, and I suppose my concern at the time was whether a small company like Palace Software could survive.

* Designer of *Micro Machines*, which was first released for the NES in 1991.

Genie itself was a bit of a gimmick, just to make these games seem better, but then we made the mental leap to realising we could actually do this to other people's games if we had an adapter sitting between *Super Mario Bros.* and the NES. Maybe we could make Mario jump higher or give you 10 lives. We applied for a patent and licensed it to a toy company in San Francisco called Lewis Galoob Toys, and it became very successful.

## Oliver twins

When we went to America for the first time to a trade show, Nintendo were launching the SNES, and the NES was there. We were just looking at it going, 'This is a huge market!' The Codemasters games then were very much European. Actually, very much UK-centric, though we had fairly good success with *Dizzy* in Germany and Spain. But America was a whole new ball game. We were looking at the Nintendo market and the fact that *Mario* had sold millions of units, whereas we tended to look at tens of thousands, possibly hundreds of thousands and that was absolutely maximum. They were really slick, and we were thinking, well, we could go for ST and Amiga, or we can go for this new console market, and we decided at that point to go after the console market.

It wasn't out of our reach to do a similar game, so we wanted to tackle the biggest market, the biggest market being America, and of course if we could get that then our sales were going to be tenfold. We were still publishing our games with Codemasters, and in fact they had taken a stand at the trade show. Our trip to America was very much trying to get our Codemasters games into the American market, but we all came away, Codemasters included, with the idea that we should be on the NES.

Even when I was a school kid I looked at British Leyland going bust and all these industries, and it was like, you've got to sell to the world. If you're going to make something once and design it once you've got to sell it to the biggest market. So we were just trying to do the same, to make games for a worldwide audience, not just the small niche market of the UK.

When we were still teenagers we went on this funny little business course at the local college, and I remember going to see a speaker talking about the fact that the British car industry was being flattened by Japanese cars, and that we are very good at innovating in Britain but very bad at exporting. That was always on our mind, and we were always quick with the *Dizzy* games to get them translated and out in France, Germany.

PD If you think about it, even Sir Clive Sinclair, I mean, he was shit at getting stuff out of the UK. The BBC Micro. That was never found anywhere else in the world, even though it was awesome.

AD The next couple of years were a little bit of a struggle, and I don't want to go into it too much, but we decided that actually there were other publishers like Activision and EA that were already there. So, we started talking to them, as there seemed to be a bit of a struggle with Codemasters.

← 327

## David Darling

330 →

We approached Nintendo to become a developer at CES. To be honest, I'm not the best sales guy in the world, but we approached them and they just said they hadn't got time to talk to us. All their meetings were booked up. They were working with just a handful of Japanese and American companies, it wasn't like nowadays with Apple, where anybody can become a developer. So they basically showed us the door, and we thought we didn't really have any choice, and would have to work out how to program this machine, whether they liked it or not.

Requiring a licence was a contentious issue. Accolade were doing unlicensed games, and Electronic Arts had reverse-engineered the NES and were ready to launch unlicensed games and use them as a lever to get a licence. The only reason licensing really happened was that Nintendo was a Japanese toy company. They weren't used, like Sinclair was, to just trying to sell computers. Sinclair didn't mind you making good games because then people would buy more computers from them, but because Nintendo was a Japanese toy company, they wanted to control the whole market themselves.

So they applied for a patent to a lock and key chip, and that was how they were able to control the licensing, because to make a Nintendo game you had to put a key chip in the game cartridge, which unlocked a lock chip in the NES. If you replicated it, you infringed their patent, because they had the exclusive right to assemble, distribute and sell it. So we were trying to think of ways round using their patent.

With Game Genie it wasn't really an issue, because you still had the game cartridge in the NES, and the Game Genie was just in the middle. We manufactured the Game Genie in Taiwan, so my brother had gone there for a few weeks to set it up, and a guy there called Dragon Chen came up with a way that you could confuse the key chip rather than unlock the lock, so it didn't shut down the Nintendo. It would just stay in this confused state and the game would just run. We found a way to electronically make the game work without using Nintendo's patent.

We had already developed some games for NES, *Treasure Island Dizzy* first of all. While you are developing there isn't a legal problem with lock and key chips, it's only when you start manufacturing. But we actually released Game Genie beforehand and then got stuck in all the Game Genie litigation for a couple of years. So that slowed us down for a bit. But by the stage we were ready to release games we had *Micro Machines*, *Dizzy* and a few other games like *Stunt Kids* ready, and we released them through a company called Camerica.

I am just guessing as to why Nintendo sued us over the Game Genie, but I think they were afraid that it would open the floodgates on their licensing programme. They had convinced everybody that you needed a licence, so for them it was like a poker game, where they had to up the ante. It was incredibly risky for us, but I don't know, it was like being on a roller coaster: you can't get off. We wanted to win the court case, because we had spent years creating

## David Darling

Nintendo sued Lewis Galoob Toys over derivative copyright infringement. If you write a book like *Harry Potter*, you have the exclusive right to make copies of it and write sequels, and nobody else can copy it without your authorisation. Nintendo was saying that because Mario was jumping higher, Game Genie was creating a new game which was similar to the original game and we were creating a derivative work, or Game Genie was enabling players to create a derivative work. Our argument was that for a derivative work to be infringing it needs to be permanent, and here it wasn't, because when you unplugged the Game Genie, Mario went back to how he originally was.

It started off with a temporary restraining order, then an injunction, then court, and then to an appeal to the Ninth Circuit, then it went to appeal to the Supreme Court, and after, like, three years we won and Nintendo had to pay $15 million in damages and the product could be sold in the US. Lewis Galoob Toys sold $140 million of them, and Game Genie was the fifth best-selling toy in America in 1991, so it was good in the end.

this product and we wanted millions of people to enjoy it. It wasn't just about the money, and we put our life and soul into making the games and trying to win.

Jez San

One of our best achievements was being able to make a platform do something that it wasn't designed to do, which opened it up to new forms of games. Early on, when the Game Boy had been announced but hadn't come out, we reverse-engineered it, emulated what we thought it would be, and built a game of *Tetris* running on a fake Game Boy emulator on an Amiga.

Then, when the real Game Boy came out, it didn't take us very long to get our game running on it, just days. We went to CES and I found the most senior person I could find at Nintendo and showed them our game running on the Game Boy. We weren't a licensed developer, and we had no documentation, so we were not supposed to be able to make a game on a Game Boy. Also, there was some copy protection built into the Game Boy which is related to the Nintendo logo dropping down on the screen before the game starts. If the 'Nintendo' isn't there, the game won't start, but we managed to drop down the word Argonaut and our game would start. We defeated Nintendo's ingenious protection scheme with literally one cent's worth of hardware: a resistor and a capacitor.

So when I showed it to Nintendo, their world fell apart. The thing that stopped developers like us making games for their system didn't work. I got back to England and a few days later I got a phone call from Nintendo asking me to go to Kyoto the next morning to meet Mr Yamauchi, the president. I spent quite a lot of time with Nintendo Japan, and they were very nice to me. They took me around Kyoto, showed me all 2,000 of the temples in Kyoto, every single one. They do look quite similar, it has to be said.

For my meeting with Yamauchi-san I was dressed up in a suit, which was a rarity for me, and they took me into his room, which was boiling hot and I was very uncomfortable in my suit. Effectively, this old man made me feel like he was a mafia boss or something. His daughter was the translator and he said he wanted me to make 3D games for Nintendo, and to teach Nintendo how to make them. He asked me how much I wanted, and at this point I thought of the biggest number I could possibly think of, which was a million dol-

* Nintendo's handheld was first released in Japan in 1989, quickly followed by North America later that year, then Europe in September 1990.

lars, and then I doubled it and said, 'Two million dollars,' nervously thinking he was going to tell me to go away. But he said yes, and I realised that I could have named any number. I was probably too cheap, but I was like 21 at the time, and for me $2 million was a hell of a lot of money.

I got back to my hotel that night and I got a phone call from my brother in London, and he said, 'Jez, were you expecting $2 million in your account?' It turned out that Yamauchi-san just sent the money and didn't wait for a contract. We negotiated the contract after that and did a three-game deal and a technology transfer. I went to Kyoto every month to teach Nintendo how to do 3D games, literally in a classroom.

We had to jump through hoops to make the NES hardware do 3D. The display is character-mapped so it's designed for scrolling, but we worked out a way, which we patented, of converting that character map into a bitmap. *Star Fox* at the time was codenamed 'NES Glider', as it was *Starglider* on the NES, and we showed it to them and they liked it. It was pretty good considering it was running on a NES. They wanted to do more, but it was running as fast as the hardware would allow it.

So we said we could always design a 3D chip. I said that with a 3D chip we could make it go 10 times faster – I made up that number, just plucked it out of the air – and they said, 'Fine, here's a million dollars, go make us a 3D chip.' We called it the Mario chip, the 'Mathematical Argonaut Rotation IO' chip, and it later got renamed by Nintendo the Super FX chip.

We developed 'NES Glider' on the NES, but Nintendo had showed us the Super Famicom˚ before it came out and told us that they were thinking about putting our 3D chip inside it for the American market, but it turned out it was too late, so the 3D chip had to go in the game cartridge. That meant the game cartridge would be more expensive to make, and only Nintendo could afford to subsidise the cost, so the only games that used the Super FX chip were by Nintendo.

Anyway, it did 3D math and rendering, and it was a fully programmable RISC processor. At the time, it was the bestselling RISC processor, selling far more than the ARM was selling. In the end, it ended up being 40 times faster, and we surprised even ourselves, and the chip allowed *Star Fox* and several other 3D games to come out on the Super Nintendo system.

˚ The Japanese name for the Super Nintendo.

When the Sega Mega Drive showed up,[*] it was natural for Probe Software to say, 'Here, take one. What can you guys do with it?' It was a 68000,[ˑ] so great! We could handle the Mega Drive, and started to develop for it. What was really funny was the manuals, which were written in Japanese, so I couldn't understand a word. I was trying to look at the diagrams and work out what was going on, and I actually misread a section and found a way to get more data through a Mega Drive than you were supposed to be able to, and I ended up with a bit of a competitive edge against other Mega Drive programmers, which I think was for a few years, before it was published by Sega as being an official way to transmit data. In games like *Aladdin* and *Cool Spot* we were using that trick.

[*] The Mega Drive was released in Europe in 1990, two years after its initial Japanese release.

[ˑ] The 68000 processor was the same type as that found in the Amiga and Atari ST.

That's an interesting part of making games: it's not always a fully level playing field. Sometimes you're competing against people who know the hardware better than you, who maybe even work at Sega or Nintendo. So that's another interesting dynamic that's always going on: it's not just about making the game, it's about trying to find ways to drive this piece of hardware to its limits. But if you came from the old days, when you had no memory and nothing but limitations, this was an acceptable paradigm; like, it was okay to assume that you're going to have to really drive this piece of hardware. If it can't do what I want, how do I make it look like it's doing what I want? That's very quickly where games went, they turned into an arms race against all the other programmers that were out there, to see who could make this hardware look the most impressive.

← 328

## Oliver twins

PO When we went to the NES we were expected to learn a new language and a new way of doing the art pipeline and everything else. It really slowed us down. The first game was three or four months, when we were making them every month before.

AO Yes, we wrote *Fantastic Dizzy* on the Nintendo system[ˣ] and it took about eight months and we needed some help, but we had quite a lot of money.

PO We decided that we needed to get an artist in, but of course we were still working from a house at that point and it wasn't really

[ˣ] Released in April 1991, *Fantastic Dizzy* was originally slated for a release in time for Christmas 1990, but was held up by Codemasters' legal case with Nintendo.

right to invite people into your house. So we decided that with the money we had at the time, which was significant money, we were actually ready to do this properly and set up an office and start hiring, and build up a team of 8, 10 people. Running the business was a very interesting exercise. I took the main responsibility for finding an office, negotiating the contract, sorting out all the utilities and recruiting for staff, and you'd try to keep your hand in and keep doing the games. We got to about 10 or 12 people in about '94, just at the point the PlayStation was coming in. We decided the PlayStation was an awesome machine, with 3D graphics and a CD to save your games on to. It was going to be a hit. We were offered so much work, and we were already good at the biz dev trips and going into publishers and presenting ourselves. Within two or three years, we'd hired 50, 60 people and actually ended up growing out of that office. It was a great time.

Although, one of the reasons why we grew wasn't just because there was lots of money on the table, but because there were lots of hits and misses, and you're always worried about a miss. We started having a lot of bills and paying wages and it's like, 'If we put everyone on to one game and it fails,' we just heard horror stories around us all the time, and we'd think, 'Oh dear. I'd hate for us to get burnt like that.' So we had a second team, and then a third, so if a publisher or a game failed on us those people could move across to another team and carry on for a couple of months.

## Mike Montgomery

We were in our office in Wapping for many years – in fact it's the only office we ever had. It was Metropolitan Wharf, an old Victorian warehouse in a cobbled street. When the building shook, like when a bomb went off in the Docklands, all these cocoa shells that rats had taken up into the rafters would fall out of all these holes. Metropolitan Wharf was used in TV adverts because it was a pretty trendy place, but when you got into our office, because we didn't have much money, it was dark and dingy and the floors weren't smooth. There were holes all over the place. We bought some cheap carpet from some dodgy dealer one day and it stayed down for probably 10 years. But it was a nice office, large and cheap. At the beginning, when there were only three or four of us, you could've had a football match in there, and later on we moved over to look out over the river, which was better still.

At the beginning of projects everything would be a little more relaxed, and people drifted into the office and left about the same time, and as the project went on it got more and more manic, to the extent that we had a few beds in the office. Quite often people just didn't go home, and for me to do five or six days in a row was common. But also that was the atmosphere. We worked as a team and there was always a nice atmosphere. I know they say I carried a baseball bat around with me and used it a few times – I can't remember doing that, but I guess there's no smoke without fire – and I was relatively strict, but I was also lenient about working as a team. It's when you don't work together that it becomes a nightmare, and if you had a rotten apple you had to get rid of it.

Most of the games we played in the studio were our own games, which seems silly, but we wanted to write games we wanted to play. We played a lot of *Sensi Soccer*, there was a lot of *Kick Off*. It was mainly two-player games like that. Us three founders didn't do any work for three weeks when *Dungeon Master* came out. But we enjoyed playing our own games as well as other people's. We didn't pick through other people's, mostly because we didn't want to plagiarise, so we kept away a bit, and anyway, when you're a developer, you don't get the time sometimes to play games.

←162

## Nigel Alderton

After *Commando* I was completely burnt out. I should have taken a couple of months off but I went into writing *Ghosts'n Goblins* on the Amstrad, and that was a real struggle. I wasn't working in Elite's office, I was working on my own in a little office I had hired. It was a battle, and it just took the fun out of it all, so I needed a change of direction after that, and I left programming.

I had a conversation with Steve Wilcox, and they were publishing all sorts of other games. He had loads of programmers working freelance all over the place and he was trying to keep track of them. I said that he should hire somebody to do that, and he said, 'Well, okay, you can have the job if you want it.' I thought, 'Oh, that's an idea. Maybe I could do that instead?'

As time went on, the game industry obviously evolved into more of a professional business, and I think I wanted to be more professional, to be a manager rather than being a programmer. So I was keeping track of the programmers, logging how far I thought they had got, chasing them up and working out why they had hit a wall, and trying to encourage them. I was on the other side, so it was

* Due to the technical demands of full-screen scrolling on the Amstrad CPC, this 1986 conversion suffered with low resolution graphics and a restricted colour palette.

interesting for me to find out what it was like trying to get programmers to do stuff when I had been a programmer.

By the time I left the games industry it was more dominated by the consoles coming in from Japan and you needed much bigger teams of people. It was still a bit like the Wild West, still a bit mad, but it was just bigger, mad teams rather than people working on their own, and I just lost interest. There was no room for the individual coder beavering away on his own, unless you could come up with a *Tetris*, which is just one in a million.

I also got fed up with being on the management side, and out of the games industry, and out into the proper grown-up world. I still felt as if I was a kid, really. Maybe it was because it's what I had done as a hobby and as a kid at school, and so I just associated it all with being a child, and I wanted to get away from that.

## Martin Kenwright

I thought that I had nothing to lose and everything to gain by leaving Rowan, I thought I could do this all myself. I gave my notice and took up some jobs for Microdeal, and I did three games in something like six months, including *Turbo Trax* and a scenery disk for *Goldrunner II*. I felt so motivated and driven after what had happened, and I also saw everything that was wrong with the likes of *Falcon*: how elitist it was, how difficult it was. Why is no one making a flight sim that a 10-year-old would be blown away by, and would humble a 30-year-old? I had worked on all these serious Harrier, Spitfire and Falcon games, and they were all a bit intensive for me. Could I do something really cool and exciting?

At that point, Russell Payne left Rowan as well, and another guy too, and I said, 'Look, why don't we do it? Why don't we make our own killer game?' It became the classic bedroom story: from my bedroom in a little council house I started making *F29 Retaliator*, although it wasn't originally called *F29*, it was called 'F22 Retaliator', but the publisher, who we didn't have at the time, thought 'F29' looked better. It didn't really matter that the plane on the box didn't really look like the name. Hey, what days.

I knocked the demo up in just six weeks, totally from scratch, with Russ. It was very plain, but we took it into Ocean and met some bloke called Gary Bracey. I remember his braces and scouse accent; he was from the posh bit of Liverpool, not the council estates like me, and before I knew it he got Jon Woods down and he shoved a £2,000 cheque in my hand and asked who to make it out to. I'd been thinking of all these company names, and literally put on the spot, we created the name Digital Image Design just so they could put a name on the cheque. We went and had pizzas, and I couldn't believe it, I had a £20,000 publishing deal. Maybe it would keep us going for a year or two.

It was an amazing time of camaraderie, and the pressure was on. The early demos looked fantastic and the magazines wanted a piece, the publisher was having wet dreams tying up all kinds of deals, but through all of this, because it was our baby and we were all happy, it didn't matter. We lived in our own little world, we just ate, slept, drank *F29 Retaliator*.

We started taking on our first staff, and I went back to college, where my art teacher had marked my A-level mocks right down and said, 'Martin, you can't draw spaceships all your life.' So I went in there saying, 'I'm making computer games. Have you got any good artists coming through?' I wanted to give some artists the same chance I had, and we actually took on a couple, and got a little unit near the end of developing *F29* in 1989. It was 250 square feet, and just a pit really, 100 yards from where Evolution Studios<sup>×</sup> is now.

The relationship with Ocean was interesting. Gary was flapping, he was stressed about anything we were doing. I think Ocean saw the opportunity to become a bit of a global player, because the type of game we were doing had global appeal, it wasn't a local little Noddy game. For the first time, people realised they could make true global franchises, and have sales figures on another level from the 8-bit days. So he was under pressure. He would turn up at the office unannounced and there would be no one in at lunchtime, but little did he know that we had been there for 80 hours non-stop.

We also didn't know how long it would take to finish, and it probably didn't help when people like Phil would say we thought it would be ready next week, so, you know, all the buttons would be pressed and then Commodore would say they would love to bundle it with every Amiga, so you can kind of imagine the pressure.

We didn't have the opportunities of a big QA department, we just tested it day and night, as much as we could. We got testers in from Ocean, too, and we just knew we had a brilliant game, but it was a bit of a rough diamond. It was almost a race against the clock, though, to get it complete before we ran out of money.

× The studio that Martin Kenwright would go on to found in 1999 after the sale of Ocean to Infogrames.

Thinking back, the deal was a proper stitch-up, although Gary, I have to tell him that they actually gave us 2% more in royalties. Gary said 12%, and we would have said yeah to anything because it was our first publisher deal. But in the documents it was 14%. Yeah, that's right Gary! It was 14% royalty and a £20,000 advance. In the end, though, it was me with begging bowls trying to get an extra grand or two to put petrol in the car. It really was touch and go. That naïvety got me through, though. If I knew what I know now, we would have never gotten out of bed.

At the same time, I was also looking at what's next, and about where we were going. All of a sudden we were taking staff on, and we had to become VAT-registered, and very strange things started happening: the whole idea of actually running it as a proper business. I hadn't even considered the idea of actually saving receipts properly. Administration was an afterthought, and boy did that come and bite me up the backside.

The tax men actually turned up to close me down because I hadn't done a VAT return, and the only reason they didn't was because I managed to sit them down with cups of tea, and gave them the game to play because it was near-finished. They stayed for four or five hours while I ran around, calling my little high-street accountant, going through shoeboxes full of receipts, ringing round mates trying to get a bit of money. In the end they turned around, smiled, and said that was a lovely cup of tea and that game's fantastic. 'It was the best afternoon we have had in six months, and don't worry, we will give you another three months.' People have no idea how much of a close run thing it was, trying to make games in those days.

Jon Hare

Those small publishing companies run by individuals – Chris Blackwell of Island Records would be the best example in the music industry – guys who are building a label but they're still art-first people. We had people of that mentality up until the mid '90s, and it coincides with when the UK was strong in publishing.

From the period of '85 to '95 we had something very akin to the music model in games, where the developers would go to the publishers and show them their new product, which was at some stage of completion, normally about a third of the way through, and they would look for a publishing deal.

There'd be a royalty deal and they would get paid in advance against those royalties. So, say if you were paid £50,000 as an advance against 25%, for example, that means you're going to get 25% of the money coming in. So for the first £200,000 that came in, you'd get nothing because you've already had your 25%, which was the £50,000 you got paid up front. The advantage was the security of that money, which enabled you to finish the game, to not stress and make it good.

To my mind these are the best-balanced deals. The publisher's getting what they want. They know their outlay and development cost, and the developer also knows his income, plus he's got internal costs to pay all his different programmers, artists and whoever else is working for him, but if he's smart he'll work it out so that he's got a little bit of profit in that money. And then you're secure. And if the game sells zero copies, you're okay. Everyone's got paid, everyone paid their mortgage, no one died, everyone's happy. If you do this a few times, back to back, the better ones will start to earn small royalties on top, because you'll have paid off that advance.

← 334 ## Mike Montgomery 344 →

There is one really good thing that The Bitmap Brothers learned, and it is the two letters I and P. We kept all of ours, 100%, and we still do to this day. All my games, I have the IP. I haven't let a publisher have any of it. So when we went to Image Works and we wanted to do *Xenon 2*,[×] it wasn't a problem because the IP was mine. I am not being big-headed, but all of our games are by The Bitmap Brothers, not by Image Works.

The IP is your bread and butter, and it came down to the philosophy of The Bitmap Brothers: we wanted to promote the developer and the people who worked there, rather than the publisher. To be fair, all the publishers we worked with agreed with that philosophy, until we got more famous than them, and then they didn't like it.

× The original was published by Melbourne House, then an imprint of Mastertronic.

← 338 ## Jon Hare 341 →

When we were working on *Sensible Soccer* or *Cannon Fodder*, I took a floppy disk to the bank manager's office at Lloyds and asked for a loan: 'We're doing this stuff, we've got these games, people say they're going to be great, can we have some money?' And I was totally blanked. But in a way I'm glad. As it turned out, we never borrowed money all the time we ran Sensible. We ran Sensible over 13 years at an average of 49% profit a year, and never borrowed a penny.

In my experience with Sensible, we were at our strongest with six people. We were good when we were two. With six people we produced *Mega lo Mania*, *Sensible Soccer*, *Wizkid*, then *Cannon Fodder*. Tonnes of profit. If you're talking about how to run a good games company, that's it. Costs down, income through the ceiling, lots of fun, lots of hard work.

## Peter Molyneux

*Populous* was an incredible success, but Electronic Arts would phone up and say we had all this money but they omitted to say that because of the horrendous contract we signed we weren't going to get any of it for months and months. We had signed up with them to do this sequence of other titles, and so we immediately went into a game called *Powermonger*, and that meant we had to expand our team. We had to bring on new artists, and one of them was Paul McLaughlin, who I still work with today. We had to work fast, and we were starting to become a proper little business. There was no money really to do much else; the money we did have was the upfront balance from signing up *Powermonger* with Electronic Arts.

It was probably the hardest I have ever worked in my life. *Powermonger* could have been brilliant, but it missed out that vital ingredient that *Populous* had, which was us playing it. We literally wrote it and then released it, and we didn't go through that step of playing and refining it. I think that was a huge mistake, because if we had played it I think we could have stumbled upon the RTS. *Powermonger* was so close to being an RTS, and it could have been a lot more successful than it actually was. Even so, it was a number one seller, sold hundreds of thousands of copies, but it was such a shame. If we had just spent that extra few months playing it, it would have been so much better.

The interesting thing about those days – and this still exists today – is that publishers didn't tend to demand you do things on a certain day, but instead they gave you a big carrot. The carrot at that particular time was, if we made *Powermonger* by Christmas they would spend a huge amount of money on marketing and release it globally, so it would be a big, big success. Of course we were all dizzy and high from the success of *Populous*, and of course you want another success. It feels great, you know, to have journalists come round and get them drunk and get high review scores. So they didn't demand that we do it. It was just something they gave a big incentive for, and so I think we did the whole thing in around nine months. I mean, nine months doesn't sound very long in the context of today's AAA games, but you know it was actually a long time in development terms during those early years.

*Mega lo Mania* was our first full Amiga game. It was a very, very difficult game to make, the hardest game I've made, to be honest, in terms of hours, because we really changed it around a lot. And that was good. That was a good hit, but it came out two months before the Mirror Group imploded, before Mr Maxwell jumped off his boat, taking all our royalties with him, I might add. Eventually we re-signed it to Ubisoft and it got republished, but it had lost its momentum. Nevertheless, it was received well, and then after that we did *Sensible Soccer*, *Cannon Fodder*, then *Wizkid*.

We started to think about the idea for *Sensible Soccer* while we were finishing *Mega lo Mania*. People forget we'd already made *MicroProse Soccer* about four years before *Sensible Soccer* came out, so we'd done one before. Chris Yates, Chris Chapman and me were all keen football fans, and Chris Chapman and I were working very late nights with *Mega lo Mania* and we were playing a lot of *Kick Off 2*, which we liked but it had some irritating features.

˥ Released in 1991, *Mega lo Mania* was an early real-time strategy game.

*Mega lo Mania* was a really complicated game, with you deciding who was going to fight, who was going to mine, or man turrets, and the right-hand side of the screen was representative of what you had ordered. I was the artist for that game. It was a lot of information to impart, but because of memory we could only have 16 sprites, I think it was, so to show battles of 100 versus 60, we'd have 10 versus six sprites. And you'd also see your castle, mine, factory or design laboratory, and these guys running around had to be proportionally scaled to the buildings, 12 pixels high, and that's how they came about.

So when I was hanging around at the end of that process, waiting for the bugs to be fixed on *Mega lo Mania*, we were playing *Kick Off 2*, and we were thinking of a new football game we wanted to make. I started dressing the *Mega lo Mania* men up in football kits, purely because it was the easiest way to get a footballer into a game. I made a pitch proportional to those men, correct to real-life scale, and at the same angle as *Mega lo Mania*, and that's how the look came about, because it was the easiest way to make it happen.

Once we had the game running, we found it was extremely good for strategy. The viewpoint gave you vision, the position of your other players and the opposition, and you could see the goal from far back. That was a lot of the reason Sensible Soccer is remembered for being a fast-passing game to play. Then, of course, we took that to Cannon Fodder. We always made it with the screen scrolling so that it slides back so you can see more in front of your sprite.

I thought Kick Off and Kick Off 2 were great games and I enjoyed them, but they frustrated me, too. Very much, the problem we had with Kick Off was the fact we couldn't see the pitch. You would pass a ball and you couldn't see who you were passing to! It's not how you play football. Sensible Soccer was faster than real football, but the decisions you made were very similar, seeing people in front.

When you're at the top, as Dino was and then we were with Sensible Soccer, and you're superseded – we got superseded by FIFA – it's a bit like real football. It became about licences and TV with FIFA. I mean, we had 1,500 accurate teams in Sensible World of Soccer. I was a big Subbuteo player and football fan when I was a kid, and I liked the idea of having all the teams, so the international side of Sensible Soccer was really important. I'm really proud of a number of things, so we were the first game to have black players, for example, which sounds like a triviality now, but you used to play with John Barnes but he was white, which ruined the illusion of whoever the team was. We also had guys in the game with blond hair and dark hair. Suddenly your brain fills in the gaps and you see John Barnes and you're playing as Liverpool.

Licensing and likenesses with sports was always a grey area, but it got to a time, when we first put Sensible Soccer on the Mega Drive, when Sega were much more cautious and the laws changed, and we had to mess around with the names.

## Dino Dini

I left Anco in 1992. The story behind that is all to do with my arch nemesis, Sensible Software. They had their own development team and so on, and I was still one person outsourcing the graphics for Kick Off. They did a take on my game, and I have to say it's pretty similar in a lot of ways, but they were used to using small sprites and they changed the viewpoint. I was always afraid of using small sprites, because I thought people wouldn't like them; they'd complain about tiny sprites, but Sensible Software went with small sprites and the bigger view, and they created Sensible Soccer.

So they were pitching the game in various places, and they ended up talking to Anco. I remember having this conversation with Anil Gupta where I was a bit upset about finding this out. I said, 'Are you planning to do a deal with Sensible Software for *Sensible Soccer*?' And he said, 'Well, we are talking to them.' I said, 'What about loyalty?' And he said to me, 'I don't owe you any loyalty.'

That was entirely the wrong thing to say to me, because at that moment my relationship with Anco was dead. That is all it took. I didn't want to hear that. It was very profoundly upsetting. It's part of what goes on with this business, and, yeah, in business you have got to be robust. But business and art, they don't work very well together, and you have got to respect the art, and respect the relationship. It was terrible, so that is why I started looking for an alternative.

One of the advantages was that I worked on *Kick Off 3* without being paid advances by Anco, so I could pick up my bags and go somewhere else, and in the end Anco didn't do a deal with Sensible Software, but they kept the *Kick Off* name. What could I do? That's where I got split off from the name. You could blame it all on Sensible Software!

Well, the first thing I did after *Sensible Soccer* came out was to decide to incorporate a choice in *Goal!* so you could play it in the old view, the *Sensible Soccer*-type of view, with a zoomed-out camera, and also a side-on view, if people wanted. But yes, *Goal!* on the Amiga and ST was actually *Kick Off 3*. If Anil Gupta hadn't said that to me I would have stayed with Anco, and things may have been different. I don't know. Steve Screech stayed with Anco. You know, I never looked at his *Kick Offs*. I have never looked at them. I don't want to. Why would I want to?

The majority of the press was kind to me, but there was the odd exception. It was nothing ... it was to do with a particular ... I'm not going to say who it is; everybody knows who he is. But he was absolutely fanatic about *Sensible Soccer* and trashed anything that I did pretty much in reviews. That's perhaps a little unfair, not pretty much everything. I am not going to say who it was, everybody knows who it was.[x]

It is difficult. I take the most comfort from that quote of Ralph Waldo Emerson: 'The reward of a thing well done is having done it.' I take comfort from that, it was something that I did well, but I think over the years it has been difficult, because in order to really appreciate that, I have to detach myself from it first. It is also painful. I made mistakes, or I didn't get the break, or whatever. I didn't

x This would be Stuart Campbell, then acting editor of *Amiga Power*.

fulfil my dreams as a videogame developer, and then, in a way, when you look back at a success it rubs it in. Do you understand what I am saying?

But I think I have reached the stage now where I am old enough. In fact, yesterday I saw two guys playing *Kick Off 2*, and I just stood behind them and I watched them, how they responded and they went, 'Oh!' and all this excitement as they were playing it. It looked like they were having a lot of fun, and that really made me feel good. I have to let it go, I think. I don't know whether I am ever going to make another football game. Part of me really wants to, but I have to have the connection. I need to feel the energy; there has to be the fuel for the creativity, and I don't have that for video-games from within any more.

So if I ever make another game ... In fact, I am working on some little things, but they are little things, not games I am going to spend two years working on. I am working on an arty game, and it is not for sale. It is just as an art piece, you know? That will be a good thing to do, but yeah, in a way my heart broke a little bit. I think about this industry and there is pain there as well. Does that make sense?

## Mike Montgomery

‹ 339 577 ›

We used to talk about Sensible in the studio, and we were quite good friends, but I never knew until recently that they actually hated us. That isn't true, they didn't *hate* us, but Jops* told me the other night that they thought The Bitmap Brothers were a bunch of wankers. I think possibly a few other developers thought that way as well, because of our arrogance, but our arrogance was helping developers across the whole industry, not just ourselves, that's what is sometimes forgotten. We also admired Bullfrog, of course, and I was personally friends with a lot of the smaller developers around, especially the single-band people.

* Jon Hare's nickname.

## Jon Hare

‹ 341 552 ›

I've still got our old phone book, and in it The Bitmap Brothers are called 'The Bitmap wankers', with a big star around it. This is typical of Chris Yates's humour. But there's a reason for this! We were very resentful of other people's success in the media when we were younger. We had *Wizball*, *Parallax*, *Shoot 'Em Up Con-*

*struction Kit* and *MicroProse Soccer* out, and the Bitmaps came along with their shades and the stuff they did with the helicopter and that, and before we knew them personally we just saw them as having created this rock star persona and stolen our thunder. We'd had a bunch of hit games before them and we hadn't done that. We were jealous. I was also jealous of the guys at Codemasters at some stage for similar reasons of getting attention. Like a pathetic 15-year-old, but never mind.

Of course, I've worked with the Bitmaps for 15 years. We first met them at Mirrorsoft when we were doing *Mega lo Mania* and they were doing *Xenon 2*, but rather than be jealous any more, we decided to copy them, and we did our own photoshoot, with us wearing caps with 'MLM' on and shades. We could pretend to be rock stars, too, and actually we took it a stage further by doing videos for *Cannon Fodder* and *Sensible Soccer*. But we missed a trick and they got there first, and that's why we thought they were wankers, and then they ended up being our mates. We published with Renegade, which was the Bitmaps and Rhythm King records,* but we kept the phone book entry, because it was funny.

* Renegade Software published Sensible Software games from 1992's *Sensible Soccer: European Champions* onwards.

← 301

## Geoff Crammond

375→

*Stunt Car Racer* was the last made-up game that I did. At the time I was quite aware about the need for marketing, and there were so many games that were based on licensed deals or sequels, and I was questioning the whole idea of an original game like *The Sentinel* succeeding. Actually, during the three years making *Stunt Car Racer*, I questioned it a bit myself, not knowing how well it would do.

So after *Stunt Car Racer*, when I had a call from the publisher* about doing a Formula One game, one of the attractive things about it was that the marketing was sort of already done. It was such a well-known franchise, and they were talking with McLaren about a possible tie-in. It meant that I suddenly had the opportunity to do the game that I had wanted to do since *Revs*. The hardware had advanced to the point where I could see the potential to do things which I couldn't have dreamt of doing when I did *Revs*, so it was quite an exciting prospect.

* The publisher was MicroStyle, which was MicroProse's UK-based label for externally developed games.

I developed *Formula One Grand Prix* for the ST, and so that was my direct platform, but I used the PC as the development environment. I had a special interface, so I basically built the code and then I sent it to the ST. That was a good way of working, and then once I'd done that I converted it to Amiga.

I remember we went to McLaren for a meeting, and I had a car I could rotate on the straight at Silverstone. The meeting went well but the deal fell down because MicroProse decided the percentage McLaren wanted wasn't viable. But because we liked the way the game was going, we just decided to go without any kind of licence. In those days you didn't go to Bernie and ask for an F1 licence. That would change, but we just put it out. You had to type the real driver names if you wanted them, but we had 16 circuits mapped to the real ones. Of course, at that point it wasn't textured graphics, so there were no in-game logos, trademarks or anything like that to worry about. With just solid-fill polygons we were trying to get representation of the livery of each car. When we came to do *Grand Prix 2*, you had to have a licence. The F1 people had realised the potential, I suppose, and what was interesting was that they made us buy a licence for the first game in order to give us one for the second game, so we didn't actually get away with it, in the end.

Since I was doing an F1 sim, I was trying to base it on real life. All the cars are always racing round the 3D tracks, even if you can't see them, which was a necessary step if you want to be able to move the camera anywhere at any time. The simulation is happening the same way, independent of where the camera is. That means the AI for all the cars is active all the time, because they are all having to interact, overtake and try to miss each other, take the corners and so on, for every car, all the time.

It all took about three years, the same as *Stunt Car Racer.* I suppose I had a head start on other race driving games, but there had been others. I suppose the obvious one was *Indianapolis 500* by Papyrus, so that was similar, but *Formula One Grand Prix* was going to have 16 tracks rather than one track, with a full season mode, and TV cameras and marshals. I felt that, well, someone else might bring out an F1 game, but it's not going to be like this one, so I didn't worry too much. It's funny really, actually, when I was programming and creating it, it was almost as if the people who played my previous games were all sitting on my shoulder, so I felt a responsibility to make a good job of it.

## Peter Molyneux

I can remember a slight feeling of shame doing the sequel to *Populous*, *Populous 2*, because in the press it was considered a crime to work on a sequel. It was unoriginal, it didn't innovate. So doing a sequel to *Populous* felt dirty. But, you know, it's something that publishers wanted, it's something that fans wanted, it's something that it felt like it should be done. My approach, which was flawed, was just to add 100 more features, rather than make what was there even better and more polished. The lesson I learned from that is when you are doing a sequel you have got to find out what it is that people really enjoyed and make that better, rather than just stuff it with lots more features.

But while this was all going on there were some incredible things happening. *Populous* was released on lots of different formats and in lots of different places around the world. It was a huge success in Japan, a massive, massive success. You know, there were comics about *Populous*, figurines, concerts with the Tokyo Philharmonic Orchestra. There was an international competition; it was absolutely huge. All this was going on at the same time as us developing *Powermonger* and *Populous 2*.

It was also the first time I really started hearing the word 'industry'. We were no longer in our bedrooms; those little two-person teams were now, you know, the dizzy heights of 10-person teams! People were starting to talk about developing a game for a year. That was a long old time! There seemed to be genres popping up every minute. This was the time of *Wolfenstein*, and the first-person shooters were starting to come along, and the first RTSes, so it was an incredibly exciting time. I think it was around about then that the first GDC happened in a small room in California, and you know that really was the birth of the development side of the American industry. The publisher side was already there and they had consumer-facing shows, but it was really starting to become an industry in the early '90s.

× Wolfenstein 3D, id Software's first-person shooter, released in May 1992 for the PC.
* The Game Developers Conference, a major industry event that takes place annually in San Francisco, started in the living room of game designer Chris Crawford in 1988.

Yes, there was obviously a sense of risk, but I think for us in the early Bullfrog days it was an amazing time, because there that sense of risk was in disappointing people more than financial risk. At that time, money was coming in from *Populous*, from *Powermonger* and *Populous 2*. We were talking about different formats all the time, and even though we made tiny amounts of money out of those different formats it felt like we had found something which people loved. Lots of people said you can only make one successful game in your life, and you know it's possible to make a second success. That seemed to be more of a motivator than the risk side.

Life for me at that time was just about work, that was all it was. It was amazingly rewarding; you know I can't begin to explain how incredibly exciting it was to realise that you had fans who would wait for one of your games to come out. Now, you compare that to selling two copies of *The Entrepreneur.* Why wouldn't I work all the time? So I think I worked as hard, if not harder, after the success of *Populous*, than I had ever worked before in my life.

Enthusiasm was so strong in all of Bullfrog, actually. The team we built up was this crazy mix of people, you know, there were people from the Youth Training Scheme. Sean Cooper, he was from the Youth Training Scheme and also a Clothes Show model of the year finalist. He was the complete opposite of us geeky people. And there were a number of testers who would come in and play. It was an amazing time and an amazing team that we built up.

## Sean Cooper

← 287   349 →

It was funny. My girlfriend at the time entered me into this modelling competition, so we went to London and as soon as we walked in the room someone came up to me and said they wanted me to come on the show. 'Walk up and down a bit, let's just see.' There were like thousands of people there, and I hated being around crowds and stuff. I walked up and down and a woman came up to me and she said I was perfect. 'Absolutely perfect. We want you for our final 16, definitely.'

I think I was 19 and it was televised, and I was fifth, thrown out in the sec- ond round. I wasn't confident enough, and in the magazine, I've still got it, it says, 'Are you looking forward to a career in modelling?' and I say, 'No, not really. I'm just going to go back to my day job.' It's not what you'd want to hear! I just went along for the ride.

Afterwards, I said to Peter, 'Look, I'm quitting, I'm going to London to become a famous model.' And he must have thought, 'God, you utter dick.' But he said, 'Go away for a couple of weeks and try it, and we'll keep in touch.' I went for quite a few interviews, and I'm quite skinny, and they said I'd have to work out a bit, and I said, 'I'm not doing that.' I had a portfolio and they said I had a good chance of making a success of it, and I remember saying, 'I don't want to. I've written games.' So I went back.

We had moved into the loft, which we squeezed nine into with an office downstairs. God, it got so hot in the summer; I'd almost be sitting there in my boxer shorts, trying to keep cool. Then we moved to the Technology Centre, in this big white room with a few windows in it. It was split into two parts, one with a receptionist – I'm not sure why we had a receptionist, but we did – and Les was there, and there was a little meeting table, and we were sitting in the back bit, less than 20 people. We had quite a comfortable environment working on *Syndicate*. Peter was sat in the middle and we had a laugh.

I didn't really see the studio as being that special, though. I honestly thought we were the only ones doing this. I was very naïve, but I'd still look at other games and say they were rubbish, that they were nothing compared to what we were doing.

← 347

## Peter Molyneux

371 →

*Syndicate* got started after *Powermonger* was finished, while we were having a pizza in the centre of Guildford, based upon this little demo that Sean Cooper had made. It was originally called 'BOB', which stood for 'Blue and Orange Bloke'. Sean Cooper was this über coder with this amazing work ethic. He would do things in hours that took people like me weeks to do.

So he was working on 'BOB' and he had this little character moving around an environment, and we started to have this idea of a multiplayer game and giving these little characters guns. You would be able to run around and shoot each other, and then that turned into a little squad of people, and you could adjust little variables in those squads, like their stamina. We had this crazy idea for a story about these chips in people's heads. All this came together as we developed the game. It was another multiplayer game that we played a lot of and refined. If you look around the Surrey Research Park in Guildford, you'll notice that it looks a little bit like *Syndicate*'s city.

← 348

## Sean Cooper

371 →

Peter asked me what my next game would be, and we sat down in a pub and he wanted to do a game based on *Blade Runner* in a living world, and *Syndicate* came from there. I didn't really know what I wanted. I wanted Arnie with a chaingun; it certainly wasn't *Blade*

*Runner* for me. But Paul McLaughlin had joined by then and he was bent towards that cyberpunk stuff. But all I could think about was having civilians moving around and we could be killing them, we could be assassinating people, taking all these movie scenarios and wrapping them into this game. I was saying to people, 'Think of a mother with a pram, and this guy comes around the corner with a machine gun and just kills everyone, and there's this pram lying on the floor afterwards. That's how violent it should be. These things are ruthless, they're going to kill everyone.'

So that became the 'Blue and Orange Bloke' demo, which was to prove how they would move around as a squad. That was the thing we were going to have problems with, so for a year we just worked on team dynamics, and we were switching machines all the time. Peter had done an OEM deal with *Populous* which had brought him into contact with these PC companies, so we had all these PCs turning up and Peter said, 'Let's move to PC, they're faster!' I took one look and thought, 'Right, this looks interesting. Oh, it's got 32-bit registers. Oh my God, that's going to make what I'm struggling with so much faster.' So eventually it was in high res, 640 by 400, in 16 colours, because we could. It was the first time we had the ability to work in that kind of resolution. It was all shifting towards the PC. There was nothing that could stand in its way, really. The Amiga wasn't a very good machine, really. It was becoming backward and Commodore were attempting to make these business machines, but not very well.

PC was amazing, and we ended up making it run really fast. Glenn worked out some techniques that helped, and we had this Z-buffering technique. I was very much in my element, from level design to art to programming. I know a lot of the artists still complain about the way that they were treated, and Paul has said quite a few things about me that were very true about me at the time. I didn't want anything to slow us down, so I made sure I was very

## Rob Hubbard

I liked the Amiga. It was a real shame. If they had put MS-DOS on it, it would have succeeded, but they got killed by the IBM clones. The Amiga, like everything else, was way ahead of its time. One of the things that was appealing was that the Amiga was still a home computer, so there were great creativity products there, like Deluxe Paint and Instant Music. So it was in this phase of being really innovative with software, not just games.

prescriptive about what I wanted. But I found building the art and level design tools a lot of fun.

When we came to the AI systems, after getting the movement right, I thought we could just have a real city with bending roads and people moving wherever they wanted. But then people just started throwing problems at me, like how are these civilians going to navigate. 'Oh we'll cross that bridge, it won't be a problem!' I was always can-do! Then I started drawing it and realised we couldn't have bendy roads. We couldn't store all the graphics in memory, all the rotations of the cars, the different tiles. We had to come down from eight rotations of the cars to four, and we could only have eight cars. I felt a bit demoralised at one point that we couldn't have millions of cars and civilians, but we built a system where we could have loads of different sorts of civilians by changing their heads and bodies and legs. The artists must have loved me for it because I gave them a crappy tool to lay them out with, which worked a bit like Deluxe Paint, but was the hardest thing to use.

The train was a nightmare, getting all the pieces of it to move together. You'd get this shudder along the train and sometimes it'd split apart if it was going too fast. Getting people on the train, I wanted the doors to open, but there were graphic problems so they would just go through the walls of the train. Interacting with the world with a mouse was causing a lot of problems, too. The cars on the roads worked through having triggers on the tiles to say they were approaching crossroads so they could look a few tiles ahead to see if there was anything on the cell, and if there was they would slow down. We ended up with civilians just crossing the road because I couldn't find a way of navigating them away from the cars. They would just navigate with a really crude wall-hugging system, terribly unreliable! I wish I'd known then what I know now.

But having things like 200 civilians getting into cars because there were no restrictions – I could have put a cap on it, but I thought it was just so much fun, using the Persuadertron and get- ting into a car, turning up somewhere and then your whole squad's completely stealthed, and you can start mowing everyone down. That's fun! That's what happened when we were just playing it. Sod the realism, we can't get there. We just made it fun.

There was no mystery to making a game like *Syndicate*. It was all restrictions; we wanted to do a lot but we couldn't, and we just didn't know enough. We were so inexperienced in the systems we needed, like navigation, and we couldn't look anything up because there was no internet. Glenn and Kevin would explain these con- cepts to me in layman's terms, because I didn't have a clue. But it's great when you play a game and lose yourself in it, and a lot of people in the office were still playing it a year after release!

I think what really drove the schedule was Les coming in one day and saying we needed it done now. I was still in that mode of playing it a bit more. We played and played it, probably the longest time I ever spent playing a game, so we were there every night, basically playing multiplayer. I'd get my friends in, whoever. And so many times it'd be like, 'This is shit!' We'd quickly change it, put a new build up and in a matter of a few minutes you had a better game. We tuned the hell out of it.

## Jon Hare

With *Cannon Fodder* we experimented with this group thing, so you had a few guys behind another guy, which were probably dots originally, and we tried this firing from the different angles and we saw that you got this pattern of bullets, and it really developed from there. It quickly became a military game, and once you've got a military game then you start to bolt the other obvious things on, like mines and tanks and helicopters, and different sorts of guns, bazookas.

It's the game that I've done the most level design on, but I've lost my drawings of the layouts, which I did on squared paper. I like to work with pen and paper when I can, actually, because it gives you control. I remember sitting in Chelmsford Library, drawing them, one by one.

Later, we had the idea of the guys queuing up at the hill and we gave them all names because they ended up being just guy after guy, so why not give them names? It's a nice touch. Then we had them going up in rank if they survived the battle, because that seemed a good idea. Then we had the idea for showing gravestones when they died, mostly because the screen was really empty, just to fill it up full of gravestones, if I'm honest. Then we decided to link the gravestones with the rank that they achieved before they died, and then we put the music on which gave it this sad feeling, and it entered this whole other feeling of, 'Oh my God, look at all the people who are dying ...'

From all these ideas combining you got this concept of reflecting on what really happens in war. It was nothing you'd ever write down in a design document. That happened purely by the iterative process of making a game and letting it evolve and letting it come out itself.

Once we'd done the whole game we could see this hill theme had become quite a thing, so we stuck some poppies on the cover. It's very logical for us in the UK to think about the poppy and associate it with warfare and with people who died in wars, but the Royal British Legion came after us, saying, 'That's our poppy,' because we actually put a plastic poppy on the cover. 'That's our poppy, you can't use it and it's an insult to the war dead to put this in a computer game.' They really hassled us, and in the end they decided that they wanted a donation from us, so we just gave them, I think it was £500. I've never bought a poppy since. I bought them all in 1992.

←269 ## Julian Gollop 386→

When we finished *Lords of Chaos* we were thinking of moving towards the PC, and we were looking for a new publisher. Blade had clearly had financial problems, because we weren't getting paid for some of the sales of *Lords of Chaos*, and one of the distributors told us that they'd been trying to get hold of copies but weren't getting them from the publisher, which was a bit alarming. But, you know, the major motivator was that smaller publishers are a bit risky, and a bigger and more stable publisher was going to give us a longer term prospect for our future development. So we drew up this little shortlist and at the top was MicroProse, because of *Civilization*, though we were skeptical that they'd take on our little project.

We wanted to evolve *Laser Squad*, so we had a demo for it with isometric graphics that was running on the Atari ST. We had line of sight for the characters and bullets, so there was the idea of cover; it was definitely a sophisticated system but still only just a two-player demo, though we thought it was enough. So we showed the demo to the guys at MicroProse, Pete Moreland and Steve Hand. Fortunately, Steve Hand was a big fan of *Laser Squad* and they thought it was a strong proposition.

They had an interesting influence on the direction the game[×] took, because I learned later that MicroProse UK were a bit of a red-headed stepchild, and they were desperate to try and emulate the success of their US arm. Up to that point the UK arm was making much less serious games, not really capable of matching anything that the US MicroProse office was producing, so they

× Which became 1994's *UFO: Enemy Unknown*, known as *X-COM: UFO Defense* in the US.

were looking for something which could compete. So they said, 'Well, we want you to make the game much bigger, to have a strategic aspect and a research tree, like in *Civilization*,' so it had this feeling of an expansive strategy game. They also suggested the theme of UFOs, because, like *Civilization*, they wanted it a little bit more familiar to people and therefore they wanted to set it on Earth, but still science fiction.

We had a really strong theme between what they wanted and what we came up with and my own research. They wanted it a little bit more Gerry Anderson, and I wanted it a little bit more *The X-Files*-style, even though I wasn't aware of *The X-Files* at the time. This sort of conspiracy background, with little alien greys and this idea that they are sinister intruders rather than coming out all guns blazing, trying to blow us to bits. But the idea of the central X-COM organisation came from the Gerry Anderson side, I guess like SHADO. So from our initial discussions with MicroProse UK, we had this amazing foundation for the game.

I thought everything they were saying was absolutely great, though I was a little bit worried about the ambition. But we said, 'Yeah, we can do it!' We told MicroProse that we wanted to lead on PC, because we saw it as the new machine for strategy games, because of MicroProse, really, and some of the games they published. PC seemed to be the obvious choice compared to Amiga or ST, and we were right, I guess. PC did become dominant quite quickly. We made that decision in 1991, so I guess in Britain the Amiga was still the games machine to have, and PC wasn't, really, but we were looking to an American market. I guess we were impressed with the fact that *Railroad Tycoon* and other PC games were considered the highest-quality games in the US at the time, so we saw the PC as the future, and that the Amiga was going to be history.

They asked if we had experience with PC, and we said, 'Oh yes, of course! No problem.' But we hadn't, actually. We had no idea, but the bluff and bravado was out of desperation, really. Nick was working on the prototype for 'Laser Squad 2' and I was doing some freelance database programming, which was pretty tedious but it was earning enough money to keep us going. We really needed a better publisher, and a properly funded project. We had nothing to lose at that stage, with no real income.

The problem we had straight away was that though the PC had 640K of memory, we quickly realised the game wasn't going to fit in it, and we had to work out how we would address extended memory, and both ways involved tricky page-swapping techniques which we thought would cause all sorts of problems. But then we luckily saw something called a Watcom C compiler, which came out after we started, which gave you a flat memory model so you didn't have to worry about it. It made things much, much easier. But we still had the problem that the game was too big, so we split it into two executables, one for the tactical game, one for the strategic. So as you went from one to the other it would transfer data between them by saving it on disk, which sounds primitive but it worked smoothly enough.

The strategic level was very much in line with my thinking about meta games, adding this really interesting layer to the game that was ultimately just as important as the tactical layer. We didn't do any prototyping – we started working on the tactical part of the game, and didn't finish when we were due to, and had to start working on the strategic part. Only three or four months before the end of the project we had to link them together properly, and it was a bit of a mess. It wasn't in a very playable state, full of bugs, pretty terrible balance and lots wasn't working properly.

It was pretty much just me and Nick, and we worked with two artists at MicroProse, and towards the end the sound designer and musician, so it was a very small project. MicroProse didn't like the initial alien designs, though, so we went to see the artist to go through his ideas for types, and we picked them from his screen, and then I had to reverse-engineer these images into a sensible game story, but he came up with inventive ideas, and the only thing I insisted on was keeping the little alien grey dude, which became the Sectoid.

The producer was very laid back; he would visit us once a month and we'd go to the pub, drink a pint of beer and talk about the game, and then he'd go home. If he was lucky he'd have a version to take with him. It was very laid back, until MicroProse decided to commit to it coming out at the end of the financial quarter, and then they put a lot of pressure on us to get the game finished before the end of March. We had to spend the last couple of months working in-house, which was tough.

At one point the game was, in fact, cancelled. We didn't know about it at the time, but when Spectrum HoloByte bought Micro-Prose they didn't understand the project and told the UK to stop it. But they didn't, and when Spectrum HoloByte later told them they were desperate for releases by the end of the financial year, they told them the game they should have cancelled was still there and it fulfilled a need at the time. It was lucky to survive, I think!

# David Braben

It was great being able to make *Elite*'s sequel, and do what I wanted to do. I planned it out; I did a lot of the graphics first because I had lots of ideas on how to make them look lovely. Actually, I showed them to several people, you know, from companies that I was thinking of working with. The same graphics that released with the game in 1993 were there in 1988. It's just that the game wasn't there. But I think I made a terrible mistake, which was to carry on for the best part of five years before releasing the game, making all of it, all the galaxy and that sort of thing. Actually, that is what made me resolve never to work alone for so long, because you go a bit spare. Oh, and supporting multiple platforms. It was a bit frustrating. I thought I had something that was ageing on the bush while I was writing it, if that makes sense. I resolved not to work like that in the future.

The industry, by the early '90s, had become a bit more professional, and also I suppose it had become more corporate, and still development was seen as one of those annoying distractions that got in the way of business. But having said that I was very fortunate because something like *Frontier* attracted a lot of attention. There was a lot of excitement over it. The fact that the other games had all done pretty well meant there was a lot of positivity. I went to Konami to publish it, but right at the very last minute before release they sold the rights to GameTek. There was a little bit of an argument over that, because I didn't know who these GameTek guys were. They were a brand new company, so no track record. It was tricky. I won't say more on that, but it didn't go that well.

# Steve Turner

Moving away from Hewson was quite a change for us, because it was the first time we ever accepted money up front for anything, and it turned out to be a mixed blessing because we also signed up for future games. Telecomsoft wanted us to experiment on 16-bit, which was highly attractive to us, and also do four 8-bit games for the Firebird label. That was the deal that was never over, because they wanted two versions of each one, so I was forever producing them to fulfil the advance, and they hardly sold any of them. They kept saying we hadn't met the advance, and because they had given us money up front, they wanted more of a say in the games.

I can remember them coming to us and saying they felt we were charging far too much money per month, but I had to get staff in to write the games they wanted. We had about six people, and I had costs down to the bone. At the same time, we were moving into 16-bit, and suddenly one person can't do a game any more. You needed a graphic artist and it would take them almost as long as the programmer, and the music needed to be proper, so you needed a musician. So instead of one person you had at least two full-timers.

The early days were much more like writing, and we were more like authors; you didn't need any money because you know you just went away and you wrote the program on a few hundred quid's worth of kit. But suddenly we needed development systems to write on, specialists, art packages for artists to work on. It was a completely different kettle of fish. With every game we found that the cost of producing it was going up exponentially, so much so that at one point I worked out that if I had saved all the money that I had ever got from royalties it still wasn't enough to do the next game.

So we were more and more reliant on the publishers financing the next game, but at the same time we only got a small share back in royalties to pay this money back. We kind of lost our freedom, and with that, creative ideas. They would say, 'No, we want this kind of game, which got a good review,' and more and more they were trying to dictate the look of the game and the way it played.

It just wasn't the way we did things. We liked to do something brand new and off the wall, and if we had a new game idea, we'd take it round several publishers and say, 'No one has done it before,' and they'd have no interest whatsoever. They wanted something like last year's hit, but we wanted to do this year's hit, or next year's.

It was a radical change in the industry; it was very fast becoming a big boy's industry, and the men in suits were controlling things. In the early '90s it went from little houses like Hewson's, which was a family business – his dad used to do the duplication out the back and at one time his brother worked there – to medium-sized publishers up in London with plush offices, and then there was a third transition, when American companies started to come in with vast amounts of money. The UK publishers had grown up so quickly, it was kind of like an immature business that had kind of grown up too fast, and they were still trying to treat programmers like they were bedroom programmers who didn't need money.

But we had matured into companies that needed a technical infrastructure. We used to spend as much time writing games as writing the technical tools to produce them. I actually used to make money selling them to other companies, and some people actually changed from game writing to writing development kits.

Branson got roped in quite a bit while we were publicising *Jimmy White*. Virgin management felt that by getting in the big guns it was really going to do this thing. So yeah, there was one afternoon where myself and Jimmy White pitched up at Branson's house in Holland Park, about lunchtime. We had already stopped in a bar on the way, which was a bit naughty, and Jimmy had about 18 pints or something, which wasn't good for later on. But as soon as we got in through the door, Branson's there, knowing he has got the afternoon off. He was ecstatically happy because apparently he had that morning signed The Rolling Stones back on to the Virgin label and sold the company to EMI, so he was pouring drinks left, right and centre. Boy, did we get drunk while a crew was trying to film a TV news piece. They were trying to film Jimmy doing trick shots and he just couldn't get a ball in because he'd had one drink too many and was cross-eyed.

Branson had a drink or two, too, and was making jokes about why Jimmy couldn't get the ball in. There was this great bit where Jimmy tried 20 times to get the ball in the pocket, and he turns around and says, 'Well, the pockets are too tight!' And Branson turns around and says, 'Well what do you expect, it's a virgin table,' and the TV crew cracked up. It was just one of those afternoons where everything was a laugh, but the funniest thing was that neither of them had ever used a mouse. We're talking '91, before Windows, but the Amiga and the ST had one, so they filmed Jimmy and Branson sat on the edge of a seat peering into an Amiga monitor, and I was underneath the table with my hand like this, trying to do something intelligible with the mouse under the table. Good old days. We didn't leave until about ten o'clock that night.

## Charles Cecil

I wasn't quite sure what we should call our first game at Revolution. I had just the working title, I think it was like 'Vengeance', or something really crap like that. When the time came to publish the game, Mirrorsoft asked us what we could call it. So we came up with a list of names and at the end I said, 'I wish we could call it "Lure of the Temptress"', and of course the marketing people, being marketing people, came back and said, 'We love it,' and I said, 'Look, I agree with you that it's a great name, but there are two problems: one, there's no luring, and two, there's no temptress.'

So they said, 'Can't you put one in?' Now, the game was almost finished! So I said, 'Well, I can but it's going to delay the game,' and, do you know, that was the best thing, because in the three months delay we got, which Mirrorsoft paid for, they collapsed. Mirrorsoft was owned by Robert Maxwell, and he fell off his yacht and died, and it turned out that the whole of the Mirror Group empire was based on some very dodgy accounting. This amazingly powerful publisher went into administration just before they published *Lure of the Temptress*, so the rights by contract reverted to us!

So the game hadn't actually been published and Mirrorsoft had already commissioned us to start working on our second game, which was going to be called *Beneath a Steel Sky*, with a comic book artist, who's a great guy, a great friend, Dave Gibbons.[x] So we were actually in quite a strong position, because we came out of Mirrorsoft with these two titles: one ready to publish, one well into development. Sean moved on to Virgin Interactive with Tim Chaney. Sean was very much our mentor and a terrific supporter of the company, and it was absolutely natural that we then moved to Virgin to work with him, and they published *Lure of the Temptress*,[*] and then finished *Beneath a Steel Sky*.[ˈ]

For a couple of years we had a really great relationship with Virgin. They had an exceptional team of really talented people and as a developer we'd arrive at their offices in Kensington and immediately you'd be surrounded by people with energy, saying, 'Oh, it's great to see you, we didn't know you were coming, let's show you the packaging! Let's show you our idea, let's show you our marketing plan.' It was incredibly, incredibly exciting to work with this team.

But unfortunately the Virgin days came to an end when Virgin were sold to Viacom, and there were various problems. The lawyers came in, the accountants came in, and eventually the whole thing collapsed, as it had done with Mirrorsoft, as it had done with Artic. These things go in cycles which don't last for very long.

[x] Dave Gibbons is best known for creating the legendary comic book series *Watchmen* with writer Alan Moore.
[*] Released in 1992 for the Amiga, Atari ST and PC.
[ˈ] Released in 1994 for the Amiga and PC.

← 350

# Rob Hubbard

391 →

I first met Mark Lewis from Electronic Arts at an award show in London in '87. I got an award for something or other, and he expressed an interest in me going over to them in the States for a couple of months to see what it was like. That was when I did *Skate or Die!*[x] with the samples, and they basically offered me a job.

[x] Hubbard's intro music for the Commodore 64 version of *Skate or Die!*, which was released in 1988, famously featured electric guitar samples, an effect that few programmers could have imagined achieving at the start of the 64's life.

Part of it was the fact I was interested in 16-bit, and the natural progression from 8-bit. One of the things that they were talking about in the States was the LaserDisc and compact disc technology. They were, you know, 10 or 12 years ahead of their time on that. Trip Hawkins was the guy running EA at the time, and he was just a complete visionary. The thing that came across was the passion and the vision that these people had, and it really attracted me.

## Peter Stone and Richard Leinfellner

I was sitting in the Palace office one day at the Scala cinema, and my phone rings and the voice at the other end says, 'Hello, this is Trip Hawkins from Electronic Arts. I'd like to come and see you.' And I said, 'Okay, when would you like to come?' And he said, 'Well, I'm downstairs in a phone box.'

We turned Trip down, didn't we?

We did.

We were visionaries in those days! Big American companies started coming over and I could see the writing on the wall, that either we would have to grow substantially or we'd probably be left on the sidelines.

Companies were becoming bigger. You needed more clout, you needed more money for development, more money for marketing, you needed to have a greater output of product. By then there was the predecessor of E3, which was CES, and you had to have a big stand. Electronic Arts was getting big, as were other companies, we were still very small in that game.
I think Palace Software was an illustration of what the UK is good at. We're very good at doing things in a pub, a small team

## Eugene Evans

A number of American companies starting to come over and set up. They generally set up in the UK first because it was English-speaking, so it was easy for them to enter. You had the Commodore 64 coming over, the Atari ST, the Commodore Amiga, and they were beginning to surpass in capability what was being offered by Sinclair and the QL, which essentially failed. In fact, part of my decision to move to the US was because I needed a reset. I needed to go somewhere where nobody knew me and I could just start over and there were no preconceived notions of who I was, what I could do. So I joined a company in Chicago.

sitting around having a beer and bouncing around ideas. But when it comes to growing something much bigger we are not so great at that, necessarily.

## Shahid Ahmad

We didn't know when the Spectrum and Commodore 64 were going to disappear, so people tried to ride them out for as long as possible, and I think a lot of us didn't embrace 16-bit machines quickly enough, and realise just what we needed to do to step up to the next level. If you looked at the production values for games like *Defender of the Crown*; companies like Cinemaware and Electronic Arts embraced that era more quickly. For us, our cottage industry was based on Commodore 64 and the Spectrum, and we had a lot of experience in this area. Publishers were aware that there was a real business to be had here, and business works best when you have a model you can repeat, where you do the same thing year over year. But they were wrong, because publishers in the US realised this isn't just a business, it's about being ahead of the technological wave, and if you're not, you're dead.

The Americans got that, and the Japanese got that. I think our developers were keen on doing it, but we needed more and more money to make this stuff happen, and fewer and fewer of us were able to do it. I think EA are a good example: they were willing to make the investment, and that's why eventually in the late '80s, early '90s, they started investing in British companies. American publishers were prepared to invest in the leading edge, which required larger teams, and smaller developers really needed to team up. Those that did went on to succeed, and the developers who didn't started to fall away.

← 333
## David Perry
389 →

The thing I think about is that it's a very, very big world out there, and there are a lot of people who want to be entertained. There's something about the United Kingdom, that either you break out into the whole world or you can't. I look at people like Cliff Richard: when I was a kid, Cliff Richard was a superstar. I mean, there wasn't a single human being in the United Kingdom who didn't know him, and yet you'd go to America and they'd never heard of him. So it's a very binary thing – either you break through or you don't.

So with games what was going on in America was always kind of tantalising to me. I didn't know anything about their industry; the only thing I knew was that computer parts cost an awful lot less. So Probe Software was very much a developer for hire, making games for publishers, and Virgin offered *The Terminator* movie rights to us. I was a big fan of *The Terminator*, so how exciting to make the game for it! Virgin were British, of course, but they'd set up their game operation in America, and *The Terminator* opened a big door for me because it put this little development team in the UK on the radar of a company in America.

It's funny how these things that you do all start to tie together as your career evolves. Years later I got invited to a party at Lightstorm Entertainment, which is James Cameron's company, and I remember thinking to myself, 'I bet, as a creative person, James Cameron doesn't want to be standing at a cocktail party in a tuxedo with a bunch of random people.' So I wondered whether I should wear a tuxedo or not, and I ended up going wearing green leather. He came straight over to me and said, 'Who are you?' It was ideal! 'I'm from the videogame industry, I actually made *The Terminator* game, I guess your first videogame!' And he goes, 'Let's get out of here,' and we left the party together.

So, anyway, I got a call one day from the head of Virgin Games in the US, and he said, 'Would you like to come to America? We have an emergency. We need your help. We have a McDonald's licence and we need somebody to come and make the game. Whatever you earn today, we'll beat that and we'll get you a car and an apartment, so just leave, lock your door, go to the airport and come to America.' It was a very difficult decision for me. It could be huge, but they asked me but not my partner, Nick. So what do you do? Do I go? Do I stay? But I wanted to understand what the California thing was, and it was a short-term contract, so I locked my door and flew out.

The game was called *Global Gladiators*. Of course, Virgin was watching very closely, but I got to work with a whole bunch of new people and animators, a whole team of people doing very high-quality animation, and as a result the game ended up looking really cool. But McDonald's came to see it and they were like, 'This is terrible! Where's Ronald McDonald and where are the burgers and fries in the game?' We were like, 'But nobody likes Ronald

McDonald and the burgers and fries. That would be lame!' So they hated it but we went ahead and shipped the game anyway, and it got awarded 'Game of the Year' by Sega. To have a game of the year as our first game ... By the way, McDonald's never got over it. They ended up making another game with Ronald McDonald and burgers and fries and all that.

After we won their award, Sega came back and asked, 'Would you like to do a game with us? We have the 7 Up brand. Would you like to make a game for them?' So we made a game called *Cool Spot*, which is the little red dot on the logo, for Sega. You start to see jigsaw pieces falling in place again, because Sega also had the rights to Disney's *Aladdin*, which was the hottest movie at the time, and they asked us, after *Cool Spot*, whether we would like to do *Aladdin*, and *Aladdin* allowed us to start to break new ground.

Jeffrey Katzenberg [*] was involved, along with the directors, and they asked us what we wanted. We of course said, 'Well, can we please have your animation and not ours? Can we have Disney Feature Animation actually do it for us?' The result was animation that was really hard to compete with. I mean, I'd hate to be an animator in the game business when we shipped *Aladdin*, because it was Disney at their best, appearing right in the videogame, incredibly fluid animation.

This is something that I've realised has defined my career: it's that I've learned about each different role in the games business. When I work with animators, I try to understand, I don't just say, 'Give me the animation.' I want to understand how it's done, how it works, how they think, what they're passionate about. When you work with people like that – musicians, too – they don't want footsteps that make the same sound, they want correct footfalls, balancing the sound to make it feel good, and I would be the programmer who would take the time to do that with them. They would love that because the more you care, the more your team realises that you care. It was a very, very enlightening period for me as I realised these people I'm getting to work with were incredible, and that at each part of the puzzle I was getting surrounded by great talent.

I also convinced Virgin to hire my friend Nick Bruty, so he came over, and so career-wise it was all looking good. The only twist was that I never went back to the United Kingdom. I kind of forgot that I had a house there, and a car sitting in the garage. I flew back

[*] Chairman of The Walt Disney Studios during production of the *Aladdin* film and game.

and my house was just nasty. It was filled with cobwebs, my car was dead, and the tyres were flat. So I just told a local estate agent to get rid of it. That was it, I was in love with the American games business and trying to become a part of this more international industry, as it was very rapidly becoming.

# Part 8

# End of the Era

I felt quite sad about the
feeling of it all becoming a
proper industry, because a lot
of the playfulness and
friendly competition had kind
of gone away. It was a lot more
serious to a lot more people,
a lot more money was being made,
and I almost felt like it was
leaving me behind because
I just wanted to carry on making
Llamasoft games.

So we had the success of *Populous, Powermonger, Populous 2* and *Syndicate*. Now, remember that Electronic Arts almost owned us anyway because of this stupid contract we signed back in the *Populous* days, and they said, 'Here is some money, wouldn't it be simpler if we just owned you? You could have lovely offices and stuff like that.' And we said yeah. At that time we had, like, seven offers on the company and I was flying all over the world going to people with higher and higher offers. It was like a rock star era!

## Sean Cooper

I didn't want to do anything else. I didn't go out, I had this mop of hair and all my friends would go out to nightclubs and I would be stuck in the office, out of sheer enjoyment. The only time it became un-fun was when EA turned up and this bunch of guys turned up who seemed so much better than me. I didn't feel important any more. Peter said to me recently that one of the biggest mistakes we ever made was selling Bullfrog. I remember him at the time asking whether he should sell it and I said no. But then they sold it and Les and Peter gave me this cheque, I was 24, and it was a lot of money, and some EA shares, I just thought it was so generous, and I realised I'd worked hard for it. But something broke, people lost interest, and it disbanded. I had a hand in that disbanding, though. I said we should be bigger, that we should be thinking bigger, but most people were demoralised.

I just think that you have to become a different person to be successful in that environment. The problem was that I was made a vice president at Electronic Arts, and I kind of took it a little bit seriously. I was flying over to California every month, and inside it made me very confused and quite angry that I wasn't who I was before, which was a guy who sat in front of a computer and thought about these crazy games. I felt that I had semi-forgotten who I was and what I was good at.

This is going to sound bizarre, but when you go in such a short amount of time from someone who cannot afford anything, buying on credit, and you know I never opened the mail because it was too frightening, going from that to someone who could afford anything but was alone and didn't have anyone to share the money with ... That was a very emotional time. And then to be part of a huge organisation as well, it was quite harrowing.

So when Electronic Arts bought the company they said they would love for us to be in a big spangly office. Of course I came from this place above Cath's flat, so you know, that was lovely. And they wanted us to expand, so in the course of a few months Bullfrog went from 40 people to over a hundred. It became a place that I didn't really particularly enjoy.

One night I invited this guy called Tim Rance* over to my house and we had a few beers. I said, 'I have had enough of Electronic Arts. I'm going to write my resignation.' So I wrote it out just as a laugh really, and the bastard pressed return and sent my resignation off to the president of Electronic Arts! I didn't intend to send it, but then I thought, do you know, it's the best thing I could have done.

But because it had been done in such an abrupt way, Electronic Arts were scared that I was going to poach all the staff, so they told me I couldn't come into Bullfrog any more. But I didn't want to leave until I had finished the game I was working on. It was called *Dungeon Keeper*,* and I said I would finish it at my house. They said, 'Well, that's the only way you can continue to work here, because we don't want you in the office.' And that's exactly what happened. I finished *Dungeon Keeper* at my house, and I wasn't allowed into the Electronic Arts office. It was all a bit silly, to be honest!

* Tim Rance was a Bullfrog programmer, responsible for the technical code of early games.
* A multiplayer version was cut from the game as time ran out.

## Jon Hare

We made good games at Sensible, but also the market was a lot less volatile. People were buying into the fact that they could trust us to make good stuff, and largely we did. We did over-extend ourselves and mess up a bit towards the end. We had the odd blip in the middle, I guess, or something like *International 3D Tennis* was a bit too esoteric, shall we say, or experimental.

We were probably over-stretching our resources at the point we were making *Sensible Golf.** The 3D version of *Sensible Soccer* just wasn't very good compared to the rest because we were new with 3D. *Sex 'n' Drugs 'n' Rock 'n' Roll** didn't work because we didn't sort the programming out. Our programming was awful on it, actually. So yes, we did make mistakes. We made a very bad transition into 3D. People like to say with Sensible, 'The rise and fall,' but I don't think we fell. We ran the company for 13 years,

* Released in 1995, *Sensible Golf* was awarded a score of 55% by *Amiga Power*, uncharacteristically low for a Sensible game. It summed up with, '75% satisfaction that Sensible have settled for technically mediocre but charming, relaxing golf. 25% annoyance...

and it spent eight years at the top, and all our hit games were 2D games. We didn't do the transition; it was a bridge too far for us.

What happened in the mid '90s was that all the big media companies, like Warner and Bertelsmann, moved in almost simultaneously, attracted by the newer consoles, the PlayStation and Mega Drive, starting to take off big-time. They saw the home computers as being outside of their normal remit, and their vision was to impose their structure on the game business. But in my opinion the problems were because they didn't understand our medium. Games are more complex to make than music or even films. The budgets may be not so large, but in a game you've got hundreds of thousands of things having to run in synchronicity, but big media companies always wanted to treat games like their little brother.

I mean, we at Sensible, we signed a £3 million deal with Warner. We'd never even thought we'd get that money and we just said, 'Yes.' It was a good deal, but unfortunately we didn't come up with the products because of our problems with 3D. We signed because we couldn't believe the money, but within that three-year period we pretty much lost the UK games industry. A lot of games were now licences and were console-led, and US- and Japan-led, not Europe-led.

The names we had as developers, well, they were crushed by these big publishers. They didn't want us to be names, because what mattered to them was their own. So the concept of us as named developers, like Sensible or the Bitmaps, or whoever else, was disappearing. If you look at the names that stayed, people like Rare, they were making games for Nintendo, based on their brands, and our brands were out, and for me as someone who made my money by being a good game designer, making original games, there was no market at all.


## Archer Maclean

I must admit '91 was tough.* We had people in negative equity on mortgages; I mean, obviously for once I had royalties coming in, and that was good, but I think from publishers' and distributors' points of view, people were tightening their belts, bad debts were

popping up everywhere and smaller companies were going to the wall. It was tough.

But not only that, you also had this transition from the one-man bedroom coder-type character into the absolute requirement of having to create content. There was a huge demand to create games with full-motion video, which was a bit of a joke with hindsight, but you know you had to have massive depth and a massive number of levels and lots of extra graphics and much better animation. One bloke couldn't do it, and I was one of the last to do a whole game on my own. I think the last was probably Geoff Crammond with one of the *Formula One* games, but by the mid '90s you had to be running a team or working with a bunch of other guys.

I think it became difficult to continue writing Amiga and ST games in the UK. They had been around for years, and when the PlayStation came out in 1994 I can remember being invited to various secret technical meetings and realising it was a massive game changer, compared to the Amiga. It started the era of giant corporate companies producing home consoles, machines that would last three years and then you would have the PlayStation 2 and then PlayStation 3. The whole thing was much more corporately organised; a machine would be launched, sell millions of games on it and then it would move straight on to the next one. The whole bedroom thing started falling apart at that point.

## Jeff Minter

I kind of felt quite sad about the feeling of it all becoming a proper industry, because a lot of the playfulness and friendly competition had kind of gone away. It was a lot more serious to a lot more people, a lot more money was being made, and I almost felt like it was leaving me behind because I just wanted to carry on making Llamasoft games. I didn't want to become a big software house or go and work for one, and so for a while I felt quite sad about all that, but somehow I managed to soldier on and find my own way to survive. Obviously I never made it big and I never made a lot of money, but I'm still enjoying what I like doing.

Not many small developers survived. You needed these big teams to make the games, and large teams means larger development budgets. Smaller teams probably can't sustain themselves, so the smaller ones got absorbed by the bigger ones or stopped doing anything at all. As an individual I was okay because my overheads were low. I wasn't trying to run a team, so it was just my expenses, so I was able to survive, but for a small team and at a time when the budget for creating a game was increasing, it became very difficult and it kind of started the dichotomy I think that remains to this day, but now in the most extreme way, where you have big development teams doing £40, £50 games on consoles, and you have small indies, and it's kind of almost like two separate things now. But at least both sides have survived, which is nice.

There have been a couple of times where I was offered a chance to work for larger companies, and I never really felt that my heart would be in it. It just wasn't what I wanted to do. But I did work for Atari. I really enjoyed working for them, but then again I sought that out. After I did *Tempest 2000* [x] I thought I really liked Atari and that it would be nice to work for them and asked whether they'd employ me to do more Jaguar stuff. They did, but when Atari folded, [*] Activision asked me if I'd be interested, and I kind of was, but then some friends of mine who were engineers at Atari were coming up with this whole weird Nuon [v] thing.

Although Nuon was much less likely to be a commercial success and probably wouldn't make me much money, I was more interested in playing with weird hardware with some of my mates than I was going to work with Activision. Maybe I made the wrong decision, maybe I'd be living in America spending millions of pounds now, I don't know, but I like what I do. I think to me that's the bottom line. I have to like what I do, and I think working in a large company on a small part of some big game, it's not really what I'd like to do. For me game design always has been and always will be personal. It's me making little Jeff Minter games, and I think that's always what I'm going to want to do.

[x] A reimagining of Dave Theurer's classic arcade game *Tempest* for the Atari Jaguar console, released in 1994.

[*] In 1996, with the Jaguar and Lynx having failed, Atari was sold to JTS Corp and effectively dissolved as a videogame company until it was sold again to Hasbro in 1998.

[v] A DVD player with 3D capabilities released in 2000, for which Minter made *Tempest 3000*.

← 345

## Geoff Crammond

376 →

A sequel to *Formula One Grand Prix* was a bit of a no-brainer, really, because I had been thinking after *Stunt Car Racer* about the way the market had changed to being about licence deals and sequels. Since *Grand Prix* was actually the most successful of all my games, it made sense then to do *Grand Prix 2*, [x] and the publisher wanted me to do it as well. The bad news was that it took another three years.

There were a lot of new physics. This happened every time I did a game, actually: I put more in, trying to get better realism, but the major difference in *Grand Prix 2* was the fact that it had texturing.

[x] Released in 1996 for the PC, *Grand Prix 2*'s physics engine was so sophisticated it allowed cars to leave the ground, though they couldn't turn over. The game was a critical hit and went on to develop a strong modding community.

Up to that point there hadn't really been a lot of textured games, but Papyrus brought out an Indy game with texturing, and I knew then that there was no way I could bring out another *Grand Prix* game without it being textured. So I had to learn how to do it. It was before hardware graphics cards, so it was like going back to the 8-bit days, where there was always a competition in terms of what technology you could bring.

Anyway, for *Grand Prix 2*, building the software engine was probably a fair amount of the three years, as well as developing the simulation. I enjoyed the feedback of trying something and having it work, and I think with graphics you get that reward even more than other things because it's so in your face. Texturing was interesting because it was a new thing for me.

Geoff Crammond

PC had become the natural machine, because whatever target machine you were going for you'd be developing it on a PC anyway. PC was a stable platform in the market, and it was going to be around for a long time, and I presume the publisher wanted it. But when the hardware cards came along, apart from the fact that they were fast, they were actually less flexible than what I was able to do with my software engine. By the time it

For *Grand Prix 2* and *3* I still had the same team, like Pete doing the menus, Norman doing the tracks, and I did the rest. My other brother-in-law Dave was my test driver, and he did that in his spare time, because he is actually an engineer, but he was very good at putting in the hours, giving me good feedback and helping me to develop the physics. So really, it was a team of four, all together.

came to *Grand Prix 3*, I was putting wet weather graphics in my software engine, working on reflections and having puddles and so on. Hardware cards have evolved with things called shaders, so you can program what each pixel does, but back in the software engine days I had shaders whereas the early hardware cards were a fixed pipeline so they didn't have them, and so I couldn't do effects quite as directly and as easily as I was used to.

Anyway, *Grand Prix 2* was probably one of the most stressful deadlines I had. I think I had a bit of a deadline with *Formula One Grand Prix* as well, and maybe I was two or three weeks behind on that one, but with *Grand Prix 2* they wanted it ready for Christmas, so, you know, they needed it in November. They actually got it in

July the following year, so it gives you an idea of the pressure I was under to deliver. But I didn't feel it was ready for market, because I wanted to get the crash graphics in, so when a car collided it could break up. I just felt the game wasn't complete or rounded enough. It just came to despair and hair pulling and stuff like that, but I carried on. July meant after the summer, which wasn't the best time to bring out a game, but they shipped 300,000 units the first weekend and all thoughts of being late disappeared, really.

I think it eventually sold about two million around the world, so it was the most successful in the series. Certainly, the publisher wanted me to do *Grand Prix 3*, but I have to say I was rather tired at that point and had to have a bit of a break.

← 275

## Fred Gray

Partly, I think, people were burnt out, and partly I think it was down to the expansion of the console market. I remember somebody at Denton asking whether I fancied doing some music for a console, and I asked what the processor was, and he said it was only a 6502 and only good enough to be in a washing machine. I went, 'Oh, forget it.' You know, I couldn't be bothered. Some of the earlier consoles were pretty awful, weren't they? Especially the handheld ones. It was getting stranger and stranger from a hardware point of view, because the Amiga was actually tailor-made for games, and a lot of the console stuff was just sort of secondhand electronics, like, 'What are we going to use for this console? Let's buy cheap.' It was all getting very frustrating at that time.

But what was happening with the game industry in Britain was more and more of an affinity towards 3D games, and obviously even the Amiga couldn't cope with that too well. I remember buying my first PC and a Voodoo card and I went, 'Wow, look, 3D graphics!' and then we didn't look back. Platform games? Forget that! The spirit went because the hardware that came out for the PC was making 8-bit machines and that type of game look absolutely stupid.

← 344

## Mike Montgomery

There is one mistake that The Bitmap Brothers made and it was a big one. We kept on the Amiga and the ST for too long. We did *The Chaos Engine 2*,* which cost us an awful lot of money, personal money as well, only to sell something like 4,000 units. We

* Critically applauded but a commercial disappointment, *The Chaos Engine*'s split-screen sequel was released in 1996.

should have gone out and seen Sony, Microsoft and Nintendo and got on to those platforms at the early stage, but we didn't do that.

Our next platform was the PC when we did Z, which we did very well with, but we started Z on the Amiga and then switched to the PC. It took us four years to finish that game, and when we finally finished the game the publishers said, 'We can't put a game on to a CD when you haven't filled the CD.' We went, 'What?' They said, 'The public will not buy a CD that has got a floppy game on it.' So then we spent the next two years doing all of our FMVs, more levels, and stuff like this. It cost us an awful lot of money but it sold well, probably one of our biggest successes.

By the time we had finished Z, we were virtually shut out of the console market. The cost of development rose greatly when the consoles came out.

A lot of it was because we spent a little bit too long on products, and it was also because of cashflow, and we didn't have the money to pay for all the consoles, which were really expensive. You went from a setup at the beginning with just a PC or something to having to get all these development kits at extortionate rates. We just didn't have the money, sadly, because Maxwell jumped off the back of his boat. We lost a lot of royalties there. As a developer it was all out of our pockets; we worked off advances but we never had enough money in the bank to buy that stuff. And we didn't have enough staff.

We couldn't afford it, essentially. When the consoles came in, the business got out of bedrooms and you started to need finance to do things.

* A small image of an Amiga game screen appeared here in 1996.
* Robert Maxwell — who was found dead in the sea off the Canary Islands in 1991 after it was alleged he fell from his yacht from his company — gave his family companies huge loans before his death and sanctioned payments to prop up the two public companies as a raid on the assets took place during the year.

## Mo Warden

I think the first indication for us that the UK game industry was having problems was when we were working on the PC version of *Damocles*. Psygnosis were going to be the publishers, and we were almost finished. The deadlines were being met and the milestones had been paid up to a point, and it was almost complete, but then they cancelled. I realised even the big companies were beginning to fail. They hadn't got money to put into projects and they were cancelling things left, right and centre. It affected everybody in the industry.

The change came when the Japanese consoles started to take over. I say take over – they didn't completely, but they certainly became more significant. I saw other companies were getting more licensing deals, so I saw programmers and designers being very restricted by what they could and couldn't do, and it was enormously expensive buying the licence to a character or a game and to develop it for one of the consoles. If you didn't make a success it could break a company.

We continued to work as a team outside of games on a system that we called Checkwin, which basically dished out coupons in supermarkets through playing very simple games, so the three of us were still working. Bruce was working up scripts, Paul was doing the coding and I was doing the graphics. I would get a TV advert to digitise, and then that had to be displayed with some voiceover advertising, 'Get 10p off if you press the button'. It was a good idea and it took off to a degree. It wasn't hugely successful, but we were still exploring what we could do together as a team.

But I left Novagen. Bruce didn't want me to give him my notice, but he wrote me a wonderful recommendation any-way, which I still have. We didn't really want to part company, but our paths had diversified. They were going into other industries and they didn't really need a graphic designer any more, so I had become less and less useful to them. Now they are doing something totally different, lighting software. It was down to Bruce and Paul's vision, but I think they knew it was time to move on away from games because the focus was moving away from the UK. So they wanted to find other industries where we could continue to be creative as a team for as long as possible.

I left the game industry because the teams became so big that the jobs became very small and uninteresting. Suddenly you became somebody who was designing a 2D texture to be mapped on to a 3D object, which was then handed to somebody who did the lighting, which was then handed to someone who put it into a scene, and then it was animated by a team of five. I didn't want to do that all day, I don't want to sit and draw pebbles, I don't want to do crap paint on the walls. I did games from start to end, and I was involved in all parts of them.

←233

## Rod Cousens

The software industry in the UK had grown up from a bunch of hobbyists, where we had all locked ourselves in bedrooms and travelled around the country in beaten-up old cars. We were riding on Sinclair, which was not a global phenomenon, and hardware was shifting from the UK to the videogame systems that were coming through from Japan, such as Nintendo. We'd gone through a period of convergence, where US content was coming on to successful British platforms, and British content was also relevant.

The US was the most prominent videogame market after Japan in the world, and talent migrated from here to there.

As the technology progressed it brought with it greater costs: the team sizes are more significant, and the UK did not have the financial resources within in order to meet the demands of a very rapidly rising cost base. If you then look around the world at how other companies met that challenge, particularly in the United States, it's normally through the involvement of venture capital or private equity, and the UK as a financial centre for supporting that lagged behind. So the companies back in the '90s didn't have the wherewithal to grow organically, or the financial support, and there were a lot of casualties as a consequence. French companies like Ubisoft and Infogrames did, they were incredibly well supported by the French government.

## Julian Rignall

Basically, in '87 and '88 companies began to make bets on whether the Amiga and the Atari ST were going to be the successors, and that people would upgrade their old 8-bit machines to these new 16-bit ones, and hoped the market would continue and everything would be as fantastic as it was. The reality, as the end of the '80s approached, was that these machines didn't come down in price, and that mums and dads realised that the computers that they maybe bought on the promise that it'd help little Johnny with his homework were in fact just used purely for gaming. So those late '80s, early '90s consoles that were 100 or 200 quid, versus buying a 500 quid machine ... 'No, let's buy little Johnny the games machine, it'll keep him happy and it's cheap. Why buy this Amiga thing?'

That's when the games industry in the UK ran out of steam. There were so many people betting the farm on the transition to these new 16-bit micros, and it didn't really happen, certainly not in the numbers of the previous generation. Most gamers transitioned to consoles, and the market changed from being based on British hardware and American systems that felt very British, because actually the best Commodore games came out of the UK and Europe. Suddenly we were faced with Japanese machines, with very closed development systems where you had to sign up to be a developer, be approved, buy cartridges and spend an enormous amount of money. People just weren't ready for it, and the industry just tanked.

You needed specialised hardware that required an upfront cost, but worse still was that you'd spend 20 grand on a development system and six months investing in a team of six to make a game, and then you had to go to Nintendo and they'd say, 'Right, we'll make 200,000 of those, but they're 15 quid a unit and you're going to pay for them up front.' Very, very, very few people had that kind of money to invest.

When I came out to work in the States I was working at Virgin on *The Jungle Book* and did a little bit of work on *The Lion King,* and I remember sitting in meetings where they were talking about having to manufacture these cartridges and the amount of money that was involved up front. You would have to take that liability and that was one of the things that really hurt Virgin. It made an awful lot of *The Lion King* cartridges, and while it sold very well it didn't sell all of them, and they had to sell this excess inventory at a discount, which offsets the investment that you made. All of a sudden it's not working very well for you.

You also saw the brain drain, from the early to the mid '90s. A lot of the best developers went to the US and found places at companies that had big distribution and licensing deals with Nintendo and Sega. They were in need of great talent, and Britain had the talent because you had all these guys that had grown up hacking and making the best out of these limited systems. Given new consoles, they could really make them sing.

It's very complicated, but one of the big reasons I think so few people in the UK saw it coming was that it was pre-internet, so people weren't aware of what was going on around the rest of the world. We'd had almost 10 years of this cosy idea that, you know, Britain's got this really healthy market. A lot of games were still selling, new computers were coming, and everything was going to be okay. And you had an entire industry geared towards making cassettes or disks: distribution, marketing, and so on, and then suddenly these new machines came along with huge pre-existing libraries developed in Japan and America that were very, very good.

The UK industry was really behind the curve except with those few exceptions, like Rare, who made that transition four years earlier. And within a very short space of time, from very late '89 to early '91, this sudden dramatic shift, with kids saying, 'I don't want to play with my Spectrum any more, Mum's not going to buy me an Amiga but there's a NES or a Sega Master System with great

× First released in 1993 for the Sega Master System. Rignall worked on the game with David Perry.
* Released in 1994 for the Mega Drive and Super Nintendo.

arcade games that look really awesome and it's quite cheap, so I'll have that.' But the Atari ST and Amiga were both out of production by, what, 1993?


## David Darling

We were definitely aware that the number of companies in the UK had been going down dramatically over the years. So in the early '80s you could name 50 or something, like Domark and Bug-Byte and loads more. But by the end of the '90s it was just Codemasters and Eidos, really. To begin with we were just competing within the UK, so with people like Ocean and U.S. Gold and Domark, but after a while it was with Electronic Arts or whoever; computer games started becoming an international marketplace. In the UK we were a big player, but in the rest of the world we were a small player. It was like playing in a new ball park.

We had cut our teeth on consoles with Nintendo, and so with PlayStation we started doing quite big games, like Colin McRae Rally with teams of like 40 or 50 people. We had a team of 20 or 30 artists and 20 programmers, and the games just kept getting bigger and bigger. As we made Colin McRae Rally 2.0, Colin McRae Rally 3 and TOCA Race Driver, the teams got to 100 people, and then it started to get a bit scary.

It's like making a movie or something, and in some ways it's really good because you work with loads of talented people, but in some ways it restricts your creativity because you can't afford to take any risks. You're much better off doing a Colin McRae sequel rather than putting 100 people on a game about, maybe, tadpole fishing in Mexico or something completely off the wall. We couldn't spend £10 million doing that because it's too risky. A sequel will be fun, but it won't be as innovative.

Like, in '82, it cost virtually nothing to make a game because you would do it in a month in your spare time. Two or three years later, if you had to pay somebody, like to convert a game to the Spectrum, then we would pay, like, £3,000. But in the mid '90s it might be like £1 million or £2 million, and by the end of the '90s it could be £10 million.

So the development budget increased dramatically, but actually, in terms of the risk analysis, I am not sure that it changed that much. Because in '84 if your game failed then you might not make it as a publisher through to the next year. For Mastertronic, BMX Racers and the Magic Knight games were big successes, but if they hadn't been, Mastertronic might not have carried on. That was the same at the end of the '90s. If you didn't have your Tomb Raider or your Colin McRae then, well, you just had to keep going, like being on a hamster wheel, you have to keep going.

In the early days the industry was pure fun, and we were just creating things. We had periods when things weren't selling, but I was always kind of thinking I could manage, because I put enough away for it not really to be a problem. But it changed when I was running a team and we'd had our first few publishers either sell up or go out of business. We were really in serious trouble; we weren't in debt but we didn't have any money, and I was living on a month-to-month basis. We were doing licensed products and selling utilities, hiring out our artists and musicians to other houses. We even did some advertising work, a little program for HMV, where Nipper the dog collects things from the bad cat. All that paid our way, but I got an increasing sort of sense of what happens if this cheque doesn't come in, and it was getting worse and worse.

But we had another brief good period when we were working with Virgin and we got a lot of 8-bit console conversions from them. It was kind of like a little bit of light relief after 16-bit Amiga and ST. But that stopped almost overnight; suddenly they didn't want to pay what they paid last time. Whether other people were undercutting us, I don't know, but we were living month-to-month again. Sometimes I didn't have enough money and I went through long periods of not paying myself. I owned the office, which I bought in the good times, so at least we didn't have to pay rent. The company ended up owing me a lot of money, and I was always thinking, 'Well, the next game has got to sell.' Game after game kind of sold, but not enough to get our heads above water.

It was almost 10 years of that, and you think just how did we manage? We had programmers who used to work for a wage plus royalty, which used to work very well, and when the royalties did come I was very honest and I used to pay them, sometimes even after they'd left. So I had a reputation for that, and in the end, when we sold the majority of the company

← 360

## Peter Stone and Richard Leinfellner

PS It was part of the downfall of Palace Software. There were a number of things happening at the same time. There was the transition to 16-bit, Richard and Steve were moving on, and we couldn't really cope with it. The *Barbarian* games were the high point of Palace Software – we continued for a number of years afterwards doing different things, but mainly distribution deals, selling our back catalogue or other people's products. That's how we survived for the next few years, really.

for finance and effectively we would have been bankrupt, the programmers said they would work for nothing. I had to tell them to go home; the company was insolvent.

It was a shame, but it was nice there was still a team spirit, and people expected me to kind of bubble up and just start another company. But the years had drained me, and I really didn't want any more of the feeling that I couldn't pay wages. When I got a job a few weeks later it was the first time I'd had a decent wage for absolutely ages. It was just such a relief.


## David Braben

I felt I couldn't work on my own any more, so I formed Frontier in late '93 – or actually formally incorporated it in January '94. To be honest, I haven't really looked back, because then you can build up a team. You don't have to do a whole load of contracts with contractors every time you make a game. People stayed together, and it was great, especially as there was a proliferation of new machines. There was PlayStation coming on the horizon. Sony were unbelievably slick. I think actually they changed the way the marketplace worked. Previously, the idea of showing things to developers was something where there would be a little circuit board and people would gather around a table, but Sony did a proper, slick presentation, almost like the launch of a new car. You know, with dramatic music and lights. It was another world, not the way you might launch a piece of software. I thought that was very interesting, amazing. They obviously spent a lot of money on their hardware. We got their development kits and they worked! That is very unusual.

But we focused on all of the hardware. I mean the real point, the great thing about development, is you can back all the horses. This is from sort of bitter experience with *Elite*, but *Frontier* was quite platform-agnostic, so the parts of the code that are machine-dependent were separate, totally separated from the gameplay code. That made it very easy to port *Frontier* on to different platforms.

So when it came to founding Frontier Developments, a lot of the principles were already set. So we were probably one of the first game companies to have an engine that was properly separated from the games, with its own API structure, and maintained from game to game. That tech is still in use today, and that is quite a long time. You have probably heard the stories of the 14th century axe where the head was changed in the 18th century and the shaft was changed in the 19th. So actually there is not very much, if any, of it left other than in spirit. But the point is there has been a continuity of how the tech worked. What that really means is you can amortise a lot of the effort across multiple games. But also it means that when you start a game, you are starting from quite a high point, not from scratch every time.

Sean, Noirin Carmody, who then became my wife, and I were sitting, I remember, in a restaurant on the King's Road, and Sean was saying, 'What are you going to do next?' 'Well, we've got a few ideas.' He said, 'I've just read *Foucault's Pendulum.*[×] What do you know about the Knights Templar?' I said, 'Well, I know a little bit about them.' He said, 'Actually, if you read a bit more, they're really, really interesting.'

So I read *Foucault's Pendulum.* I mean, it's a load of nonsense, but the *Holy Blood and the Holy Grail*[•] ... The interesting thing is that the Knights Templar weren't part of the public consciousness at that point, and so of course we wrote *Broken Sword,*[ˎ] involving the backstory of the Knights Templar, and really it entered the zeitgeist in a small way.

We had talked to Virgin about the possibility of releasing *Broken Sword* on PlayStation. Sony did a spectacularly good job at promoting the PlayStation to younger people and

× A novel by Umberto Eco first published in English in 1989.
• A 1982 book which claimed Jesus married Mary Magdalene and their descendants became a royal line with a claim to the French throne.
ˎ Released in 1996 as *Broken Sword: The Shadow of the Templars* on PC.

building a market that hadn't existed before. Before, you had older people who played PC games and younger people that played Nintendo, and the middle hadn't really been exploited. Sony went for them and built upwards, and they did a great job. We felt that *Broken Sword* might make a good game for it.

Virgin were very dismissive, because as far as they were concerned, the PlayStation was all about 3D games, and so they turned it down. So I approached Sony, and they weren't initially all that keen but they thought it might just work, and in the end they commissioned it. The game went on to sell half a million copies – it was just phenomenally successful. Working with Sony was wonderful, because you had three or four key people, even though they had all these games coming through. We were dealing directly with the head of PR, Liz Ashford, and the head of marketing, who was a brilliant guy, Dave Patton, and Chris Deering was running the whole thing. They were a very small group of people and it was really important to us that this game that everybody was a little bit uncertain about, hit Christmas.

Then I got a really cross email from Dave Patton, saying, 'It's not going to hit Christmas, we're going to postpone it to January,' so I phoned David up and said, 'Look, I'm confident it's going to be Christmas,' he said, 'Well, my testing people say it's not.' I said, 'Are you going to be in the office for the next few hours, because I'll get on a train and I'll come down and see you?' So I got on a train and I walked into his office and I said, 'What do I need to do to convince you?' He said, 'My test guys say it's going to miss.' So I picked up his phone and I phoned the QA people in Liverpool and I said, 'Can you give us an honest opinion, now?' and the head of QA said, 'Well, I thought it was going to miss but actually the newer version's really good, I think it's going to make it!' I said, 'Talk to David, will you?' and David said, 'Okay, it's back in before Christmas.' And that was wonderful, because that was the era, the mid '90s, that Sony in particular were really developer-friendly.

## Julian Gollop

When *X-COM* was published in America it became a big success for us. We became around 20–25 people at Mythos Games, and worked on a sequel, *X-COM: Apocalypse*. But we had some trouble with MicroProse because they were taken over by, ultimately, Hasbro, and drove a hard bargain on *Apocalypse*, so we started looking for an alternative publisher. Because of the initial success of *X-COM* we were hot property, and one was Virgin Interactive, which at the time was the biggest European publisher. They were very, very keen to sign us up and we entered a big negotiation between MicroProse, Virgin and us where they were offering ever and ever bigger sums of money. Eventually we signed a four-game deal with Virgin, and they gave us a huge signing fee, I think it was £300,000, just for signing the contract, which at the time was a major bonus.

So we saw Virgin as a really cool publisher, because they had a big reputation with Westwood Studios' *Command & Conquer*, their marketing was controversial but they had a big reputation. They had a load of chutzpah; it looked like they were really going places.

We worked on *Magic & Mayhem* and *X-COM: Apocalypse* at the same time. It was pretty difficult for us; we managed to increase the studio size to around 30, and I was still coding on *Apocalypse*, which was a big mistake. I should have been paying much more attention to the overall direction of the company and design, but

I think that's the problem of scaling that probably a lot of developers have at that kind of level. I was still too stuck in my old way of doing things, which was coding, design and testing, and not trying to think how the process of game development can scale properly.

I felt I was being pulled in lots of different directions, and I clearly wasn't good at everything. The thing that I was best, and I still think I am best at, is game design, and that was suffering a little bit, especially with regards to *Magic & Mayhem*. I kind of regret it, because *Magic & Mayhem* didn't really turn out the way I wanted, and it was the first game that I really experienced a lot of intervention by the publisher in what we put in and how it was designed.

It didn't sit very well with me. With *Magic & Mayhem* I wanted to evolve *Lords of Chaos*, this time setting it in a real-time strategy game framework, and fit it with what Virgin were doing with *Command & Conquer*. I wanted to put many more RPG-type systems in, like more intricate character progression, a bit less emphasis on preconfigured storylines and levels and a bit more of the random elements that we had in, say, *X-COM*. I think we had a really great game system, but the marketing department basically ruled Virgin and told us that we couldn't make it too RPG, because role-playing games didn't sell. This was, of course, before *Baldur's Gate*⃰ came out and changed the whole game.

I felt there was a strong future for games embracing the basic *Dungeons & Dragons* idea of a configurable character that gives the player choice over developing. But what really dominated were RTS games. Almost everybody was trying to develop them, and I found it very annoying, because they were all much of a muchness. We all remember the good ones, but we don't remember the hundreds of bad ones.

The problem with game development at the time was that the variety and innovation of the early computer games scene in Britain was being subverted and repressed by publishers who wanted games in a particular genre, or in a particular style. They wanted an RTS game because they sold. I think it marked a real change in the development of the industry, because the publishers with large amounts of money were starting to design games, rather than support game developers.

We were very much a victim of this idea. It was a bit of a shock for me, because I saw myself as a game designer; I thought I knew my audience, but now I was being told that people wouldn't like

⃰ BioWare's groundbreaking *Dungeons & Dragons*-based RPG, released in 1998.

this and that, like RPG elements, and it was quite different from, say, working with MicroProse.

Team sizes grew, which was driven by the advancement in platforms and technology, and for great content generation. One of the biggest things was the advent of CD-ROM, and of course the PC was a rapidly evolving architecture, so there was a drive to get the most out of it. The biggest development teams with the biggest funding were creating amazing stuff. The console cycle also had an impact, and there was a big change with the shift to CD-ROM with the PlayStation. There was always technical escalation which developers had to keep up with.

So the costs were accelerating, particularly with consoles. Publishers soon became conservative and focused much more on brand and IP development rather than original innovations. I guess the driving force behind development was that if you can establish a brand then you can predict profitability more accurately, because you've got a certain audience, and a historical record of what games sold. This was definitely the change that took place towards the end of the 1990s.

I think problems with Virgin started to happen after we published *Magic & Mayhem*, the first one. It seemed that it started with Westwood Studios splitting away from Virgin;[x] something was going wrong with Virgin Interactive. They had a meteoric rise, and then fell pretty rapidly because, basically, a big source of income seemed to be coming from Westwood Studios and the *Command & Conquer* franchise.

I think that marked the end of possibly the last really big UK-based publisher, and we suffered as a consequence. We had done only one game out of the four games in our deal. Virgin was sold to Titus Software,[*] who were just not really interested in anything except Virgin's IP. They weren't going to fund us on development so we had to liquidate Mythos Games, because we couldn't sign with another publisher. So the fall of Virgin Interactive had a big impact on us. It really showed the difference between the hype and the reality.

[x] Electronic Arts bought the studio, which made the leading RTS *Command & Conquer*, in 1998.
[*] The French publisher-developer behind *Titus the Fox* and *The Blues Brothers*.

After *Aladdin*, I got a green card, which was interesting because it opened up the option of leaving Virgin and having my own company. I was actually welcome in the United States! I also got a couple of job offers, one from the Sega Technical Institute˙ from a guy called Roger Hector.˟ It was shocking because it would have made me technical director, and, technically, Yuji Naka's boss!˙ I was like, 'What?!' I mean, Yuji Naka was one of my heroes. So that was really tempting.

Then there was a second offer. Playmates Toys was the company that made Teenage Mutant Ninja Turtles and, I would imagine, billions of dollars from them. Again, a jigsaw piece fell into place, because I was a guy who made a *Teenage Mutant Ninja Turtles* game back in the UK and had a number one hit from it, and this company had the Turtles licence ... So should I join the Turtles guys, stay at Virgin, or should I go to Sega? But I ended up making another option. I met with the head of Playmates and I said to him, 'Would you be willing to fund us to make a game for you? So I won't work for your company, I'll start my own, but we will give the output to you, so that you can publish it?' He was interested in doing that and the result was a three-game deal and our company, Shiny Entertainment.˟˟

Then it began, the search for the first game. What were we going to do? We'd just finished *Aladdin*, so people assumed we would do something like that, but we didn't have any Disney rights. We looked at everything; we assumed the game would be licensed, of course, because we'd just done three back-to-back licensed games. One we were seriously considering was *Knight Rider,* you know, the TV show with the car with the light that goes back and forth? Then I went to Universal and they showed me all these different properties that they had but none of them was really quite exciting. I would sit through these long meetings with Sony and everybody else, looking at all these different properties, trying to understand which was the best one for the talents of our team, but nothing really got me.

Then, one of our team members wanted us to hire a new animator, called Doug TenNapel. I'd never heard of him, so I said, 'I

˙ Sega's development division based in the US, where games including *Die Hard Arcade* and *Kid Chameleon* were made, and where Sonic Team created *Sonic the Hedgehog 2.*
˟ Sega Technical Institute's general manager at the time, who'd previously taken leading roles during the early days of Atari and Electronic Arts.
˙ The programmer of *Sonic the Hedgehog.*
˟˟ Founded in October 1993 in Laguna Beach, Southern California.

have to see something, so have him draw something and animate it, and I'll have a look.' The first thing he drew was Earthworm Jim, this worm in a suit, and we were like, 'Hmmm, that's really cool, I like that! You're hired! And we'll make a game based on this character!'

It was a really fun relationship, because there was a bit of butting of heads between myself and Doug. Doug always wanted to make the character very funny and cartoony and slapstick, and sort of the bumbling idiot, and I wanted to make it that he's a superhero, tough, big muscles, and going to save the day. I realised that it's not about one person's opinion; the whole team would start to impact and change the dynamic of the game. There were all these weird influences in our company, we had Johnny Cash music playing, we had LaserDiscs of Tex Avery cartoons playing all day long. In a Tex Avery cartoon you don't get punched; you get punched across the room, your head goes all the whole way across and back again.

Everybody had to draw in our meetings, you weren't allowed to just write things down, so even the programmers would come in with drawings of their ideas. They were horrible! I mean, my ability to draw is zero; when a programmer draws something it makes everybody have a fun time, because they're going to make fun of these images. We would get a conversation going from that which would inspire people; new ideas would come from it which would never have happened if the programmers hadn't contributed, or if the artist had just drawn it perfectly.

That mix created an interesting dynamic of unpredictability over what would come out, and that's why I think the DNA of *Earthworm Jim* games was this weird funniness. You would have no idea where we were going and what we were going to do next. It would tease you on: 'I just want to finish the level to see what on Earth happens next.'

I think that we had struck on a very important piece of the games business, that humour matters. I don't know why more people don't go for humour, because having that humour element – it doesn't have to be laugh out loud – is what really helped make *Earthworm Jim*. So *Earthworm Jim* was successful for Playmates, and when we suggested *Earthworm Jim 2*, the answer was yes. We were also interested in licensing it, but we had this interesting problem. We really wanted a TV show bad, but there's a catch-22 where you can't have a TV show unless you have a toy line, and you can't have a toy line unless you have a TV show. The videogames weren't enough.

So I ended up having dinner with the head of Universal Cartoon Studios* and the head of Playmates Toys, and everyone looked each other in the eye and said, 'I'll do the toys if you do the TV show, and I'll do the videogame ... are we all cool with this?' So boom, we had a TV show with Universal, and the minute you get a TV show and a toy line, everybody wants to license your stuff. We ended up with Marvel making comic books, we had Taco Bell and Carl's giving Earthworm Jim toys away with fast food, we had lunch boxes and Halloween masks, napkins and bed covers and underpants. This was a new idea for a game developer, to take our property and license it out. Our history was always bringing stuff in. This was a new company, our first property and boy we'd hit our stride.

* Which then became Universal Animation Studios.

## Rob Hubbard

As soon as I went to the States I kind of lost touch with the UK side. We had a good run, you know, before a certain Japanese company released something called the Famicom, which changed the whole nature of the business. It moved away from the home computer and the hobbyist into a little box dedicated to one function, and that was kids playing games. It's what led to the massive expansion of companies like EA to move away from home computing and creativity products, and that vision of what they used to call 'Real life in a box,' and 'We see farther,' into purely videogames.

And all the endless sequels ... I remember the first time they did a sequel to *John Madden Football*, and I thought it was never going to sell because it was the same as the original, and of course it did. After that the floodgates opened, and EA never looked back. Every sports game since 1992, you know, *NHL Hockey*, *FIFA*, *Need for Speed*, the list goes on. They started to build teams around franchises, so the *Need for Speed* guys would have their own graphics and audio guys, who would just work on that.

To me, it was, 'How can you possibly put any more creativity into a football game that you have been doing for five years?' People are now just part of a machine, trying to get the game out. The hours started getting long, because the machines were getting very complicated, and it became very, very involved getting these games out. People were working months and months on end, without any time off, and a lot of the passion was going out of them. If you want a good game, you need somebody who is bright and has lots of passion. Then, you can't go wrong, can you?

I had tried to innovate, like there was the interactive loading music I did on *Delta*[x], where you could move the joystick and change the chords and instruments. It was a forerunner to interactive music, which I had a very keen interest in, the idea of playing the game and the music starting to change as the action is changing. It's very, very difficult to do, and unfortunately it pretty much got killed off by all the big companies. They started licensing various famous rap artists and people like that, so there was a move towards licensed music. The marketing people took over the games industry, to a large extent, and changed a lot of things.

[x] A 1987 scrolling shooter for the Commodore 64 from Thalamus.

‹ 274

## Gary Penn

I think the decline happened possibly because we in the UK didn't take games seriously enough, and maybe weren't aggressive enough in the way that we marketed the goods. I don't think the UK is as aggressive as, say, the US is in terms of sales. The UK tends to make stuff quite modestly, and I think there is a degree of artistry, where you make things to stand the test of time, rather than to be sold and exploited in the short term. So they were made with less of a kind of commercial eye, sometimes, or perhaps we're just too modest. The American side dominated so readily because America tends to be very good at selling dreams. Whether those dreams were actually realised through the products is another discussion entirely.

The UK side of things was always small-scale, so we had single-load technology, tape-based stuff, whereas in the US they had disks, generally, and more memory to play with. We were dealing with tighter budgets, whereas the US had that Hollywood and entrepreneur mentality. And a lot of guys from the UK went to the US, and that didn't help.

I always think the UK back then was almost a mirror image of Japan, producing the same degree of quirk. We were producing things like games about brushing your teeth, which you would expect from Japan. If you take something like *Manic Miner*, it has some fantastically quirky British humour in it, and you never got that kind of stuff in the US. The games from the US have scale, you know? Maybe that's a reflection of the country, while the UK is a small Island, and Japan is another island. Maybe it's a coincidence that these two islands were producing this kind of quirky stuff almost in isolation.

It felt almost like we were amateurs, but in a very positive way, whereas the corporate side in America was always more pronounced. You always got the sense that these guys could attract the money and knew what to do with it, while we were doing it for ourselves.

I had a very private concern with Shiny at the time, which was that the company was an S corporation,* and my personal finances were tied to it all. I was very worried about where the game industry was going, because I had a team of the best pencil and paper artists in the industry, and yet everyone was talking about this 3D thing. We got some software and tools in so that the animators could try it, and the feedback was, 'We don't like this, this isn't interesting to us, and we don't like these tools.' So I had a little bit of a panic, and felt that we wouldn't make it as a company because 3D wasn't our skill set.

That was probably the biggest mistake I've made in my career. I underestimated the team, because it turned out they ended up, I think, doing some of the best 3D in the industry for its time. The first game they made was *MDK,* the first game with a sniper mode, so they invented the sniper mode. Remember, the company was about licensing out, so when Apple made the iMac, every single one had *MDK* on it, and we licensed to Microsoft for their joysticks, video card companies; everyone was licensing our game to put it into their boxes. But I had sold Shiny Entertainment to Interplay, and boy that was a mistake. We actually were going to survive; the company did very well as a 3D company. But you can't take it back, right?

But it was a tough time, because the animators ended up starting their own company doing claymation while our team became focused on 3D. We were trying to innovate in technologies, like tessellation, which meant more and more detail in the characters, very smooth surfaces compared to what else was out there.

And so there we were, innovating in 3D, but I made bad decision number two. It was this idea that the more games you make, the more money the company will make.￪ But it doesn't work that way. You dilute your team, and you end up with all these headaches and the games aren't as good as you'd want them to be. There are lots of decisions to make: which is the right property? Which is the right platform? What are you going to do next, and what's the perfect team mix? We went through a very rough period while we were trying to work it out.

We also couldn't shake that idea that we could make whatever we wanted. In the old days you just made anything you felt like; we could make a game about hair if we wanted. It just didn't matter,

* A status affecting taxation where income and losses are passed through shareholders.
￪ In three years, the studio released five games: *MDK, Wild 9, R/C Stunt Copter, Messiah* and *Sacrifice.*

someone would buy it. But we had marketing forces coming in; PR people were doing analysis, and you're like, 'What!? No one wants the product?' But I kept kicking off more products, like I was into model helicopters, so suddenly we started making a model helicopter game and maybe there wasn't a market for it. We didn't do any analysis, we'd just start working on the game.

So this was a very strange period, where the team was diluted and we were trying to get this stuff out. Luckily the games that we made, each of them had some kind of hook and so we had fans of them, but if you looked at the mass market I felt that they weren't right. We weren't acting as a developer supporting our publisher, we were almost pulling against them because we were just doing whatever we wanted. The answer was to do a licensed game again. It was our DNA. In my career, every time we hit a licensed game, boom, great things happened.

Jon Hare

We were inventing new game genres every other month back in the '80s and '90s. The only reason it stopped is people stopped wanting to pay money to take risks on people being highly creative, whereas in the early days everyone was being creative, and it was new, so the people investing money in it from the publishing side were willing to take risks because it was their only way into the market. There was a huge mentality shift from about 1995, where we've gone from 'anything is possible and we can take anything in real life and we can turn it into a game,' to 'we've got to take a game and turn it into another game.' It automatically restricted your choices to existing games and how you're going to modify them. In the old days people were just excited to see something new, like 'Wow, that's great, yeah let's do this!' There was a lot more of that mentality rather than having one or two slots to fill in a year and they know exactly the kind of thing they want, and if you've got something which happens to fall in that narrow slot, then you might be lucky and get some money.

The thing about Americans is that they take business very, very seriously. Electronic Arts' upper senior management was populated by some people who had been programmers and artists, but the vast majority were people from other industries. If you look at 90% of the UK publishers, the top management were people who had been in the industry for a long time, who could remember the trestle tables. That means that they didn't have the diversity of talent that you need to take a company from turning over $10 million to $100 million, and in Electronic Arts' case, turning over a billion. If you're going to do that you have got to be a global enterprise, thinking as much about Asia and Europe as America. You cannot be a band of people who used to be programmers. That's the first reason.

The second reason is the British are great at creativity. We thrived in the home computing era, and the Americans are brilliant at exploiting that creativity. Time and time again in our industry and many others, we have been bought out and then taken to higher heights by Americans. That's just the way the world is.

## Julian Rignall

I'm going to sound like a right wanker saying it, but British developers sometimes look at things in a very insular way. That's great if you want to make a success in the British market, but not many people really understand what it takes to make a game that's successful outside of the UK. There's certain taste levels in Japan and America that are just different.

I hear a lot from developers that want worldwide success and I think that requires talking to or employing people, or spending time in other countries, really talking to gamers and understanding those differences. It took me years to figure out why American magazines are like they are. When I first came out here I'm like, 'American magazines, they're crap, nobody says anything funny, and there's this reviewing tolerance.' We were like, 'It's brilliant' or, 'It's absolute crap!' But that doesn't work out here. I couldn't understand why, but then I figured it out. It's because people just don't look at the world in the same way that we do.

I think there's huge potential success to be had in the indie and iOS markets, which are far, far more open to innovation and quirkiness. Actually we've already seen a few little things coming through from British developers. Jeff Minter's suddenly found himself back, it's a small market, but relevant again after years out in the wilderness unable to do much. But he can crank out these iOS games that echo what he did 20 years ago, because the industry is now old enough that rather than building games on technology and everything having to be new, we can look back. It's a little bit like genres of music, you know? Make a game like a 16-bit game and somebody will be excited about playing that again. Or an 8-bit game. They've almost become genres in and of themselves, and I think in that sense the sky's the limit: you can really be inventive and crazy.

I think Britain is very good at its quirky, strange, sometimes esoteric, sometimes smarter than the average bear games. These more novel and interesting ideas are a sock to these massive multi-multi-multi-million dollar blockbusters. They're like blockbuster movies. *Prometheus*? Fantastic movie, it looks great, but you know what? I love *Doctor Who*. It's a fantastic show, it's brilliantly written, it's kind of weird and quirky, and certainly some of my American friends absolutely love it, and some of them just don't get it at all, but it's British, it's quirky, and I think we can do the same thing with games. It's like we don't need to compete on the same level, we find what we're good at and that's what we make.

← 385

## Charles Cecil

Right at the very beginning, there were two types of games. There were arcade games that we copied, and there were original games. In the UK, I think we have a history of writing games and being successful, and I think that's because we innovate. We innovate both from a technical and a creative perspective, and if you look back at some of those very early games, like *3D Monster Maze*, for example, which was extraordinary, the first first person game, where you run away from a tyrannosaurus chasing you around a maze. We were in many ways creating the games that we wanted to play, and they were driven by the vision of either one person or a team of two, but never more than that, coming up with a design, programming it, coming up with the graphics, the music, they would then test it, they would hone it and then they'd give it to a publisher to publish.

As teams grew, that vision became less important and much more driven towards commercial rather than aesthetic ends, and I always believe that you need a commercial and aesthetic vision, but it became too commercial, too safe. Currently the market is really polarising, from the mega expensive, hundred-million-dollar *Grand Theft Auto V*s: fantastic games, I mean, extraordinary games, driven by huge teams, very technical but also exciting but also building very much on the building blocks that have come before. And at the other end you've got much cheaper games, games costing tens of thousands or maybe a few hundred thousand, and those can be much more experimental. That's much more the indie scene.

An indie scene is where we all came from at the beginning of the '80s and it was driven out in the '90s. But through the opportunity to develop a game relatively cheaply, you get kids just coming together: an artist, a programmer, a sound person. They can just give it a go and because there's a very low barrier to entry, and they're able to distribute the games so effectively now through the digital medium, actually there's wonderful opportunity for people to create games in an indie scene and I think this is just going to continue.

Both from a development perspective and from a gamer's perspective today is as exciting as it has ever been, and it really in many ways feels like it was in the very early days, when we were forging the way, we were pioneers. We didn't know what to build on, we didn't have a template.

# Epilogue

The end of Britsoft wasn't sudden. It wasn't some kind of cataclysm, leaving nothing but scorched earth where the superstars of the Spectrum, Commodore 64 and Amiga had once ruled. Instead, it was a slow transmutation, as one generation blended into the next.

Many of Britsoft's leading lights vanished in the early '90s: some had burned out; some couldn't adapt to working with larger teams; some were simply uninterested in making games that weren't on their own terms any more. Many, however, quietly changed their roles; former programmers went into management and passed their experience on to a new set of game makers ready to devote themselves to Nintendo, Sega and Sony.

The playground might have expanded, but the hits kept coming: *Tomb Raider*, *GoldenEye 007*, *Worms*, *Grand Theft Auto*, *Micro Machines*, *Driver* and so many more. Eidos and Codemasters would take leading roles as international publishers. The crown jewels of what remained of the UK game industry were treasured by Nintendo. Now home to Electronic Arts and Sony's European operations, the British landscape remained imprinted with Britsoft's achievements: Guildford, home of Bullfrog; Leamington Spa, home of Codemasters and Blitz; Cambridge, home of Frontier Developments; and Dundee, home of DMA Design. All grew as vibrant centres of game making.

But the era of the small developer was over. A tiny number of individuals, like Jeff Minter, were able to persevere, but few others had the talent, the following or the financial muscle to make and distribute their own games. Expensive, team-built games were now the order of the day; and while some of Britsoft's pioneering names did become a part of this new world, the time of the lone programmer, the independent tinkerer producing homebrew games, was over. In the new era, the era of the Super Nintendo, PlayStation and Xbox, consoles ruled, and the Wild West was won.

--------------------------------------------------------------------
Peter Molyneux       33, 49, 56, 71, 84, 92, 99, 196, 229, 236, 243, 265, 279, 288,
                     340, 347, 349, 371, 395

Born in 1959 in Guildford, Peter Molyneux is the co-founder of seminal
Guildford-based studios Bullfrog and Lionhead, and a designer of well-
loved and ambitious strategy games including *Populous*, *Dungeon Keeper*
and *Black & White*. He was awarded an OBE in 2004 and helped spur the
growth of Guildford as a centre of game development in the UK, while
inspiring a generation of makers and players alike with his ability
and passion for high-concept ideas and features. After becoming creative director of Microsoft Game Studios Europe, Molyneux left to found
a new studio in 2012 called 22Cans, turning to crowdfunding to realise
smaller-scale but still conceptually progressive projects including *Cu-
riosity* and *Godus*.

--------------------------------------------------------------------
David Braben         40, 49, 85, 88, 90, 102, 135, 138, 176, 284, 356, 384

David Braben was born in Nottingham in 1964 and is the co-creator of
*Elite*, the pioneering 3D space trading and combat game. He went on to
write a succession of technically and creatively advanced games, including *Zarch* and *Virus*, and founded Cambridge-based Frontier Developments
in 1994, which became one of the UK's largest developers. Taking on both
contract work and passion projects, Frontier Developments has produced
a remarkably broad range of games, including the *Rollercoaster Tycoon*
series, *Kinectimals*, and *Elite: Dangerous*. Braben is also one of the
founders of the Raspberry Pi Foundation, maker of a small, single-board
computer designed to develop computer skills among children, and was
awarded an OBE in 2014.

---

Archer Maclean

Archer Maclean was born in 1962, and his interest in computers quickly led him to games. His creations are best known for their technical prowess: *Dropzone* for its super smooth scrolling, and *International Karate +* for displaying more sprites than the Commodore 64 was supposed to be capable of handling. Maclean's biggest success was the sophisticated 3D sports simulation *Jimmy White's Whirlwind Snooker*, which led to him founding a company, Awesome Developments, to create a succession of snooker games. It was bought by Ignition Entertainment in 2002, and Maclean resigned in 2005, just after releasing puzzler *Archer Maclean's Mercury* as a PlayStation Portable launch game.

---

David Darling

Born in 1966, David Darling founded Codemasters (then Code Masters) at the age of 19, along with his father and his twin brother, Richard, having already established a family business making and selling games. The Darlings epitomised the entrepreneurial spirit of some early developers, and became well known for publishing low price games. As well as writing their own titles, they discovered talent including the Oliver twins, who produced the *Dizzy* series. Codemasters became one of the UK's longest established studios, though Darling sold his interest in the company in 2007. He was awarded a CBE in 2008, and in 2011 founded Kwalee, a small smartphone game developer based in Leamington Spa.

---

Jeff Minter

One of the most beloved British game developers, Jeff Minter began a long career writing idiosyncratically styled but carefully crafted games in the early 1980s. Under the name Llamasoft, he worked with a particular focus on shoot 'em ups, including *Attack of the Mutant Camels*, *Tempest 2000* and *Space Giraffe*. His fiercely independent attitude has tended to confound the mainstream commercial industry. But his technical skills, coupled with his passion for experimenting and tinkering with new platforms and designs, led him to contribute and provide consulting on various hardware launches, including the Atari Jaguar and Xbox 360.

---
Charles Cecil

---

Best known for the *Broken Sword* series, Charles Cecil began his career in videogames in 1981, writing text adventures. He later became a
software development manager for U.S. Gold before founding Revolution
Software in 1990, making *Beneath a Steel Sky*, *Lure of the Temptress* and
*Broken Sword*. Revolution was renowned for pushing the genre into 3D and
for its use of sophisticated animation techniques; however, mainstream
interest in adventure games declined and led to financial struggles for
the company from the late '00s. Revolution was later buoyed by the rise
of crowdfunding and self-publishing. Cecil was awarded an MBE in 2011,
and his avuncular personality and astute views have helped him to main-
tain a central role in the British game development community.

---

David Perry

---

Born in Northern Ireland in 1967, David Perry was still at school when
he got his first job at Mikro-Gen. He swiftly demonstrated an aptitude
for making games with high production values, backed up by programming
smarts and an eye for business. Keenly aware of the industry outside the
UK, he left to work in the United States in the early 1990s, applying
his skills to licensed games like *Disney's Aladdin*, before establishing
Shiny Entertainment in 1993, making titles including *Earthworm Jim*, *MDK*
and *Enter the Matrix*. He sold Shiny in 2002, resigned in 2006 and in 2008
founded cloud gaming service Gaikai, which was bought by Sony in 2012.

---

Geoff Crammond

---

While many of his contemporaries were fresh out of school, Geoff Crammond
came to games with a degree in physics and a previous job as a Fortran
programmer. He quickly became one of the scene's leading programmers,
specialising in cutting-edge 3D with flight simulator *Aviator*, progressive abstract puzzle game *The Sentinel* and car sims *Revs* and *Stunt Car
Racer*. He is best known for the *Grand Prix* series, which was famed for
its bleeding edge physics simulation. He worked on the series right up
to 2002's *Grand Prix 4*, after which, tired of deadlines and the rising
complexity of game development, he left the commercial game industry.

---

Julian Gollop          50, 144, 150, 151, 195, 232, 252, 269, 353, 386

Julian Gollop cut a very single-minded path through his long career in videogames, specialising almost exclusively in strategy games. Inspired by board and card games as well as *Dungeons & Dragons*, he released his first game in 1983. He has since created *Chaos*, *Rebelstar* and *X-COM*, all classic turn-based strategy series, steadily honing them and expanding on their designs over the years. He founded several studios, punctuated by a period working at Ubisoft's Bulgaria studio, which saw him contributing to the *Assassin's Creed* and *Ghost Recon* series. He left to found another company of his own, Gollop Games, which debuted with the Kickstarter-funded *Chaos Reborn*.

---

Julian Rignall          34, 46, 48, 68, 180, 190, 232, 235, 237, 325, 380, 395

Julian Rignall's competition-level gaming skills led to him contributing gaming tips and guides to *Personal Computer Games* and *Computer and Video Games*. Ex-*Personal Computer Games* editor Chris Anderson brought him on to the launch editorial team of *Zzap!64*. There, 'Jaz' Rignall's fiery opinion and quips, aided by Oliver Frey's distinctive review portraits, helped immortalise him as a gaming personality for a generation. He became *Zzap!64*'s editor, before joining *Computer and Video Games* in 1988, and launching *Mean Machines* in 1990, which focused on Japanese consoles. He also frequently appeared on TV shows including *GamesMaster*. In the mid '90s he moved to the US to become vice president of design at Virgin, before taking a series of management roles in games media, from IGN to US Gamer.

---

Dino Dini          36, 69, 291, 293, 342

Dino Dini's first commercial game was *Kick Off* for the Atari ST, which revitalised the football game. Not bad for a programmer who didn't even follow the sport. Its innovation was modelling the ball separately to the players, offering the genre a new sense of realism. He went on to make *Kick Off 2* and *Player Manager*, before leaving Anco to make *Goal!*, a game which, though popular, had to contend with *Sensible Soccer*'s barnstorming success. Dini left the UK for the US in the mid '90s to make PlayStation football game *Three Lions*, and returned in 2001 to found Abundant Software, which closed after its project, 'Total Control Football', was cancelled. He then became a lecturer on game programming in the Netherlands.

---
Mo Warden

An artist - or, more specifically, a computer graphic designer - on early
3D games at Novagen Software, not only was Warden a rare example, for
the time, of a woman taking a lead role in game making, she also learned
her craft as a single mother of two. She started out producing art for
developers including Jeff Minter and Anco, before joining Novagen to
work on games including *Damocles* and *Backlash*. Later, she contributed
a column to *ST User* on game art. After Novagen's transformation into
an interactive retail platform maker in the mid '90s, she left games to
become a web designer.

---
Rob Hubbard

Rob Hubbard was one of the Commodore 64's most celebrated personalities.
Creator of music and sound across some 70 games, he did much to sculpt
the distinctive character of the system. He pioneered audio programming
techniques that stretched the SID audio chip to produce effects far
beyond its designed limits. Formerly a professional musician, his first
game was Gremlin's *Thing on a Spring* in 1985, after which he immediately
found himself in hot demand. He moved from Newcastle to California in
1988 to join Electronic Arts, where he led audio until returning to the
UK in 2002 and, for the most part, moving on from the videogame industry.

---
Martin Kenwright

Martin Kenwright emerged just as 16-bit machines began flowering, his
background as an artist giving him the sensibility to develop early 3D
and make it beautiful. He started his career in 1987 working at Rowan
Software, porting 3D flight sim *Falcon* to the Atari ST. He left in 1989,
founding Digital Image Design to make cutting edge flight sims of his
own, starting with *F-22* and going on to make *EF2000*, the first 3D-accel-
erated game, which was also sold as a military training tool. By then
he'd gained a taste for entrepreneurship, co-founding *MotorStorm* maker
Evolution Studios in 1999 and digital media studio Starship in 2013.

```
----------------------------------------------------------------
Fred Gray                  34, 106, 155, 159, 174, 176, 178, 180, 238, 273, 377
```

When Fred Gray joined Imagine Software, he became the UK game industry's
first ever in-house music composer. His first title was 1984's *Pedro*, but
when Imagine suddenly collapsed later that year, he went on to compose
for Denton Designs, where he worked on titles including *Enigma Force*,
*Shadowfire* and *Madballs*, developing a musical style that was bouncier
and lighter than the harder and more progressive sound of his leading
contemporaries. When the 8-bit generation came to its end, Gray lost
interest in making music for games and left the industry.

```
----------------------------------------------------------------
Martin Galway              46, 53, 104, 153, 155, 157, 158, 160, 161, 163, 164, 165, 167,
                           177, 193, 241, 275, 302, 303, 325
```

Martin Galway was perhaps the most musically progressive Commodore 64
game composer. Influenced by Vangelis and Tangerine Dream, and charac-
terised by an impressive attention to technical detail, his most celebrated musical works came on *Rambo II* and Sensible Software's *Wizball*.
Perhaps surprisingly given his family background - his uncle is a classical flautist, and his father a music teacher - Martin's first interest
was programming. However, he decided to join Ocean as a composer after
finishing school. For a time he was a partner at Sensible Software, but
ended up moving to Texas to join Origin Systems, and later, Certain Affinity and Cloud Imperium Games, where he worked on *Star Citizen*.

```
----------------------------------------------------------------
Mel Croucher              57, 60, 62, 66, 133, 134, 182, 203, 233
```

There were many visionaries in the early British game industry, but Mel
Croucher was the exemplar, seeing the potential for home computer games
long before the computers and trade existed to support them. Originally
an architect, he started out broadcasting code for simple quiz games
over local radio in 1977, before discovering there was a market for selling the games on cassette tapes. He is best known for the 1984 title
*Deus Ex Machina*, a multimedia experience that explored life from birth
to death, incorporating celebrity talent and his own music. Rejecting
what he saw as the rising commercialism and violent tone of the industry he'd helped spawn, he largely left games behind until 2013, when he
announced a sequel to *Deus Ex Machina*.

---

Mike Montgomery

Mike Montgomery spent 15 years in retail at Woolworths before becoming a programmer at the London developer Laser Genius. He established The Bitmap Brothers in 1987 with Eric Matthews and Steve Kelly. His experience in sales gave him rare marketing insight, and allowed him to make The Bitmap Brothers a savvier kind of studio than the game industry had seen before. The team self-promoted as rock stars, and established a distinctive house style across titles such as *Speedball*, *Gods* and *The Chaos Engine*. After the studio faced financial difficulties in the mid-'00s, he established Tower Studios, a game development consultancy, with Jon Hare. He also began developing and re-releasing Bitmap Brothers games on PC and mobile platforms, and joined racing specialist Slightly Mad Studios in 2013.

---

Rod Cousens

From the beginning, Rod Cousens was at the forefront of the UK game industry's business culture. He helped establish Quicksilva as a publisher in 1981, and spearheaded the earliest industry events, including awards and fundraising efforts such as 1985's Soft Aid. He also saw opportunities outside the UK, whether exporting British-made titles, or bringing overseas games in. He carved out a position for himself at Activision, eventually becoming its international president, before moving on to Acclaim in 1998. In 2005, he joined Codemasters as CEO when venture capitalists invested in the company, leaving in 2015 to lead *RuneScape* maker Jagex.

---

Sean Cooper

Sean Cooper perfectly exemplifies Bullfrog's habit of taking on new talent and seeing it shine. He joined the company on work experience during his Youth Training Scheme computer course, first making 1990 16-bit platformer *Flood*, learning programming as he went along, before leading the creation of *Syndicate*. Despite a brief dalliance in modelling, he stayed at the studio until Electronic Arts subsumed it in 1995, but soon returned, later working on *The Godfather* and *007*. He left in 2005 to freelance, making Flash-based web games like the *Boxhead* series, and a graphics engine for Flash called Fliso, which was bought by US social game developer Lolapps.

---

Malcolm Evans                80

It was possibly the earliest 3D game for home computers, and the first
survival horror title: *3D Monster Maze* stunned everyone who experienced
it, and defied assumptions of what the ZX81 could do. Its creator, Malcolm Evans, who was 37 at the time, had developed a career programming
jet engines, satellites for Marconi and classified software for the
Ministry of Defence, but *3D Monster Maze*'s success led him to found New
Generation Software in 1982 with his brother, Rod. It published games
for the Spectrum and Commodore 64, including Evans' *Trashman*, until it
closed in 1986, when Evans returned to software engineering for British
Aerospace, and later, Science Systems.

---

Steve Turner                51, 61, 66, 82, 139, 142, 150, 184, 239, 245, 247, 267, 271,
                            325, 356, 383

It's rare to find a game maker as multi-skilled as Steve Turner, who was
a programmer, musician, business professional and manager. His games,
such as *3D Space Wars*, *Avalon* and *Quazatron*, were smartly designed and
programmed, an achievement made all the more impressive by the fact that
Turner, working alongside Andrew Braybrook, was also running Graftgold,
steering it to becoming one of the '80s' most successful developers.
Turner was unable to keep up with changes to the industry that came with
the transition to 16-bit, and he closed the company to take a job writing
banking and financial software before retiring in 2011.

---

Tim Tyler                   100, 145, 204

One of the more eccentric figures of the Britsoft era, the teenage Tim
Tyler made several false starts as a game writer before producing 1983's
*Repton*. Its success propelled him to make a sequel before he attended
university, and once there, he continued to write games. He released
only one, *Caverns*, but it failed to sell, a failure that made him dismiss
his previous accomplishments as pure luck. Disenchanted with the game
industry's focus on violence, he moved to the US, where his programming
and writing allowed him to explore a diverse range of interests, including but not limited to: geoengineering, transhumanism, memetics, shoes,
and the building of dizzyingly complicated homemade keyboards.

---

Nigel Alderton                35, 44, 87, 101, 157, 162, 335

With his big hit, *Chuckie Egg*, Nigel Alderton discovered a way to get
a player sprite to scroll completely smoothly across the screen. The
game was a great success, but nonetheless he left its publisher to make
a sequel without him, and instead joined Ocean, before leaving to port
*Commando* to the Spectrum and *Ghosts'n Goblins* to the Amstrad CPC for
Elite. There, he became a development manager but, finding that the game
industry was becoming both too immature and too focused on large game
projects, he decided to leave and work as a general programmer.

---

Jon Hare              35, 38, 108, 164, 166, 276, 302, 338, 339, 341, 344, 352, 372, 394

Co-founder of Sensible Software with his best friend and band mate Chris
Yates, Jon 'Jops' Hare was sole designer and artist for its breakout
games *Parallax*, *Wizball* and *Microprose Soccer*, and creative director for
its most celebrated releases, *Cannon Fodder* and *Sensible Soccer*. After
selling Sensible to Codemasters in 1999, Hare kept just as busy, working
as a design consultant and creative director at Jagex and Codemasters,
and founding several studios, including mobile studio Me-Stars and Tower
Studios, which he established with the Bitmap Brothers' Mike Montgomery.
He also established BUGS, a network connecting graduates with jobs in
the game industry.

---

Gary Penn             40, 48, 60, 72, 233, 236, 252, 274, 392

Gary Penn was a member of *Zzap!64*'s founding editorial team, where he became well known for his passionate writing, which showed a particularly
deep appreciation for game design. He went on to edit 16-bit focused
magazine *The One*, before leaving to go freelance, creating manuals for
Virgin and producing *Frontier: Elite II* at Konami. He joined DMA Design
as creative manager, working on 1997's *Grand Theft Auto*, *Body Harvest*
and *Tanktics*. After Infogrames bought DMA Design, Penn and other DMA
alumni founded Denki, developer of *Denki Blocks* and *Go! Go! Beckham!* He
was awarded 2007's Games Media Legend award, and also authored *Sensible
Software 1986-1999*.

---

Eugene Evans

One of the emblematic stories of the Britsoft movement concerned a teen programmer whose success earned him a Lotus sports car. The teen programmer was Eugene Evans, although the story was somewhat fanciful. One of the first employees of Imagine Software, Evans held a leading position there until it collapsed in 1984. He then joined Psygnosis before leaving the UK for Chicago, feeling hounded by his high profile past, to work at little-known developer GraphicFinal. A succession of management roles followed at Viacom, Infinite Ventures, Mythic Entertainment and Electronic Arts, until in 2013 he turned his attention to non-gaming technology and media startups.

---

Oliver Frey

Fantasy and sci-fi artist Oliver Frey is responsible for much of early videogames' visual identity, despite working almost exclusively in print. He created *Zzap!64* and *Crash*'s colourful covers, using his visual imagination to bridge the gap between the games people played in their heads and the crude pixels they saw on their screens. Born in Zurich, he moved to the UK to study at the London Film School in the early '70s. It was there that he met future colleague Roger Kean. After film school, Frey became a freelance artist, contributing to *Superman: The Movie*'s opening credits; then in 1983, Kean asked Frey to join him in founding *Crash*. Frey made his name at *Crash*, and the pair continued to work together producing illustrated books after it folded in 1992.

---

Oliver twins

Under *Dizzy*'s jolly, breezy exterior lies a flair for efficient production. There is also a keen awareness of how to speak to young videogame players, and of the value of establishing franchises. These qualities came from Philip and Andrew Oliver, self-taught twins from Trowbridge in Somerset. Following their 1985 breakout hit, *Super Robin Hood*, they published a multitude of games through Codemasters until 1990, when, at 22, they established Blitz Games Studios. With Andrew focusing on business and Philip on technology, it became one of the UK's largest developers, producing a mass market blend of both official tie-ins and original games, as well as providing medical training aids and licensing its technology to other studios. Blitz closed in 2013, but the Olivers soon bounced back with a new company, Radiant Worlds.

---

Rather schlocky and more than a little canny, Palace Software emerged when Peter Stone, MD of a London VHS retailer, noticed the fervour of the kids who flocked to buy the computers and games he'd begun to stock. One of his sales team, Richard Leinfellner, proposed they begin making their own games, and so they started a studio, introducing a fresh marketing concept – the movie tie-in – when they released 1984's *The Evil Dead*. Their biggest hit was *Barbarian*, famous for its use of glamour model Maria Whittaker in its advertising. Stone went on to join Konami, and Leinfellner took various leading positions at Mindscape, Electronic Arts and translation service Babel Media.

---

When he became editor of *Personal Computer Games* in 1983, Chris Anderson's discovery that magazines were failing to cater to the rapid growth of gaming led him to develop a new vision, of passionate writing, by people who loved games as much as their readers. He realised his ambition by founding *Zzap!64* in 1985 from his home in Somerset. When publisher Newsfield consolidated *Zzap!64* into its Ludlow office the same year, Anderson chose to leave, instead founding Future Publishing and launching its first magazine, *Amstrad Action*. Future quickly grew into a major specialist media company, but Anderson left in 2001 amid financial difficulties and through his non-profit Sapling Foundation bought TED, a set of global conferences focusing on the converging fields of technology, entertainment and design. As curator, Anderson has helped to grow TED into an international phenomenon, expanding its horizons to include more general talks on scientific, cultural and academic topics.

---

Maker of adventure games *Chimera* in 1985 and *Pandora* in 1988, both for Firebird, as well as the port of *Jet Set Willy* to the Commodore 64, Shahid Ahmad made a name for himself as a technically able and creative game writer. He is best known for his work at Sony from the mid '00s, where he worked as a liaison between Sony's corporate side and its external developers. He eventually became the leader of its strategic content team, the department responsible for signing indie games to Sony's PlayStation formats.

---

Andrew Braybrook          140, 144, 246, 248


One of the Britsoft era's most celebrated game writers, Andrew Braybrook created *Paradroid*, *Uridium* and *Gribbly's Day Out* for the Commodore 64, working with Steve Turner at Graftgold. Each of Braybrook's original games had a fascinating hook, whether *Uridium*'s miraculously smooth scrolling or *Paradroid*'s inspirational and elegant robot possession mechanic, the result of his careful and iterative approach to design. He remained at Graftgold until its closure in 1998, content to shrug away the fame his games had earned him, before he turned away from games entirely, joining an insurance software firm as a senior programmer.


---

Geoff Brown               193, 240


Co-founder, along with wife Anne, of publisher U.S. Gold and distributor CentreSoft in 1984, Geoff Brown was responsible for spurring great change. With his eye for the potential in licensed games based on sports events such as the Olympics and the football World Cup, he helped to expand the game market, while U.S. Gold's rampant commercialism helped professionalise the industry. U.S. Gold's original mission was to port American games to British systems, but it soon started to commission original games too, leading to Brown founding and buying development studios including *Tomb Raider* maker Core Design. He sold his operations to Eidos in 1996, going on to found more new gaming companies, including Kaboom and FairPlay.


---

Jez San                   41, 47, 93, 282, 331


Jez San founded his first company at the age of 16, naming it Argonaut as a play on his initial and surname; with his background in hacking, he decided he needed the company in order to appear professional when consulting for British Telecom about its IT security. His first game, written with two friends, was *Skyline Attack*, but his first success was early 3D shooter *Starglider*, which allowed him to grow Argonaut and develop its reputation for cutting edge technology. He worked to introduce 3D capabilities to Nintendo consoles, and helped design the SuperFX chip for the SNES. Argonaut became one of the UK's leading developers until it closed in 2004. San went on to found online poker company PKR.

Hardware
UK launch date

Magnavox Odyssey
1973

MITS Altair 8800
1974

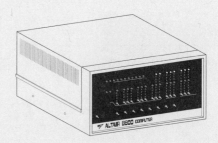

Binatone TV Master
1976
Pictured: MK 6

Tandy Corporation TRS-80 Model 1
Aug 1977

---

Nascom 1
Dec 1977

---

Commodore PET
1977
Pictured: CBM 4032, May 1980

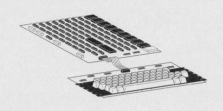

---

Research Machines 380Z
Feb 1978

---

Science of Cambridge MK14
Feb 1978

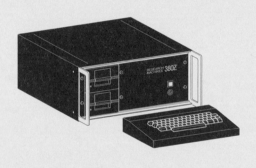

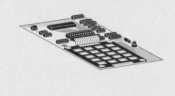

---

Apple II
1978

---

Atari 2600
1978

Acorn System 1
Mar 1979

Compukit UK101
Aug 1979

Acorn Atom
Jan 1980

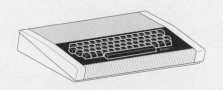

Sinclair ZX80
Jun 1980

Commodore VIC-20
Jan 1981

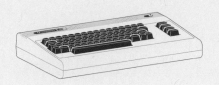

Sinclair ZX81
Mar 1981

------------------------------------
Texas Instruments TI-99/4A
Jul 1981

------------------------------------
Atari 400
Sep 1981

------------------------------------
Acorn BBC Microcomputer System
Dec 1981

------------------------------------
Sinclair ZX Spectrum 48K
Apr 1982

------------------------------------
CBS ColecoVision
Aug 1982

------------------------------------
Dragon 32
Aug 1982

--------------------------------

Jupiter Ace
Sep 1982

--------------------------------

Oric-1
Feb 1983

--------------------------------

Camputers Lynx
Mar 1983

--------------------------------

Commodore 64
Mar 1983

--------------------------------

Acorn Electron
Aug 1983

--------------------------------

Sinclair QL
Jan 1984

Amstrad CPC
Apr 1984

Atari ST
Jul 1985
Pictured: 520ST

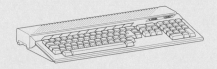

Commodore Amiga
Sep 1985
Pictured: Amiga 500, Oct 1987

Acorn Archimedes
Jun 1987
Pictured: Archimedes 305

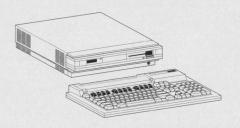

Nintendo Entertainment System
Aug 1987

Sega Master System
Dec 1987

Acorn Archimedes 3000
May 1989

Amstrad GX4000
Sep 1990

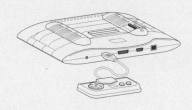

Sega Mega Drive
Nov 1990

SNK Neo Geo AES
1991

Super Nintendo
Entertainment System
Apr 1992

Photo Scrapbook Captions

1
Stanley Schembri, programmer at Palace Software.

2
Reviewer Matthew Uffindell taking screenshots for *Crash* in September 1984.

3
Oliver Frey working on a page from *Crash*'s *Terminal Man* comic in early 1985.

4
Oliver Frey airbrushing background colour for *Crash*'s Christmas special in November 1985.

5
From left: Chris Anderson, Denise Roberts, Bob Wade, Matthew Uffindell and Oliver Frey at *Zzap!64*'s launch party.

6
Commodore founder Jack Tramiel with models of the Commodore CBM-II.

7
Roger Kean and Oliver and Franco Frey pose for a PR shot for *Crash* in Franco's Pontiac Trans Am on Ludlow's Broad Street.

8
Roger Kean and Oliver and Franco Frey promoting the 1983 launch of *Crash* magazine.

9
From left: Chris Yates, Martin Galway and Jon Hare of Sensible Software.

10
Chris Chapman of Sensible Software during the filming of *Cannon Fodder*'s accompanying music video.

11
Andrew and Philip Oliver in 1992.

12
Palace Software's office; Peter
Stone is sat front-right.

13
*Stonkers* writer and Denton
Designs co-founder John Gibson.

14
The Imagine Software team.

15
Elite's sales office in 1992,
note the monthly sales target
on the whiteboard.

16
Anne and Geoff Brown of U.S. Gold.

17
The PCW Show at Olympia,
September 1986.

18
Automata exhibiting with Piman in
1983.

19
Promotional material from the
1986 PCW Show.

20
Stanley Schembri and Steve Brown
of Palace Software.

21
On left: Richard Leinfellner.

22
Geoff Crammond writing
*Aviator*.

*Britsoft: An Oral History*
Edited by Alex Wiltshire

Based on the 2014 documentary feature film
*From Bedrooms to Billions*, written and
directed by Anthony and Nicola Caulfield.

Published by Read-Only Memory

Design and Art Direction: Julia
Commissioning Editor: Darren Wall
Proofreading: Jim Caunter, Richard Stacey,
Silvia Novak, Leonard Owen

ISBN 978-0-9575768-2-7

ROM05

© Read-Only Memory 2015

A catalogue for this book is available from
the British Library.

Printed in Spain by Imago

frombedroomstobillions.com

readonlymemory.vg

Images used with the kind permission of:
Ian Agland, James Arran McDonnell,
Stefan Bates, David Braben, Ben Coffer,
Geoff Crammond, Mel Croucher, Mat Dolphin,
Franco Frey, Oliver Frey, Roger Kean,
Andrew Knowles, Peter Stone, Dustin Vogel,
Marc Wilding.

Every effort has been made to trace copyright
holders and to obtain their permission for
the use of copyright material. The publisher
apologises for any errors or omissions
and would be grateful if notified of any
corrections that should be incorporated in
future reprints or editions of this book.

The publishers would like to thank: Anthony
and Nicola Caulfield, Tom Cleaver, Andy Lemon,
Jonathan Silverman, Camilla Smallwood.

The editor would like to thank: Hannah, Jack,
Hester, Gary Penn.